Linguistics and Biblical Hebrew

The beginning of Genesis in the Leningrad Codex of the Hebrew Bible.

Linguistics

and

Biblical Hebrew

Edited by

Walter R. Bodine

Eisenbrauns
Winona Lake, Indiana
1992

Second Printing, 1998

Library of Congress Cataloging-in-Publication Data

Linguistics and Biblical Hebrew / edited by Walter R. Bodine.
    p.   cm.
   Includes bibliographical references and index.
   ISBN 0-931464-55-2
   1. Hebrew language—Grammar. 2. Linguistics. 3. Bible. O.T.—
Language, style. I. Bodine, Walter Ray.
PJ4521.L56 1992
492′.4—dc20   92-29716

Contents

Preface

Many people have had a part in the preparation of this volume, and my hearty thanks goes out to each of them. While my graduate training was primarily philological, Frank Cross, William Moran, and Bruce Waltke were philologians who were sensitive to linguistic perspectives and who cultivated that sensitivity in me. The two approaches were so integrated as to be indistinguishable in the teaching of Thomas Lambdin. I thank Earl Bills for many hours of tutoring during my concerted study of general linguistics beginning in 1979. Ilah Fleming and Robert Longacre have given me encouragement over the years.

John DeAcutis volunteered typing help with my essay, the introduction, and several other parts of the manuscript, including the entire bibliography. It has been a pleasure to work with Jim Eisenbraun. He and his staff have improved the manuscript at many points.

Walter Bodine

Abbreviations

AAL	*Afroasiatic Linguistics*
AOS	American Oriental Series
BASOR	*Bulletin of the American School of Oriental Research*
BDB	F. Brown, S. R. Driver, and C. A. Briggs, *Hebrew and English Lexicon of the Old Testament* (1907)
BHS	*Biblica Hebraica Stuttgartensia*
BL	H. Bauer and P. Leander, *Historische Grammatik der hebräischen Sprache des Altes Testamentes* (1922)
BO	*Bibliotheca Orientalis*
EA	El-Amarna tablets; cited by text:line number from J. A. Knudtzon, *Die El-Amarna Tafeln* (1907–15)
EncJud	*Encyclopaedia Judaica* (1971)
ErIsr	*Eretz-Israel*
GB	W. Gesenius and G. Bergsträsser, *Hebräische Grammatik* (1918–29)
GKC	W. Gesenius and E. Kautzsch, *Gesenius' Hebrew Grammar*, trans. A. E. Cowley (1920)
HALAT	W. Baumgartner et al., *Hebräisches und aramäisches Lexikon zum Alten Testament* (1967–)
HAR	*Hebrew Annual Review*
HUCA	*Hebrew Union College Annual*
IOS	*Israel Oriental Studies*
IPA	International Phonetic Alphabet
JANESCU	*Journal of the Ancient Near Eastern Society of Columbia University*
JAOS	*Journal of the American Oriental Society*
JBL	*Journal of Biblical Literature*
JNES	*Journal of Near Eastern Studies*
Joüon	P. Joüon, *Grammaire de l'hébreu biblique* (1923)
JQR	*Jewish Quarterly Review*
JSS	*Journal of Semitic Studies*
JTS	*Journal of Theological Studies*
KB	L. Köhler and W. Baumgartner, *Lexicon in Veteris Testamenti Libros* (1953)

KTU	M. Dietrich, O. Loretz, and J. Sanmartín, *Die keilalphabetischen Texte aus Ugarit, Teil 1: Transkription* (1976)
Leš	*Lešonénu*
Lg.	*Language*
LXX	the Septuagint
Meyer	R. Meyer, *Hebräische Grammatik* (1969–72)
MT	the Masoretic Text
UF	*Ugarit Forschungen*
VT	*Vetus Testamentum*
ZAW	*Zeitschrift für die Alttestamentliche Wissenschaft*

Walter R. Bodine

The Study of Linguistics and Biblical Hebrew

People have studied language for virtually as long as they have written about anything.[1] Yet what we now call modern, general linguistics is usually traced back only to the nineteenth century,[2] if not to the turn of the twentieth century.[3] Prior to these two periods, comments on languages emanated from philologians[4] as well as from philosophers; thereafter there have been those who studied language as a phenomenon in and of itself as their primary field, rather than focusing on one or more specific languages or a certain body of written texts.

Since the emergence of linguistics as a field in its own right, biblical scholars have occupied an intermediate ground. They have functioned primarily as philologians in a broad sense. At the same time many of those who have written the grammars and produced the dictionaries that are still widely

Author's note: Edward Greenstein and Robert Longacre made helpful suggestions during my preparation of this introduction.

1. See B. Landsberger et al., *Materialien zum sumerischen Lexikon*, vol. 4 (Rome: Pontifical Biblical Institute, 1956), for the study of Sumerian grammar by Babylonian scribes.
2. The rise of the historical/comparative study of languages should, I believe, be recognized as the study of language as such, i.e., the normal understanding of what is meant by "linguistics."
3. Often historians of linguistics point to F. de Saussure (1857–1913) as the starting point of modern linguistics, and it is true that many of the salient characteristics of the field were first clearly articulated by de Saussure.
4. On distinguishing linguistics from philology, see W. R. Bodine, "Linguistics and Philology in the Study of Ancient Near East Languages," in *"Working with No Data": Semitic and Egyptian Studies Presented to Thomas O. Lambdin* (ed. D. M. Golomb; Winona Lake, IN: Eisenbrauns, 1987) 39–41, and the literature cited there in n. 1.

used have been cognizant of current developments among linguists and, in some cases, have been astute in their own linguistic perceptions.[5]

I believe it would be readily acknowledged by most biblical scholars that linguistics is a sister discipline that is vital to their field. Whether or not any given biblical scholar is directly involved in linguistics, most would accord it a place alongside archeology, historiography, literary criticism, the social sciences, and whatever other fields might be regarded as essential complements to biblical studies proper.

There have been forces, however, which have tended to stymie dialogue between biblical scholars and linguists. In particular, the commitment of linguists to speech as the primary data of linguistics, to synchronic analysis as their main approach, and to an increasingly formalistic orientation have hampered communication. Biblical scholars are bound to written texts by the very nature of their evidence;[6] they are constrained to deal with diachronic issues at almost every turn;[7] and they are, for the most part, more oriented to interpreting empirical data than to constructing highly formal theories. On the other hand, biblicists often have not seen the difference that linguistic sophistication can make in interpreting literature.

The present volume is an effort to facilitate communication. Its purpose is to offer an introduction to major types of linguistic analysis and samples of how such analysis might be carried out in the text of the Hebrew Bible. Thus, there are two essays for each topic, the first showing how a linguist might approach an aspect of language study[8] and the second illustrating an application of that kind of study to the biblical text.

Most of the essays were originally delivered as oral presentations to the Linguistics and Biblical Hebrew unit at the annual meetings of the Society of

---

5. A case in point would be Bergsträsser, for whom see P. T. Daniels's observations scattered throughout his notes in Gotthelf Bergsträsser, *Introduction to the Semitic Languages: Text Specimens and Grammatical Sketches* (trans. P. T. Daniels; Winona Lake, IN: Eisenbrauns, 1983; originally Munich: Hueber, 1928). Another would be Bauer and Leander's application to Hebrew of the linguistic methodology in vogue in their time (cf. in this regard E. Ullendorff, "Comparative Semitics," in *Linguistica semitica: presente e futuro* [ed. G. Levi della Vida; Studi Semitici 4; Rome: Centro di Studi Semitici, 1961] 17).

6. This is not to argue here that written data should be treated on a par with spoken data by linguists, but only to point out the situation that biblical scholars face. The question of the nature of written data is addressed briefly by M. O'Connor's essay below. Differences of opinion on the subject exist among linguists and even among contributors to this volume.

7. This is especially true in Hebrew Bible studies, where the text is a conglomerate of materials whose composition spans roughly a thousand years, regardless of one's scheme of dating. The New Testament was produced in a relatively compact period of time and, for this reason, lends itself more readily to synchronic linguistic analysis.

8. These introductory studies are just that. They are not intended to be comprehensive, nor could they be within their allotted space.

Biblical Literature over the period 1983–1987 and have not been substantially revised since then. The dates of the presentations were as follows: 1983: Greenstein and Enos; 1984: MacDonald; 1985: Garr, Rendsburg, and Bandstra; 1986: O'Connor, Lieberman, and Bodine; 1987: Scanlin, Faber, and Huehnergard. We are pleased to have Drs. Barr, Devens, Longacre, and Revell join the endeavor. Two of their papers as well were initially presented orally, though in other settings: Barr at the 1985 Society of Biblical Literature annual meeting and Longacre at the International Organization for the Study of the Old Testament in 1986. Submission dates of the written manuscripts may be found at the conclusion of each article. We were grieved at the passing of Stephen Lieberman while this volume was in press. He was a good friend and a gifted scholar. We will miss him, and our field suffers loss.

Because there is no consensus on the transcription of Biblical Hebrew at present, the transcription systems employed in the following essays have not been standardized, although the system recomended by *JBL* is used most often, in keeping with the plan of the volume at an earlier stage.

Two approaches to *phonology* (the study of the sound system of a language) are introduced and applied to Biblical Hebrew in the first section. The two introductions to these approaches, by Devens and Greenstein, may profitably be read together. Devens compares her descriptive approach with a generative one, and Greenstein illustrates his generative methodology from Biblical Hebrew. The application article by Enos is closely patterned after Greenstein and gives further indication of how a generativist would approach the Hebrew data. Revell's study deals with a specific issue in Biblical Hebrew descriptively.

Morphology (the study of the smallest meaningful units of a language) is a staple of traditional Hebrew grammar. Garr introduces the linguistic underpinnings, and Rendsburg shows how this kind of analysis can bear on the far-reaching question of linguistic diversity within ancient Israel.

Syntax (the study of the structure of such units as phrases, clauses, and larger combinations) is surveyed in Bodine's article in terms of how it has been approached and some of the issues that are still unresolved. Bandstra's essay could as easily have been placed in the section on discourse. Word order and emphasis are usually addressed as syntactic questions, but Bandstra's essay demonstrates how discourse analysis bears directly on the study of syntax.[9]

---

9. The major study of Biblical Hebrew syntax by B. K. Waltke and M. O'Connor, *An Introduction to Biblical Hebrew Syntax* (Winona Lake, IN: Eisenbrauns, 1990), appeared too late to be considered in the present volume (see my review in *Hebrew Studies* 31 [1990] 253–59). The same was true of P. Cotterell and M. Turner, *Linguistics and Biblical Interpretation* (Downers Grove, IL: InterVarsity, 1989) and Moises Silva, *God, Language, and Scripture: Reading the Bible in the Light of General Linguistics* (Foundations of Contemporary Interpretation 4; Grand Rapids: Zondervan, 1990).

Scanlin's discussion of *semantics* (the study of the expression of meaning in language) focuses on the semantic-domain approach employed in the United Bible Societies' recently published lexicon of New Testament Greek.[10] Barr, adopting a conversational tone, shares insights into the inner workings of the Oxford Hebrew Dictionary project when it was underway.

Discourse analysis (or text linguistics) is the linguistic study of units that are larger than the sentence. MacDonald's introduction points to the diversity of approaches being employed in the field. Longacre's study shows how a discourse linguist might approach the subject of the Hebrew verb.

The next two essays discuss and illustrate in turn the kind of study that launched the modern period of linguistics, the *historical/comparative approach* (the study of language development over time and the systematic comparison of related languages). It seems that historical/comparative linguistics is presently in the midst of a resurgence among linguists, and this is a welcome development. Faber suggests new ways of looking at old issues in her introduction, and Huehnergard probes the ramifications of a historical reconstruction within the Hebrew verbal system, that of the *Piel* stem.

In the final section, *grammatology* (the study of writing) is explored in its relationship to the Hebrew Bible. Linguists differ over whether written material is a proper subject of linguistic inquiry because of the view often held among them that only speech constitutes primary linguistic data. Whatever position one may take on this question, it is essential that grammatology be addressed by those who deal with written texts. O'Connor explores the nature of writing systems and discusses contacts of grammatology with semiotics, ethnoscience, and literary criticism. Lieberman's essay interacts with issues in linguistics and early Jewish sources in an analysis of the historical layers in the writing system of the Hebrew Bible.

Over the years during which these essays were being prepared a bibliography was gathered with the help of many participants in the Society of Biblical Literature unit. Thanks are due to H. Scanlin for making it available to those who requested it during that time. In the bibliography published here, entries have been organized in keeping with topics treated in the book, with the addition of the categories of poetry and translation. My purpose in preparing this bibliography is to point to studies on Biblical Hebrew[11] that are

---

10. J. P. Louw and E. A. Nida, *Greek-English Lexicon of the New Testament Based on Semantic Domains* (2 vols.; New York: United Bible Societies, 1988). Because of the very specific focus of his essay, Scanlin has included a selection of further readings with brief annotations for those who wish to explore the field of semantics more widely. The selections by Lyons would, in most cases, be a good starting place. His two-volume work offers a broad overview of the field.

11. By Biblical Hebrew I mean here the Hebrew of the biblical period, insofar as it can be reconstructed, and that of the Tiberian Masoretes.

explicitly linguistic in their methodology or, at least, that interact with perspectives from general linguistics. The inclusion of a particular item does not imply agreement with its conclusions or the judgment that its approach is superior to more customary philological studies. Philology cannot, and should not, be replaced by linguistics in biblical studies. However, in the field of Biblical Hebrew studies as a whole, the potential of general linguistics for producing new insights has yet to be realized. Those who are forging this path deserve appreciation, and the purpose of this bibliography, as well as the entire volume, is to create more interest in such work. The bibliography is admittedly selective. To have attempted to make it complete in any sense would have caused further and intolerable delay in the publication schedule. Suggestions from readers as to other items which merit inclusion will be appreciated and may perhaps be useful on some future occasion.

For readers who desire an integrated view of the field of general linguistics, a currently popular introduction and also a pleasurable one to read is that of Fromkin and Rodman.[12] An older introduction, which draws many illustrations from Hebrew, is that of Gleason.[13] A survey of the history of linguistics with special reference to biblical studies will appear in the forthcoming *Anchor Bible Dictionary*.[14] Those who wish to do more extensive reading can be guided by references in the following essays and, beyond that, in the major reference works recently published by Cambridge University Press and Oxford University Press.[15]

While this volume was prepared primarily with Biblical Hebrew scholars in mind, it will be relevant to scholars of the Greek New Testament and of cognate literatures, both in the ancient Near East and the classical world. Students of other literatures who desire to incorporate linguistic insights and methodologies into their work should find it useful. We hope that linguistics will respond and that increased interaction between the fields will result. It will be especially gratifying if these essays stimulate biblical scholars to delve further into general linguistics.

---

12. V. Fromkin and R. Rodman, *An Introduction to Language* (New York: Holt, Rinehart & Winston, 1988).

13. H. A. Gleason Jr., *An Introduction to Descriptive Linguistics* (New York: Holt, Rinehart & Winston, 1961).

14. W. R. Bodine, "Linguistics and Biblical Studies," in *Anchor Bible Dictionary* (ed. D. N. Freedman; 6 vols.; New York: Doubleday, 1992).

15. F. J. Newmeyer, ed., *Linguistics: The Cambridge Survey* (4 vols.; Cambridge: Cambridge University Press, 1989); W. Bright, ed., *International Encyclopedia of Linguistics* (4 vols.; Oxford: Oxford University Press, 1992).

Monica S. Devens

What Descriptive Phonologists Do:
One Approach to the Study of Language, with Particular Attention to Biblical Hebrew

Phonetics is the study of the physical properties of speech sounds, while phonology is the study of how those speech sounds are organized into systems. Phonology is heavily dependent upon phonetics, since without a knowledge of language production and perception linguists would have no framework for their phonological descriptions.[1]

There are four basic ways to "do phonology"—synchronic descriptive, diachronic descriptive, synchronic generative, and diachronic generative. In reality, however, we usually speak of descriptive (assumed to be synchronic) and generative (assumed to be synchronic) phonology, on the one hand, and historical (i.e., diachronic, most often assumed to be descriptive) phonology, on the other.

Descriptive (that is, synchronic descriptive) phonology is the focus of this paper, and I begin with a section on methodology. But we cannot look to methodology alone to understand what descriptive phonology has to offer. It is important to examine some of the theoretical assumptions that descriptive phonologists have made, and I believe that this is best done by contrasting the two principal synchronic approaches, descriptive and generative.

Author's note: I am grateful to Peter T. Daniels and Robert D. Hoberman for their extensive and insightful comments on an earlier version of this paper. Any errors remaining are, of course, entirely my own.

1. For instance, unless one knows that [k] and [s] are voiceless while [z] is voiced, a voicing assimilation rule—explaining, for example, why Israeli Hebrew /yiskor/ 'he will rent' and /yizkor/ 'he will remember' are both pronounced [yiskor]—is unmotivated.

Finally, since the ultimate concern of this book is the study of an ancient language, namely Biblical Hebrew, we must evaluate the contributions of any synchronic analysis in light of the problem of uncertain phonetics.

Since I discuss generative and historical phonology only to the extent that they are useful in elucidating descriptive phonology, the reader should consult the essays in this volume by Edward L. Greenstein (pp. 29–40) and Alice Faber (pp. 189–205) for more complete presentations.

THE METHODOLOGY OF DESCRIPTIVE PHONOLOGY

Some form of descriptive methodology is undoubtedly the most familiar phonological approach to students of Biblical Hebrew, and only a minimal introduction is needed. Basically, descriptive phonologists (1) gather data, (2) work out the phonetics of the language they are studying, and then (3) proceed with a phonological analysis that considers only those elements which have been recorded in transcription. If some aspect of the language remains unclear, more data are gathered to clarify it.

For spoken languages—the usual subject of study for a descriptive phonologist—the data consist of speech samples elicited from native speakers, sufficient in quantity and detail to ensure coverage of the entire inventory of sounds and of grammatical categories. If the phonologist is familiar with the language family, it will not be too difficult to work out a phonetic chart. If the language is completely new, however, or atypical of the family to which it belongs, this part of the linguist's job can be quite time-consuming.

Since the linguist's goal is a phonological analysis, not a phonetic study, reasonable approximation will serve. However, the dependence of descriptive phonology on phonetics is such that a major error in understanding the phonetics of the language can throw off the entire analysis. In other words, if the phonetic underpinning turns out to be wrong, the phonological analysis will need a lot of revision. Therefore, the phonologist must actively seek phonetic confirmation for phonological statements. As one standard descriptive linguistics textbook says, "The definition of the phoneme . . . will be inadequate when the observer cannot hear the language as a native does."[2]

In addition, the descriptive linguist will keep the phonological and morphological levels strictly separate. In other words, information of a morphological nature will not be considered in constructing a phonological analysis.

Finally, the methodology of descriptive phonology as presented here stems from the twin assumptions that spoken language data are available and

---

2. H. A. Gleason Jr., *An Introduction to Descriptive Linguistics* (2d ed.; New York: Holt, Rinehart & Winston, 1961) 261.

that any phonological analysis will reflect only one point in time. In this view, therefore, written forms are irrelevant. As in the example to follow, to a phonologist working on Israeli Hebrew the existence of the phoneme /ˁ/ is problematic. The fact that the written language has a grapheme ˁ*ayin* is information of historical significance only, except to the degree that it may be considered an influence on the speech of literate speakers.

Let us follow a descriptivist through a phonological analysis of Israeli Hebrew.[3] The first step is to gather speech samples from a representative group of native speakers.[4] In the course of this work the linguist notices that while the word for 'time, instance' is generally given as [paˀam] or [paam], sometimes the [aˀa] or [aa] sequence is replaced by something else. Through persistent listening and fine-tuned hearing, the linguist identifies this "something else" as a set of alternants: a voiced pharyngeal fricative, a glide, a back vowel, or a combination of these elements. Having the basic phonetic pieces of the puzzle, the linguist must now organize them.

As I have said, when something is unclear, the descriptivist seeks more data for clarification. In this case, even with twice as much data, there are no rules of environmental conditioning to explain these variants. Furthermore, while eliciting more examples the linguist uncovers a possible minimal pair—/natati/ 'I gave' versus /natAti/ 'I planted'—but while this constellation of alternants, symbolized here by /A/, sometimes stands in opposition to /a/, at other times it comes after it, as in /nataAti/. This pair of words is intriguing, but not definitive enough to claim phonemicity.

Perhaps quantification—knowing the frequency of all these different forms—will shed some light. A numerical analysis reveals that only 15 percent of the occurrences of these words exhibit some form of /A/. In other words, 85 percent of the time there is no trace of /A/. By now the linguist undoubtedly suspects a change in progress—probably the loss of whatever was there before—but this is irrelevant to a synchronic analysis.

One possibility is to divide the speakers into two groups—those who sometimes produce these variants and those who never do—and define their speech as different dialects of Israeli Hebrew. In this case, the word for 'time, instance' can be established for one dialect as /paˀam/ or /paam/, depending on the linguist's point of view.[5] Furthermore, the majority of speakers seem to fall in this category, making it an attractive option. But what of

---

3. The following discussion is based loosely on data reported in M. S. Devens, "Oriental Israeli Hebrew: A Study in Phonetics," *AAL* 7 (1980) 127–42.

4. The concept of statistical significance is often ignored by linguists of all stripes. Because of the impossibility of obtaining enough data to claim statistical reliability in anything but the most strictly delimited inquiries, one should always be cautious in stating conclusions.

5. One can certainly argue about the phonemicity of /ˀ/ in Israeli Hebrew, but I do not wish to enter into that discussion here.

the other speakers? They remain a problem, for, even when they are considered as a separate group, their treatment of this constellation of variants is still mysterious. /A/ is more frequent, but it still appears in only 35 percent of all occurrences of the relevant words, and there are still no rules to explain why any particular variant should appear when it does. It would be logical at this point to undertake a more detailed phonetic analysis, but in this particular case it would only confirm the dilemma.

The descriptive linguist has stumbled upon a very difficult problem in the descriptive phonology of Israeli Hebrew, and there is no definitive solution. Since it is easier to posit unexplained loss than it is to posit unexplained insertion, it is easier to establish a phoneme which is sometimes realized as zero rather than a new vocalic or consonantal phone which suddenly appears. Of course, I have taken this one problem out of context. The actual solution proposed would depend not only on these data, but on their place in the language's overall system.

THEORETICAL ASSUMPTIONS:
THE UNIVERSAL VERSUS THE PARTICULAR

While the methodology of descriptive phonology is undoubtedly quite familiar, and some of its theoretical assumptions transparent, other assumptions may be neither as well known nor as obvious. I now examine some issues which have tended to separate practitioners of the descriptive method from those of the generative method, though, needless to say, I will not be able to cover here all that differentiates them.[6] Furthermore, I readily acknowledge that the universe is not so starkly divided as I portray it. The best linguists continually negotiate their way productively among all the methods, utilizing the best of each approach and ignoring the excesses of each. A "neat" depiction is very useful, however, for an introduction such as this.

All phonologists share the same goals—to arrive at a comprehensive understanding of the sound system of a particular language, and ultimately of the phenomenon of human language. They all recognize roughly the same kinds of phonological processes and attempt to write rules to describe them. They differ widely, however, on the roles the universal and the particular— the language ability of the human mind versus the individual language under review—play in their work. Consider these two statements:

---

6. For example, one important difference not discussed here is the degree to which the two approaches allow the mixing of phonological and morphological levels. I have mentioned above that descriptivists do not permit mixing, while generativists are far more open to it.

A **phoneme** is a class of sounds which: (1) are phonetically similar and (2) show certain characteristic patterns of distribution in the language or dialect under consideration. Note that this definition is restricted in its application to a single language or dialect. There is no such thing as a general /p/ phoneme. There is, however, an English /p/ phoneme. Likewise there is a Hindi /p/ phoneme. They are in no sense identical. Each is a feature of its own language and not relevant to any other language.[7]

Traditional phonology is problematic in that it requires a new phonetic chart for every language. Generative phonology sets up features as a single way of describing all sounds found in human language.[8]

Clearly the linguists speaking here have different focal points. For the descriptivist, it is the particular; for the generativist, it is the universal. In a very broad sense, while descriptive phonologists tend to emphasize differences between languages, generative phonologists tend to emphasize similarities.

Descriptive phonology comes fairly close to the traditional stance of the Hebraist. Kautzsch wrote: "They [the gutturals] prefer before them, and sometimes after them . . . , a short A-sound, because this vowel is organically the nearest akin to the gutturals,"[9] which covers much of what the Hebraist cares to know. Certainly the descriptivist looks for more, for example, to what conditions does the phrase *and sometimes after them* refer, and what does *prefer* mean? One would like these observations specified in rule form. But still, ignoring for the moment the uncertainty of phonetic fact, we are fairly content with this description of the way gutturals behave in Hebrew.

The generative linguist, however, would be much more interested in cross-linguistic generalization. How does the behavior of pharyngeal consonants in Biblical Hebrew compare to their behavior in other languages? How does the preference of these consonants for a certain vowel relate to the preferences of other consonants for other vowels? For a generative phonologist, learning the particulars about Biblical Hebrew would be quite secondary.

The generative view of the relative importance of knowledge of a specific language versus knowledge of general language principles is summed up fairly well in this statement from the preface of a book on the structure of Israeli Hebrew:

While presupposing some familiarity with contemporary linguistic theory and methods of analysis, the present study assumes no prior knowledge of the Hebrew language. As such, it is intended: for a university course in the Structure of

---

7. Gleason, *Descriptive Linguistics*, 261–62.
8. J. T. Grinder and S. H. Elgin, *Guide to Transformational Grammar: History, Theory, Practice* (New York: Holt, Rinehart & Winston, 1973) 192.
9. GKC §22d/p. 77.

Hebrew offered within the curriculum of a general linguistics program; for the Hebrew scholar interested in a more contemporary linguistically-oriented study in his field; and for the general linguist interested in data and descriptions from a non-Indo-European language which, while genetically Semitic, manifests certain quite unique socio-historical properties.[10]

THEORETICAL ASSUMPTIONS:
THE QUESTION OF ABSTRACTNESS

This difference of approach to the universal versus the particular is reflected in the attitudes generative and descriptive phonologists have toward the question of abstractness. In a parallel fashion, the descriptive phonologist is more focused on the observable (i.e., data), while the generative phonologist is more focused on the theoretical.

Both descriptive and generative phonologists write rules which produce phonetic forms from phonological forms. This being the case, both camps clearly accept that the phonetic and phonological forms of a particular lexeme may diverge. They can understand differently, however, what the phonological form represents. For generative phonologists, phonemes depict psychological reality, while for some descriptive phonologists,

> in a certain sense they are the intellectual creation of the linguist. . . . The phonemes of a language are a set of abstractions which will more adequately describe certain features of the utterances of that language . . . than any other set. . . . The phoneme is not . . . a psychological concept. . . . [11]

This judgment on the psychological reality of the phoneme paves the way for the generative emphasis on theory. If the phoneme is psychologically real, then abstractness is not merely a convenient tool for description, but a statement of reality—mental reality. The further one moves from the observed to the postulated, the more theoretical one's approach.

While there is no agreement among generativists as to how abstract is too abstract, certainly they accept a far greater level of abstractness than do descriptivists. In the words of one prominent generative phonologist,

> One of the outgrowths of generative phonology was a rejection of a phonemic level. It is not that generative phonologists denied a level more abstract than the systematic phonetic one, but rather that the phonemic level was not the right one. It was not abstract enough; it was still too close to the phonetic ground. . . . [12]

10. R. A. Berman, *Modern Hebrew Structure*, with a chapter by Shmuel Bolozky (Tel Aviv: University Publishing Projects, 1978) ix.
11. Gleason, *Descriptive Linguistics*, 269–70.
12. S. A. Schane, *Generative Phonology* (Englewood Cliffs: Prentice-Hall, 1973) 7.

Or another:

> There seem to be no constraints on the degree of abstractness allowable in generative phonology.[13]

Thus, while descriptive phonologists believe that a phonemic transcription is partly a theory about the way people behave linguistically, and as such cannot contain much beyond the observable, generative phonologists hold that a phonemic transcription is partly a theory about the way people behave linguistically, and as such must contain much beyond the observable. For a generativist, the work of a descriptive phonologist might have "descriptive adequacy," but it would not have "explanatory adequacy."[14]

THEORETICAL ASSUMPTIONS:
HOW PHONEMES ARE REPRESENTED

It is not hard to distinguish analyses written by descriptivists from those written either by generativists or by historical phonologists. Descriptive phonologists present their phonemic forms and phonological rules using some variation of the alphabetic notation with which we are all familiar. Along with the analysis, they offer a phonetic chart specifying what their symbols mean for the language under study. Depending on their belief in the importance of a standard notation, they may choose the International Phonetic Alphabet, which requires little or no further explanation.[15] In other cases they may opt for the system that is most commonly used by linguists working on their particular language area. Thus, symbols used by Semitists often differ from those used by Indo-Europeanists, which in turn differ from those used by Slavicists, etc.[16] The most practical linguists use whichever system is the easiest for either their publisher or their computer.

Sometimes the choice of a symbol embodies a particular theoretical approach. Thus, when some linguists express the Biblical Hebrew grapheme ṣādê as /ṣ/, they manifest their commitment to a historical view. Use of the symbol /c/, on the other hand, demonstrates the descriptivist's refusal to make such a judgment. Similarly, linguists who transliterate Israeli Hebrew śîn and sāmek with different symbols are making a diachronic or an orthographic, but not a synchronic, statement.

---

13. L. M. Hyman, *Phonology: Theory and Analysis* (New York: Holt, Rinehart & Winston, 1975) 84.
14. N. Chomsky, *Aspects of the Theory of Syntax* (Cambridge: MIT Press, 1965) 24–26, 33–38.
15. The latest revision of the IPA is presented by P. Ladefoged, "The Revised International Phonetic Alphabet," *Lg.* 66 (1990) 550–52.
16. Cf. G. K. Pullum and W. A. Ladusaw, *Phonetic Symbol Guide* (Chicago: University of Chicago Press, 1986).

Generativists write their rules completely differently, based on distinctive feature theory, which holds that (1) all distinctions in human language can be expressed using a set of possible attributes and (2) generally these attributes function in a binary fashion, that is, they are most often marked as either present or absent.[17] This method of rule writing allows for broader rules with fewer symbols. Since, as we have already seen, generativists are more interested in the universal than the particular, in the workings of human language as a system rather than in any particular language, broad rules—otherwise known as "capturing the widest generalization"—are very desirable. In fact, they are the goal of all generative phonological analysis.

For the descriptive phonologist, however, directed more toward the particulars of an observed language, it can seem as though facts are being sacrificed to fit theory. While descriptive phonology proceeds from data to analysis, generative phonology can seem reversed. In striving to explain the phenomenon of human language it can start with the general and move to the specific, theorizing needed features in order to produce expected generalizations and then working backward in an attempt to match these to phonetic reality.[18]

WHAT ALL THIS MEANS FOR
THE STUDY OF BIBLICAL HEBREW

As we have seen, descriptive phonologists have generally been more interested in the particular and concrete than in the universal and abstract. This has been true of Hebraists as well. But in spite of their common outlook, Hebraists cannot apply descriptive methodology to the study of Biblical Hebrew without encountering some problems. Descriptive phonology is an approach grounded in observable reality, yet here reality cannot really be observed. From a descriptive viewpoint, data on Biblical Hebrew phonetics are at best idealized, and at worst imagined.

Consider, for example, one of the most frequently cited cases of possible dialectal differentiation in Biblical Hebrew, the famous story in Judg 12:1–6. The Ephraimites are asked to pronounce שִׁבֹּלֶת and reportedly say

---

17. In reality this distinction is not quite so clear-cut. Descriptive phonologists also acknowledge the presence of features. While they would not write their rules with the same feature-based notation, nor would they agree to all the distinctions proposed by generativists, they certainly acknowledge and employ concepts such as voiced/voiceless or stop/fricative. Cf. E. L. Greenstein's paper in this volume, pp. 38–40.

18. See, for example, the discussion of Jakobson's feature system and Chomsky and Halle's revisions of it in Hyman, *Phonology*, esp. 33–34, 43–44, 55, 57–58.

סַבֶּלֶת. Clearly two different phones are meant, but what are they? Descriptive phonology is helpless in such an instance.

Even when the phonetic equivalent of the written form is more certain, we cannot pretend that the written form is equal to an accurate phonetic transcription, even a broad one. Spelling changes more slowly than does pronunciation and thus masks developments in the spoken language. Rather than slicing through time at one particular moment—the goal of synchronic linguistics—a language's written form superimposes time layers, one on the other, to form an undifferentiated mass.

And even when the linguist's phonetic assumptions seem unassailable, they can never be truly validated. As wonderful as archeology is, it is unlikely that descriptive phonologists will ever be provided with audio recordings of Biblical Hebrew.[19] We are then forced into a form of circular reasoning: the written form of the language leads the linguist to construct a phonetic equivalent, which in turn allows a phonological analysis, whose outcome suggests alterations in some phonetic assumptions, which subsequently permit an easier phonological analysis.

Taking an example from Mishnaic Hebrew, we see that words normally written with the letter *bêt rāpeh* are sometimes written with the letter *wāw*. Kutscher takes this to mean that either [w] (the pronunciation he assumes for *wāw*) became [v] (the pronunciation he assumes for *bêt rāpeh*), or vice versa.[20] One must then consider either the loss of the phoneme /w/ and the resulting phonemicization of /v/, or a restructuring of our understanding of the phoneme /b/. Either being difficult, it might be better to take the perfectly logical view that *bêt rāpeh* was actually pronounced as a bilabial fricative, [β], and that the closest symbol to express this was the letter *wāw*, making our phonological analysis much easier. Unfortunately we cannot confirm our ideas, and logic is not necessarily fact.

Everything that has been said about descriptive phonology is true of generative phonology as well, with one exception. Focusing as it does on human language processes, and being more willing to deal in abstraction, generative phonology is somewhat less dependent on hard data, and is therefore somewhat better suited for what is essentially not a synchronic task.

Should one argue, then, that the study of Biblical Hebrew should be left to the historical phonologists? Of course not, and here's the rub. Throughout this paper, as part of the starkly divided universe laid out here, I have carefully separated synchronic and diachronic tasks. In truth they often overlap.

---

19. And as interesting and valuable as studies of traditional pronunciation are, they cannot take the place of bona fide native speaker input.
20. E. Y. Kutscher, *A History of the Hebrew Language* (ed. R. Kutscher; Jerusalem: Magnes/ Leiden: Brill, 1982) 121.

A synchronic analysis of a language often provides a stylized blueprint of the language's historical development, in terms of both what rules emerge and how they are ordered. Thus a descriptive analysis of a written language both feeds and absorbs a historical analysis, feeding it by suggesting new ways to formulate historical development and absorbing it by providing another framework to test ideas developed through use of the historical method. This is only one example of ways in which various methodologies enhance each other; no single linguistic approach can ever tell us everything.

When descriptive, generative, and historical phonologists—and practitioners of the many other schools of thought not discussed here—all bring their insights to bear, we will have achieved ideal conditions for the study of Biblical Hebrew. To quote Kautzsch again,

> The chief requirements for one who is treating the grammar of an ancient language are—(1) that he should *observe* as fully and accurately as possible the existing linguistic phenomena and *describe* them, after showing their organic connexion (the empirical and historico-critical element); (2) that he should try to *explain* these facts, partly by comparing them with one another and by the analogy of the sister languages, partly from the general laws of philology (the logical element).[21]

21. (GKC §3f/p. 21).

[December, 1988]

E. J. Revell

The Development of Sĕgôl in an Open Syllable as a Reflex of *a: An Exercise in Descriptive Phonology

1. INTRODUCTION

The development of *sĕgôl* in an open syllable as a reflex of *a in the MT[1] is typically treated in Hebrew grammars in two separate categories. In the stressed syllables of segolate nouns it is generally ascribed to the assimilation of *a to the following (anaptyctic) *sĕgôl*. In unstressed syllables (where *sĕgôl* usually occurs before a historically lengthened guttural followed by *qāmeṣ*), there is less unanimity on its origin, but the most common view is that it arises through dissimilation of *a from the following vowel.[2] This categorization appears to have led to a general opinion that *sĕgôl* in an open syllable reflecting *a arose only under the influence of the following sounds. The voweling of the interrogative pronoun *mh* raises difficulties for this view which have not been solved (see BL §33j/p. 266, GB pt. 1 §28a/p. 152, and Joüon §37c/p. 88; the latter notes that the relationship of *mh* to the following word is an important factor). The present article argues that a careful

1. The vowels of the MT are identified in this paper by name. They are transliterated as *u, o, ɔ, a, ɛ, e, i, ə, ŏ, ă, ĕ*. The use of *w* as a vowel letter with *u* or *o*, and of *y* with *ɛ, e*, or *i*, is indicated by a circumflex accent. Other vowel letters are ignored. The (reconstructed) vowel from which an MT vowel arose is represented by the appropriate letter marked with an asterisk. Unstarred vowel letters are used to represent vowels treated in other contexts. Thus *a in *kasp(u)* gives rise to ε, MT *sĕgôl*.

2. This *sĕgôl* is treated as due to dissimilation in BL §21n–o/p. 216, and most recently by J. Blau, "Marginalia Semitica III," *IOS* 7 (1977) 17 §4 and n. 14. Joüon §29f/p. 74 regards it as the result of "harmonisation vocalique." GB pt. 1 §27c/p. 151 considers the cause uncertain. For their opinions on stressed *sĕgôl*, see BL §16d/p. 200, Joüon §96Ab/p. 235, GB pt. 1 §23f/p. 136. For a new suggestion on the development of *sĕgôl*, see W. Randall Garr, "The *seghol* and segholation in Hebrew," *JNES* 48 (1989) 109–16.

17

description of the reflexes of *a in these three situations shows that all can plausibly be explained as resulting from the same process of development, in which the influence of the sounds following *a is of limited importance.

2. THE REFLEX OF *a IN SEGOLATE STRUCTURES

2.1 The loss of final vowels (case or mood markers) left a number of words consisting of, or ending in, a structure of form *CaCC. Where the syllable remains doubly closed, the reflex of *a is *pataḥ*, the usual reflex of *a in a closed nonfinal syllable. Typically, however, the final consonant cluster is broken up by the insertion of an anaptyctic vowel: *ḥîreq* following *yôd*, *pataḥ* before *hēʾ*, *ḥêt*, or *ʿayin* and usually after them, *sĕgôl* elsewhere.

2.2 The original vowel, which retains its original stress in the now open syllable, appears as *qāmeṣ* where the word stands in terminal position.[3] This represents the expected development of *a in an open stressed syllable.

2.3 Where a word of form *CaCC stands in medial position, the reflex of *a is *qāmeṣ* before *wāw*; but *pataḥ* before *yôd*, *hēʾ*, and *ʿayin* and usually before *ḥêt*; and *sĕgôl* elsewhere. The view that this *sĕgôl* results from assimilation of *a to the following anaptyctic vowel fails to explain its appearance where the following vowel is *pataḥ*.

2.4 The general pattern is thus clear. *Pataḥ* appears where the syllable remains closed, *sĕgôl* where it is open in medial position, *qāmeṣ* where it is open in terminal position. In medial position, the reflex is further conditioned by the following consonant, so that *pataḥ* and *qāmeṣ* appear as well as *sĕgôl*, showing clearly that all three are natural reflexes of *a. In this context (as in others discussed below) *ḥêt* has a lesser effect on the preceding *a than does *hēʾ* or *ʿayin*.

3. THE REFLEX OF *a IN THE PRONOUN *mh*

3.1.1 Where *mh* stands at the end of a clause (in terminal position), the reflex of *a is *qāmeṣ*.[4]

---

3. "Terminal position" refers to the position in which the intonation contours of the text as read (in the form of the tradition reflected by the vowel patterns) give rise to "pausal" forms, or similar morphophonemic variations. See E. J. Revell, "The Conditioning of Stress Position in Waw Consecutive Perfect Forms," *HAR* 9 (1985) 277–300 §§5–13. The pausal forms of nouns of form *CaCC typically appear at the ends of clauses. Other positions, where "contextual" forms occur, are called "medial."

4. With *ʾatnāḥ* or *sillûq*, 2 Sam 18:29, Mal 2:14, Ps 84:9, Prov 9:13, Job 13:13; with other disjunctives, Exod 16:7–8, 1 Sam 19:3. Also 2 Sam 18:22–23 (the latter with a conjunctive), where *qāmeṣ* in *mh* could possibly be due to the fact that the following word begins with

3.1.2 Where *mh* stands within a clause, and the following word begins with a consonant other than the gutturals *ᵓālep*, *hē*ᵓ, *ḥêt*, *ᶜayin*, or *rêš*, the reflex of **a* is *pataḥ* where *mh* has *maqqēp*, *sĕgôl* otherwise.

3.1.3 Where *mh* has *pataḥ*, *dāgēš* is used in the following letter, except where said letter is *yôd* followed by *šĕwā*ᵓ, or is *l*, *m*, or *š* followed by a consonant with *dāgēš forte*, and in a few anomalous cases.[5]

3.1.4 The pattern of reflexes shown here is the same as that shown in words of form **CaCC* and is evidently typical for **a*. Minimum change (represented by *pataḥ*) occurs where the syllable is closed (and not originally word final) or is unstressed, medium change (*sĕgôl*) where it is open in medial position, maximum change (*qāmeṣ*) where it is open in terminal position.[6]

3.2.1 Where *mh* is followed by a word beginning with *ḥêt*, the reflex of **a* is *sĕgôl* in eight cases, *pataḥ* in two.

3.2.2 *Pataḥ* occurs in Job 21:21, where *mh* has *maqqēp*, and, where it has a conjunctive, in *ma ḥaṭ:ɔᵓtî* (Gen 31:36).

3.2.3 *Sĕgôl* occurs in the parallel to the latter case *ûme-ḥaṭ:ɔᵓtî* (1 Sam 20:1), where *mh* has *maqqēp*. In the remaining cases, *mh* with *sĕgôl* has a conjunctive accent. The vowel following the *ḥêt* is *qāmeṣ* or *pataḥ*.

3.2.4 The available evidence justifies no more than the statement that the voweling of *mh* before a word beginning with *ḥêt* is generally similar to the pattern shown before nonguttural consonants.

3.3.1 Where *mh* is followed by a word beginning with *ᶜayin*, the reflex of **a* is typically *sĕgôl*.

3.3.2 *Sĕgôl* occurs in one case where *mh* has a disjunctive, in twenty-six where it has a conjunctive, and in eleven where it has *maqqēp*. The vowel following *ᶜayin* is *pataḥ* or *ḥāṭēp pataḥ* in five cases, otherwise *qāmeṣ*.

ᵓālep with *qāmeṣ*. In an equivocal case in Hag 1:9, *mh* has *sĕgôl* at the end of a clause, but is followed by the attribution *nᵓm yhwh ṣbᵓwt* "(This is) a declaration of the Lᴏʀᴅ of Hosts." Presumably the prosodic unit ends with this phrase, not with the word *mh*, which is thus not in terminal position. The basis of the division into prosodic units is not simply syntactic but has a wider semantic basis.

5. Anomalous omission of *dāgēš* following *mh* occurs in *y* in Zech 9:17, Job 34:33, Qoh 6:8. On the omission of *dāgēš* in the Leningrad Codex in *l*, *m*, or *š* (and also *q*) following *mh*, see A. Dotan, "Deviation in Gemination in the Tiberian Vocalization," in *Estudios Masoreticos*, (ed. E. Fernández Tejero; Textos y Estudios "Cardenal Cisneros" 33; Madrid: CSIC, 1983) 67. The other Ben Asher codexes rarely agree. *Dāgēš* fails to occur in *yôd* with *šĕwā*ᵓ in Num 9:8, Judg 7:11, Jer 5:15, Hab 2:1, Ps 85:9.

6. A similar pattern occurs in some nouns of form **CiCC*, where the reflexes of **i* are *ṣērê*, *sĕgôl* (arising from *a* reflecting **i* in a stressed closed syllable), and *qāmeṣ* (the reflex of that *a* in terminal position). See E. J. Revell, "The Tiberian Reflexes of Short **i* in Closed Syllables," *JAOS* 109 (1989) 183–203.

3.3.3 The reflex of **a* is *qāmeṣ* in two cases where *mh* has a conjunctive: *mɔ ʿim:ɔdî* (Gen 31:32) and *mɔ ʿabdəkɔ* (2 Kgs 8:13). The last case has a close parallel in *me ʿabdɛkɔ* (2 Sam 9:8), which shows the expected *sĕgôl*.

3.3.4 In this situation, no difference in voweling correlates (even generally) with the use of *maqqēp* rather than a conjunctive. The two cases in which *qāmeṣ* occurs could have been partially conditioned by the vowel following the *ʿayin*, but, if so, other factors must also have been involved.

3.4.1 Where *mh* is followed by a word beginning with *hē*, the reflex of **a* is usually *qāmeṣ*.

3.4.2 The reflex of **a* is *pataḥ* before *hûʾ* and *hîʾ* (the only cases where *mh* is followed by an open monosyllable). *Mh* has *maqqēp* in six cases, a conjunctive in one.[7]

3.4.3 The reflex of **a* is *sĕgôl* before *hɔyɔ* (with final or penultimate stress) and *howɛ* (the only cases where the word following *mh* is composed of two open syllables). Here also, *mh* has *maqqēp* in six cases, a conjunctive in one.[8]

3.4.4 The reflex of **a* is typically *qāmeṣ* where *mh* has *maqqēp* but stands before a word in which more than one consonant follows the initial vowel, as *mɔ-hɔʿɔm* (Jer 33:24), or where *mh* has a conjunctive accent, as *mɔ hem* (Ezek 8:6 *Qere*). There are, in all, nearly forty cases.

3.4.5 There is one exception (besides the cases noted above where *mh* with *pataḥ* or *sĕgôl* has a conjunctive). *Mh* with *sĕgôl* has a conjunctive in *me hɔʾɔdɔm* (Qoh 2:12), contrasting with the close parallel in *mɔ hɔʾɔšɔm* (1 Sam 6:4), which shows the expected voweling.

3.4.6 The use of *sĕgôl* and *pataḥ* appears to be determined by the length (in terms of number of consonants) of the word following *mh*, and by the use of *maqqēp*. Where the word is too long, or where *maqqēp* is not used, *pataḥ* and *sĕgôl* typically do not occur. The choice of *pataḥ* or *sĕgôl* could have been determined by the structure of the word following *mh*, or by its initial vowel (see §4.3.3–4).

3.5.1 Where *mh* is followed by a word beginning with a guttural, the reflex of **a* is affected by the vowel following the guttural only to a minor extent, if at all. The main conditioning factors are the use of *maqqēp* (as where the following word does not begin with a guttural) and the nature of the following guttural.

3.5.2 The development of *qāmeṣ* is more likely where the following guttural is articulated more toward the back of the mouth, or is voiced. Thus,

---

7. *Māqqēp* is used in Gen 23:15; Exod 16:15; Num 13:18, 16:11; Zech 5:6; Ps 39:5. A conjunctive occurs in Esth 8:1.

8. *Māqqēp* occurs in Exod 32:1, 23; 1 Sam 4:16; 2 Sam 1:4; Lam 5:1; Qoh 2:22. A conjunctive occurs in Qoh 7:10.

where consonants are articulated in the same position, *qāmeṣ* develops before the voiced *ʿayin*, but not before the voiceless *ḥêt*. Where both are voiceless, *qāmeṣ* develops before the glottal *hēʾ*, but not before the laryngeal *ḥêt*. *Rêš* is voiced, and *ʾālep* has glottal articulation, but there is no good basis for a suggestion of the qualities which made these more conducive to the development of *qāmeṣ* than the three fricatives.

3.5.3 *Pataḥ* occurs before the voiceless fricatives *hēʾ* and *ḥêt*. Before the glottal *hēʾ* it occurs only under special conditions (to which there is no parallel before *ḥêt* or before *ʿayin*). It thus appears likely that these three fricatives are conducive to the development of *sĕgôl* (which is used elsewhere) in the same degree as to the development of *qāmeṣ*.

4. THE REFLEX OF *a IN THE DEFINITE ARTICLE

4.1 Before nonguttural consonants, the reflex of *a in the definite article is *pataḥ*. The following letter is marked with *dāgēš* except (in many cases) where it is followed by *šĕwāʾ*.

4.2.1 Before *ḥêt*, the reflex of *a is usually *pataḥ*.

4.2.2 Where *ḥêt* is followed by *qāmeṣ*, the reflex is *sĕgôl* where *qāmeṣ* is stressed or stands in an open syllable, including *ḥāṭēp qāmeṣ*, as *hɛḥɔ̆dɔšîm*, *hɛḥɔ̆rɔbôt*, *hɛḥɔ̆rebôt*.[9] Where *qāmeṣ* stands in a closed unstressed syllable, the reflex of *a is *pataḥ* in *hahɔkmɔ*.

4.2.3 In a few anomalous cases, the reflex of *a is *qāmeṣ*, as in Gen 6:19; Isa 3:22, 17:8.

4.3.1 Before *hēʾ*, the reflex of *a is usually *pataḥ*.

4.3.2 Where *hēʾ* is followed by *qāmeṣ* in an unstressed open syllable, the reflex of *a is *sĕgôl*.

4.3.3 Where *hēʾ* is followed by stressed *qāmeṣ* or *ṣērê*, the reflex of *a is *qāmeṣ*.

4.3.4 Where *hēʾ* is followed by the pronoun *hûʾ* or *hîʾ*, or by unstressed vowels other than *qāmeṣ* or *ṣērê*, the reflex of *a is *pataḥ*.

4.4.1 Before *ʿayin*, the reflex of *a is usually *qāmeṣ*. This includes those cases in which *ʿayin* is followed by stressed *qāmeṣ* as in *hɔʿɔm*, by *qāmeṣ* in a closed unstressed syllable (in proper nouns in Lev 11:13, Num 3:27, Deut 14:12, Josh 18:24, 1 Chr 26:23), and by *qāmeṣ ḥāṭûp* in *hɔʿɔ̆mɔrîm* (Ruth 2:7, 15).

---

9. In the last of these, *ḥāṭēp qāmeṣ* evidently reflects *a. I can find no source showing the form *hɛḥɔ̆lî*, listed by E. König, *Lehrgebäude der hebräischen Sprache* (Leipzig: Hinrichs, 1881), 1:134.

4.4.2 Where ⁣ᶜayin is followed by qāmeṣ in an unstressed open syllable, the reflex of *a is sĕgôl.

4.4.3 In a few anomalous cases, the reflex of *a before ᶜayin is pataḥ. In several of these, this pataḥ contrasts with the use of the expected qāmeṣ before other examples of the same word. Thus qāmeṣ occurs before ᶜênayim in Gen 3:6, 38:21; Prov 10:26; but pataḥ in 1 Sam 16:7, Qoh 11:7.

4.5 Before ᵓālep and rêš, the reflex of *a is qāmeṣ.

4.6.1 It is clear that the effect of a following guttural on the *a of the article is much the same as its effect on *a in mh. ᵓālep and rêš induce the maximum change, ᶜayin and hēᵓ less change, and ḥêt minimum change. Unlike the vowel of mh, however, the *a of the article is clearly affected by the vowel following h, ḥ, or ᶜ.

4.2.6 Following ḥêt, qāmeṣ is more conducive to change in preceding *a than is any other vowel. Ḥāṭēp qāmeṣ has the same effect, whether it reflects *a or *u. Only qāmeṣ in a closed unstressed syllable induces the same (minimum) change as do other vowels.

4.6.3 Following hēᵓ, qāmeṣ also produces greater change than do other vowels, with one exception. Where it is stressed, qāmeṣ induces maximum change in preceding *a. The same is true of stressed ṣērê. Where qāmeṣ is unstressed, it generally induces medium change. Other unstressed vowels (including ṣērê), and other stressed vowels, induce minimum change.

4.6.4 Following ᶜayin, unstressed qāmeṣ in an open syllable (reflecting *a) usually induces only medium change. All other vowels, including ḥāṭēp qāmeṣ, qāmeṣ ḥāṭûp (which reflect *u), and stressed qāmeṣ, induce maximum change.

5. THE EFFECT OF A GUTTURAL ON PRECEDING *a

5.1 Gutturals are generally conducive to the change of preceding *a toward qāmeṣ, but this is true of the fricatives h, ḥ, and ᶜ only where they are followed by a vowel. Unless the standard pattern calls for qāmeṣ in the final syllable, h, ḥ, or ᶜ in word-final position is preceded by pataḥ (either regular or "furtive"). The guttural does not induce further development, even where the vowel is stressed. In structures of form *CaCC, where *a is followed by h, ḥ, or ᶜ, the vowel develops only minimally in medial position, and so does not appear as sĕgôl, as it does before other consonants. It appears that the development of *a is similarly inhibited by following ᶜayin where it is followed by *a. Where the following *a is stressed, the expected development could occur, as before any other vowel. Where it is not stressed, however, the change in a preceding *a proceeded more slowly than before other vowels.

5.2   Blau is no doubt right in his view that this effect of *a following ᶜ*ayin* on preceding *a occurred while the reflexes of *a and *u were phonetically distinct, as this explains the fact that the maximum change in the preceding *a takes places before ᶜ*ayin* followed by *qāmeṣ* reflecting *u, as before any other vowel.[10] There seems no doubt, however, that the changes in *a followed by a guttural were stimulated by the Masoretic *qāmeṣ* (ɔ), which might reflect *a or *u, not by long *ā*. The failure of the *a of the article to develop into *sĕgôl* in *haḥɔkmɔ* is due to the fact that the following *qāmeṣ* stands in a closed syllable, not to the fact that it reflects *u, since *a does change to *sĕgôl* before *ḥêt* followed by *ḥāṭēp qāmeṣ* reflecting *u which stands in an open syllable.

5.3   The situation of *a before ᶜ*ayin* followed by *a is analogous to that of the first vowel in the absolute form ʾ*aḥat*. The first *a is represented by *pataḥ* (rather than by *sĕgôl*, as in the masculine form ʾ*eḥɔd*) because in medial position the effect of the historical double closure of the final syllable in the feminine form prevented the development of its vowel to *qāmeṣ*. The *pataḥ* in this final syllable, though stressed and (presumably) long in the Masoretic pronunciation, had no effect on the preceding *a.[11] In terminal position, this inhibiting factor is nullified, so that *qāmeṣ* appears in the second syllable and *sĕgôl* in the first, as in the masculine form. In the same way, ᶜ*ayin* followed by *a has inhibited the development of preceding *a, unless the vowel following ᶜ*ayin* is stressed. This stress nullified the inhibiting factor (presumably by hastening the development of the stressed vowel toward *qameṣ*) and so allowed the expected change to take place in the preceding *a.

6.   THE DEVELOPMENT OF *a IN SEGOLATES, *mh*, AND THE ARTICLE

The survey of the reflexes of *a in the three common situations suggests that *sĕgôl* develops most readily in a stressed open syllable or in an unstressed syllable which was historically closed but is open in the MT, exactly as does *qāmeṣ*. A guttural followed by a vowel is favorable to the change in preceding *a: ʾ*ālep* and *rêš* most, *hēʾ* and ᶜ*ayin* less, *ḥêt* least. The last three are more favorable to the change where the following vowel is stressed *qāmeṣ*. In this situation, the reflex of *a is *qāmeṣ* before *hēʾ* and ᶜ*ayin*, but only *sĕgôl* before the less favorable *ḥêt*. Voiceless *hēʾ* or *ḥêt* where followed by

10. Blau, "Marginalia Semitica," 17 n. 14.

11. The probability that the vowel of a stressed syllable is always long is shown by G. Khan, "Vowel Length and Syllable Structure in the Tiberian Tradition of Biblical Hebrew," *JSS* 32 (1987) 44. However, the relation of Khan's sources to the tradition represented in the MT is unclear, so his conclusions must be treated with caution.

unstressed *qāmeṣ* in an open syllable provides a more favorable environment for change than where followed by some other vowel. This is not the case with the voiced *ᶜayin* followed by unstressed *qāmeṣ* in an open syllable. The change of **a* toward *qāmeṣ* is retarded in this situation. This explanation is preferable to that of dissimilation, since there is no reason to regard *sĕgôl* as a reflex of **a* as resulting from dissimilation in other situations. There is, then, no impediment to seeing the different reflexes of **a* in the situations described as representing different stages in the same process of change. Where conditions for change in such situations are optimal, the reflex of **a* is *qāmeṣ*. Where they are less good, the reflex is *sĕgôl*.

7. *Sĕgôl* IN OTHER MORPHS

7.1 *Prefixed Interrogative Hēʾ*

7.1.1 The reflex of **a* in interrogative *hēʾ* is *pataḥ* or *ḥāṭēp pataḥ*, except where the word begins with a guttural followed by *qāmeṣ* in an unstressed open syllable. In this situation, the reflex of **a* is *sĕgôl*. This includes the cases of *ḥêt* followed by *ḥāṭēp qāmeṣ* in *heḥŏdaltî* in Judg 9:9, etc.[12] I know of no cases where *hēʾ* interrogative stands before *qāmeṣ* in a stressed or closed syllable, nor of any in which it stands before *ᶜayin* followed by *qāmeṣ*.
7.1.2 The only exceptions to this pattern appear to be cases where the prefixed *hēʾ* was taken as representing the definite article, as in Qoh 3:21 and probably Num 16:22, Deut 20:19. The conditioning of **a* in this morph is, then, generally similar to that in the article. The differences are presumably due to the phonological differences between the two morphs.

7.2 *The Prefix š-*

7.2.1 The prefix *š-* is commonly voweled with *sĕgôl* before all consonants, including *ʾ*, *h*, *ḥ*, *ᶜ*. Except where one of these four follows *š-*, *dāgēš* is marked in the following letter. This includes *rēś* (Song 5:2) and *yôd* followed by *šĕwāʾ* (Ps 123:2).
7.2.2 In a few cases this prefix has other vowels. *Pataḥ* occurs before a nonguttural (which is marked with *dāgēš*) in Gen 6:3, Judg 5:7*bis*, Song 1:7,

---

12. This form is most reasonably explained as a perfect *Qal*, with original **a* reduced between long syllables, in GKC §63k/p. 167. On the tendency to reduce **a* before a nonreduced syllable, see J. Blau, *A Grammar of Biblical Hebrew* (Wiesbaden: Harrassowitz, 1976) §9.3.3. The perfect form is used to represent a hypothetical occurrence which is unexpected or undesirable, as *gul:aḥtî* (Judg 16:17) and other cases in 2 Sam 15:33, 2 Kgs 7:4, Ruth 1:12, etc. See S. R. Driver, *A Treatise on the Use of the Tenses in Hebrew* (3d ed.; Oxford: Clarendon, 1892) 178/§138i(α).

and perhaps Job 19:29. *Qāmeṣ* is used before *ʾālep* in Judg 6:17. *Šĕwāʾ* is used before *hûʾ* and *hem* in Qoh 2:22, 3:18.

7.2.3 Different voweling may be used in similar situations, as before *gam* (Qoh 1:17, 2:15, 8:14; cf. Gen 6:3) and *hem* (Song 6:5, Lam 4:9; cf. Qoh 3:18). The situations in which the different vowels are used are not absolutely identical (note the accentuation where the prefix occurs before *hem*), but it seems highly probable that the different vowelings are free variants. That with *sĕgôl* can be considered irrelevant to the particular development of **a* traced here. The cases described in §7.2.2 show a pattern possibly related to that shown by the vowel of the definite article, but minimum development is shown only before *hûʾ*, while maximum development occurs before *hem*, as before *hēʾ* with stressed *qāmeṣ*.[13]

7.3   Elsewhere before a Guttural Followed by Qāmeṣ

7.3.1 *Sĕgôl* occurs before *ḥêt* (whether the following *qāmeṣ* is stressed or unstressed) in *Hithpael* forms from *nḥl* and *nḥm*, and nouns such as *ʾeḥɔd*, as listed in GB pt. 1 §28a/p. 152. In *mibṭɛḥɔ* (Prov 21:22, the final vowel represents a pronoun) and *mibṭɛḥɔm* (Jer 48:13), where *ḥêt* was not historically lengthened, the following *qāmeṣ* has induced greater development than has occurred before other vowels (see Jer 2:37, Ps 71:5, Prov 22:19, Job 8:14).

7.3.2 *Sĕgôl* occurs before *hēʾ* even where the following *qāmeṣ* is stressed in the *Hithpael* form *hiṭːɛhɔrû* (Num 8:7, 2 Chr 30:18), and the nominal form *behɔret* (Lev 14:56), as well as where it is unstressed in *behɔrot* (Lev 13:38–39).

7.3.3 *Sĕgôl* even occurs before *ʾālep* in *nɛʾɔṣôt* (Neh 9:18, 26), although *qāmeṣ* occurs in *nɔʾɔṣôtêkɔ* (Ezek 35:12). *Šĕwāʾ* appears in *nɔʾɔṣɔ* (2 Kgs 19:3 = Isa 37:3), which could be the singular form of this word but is not usually considered so.

7.3.4 *Sĕgôl* occurs before *rêš* in a stressed syllable in *hɛrɔ* (Gen 14:10). The expected *qāmeṣ* occurs in *hɔhɔrɔ* (Gen 12:8, etc.).[14]

7.3.5 The reflex of **a* before *ʿayin* is *qāmeṣ* in forms from the feminine noun *rɔʿɔ* (from *rʿʿ*), whether the following *qāmeṣ* is stressed or unstressed. *Qāmeṣ* also occurs in the *Hithpael* form *ništɔʿɔ* (Isa 41:23), where the stress is penultimate.

---

13. S. Morag suggests that the voweling with *šĕwāʾ* derives from a different stream of tradition—not from the one in which the use of *sĕgôl* became standard; see "On the Historical Validity of the Vocalization of the Hebrew Bible," *JAOS* 94 (1974) 308–9.

14. Where directional *hēʾ* is not suffixed to this noun, a more developed reflex of **a* is more likely to be shown where the article is prefixed than where it is not, and this is the case also with some other nouns of form **CaC:*, as *bad*, *gan*, *ḥag*, *ʿam*. *Pataḥ* occurs in the construct form *midbarɔ* (Josh 18:12, 1 Kgs 19:15).

7.4   Other Situations

7.4.1 *Sĕgôl* occurs in an unstressed open final syllable as the vowel of directional *hē³* in 1 Sam 21:2, 22:9; 1 Kgs 2:36, 42; 2 Kgs 5:25; Ezek 25:13 and as that of a third-person feminine singular perfect verb form in Zech 5:4.

7.4.2 *Sĕgôl* replaces the expected *qāmeṣ* in a stressed open final syllable in the characteristic ending of a feminine noun in Isa 59:5, in the "cohortative" ending in 1 Sam 28:15, and in the related ending of the imperative in *dᵊᶜɛ ḥɔkma* (Prov 24:14, the only case where the following word begins with a guttural followed by *qāmeṣ*).

7.4.3 *Sĕgôl* (presumably reflecting *$*a$*) occurs in a stressed open nonfinal syllable before *nûn* followed by *qāmeṣ* in the construct form in *pad:ɛnɔ ³ărɔm* (Gen 28:2, 5, 6, 7; cf. §7.3.4), also in the third-person feminine plural suffix in *qirbɛnɔ* (Gen 41:21*bis*), and similarly before *kap* and *hē³* followed by *qāmeṣ* in the second-person masculine singular and third-person feminine singular pronominal suffixes -*ɛkɔ* and -*ɛhɔ*.

8.   THE DEVELOPMENT OF *Sĕgôl* IN THE OTHER SITUATIONS

8.1 The cases of *sĕgôl* in final open syllables are rare exceptions to the common forms. They cannot be interpreted (in the light of the present evidence) as examples of the process of change described in §6. Of the other cases, *pad:ɛnɔ* could be explained as an example of this process. This seems less likely for the *sĕgôl* in the pronominal forms. Indeed it is doubtful if it is correct to regard these simply as reflexes of *$*a$* in a stressed open syllable; other factors are probably also involved. The same is true for the use of *sĕgôl* in the prefix *š-*. There is insufficient evidence of the use of other vowels in that prefix to allow a decision.

8.2 The other cases of *sĕgôl* before gutturals (§§7.1, 7.3) are generally consistent with the pattern of development shown by the vowel of the article. They reinforce the conclusion that *pataḥ*, *sĕgôl*, and *qāmeṣ* represent stages in a single process of development. The development was conditioned by the total phonological environment, not just by the sounds that follow. This would include the structure (in terms of syllable structure, stress pattern, and vowel length) of the prosodic phrase in which the vowel occurs.[15] Consequently, the vowel which actually reflects *$*a$* before a particular guttural followed by stressed or unstressed *qāmeṣ* differs in different words.

---

15. On the importance of prosodic phrases (or "speech units") in conditioning vowel and stress patterns, see E. J. Revell, *Nesiga in Tiberian Hebrew* (Textos y Estudios "Cardenal Cisneros" 39; Madrid: CSIC, 1987 §9.1–4; idem, "Conditioning of Stress Position," 299; idem, "Stress Position in Verb Forms with Vocalic Affix," *JSS* 32 (1987) 259.

Sĕgôl may occur where the article would show *qāmeṣ*, and *qāmeṣ* may occur where the article would show *sĕgôl*, showing again that *sĕgôl* does not result from dissimilation, but from a less advanced stage of the same process of change which gave rise to *qāmeṣ*.

9. CONCLUSION

9.1 *Sĕgôl* as a reflex of **a* appears most commonly in syllables which have been secondarily opened, but this is not the case with interrogative *hē⁼*, nor with some of the noun forms considered, and may not be the case with *mh*. It is probably correct, then, to say that *sĕgôl* developed as a reflex of **a* in a syllable in which the vowel remained short at a later date than in the typical open syllable, due either to structural features (the vowel stood in a closed nonfinal syllable) or to prosodic features (the morph was typically proclitic,[16] or the syllable was never stressed). Consequently the process of change (which was due to the opening of the syllable, or to the effect of a following guttural) began relatively late in the history of the language, and so only induced the maximum development (*qāmeṣ*) in the vowel in situations particularly favorable to the change. *Sĕgôl* represents a medial stage in this process of change.

9.2 The anomalies noted in the above descriptions can be accounted for in a number of ways. Studies of various phenomena in the Masoretic Text suggest that the accentuation of that text does not always represent the same intonation patterns as conditioned its voweling.[17] Thus, when the vowel patterns were fixed, some cases of *mh* now unstressed may have been stressed, and vice versa. The process by which the Masoretes established a standard reading may have resulted in the introduction into the standard text of a form which had developed under conditioning characteristic of some slightly different strand of tradition.[18] Finally, the development of **a* may

---

16. G. Khan, "The Pronunciation of ־מַה before *dageš* in the Medieval Tiberian Hebrew Reading Tradition," *JSS* 34 (1989) 433–41, shows that *mh* with *pataḥ* and following *dāgēš* was read as proclitic in the Tiberian tradition of the Ben Asher school, but was read with a certain degree of prosodic separation at later times. Possibly this reflects the final stage of a development away from what was once general proclitic use. I am most grateful to Dr. Khan for his kindly providing me with a copy of this article in typescript, and for permission to cite it.

17. See my discussion of this point in "Conditioning of Stress Position," 281–84; and "Stress Position in Verb Forms," 250.

18. This possibility is discussed in E. J. Revell, "LXX and MT: Aspects of Relationship," in *De Septuaginta: Studies in Honour of John William Wevers* (ed. A. Pietersma and C. Cox; Toronto: Benben, 1984) 48. Cf. Morag's opinion on the origin of the use of *šĕwā⁼* as the vowel of the prefix *š-* referred to in n. 13 above.

have been affected by prosodic features which are little understood, such as the tendency to alternate long and short syllables noted in n. 12 above.

9.3   The general line of development of *a* in the situations surveyed is, then, quite clear. An open syllable, a following guttural, main stress, and terminal position are all conducive to the development of *qāmeṣ* from *a*. Where all, or most, of these factors are present, *a* gives rise to *qāmeṣ*. Where a few or none are present, *a* gives rise to *pataḥ*. In intermediate situations, *a* gives rise to *sĕgôl*. The effect of these factors on the development of *a*, and so the number required to effect development, varies with the individual features which characterize the different situations surveyed.

[December, 1988]

Edward L. Greenstein

An Introduction to a Generative Phonology of Biblical Hebrew

In biblical studies, as in many other areas of learning, language analysis has rarely thrived as an end in itself. For the most part, linguistics has served the needs of philology.[1] Grammar has been formalized in order to read and interpret a text fluently and correctly. Special attention has been paid to irregular patterns and to rare and unexpected forms. The philologist encountering an odd phenomenon can consult a specialized grammar book and find an explanation of a puzzling form or construction, or the thrust of a peculiar idiom. By correctly identifying unusual language forms, the philologist can proceed with the business of interpreting the text. Grammar ministers to meaning, and this is as it should be. Ultimately all disciplines should serve to elucidate the literatures that we study by clearing out the channels of communication, removing the clutter of unknowns that block our understanding.

Nevertheless, although languages are worth studying primarily in order to read and understand foreign texts and speakers, they are fascinating in and of themselves. One significant assumption of the generative approach to language study is that, by analyzing how people produce and perceive language, we learn something important about what it is to be human.[2] Even when linguistic analysis does not increase our understanding of *what* a particular text means, it always tells us more about *how* the language of that text means.

Author's note: My thanks to Walter Bodine for his challenging questions and to Joseph Malone for his helpful suggestions.

1. Cf. E. L. Greenstein, "The Phonology of Akkadian Syllable Structure," *AAL* 9 (1984) 1–71, esp. 7. Many of the general points that follow are treated in greater detail there.
2. See, e.g., J. J. Katz, *The Underlying Reality of Language and Its Philosophical Import* (New York: Harper & Row, 1971).

The generative method is structuralist in its orientation. Structuralism views the object of its study, whatever that might be, as a self-contained system in which all the parts interact in a thoroughly interdependent way.[3] For language this means that the various components of a language inform and relate to each other on various levels. Changes in one domain may trigger adaptations elsewhere in the language. A phonological change that leads to the dropping of short vocalic case endings,[4] for example, may lead further to the development of syntactic constraints on word order. Within a component of a language, such as its sound system or phonology, the various linguistic operations interact in numerous ways. They may have to line up to apply in a specific hierarchical sequence (see p. 40 for a case in point). The presence of one operation may block the application of another. A number of processes may be subordinated to a single overriding constraint or principle.[5] Since we are interested here in phonology, my remarks focus on that area, though they may be appropriate generally to the other components of language too.[6]

TWO LEVELS OF STRUCTURE

The generative approach sees language on two major levels. The concrete, or surface, level represents language as produced or spoken. This is the phonetic level. Beneath the surface structure is an abstract level, or deep structure, the representation of language before it emerges as speech by passing through all the appropriate phonological rules. This is the phonemic level. The theory is based on the following assumptions regarding language learning. When a child hears a language, he or she relates variants of the same word or morpheme to each other and posits a single deep or underlying form from which all the variants are derived. The actually occurring forms are derived from the underlying form by rules, which the child induces from the relations between all posited underlying forms and variants.

3. See, e.g., J. Piaget, *Structuralism* (New York: Harper & Row, 1970).
4. For this change in Hebrew around the turn of the first millennium B.C.E., see Z. S. Harris, *Development of the Canaanite Dialects* (AOS 16; New Haven: American Oriental Society, 1939) 59–60.
5. For example, widespread Semitic constraints on syllable structure (e.g., avoidance of consonant clusters) govern various phonological rules in Akkadian; see Greenstein, "Akkadian Syllable Structure." Similar constraints operate in Hebrew.
6. Good general introductions to generative phonology are S. A. Schane, *Generative Phonology* (Englewood Cliffs: Prentice-Hall, 1973) and L. M. Hyman, *Phonology: Theory and Analysis* (New York: Holt, Rinehart & Winston, 1975). More advanced discussions are, e.g., A. H. Sommerstein, *Modern Phonology* (Baltimore: University Park, 1977) and M. Kenstowicz and C. Kisseberth, *Generative Phonology: Description and Theory* (New York: Academic Press, 1979). The classic presentation on which subsequent discussions have been based is N. Chomsky and M. Halle, *The Sound Pattern of English* (New York: Harper & Row, 1968).

There is psychological evidence for the existence of both the phonemic level and rules. For example, a child learning native English learns to pluralize nouns by adding *s*. Internalizing the rule, many children will apply the rule indiscriminately, even where it does not apply, as in *mans* (for *men*), even after they have heard the correct (accepted) form many times. They must then learn the exception, that nouns such as *man, woman,* and *child* form the plural differently.[7]

The rules map the underlying forms onto their phonetic realizations in speech. Thus, hearing the words *electric* and *electricity*, a speaker would perceive a phonemic relation between the two words, posit *electric* as the underlying, or base, form of *electricity*, and derive the latter by applying an internalized phonological rule that converts the phoneme /k/ to phonetic [s] preceding the suffix /iti/.[8] The rules, then, generate correct surface forms from underlying bases, which accounts for the name of the theory, "generative."

One of the issues within generative phonology is the extent to which the underlying level can be abstract. In the case above, the base form is one that actually occurs (more or less) in the word *electric*. May we posit a phonemic representation that never appears on the surface because it is always transformed by the phonological rules? Some phonologists argue for a degree of concreteness such that only an actually occurring form may be posited on the underlying level. Others allow for assuming an abstract phoneme.[9]

7. On the psychological reality of the phonemic level and rules, see further, e.g., J. A. Fodor, T. G. Bever, and M. F. Garrett, *The Psychology of Language* (New York: McGraw-Hill, 1974), esp. 432–34; W. A. Wickelgren, "Phonetic Coding and Serial Order," in *Handbook of Perception*, vol. 7: *Language and Speech* (ed. E. C. Carterette and M. P. Friedman; New York: Academic Press, 1976), esp. 246–50; A. Cutler and D. Norris, "Monitoring Sentence Comprehension," in *Sentence Processing* (ed. W. E. Cooper and C. T. Walker; Hillsdale, NJ: Lawrence Erlbaum, 1979), esp. 113–14; and M. Halle, J. Bresnan and G. A. Miller, eds., *Linguistic Theory and Psychological Reality* (Cambridge: MIT Press, 1978).

8. That the "softening" of /k/ to [s] in *electricity* is a learned rule and not a purely "natural" and necessary process is suggested by the fact that in other locutions, such as *persnickity* and *lickety split*, /k/ does not change to [s] preceding /iti/; cf. D. Stampe, "On Chapter Nine," in *Issues in Phonological Theory* (ed. M. J. Kenstowicz and C. W. Kisseberth; The Hague: Mouton, 1973) 44–52, at 45–46.

9. For various positions, consult, e.g., P. Kiparsky, "Phonological Representations," in *Three Dimensions of Linguistic Theory* (ed. O. Fujimura; Tokyo: TEC, 1973) 1–136; L. M. Hyman, "How Concrete Is Phonology?" *Lg.* 46 (1970) 58–76; M. K. Brame, "On the Abstractness of Phonology: Maltese ᶜ," in *Contributions to Generative Phonology* (ed. M. K. Brame; Austin: University of Texas Press, 1972) 22–61; J. B. Hooper, *An Introduction to Natural Generative Phonology* (New York: Academic Press, 1976).

I incline to the position that a phoneme may be abstract, as I am impressed by the analysis of Maltese Arabic phonology presented by Brame. He demonstrates that although /ᶜ/ does not occur phonetically in Maltese Arabic, it must be assumed implicitly in order to account

Consider the paradigms of III-*yôd* verb stems in Hebrew. The final *yôd* of the stem occurs in none of the regular Masoretic Hebrew forms in the paradigms, although it does turn up in some archaic and/or pausal forms. Compare normal *yɛḥĕ zū* 'they see' beside pausal *yɛḥĕ zɔ́yūn* (Isa 26:11). In the second, uncommon, form the *yôd* appears phonetically. But is the *yôd* to be posited as phonemic in the first form? I would say yes. The paradigm of the suffixed form of a III-*yôd* verb like *ḥɔzɔ* 'to see' includes forms such as *ḥɔzīṯī* 'I saw' and *ḥɔzīṯɔ* 'you [masc. sing.] saw'. The long *ī*-vowel of the second syllable can best be interpreted as the contraction of the vowel /i/ and the glide /y/ to long *ī*. Because the language possesses a rule to rewrite /iy/ (when it is not followed by a vowel) as [ī], and because there is no other reason to find a long *ī*-vowel in the second syllable of the *Qal* conjugation suffixed verb-form paradigm, a *yôd* is implicit in the surface form and will be posited underlyingly. The fact that the pausal form *yɛḥĕ zɔ́yūn* and certain derived nouns, such as *ḥizzɔyón* 'vision' (2 Sam 7:17), manifest the *yôd* phonetically reinforces this interpretation of the verbal paradigm. (We may not be so lucky for every III-*yôd* verb.)

Clearly the phonemic representation will not always occur on the surface. It seems best to me, therefore, to posit an actually occurring form on the deep level, where possible, but to be prepared to posit a more abstract underlying form where such a representation can be deduced from the alternant phonetic forms within the framework of the otherwise accepted rules. It is precisely because we assume certain rules that we can deduce the underlying presence of the third radical *yôd* in a form like *ḥɔzīṯī*.

It is important from a generative perspective to emphasize that the grammar of a language entails the underlying forms and rules that a person

---

for a number of exceptions to the phonological rules. (The other Semitic gutturals, /ʾ/, /h/, and /ḫ/, occur phonetically in this dialect.) Here I can only summarize some of the salient arguments from Brame's model generative analysis. Brame identifies the abstract phoneme /ʿ/ in all three positions in the verbal root. By assuming /ʿ/ in first radical position, Brame can explain why the regular prefixes *ni* and *ti* occur as *na* and *ta* in certain stems, e.g., *nála*ʾ 'I close', *tála*ʾ 'you close'. If /ʿ/ is present on the underlying level, the prefix vowel would undergo the guttural assimilation rule by which /i/ becomes /a/ preceding a consonant that is "back" and "low," i.e., a guttural. If one assumes /ʿ/ as the abstract phoneme in the second radical position, one can explain forms like *soobt* 'I lamented'. Normally, a double-vowel segment, or long vowel, undergoes truncation (or vowel shortening); here, an abstract /ʿ/ lies between the vowels on the phonemic level, preventing truncation from applying. The form *tísma* 'you hear', instead of otherwise expected *tísmi*, can be accounted for by positing abstract /ʿ/ in the third radical position. The morphologically conditioned /i/ in the second syllable would be followed on the phonemic level by /ʿ/ so that it would undergo guttural assimilation and become the actually occurring *a*. Whereas Semitists may know that /ʿ/ appears in the historical root of this verb, speakers of Maltese must organize their competence in their language without recourse to such unavailable knowledge.

would induce from the speech that one hears. This has two procedural implications to which we shall direct our attention. One is the need to segregate
the synchronic grammar of a language from its history. The other is that linguistic data should be culled from a spoken language.

SYNCHRONIC AND DIACHRONIC

If a grammar is based on what a child would induce about the language that
he or she hears, we must exclude from the grammar word forms and rules
that no longer exist in the language, to which the child has no access. Thus,
to return to our example of III-*yôd* verb stems, it would be simple to establish the original presence of the final *yôd* in the verb *ḥɜzɜ* by means of a
comparative study of the West Semitic languages and a historical reconstruction of the III-*yôd* paradigm. We could trace Masoretic *ḥɜzɜ* to a much
earlier **ḥazaya*, or more precisely **ḥaḏaya*.[10] The native speaker of Biblical
Hebrew, however, had no such information but, rather, produced correct
forms by inducing bases and rules from the contemporary language. The
grammarian seeks to recapture those inductions.

The difference between a synchronic interpretation and a historical reconstruction can be illustrated simply by the example of Hebrew determination.[11] Upon hearing a number of noun forms such as *habbayit* 'the house',
hammɛlɛk 'the king', *hayyōm* 'the day' (or 'today'), a native speaker would induce the following rule: determination is produced by prefixing /ha/ to the
stem and doubling the initial consonant of the stem. The historical linguist
may trace determination back to a deictic particle, such as **hā*[12] or **hal*,[13]
which is prefixed to the stem. In time the long vowel segment, or vowel plus
l, evolved into a short vowel segment plus doubled consonant. The ordinary
speaker of Biblical Hebrew, however, knew nothing about the reconstructed
particle **hā* or **hal*. He or she knew only that to say 'the king' one prefixes
/ha/ to the stem and doubles the stem's initial consonant. A grammar com-
prises a speaker's implicit knowledge, or competence, in one's language. It is
synchronic.

10. Cf., e.g., Ugaritic *ḥdy*, where the final *yod* appears consonantally in *KTU* 1.3, III, 23–24:
    mid tmtḫṣn wtʿn, tḥtṣb wtḥdy ʿnt 'She did much combat, then looked; she fought, then saw
    [*watahdiyu*], did Anat'.
11. Cf. J. L. Malone, "Systematic vs. Autonomous Phonemics and the Hebrew Grapheme
    dagesh," *AAL* 2 (1975) 121.
12. Cf., e.g., J. Barth, *Die Pronominalbildung in den semitischen Sprachen* (Leipzig: Hinrichs,
    1913) 133; BL §31a/p. 262.
13. Cf., e.g., A. Ungnad, cited in C. Brockelmann, *Grundriss der vergleichenden Grammatik
    der semitischen Sprachen* (Berlin: Reuther & Reichard, 1908) 1:316 n. 1; see also GKC
    §31l/pp. 111–12.

THE PROBLEM OF SPOKEN LANGUAGE

The second procedural implication of the generative perspective involves the premise that "language" means spoken, natural language. This raises a special issue concerning Biblical Hebrew, which is a historical (or "dead") language with no direct record of its spoken nature. There is reason to believe that, although the Bible's Hebrew is literary, its main linguistic features reflect colloquial language. The Lachish letters and other epigraphic materials—which are the best testimony to colloquial ancient Hebrew that we shall ever have—display a Hebrew closely resembling that of, say, the Book of Kings.[14] Nevertheless, since the Bible had undergone considerable phonological development by the time we get any vocalized texts, it is precisely in the area of phonology that we lack direct evidence of Hebrew in the ancient periods. Any synchronic phonological analysis must be based substantially on reconstruction and is accordingly a risky enterprise.[15]

The analysis of Biblical Hebrew as vocalized by the early medieval Masoretes of Tiberias is another matter. It is possible that the Masoretic vocalization represents the result of a natural phonological evolution of the Bible's Hebrew into a synchronic Tiberian stage. We may then perform generative analysis of Tiberian Hebrew phonology. This is essentially what J. L. Malone has done in an unpublished comprehensive study and in numerous published articles.[16]

The only way to test such a hypothesis is to try it and see what happens, but a sort of "Catch 22" inheres in the situation. Unless Tiberian Hebrew is a systematic, natural language, it would be inappropriate to apply a generative analysis to it. On the other hand, if the generative approach is not only sound but desirable, one ought to adopt it in order to ascertain whether or not Tiberian Hebrew behaves like a natural language.

We cannot explore this knotty issue at length here, but it is worth considering a case or two in point. Malone has attempted to show that certain

---

14. Note, for example, that the Lachish letters employ the *wāw*-consecutive, a feature of Biblical Hebrew that has sometimes been taken to be purely literary; see H. Donner and W. Röllig, *Kanaanäische und aramäische Inschriften* (Wiesbaden: Harrassowitz, 1962) vol. 1: #194:6–7; cf. #200:4–5, 7–8. For attempts to identify evidence of colloquial Hebrew in the Bible, see, e.g., A. Bendavid, *Biblical Hebrew and Mishnaic Hebrew* (2 vols.; Tel Aviv: Dvir, 1967) [Hebrew]; B. A. Levine, "Chapters in the History of Spoken Hebrew," *ErIsr* 14 (1978) 155–60 [Hebrew]; G. Rendsburg, *Evidence for a Spoken Hebrew in Biblical Times* (Ph.D. diss., New York University, 1980).
15. For a notable attempt to reconstruct Judean Hebrew of about 600 B.C.E., see Z. S. Harris, "Linguistic Structure of Hebrew," *JAOS* 61 (1941) 143–67.
16. J. L. Malone, *Tiberian Hebrew Phonology* (ms., 1984—to be published by Eisenbrauns, 1993); some of his articles are cited elsewhere in the notes to this chapter.

apparent deviations from typical Masoretic forms reflect the natural processes of a living language.[17] If Malone's analyses are judged correct, the implication is that Tiberian Hebrew behaves like, and may be regarded as, a natural language. Here is one of his illustrations.

For reasons he delineates in his comprehensive study, Malone posits the first schematic vowel of the *Qal* imperative to be an underlying /o/. (Compare the *u* that is most commonly reconstructed by Semitic historical linguists.) Using the stem /š-m-r/, the underlying form would be /šomor/. (The masc. sing. form [šəmor] and the fem. sing. form [šimrī] are derived from this base form through rules of vowel reduction/deletion and, in the latter case, vowel raising, on which see further below.) When a high vocalic suffix, such as /ī/ or /ū/ is added, the first schematic vowel undergoes a kind of umlauting and is raised to [i], yielding such forms as *šimrī* and *šimrū*. The same occurs normally to the stem /ᶜoloz/ 'rejoice' when, after the application of vowel deletion, it gives rise to a masculine plural imperative *ᶜilzū*. However, a deviant form of the feminine singular imperative *ᶜɔlzī* is also attested (Zeph 3:14). Is this form a Masoretic slip, or is it an authentic Tiberian Hebrew form? Malone opts for the latter. He explains the deviant form as the product of a natural and common enough linguistic process of suppressing a rule, in this instance the rule of imperative raising or umlauting the first stem vowel of the *Qal* imperative. What surfaces is the form as it would look had it undergone all the phonological rules except imperative raising.

Lest one grow impatient and judge this explanation to be merely ad hoc, Malone cites another case of rule suppression in the *Qal* imperative. Normally, Tiberian Hebrew lowers a *ḥāṭēp* vowel, or colored *šĕwāʾ*, to *a* following an initial guttural consonant in verb stems. Thus, the pausal form that would otherwise be *ᶜᵊ̌vódū* 'serve!' undergoes schwa coloring and occurs typically as *ᶜăbódū* (Ezek 20:39). There exists, however, a deviant form *ḥɔrɔ̌bī* 'dry up!' (Isa 44:27). As in the preceding example, Malone explains this as the result of suppressing the schwa coloring rule. Since rule suppression is a natural linguistic process and attests to the existence of the rule, it is at least possible that Tiberian Hebrew is a natural language.

In all fairness to the cynical, it is also possible that Tiberian Hebrew is not entirely natural. We are all familiar with examples where the Masoretes, or their traditions, fouled up, creatively inventing forms because they were stuck with anomalous words or because they misunderstood difficult or ambiguous ones. An apparent case of an ambiguous form that the Masoretes mistakenly parsed is *hizzakkū* 'cleanse yourselves!' in Isa 1:16. The Masoretes take the stem to be /z-k-y/ 'to be pure, innocent'. But what form is

17. J. L. Malone, "Textually Deviant Forms as Evidence for Philological Analysis: A Service of Philology to Linguistics," *JANESCU* 11 (1979) 71–79, esp. 76.

implied by the double *zz* and the double *kk*? A *Hithpael*, it would seem. If so, why is there a double *zz* instead of *zd*—that is, **hizdakkú*—which is what we expect? Malone proffers an involved phonological solution to account for the assimilation of /zd/ to [zz].[18]

There is a philological snag in the anomalous, or uncommon, Masoretic form. Isaiah presents a sequence of two verbs: *raḥăṣú hizzakkú* 'wash, cleanse yourselves [of the crimes that have tainted your hands]' (see v. 15). In a context of cleansing and in juxtaposition to the verb *rɔḥaṣ* 'wash', we might expect a form of the stem /z-k-k/ rather than /z-k-y/. Compare Job 9:30: *ʾim hitrɔḥaṣtī bəmē šɔ̄lɛg, wahăzikkōtī bəbor kappɔ̄y* 'If I would wash myself with soap plant, or cleanse my hands with lye'.[19] In Job it is clear that the stem /z-k-k/ is used in parallel with /r-ḥ-ṣ/. The form *hizzakkú* in Isa 1:16 should, then, be parsed as a *Niphal* imperative of /z-k-k/ and vocalized correctly as *hizzákkū*, as Honeyman had proposed.[20] Consequently, if such argumentation is persuasive, the anomalous *hizzakkú* is a Masoretic ghost form and is not a reflex of a living language situation.

The moral of this discussion, then, is this: When a generative phonologist analyzes Tiberian Hebrew, one must guard against assuming that Tiberian Hebrew reflects a natural language just because generative analysis produces interesting results. Nevertheless, the more generative theory works in explaining living languages, the more sanguine one can be about applying it to Masoretic Hebrew. And the more generative analysis satisfactorily explains Tiberian Hebrew, the more it will impress Hebrew linguists of other stripes.

MASORETIC VOCALIZATION

While I am treating the work of the Masoretes, I should touch, albeit briefly, on the issue of how to interpret the Hebrew graphemes and the Masoretic vowel symbols in particular. The Masoretic pointing distinguishes seven vowel qualities: *a, ɔ, o, u, ɛ, e, i*, as well as *šĕwāʾ (ə)*.[21] Vowel length is not

---

18. J. L. Malone, "Systematic Metathesis in Mandaic," *Lg.* 47 (1971) 396–97 n. 5.

19. Cf. N. H. Tur-Sinai, *The Book of Job* (Jerusalem: Kiryath Sepher, 1967) 170–71.

20. A. M. Honeyman, "Isaiah I 16 הִזַּכּוּ," *VT* 1 (1951) 63–65.

21. This is the understanding of the classic grammars, GB, esp. § 10/pp. 58–69; Brockelmann, *Grundriss der vergleichenden Grammatik*; and BL. On the historical development of the seven vowel qualities, see, e.g., J. Blau, "Marginalia Semitica III," *IOS* 7 (1977) 14–31, at 14–17. On the history of the Masoretic vowel pointing, cf. W. Chomsky, "The History of Our Vowel System in Hebrew," *JQR* 32 (1941) 27–46. This seven-vowel system is accepted by Malone in his *Tiberian Hebrew Phonology* and other studies. The seven-vowel distinction is recognized, too, in W. Richter, *Transliteration und Transkription: Objekt- und metasprachliche Metazeichensysteme zur Wiedergabe hebräischer Texte* (St. Ottilien: EOS, 1983).

indicated explicitly. The assumption that vocalic length is part of the phonology although it is not distinguished graphemically allows us to explain, for example, the conditions under which certain vowels (presumed short) reduce or elide when other vowels (presumed long) do not.[22] Students of Hebrew are misled by typical systems of transliteration, such as those of the Society of Biblical Literature and various individuals,[23] which employ phonological symbols such as the macron (which is meant to indicate vowel length) to represent graphemic distinctions (such as vowel quality). It would appear from such transcriptions that Masoretic *qāmeṣ*, transliterated *ā*, is simply a long *pataḥ*, and that *ṣērê*, transliterated *ē*, is a long *sĕgôl*. The usual corollary is that both *pataḥ* and *sĕgôl* are always short and that both *qāmeṣ gādôl* and *ṣērê* are always long.

From a phonological point of view, the system of only five vowels (excluding *šĕwāʾ*), in which *ṣērê* is a long *sĕgôl*, etc., makes little sense. Why would the Masoretes employ a single symbol to render both *qāmeṣ qāṭān*—the realization of closed /o/—and a long *ā*? It is much more likely that the same symbol represents both short and long *qāmeṣ*, *ɔ* and *ɔ̄*. Moreover, it stands to reason phonologically that *pataḥ* can be, and is, long in the initial open syllable of forms like *lāḏōnɔ̄y* 'to my lord'. Concerning *ṣērê*, there is no reason that it should always be long. In the first syllable of segolate noun forms such as *séfɛr* 'document', the vowel ought to be short, as is the *sĕgôl* in the first syllable of *mélɛḵ* 'king' and the first vowel in all segolate nouns. Moreover, it is surely unreasonable to analyze the open and accented *sĕgôl* at the end of the unbound (absolute) form *yɔ̄fɛ̄* 'fair' as short but the *ṣērê* with only a secondary accent in the construct counterpart *yɔfè* as long! The graphemic system should, it would seem, be interpreted in such a way that the phonology makes sense.

The issue is worth reviewing because the improbable presumption of a five-vowel rather than a seven-vowel system for Tiberian Hebrew has misguided recent generative work on Hebrew phonology by Prince and McCarthy.[24] The analysis that follows adopts the interpretation that Masoretic Hebrew distinguishes seven vowels, which may be long or short, plus *šĕwāʾ*.

---

22. For a historical analysis of short vowel elision in ancient Hebrew, cf. J. Cantineau, "Elimination des syllables brèves en hébreu et en araméen biblique," *Bulletin d'études orientales* 2 (1932) 125–44.

23. I single out here W. Weinberg, who has devoted entire publications to the topic of transliterating Hebrew, esp. "Transliteration and Transcription of Hebrew," *HUCA* 40–41 (1969–70) 1–32 with tables. Even what he calls the "narrow [i.e., scholarly, philological] transliteration" fails to distinguish the seven Masoretic vowels and mixes phonetic with graphemic phenomena.

24. Cf., e.g., Alan Prince, *The Phonology and Morphology of Tiberian Hebrew* (Ph.D. diss., MIT, 1975); J. J. McCarthy, *Formal Problems in Semitic Phonology and Morphology*

A SKETCH OF THE GENERATIVE METHOD

A hallmark of the generative approach is its view that the phoneme is an abstract bundle of relevant phonological characteristics or distinctions called "distinctive features." These features tend to be, for any given language, of an abstract definition. It is more common usage among generativists, for example, to find features such as "front," "low," and "continuant" than to find narrower qualities such as "fricative" or even "labial." The reason for this is that the more general labels are capable of capturing larger generalizations. Following the assumption that speakers will organize and interpret their language in the most economical way, the generative method looks for wider descriptions and broader explanations, covering as much as possible at a single stroke. Without getting into all the features that one would need in order to analyze Tiberian Hebrew, we should note at least that a matrix of features must be delineated and that those features are generally taken to be binary. That is, what distinguishes one phoneme from another is the presence or absence of a particular feature of the language. A vowel, for example, may be plus or minus "low," or "round," or "long." A stop consonant may be plus or minus "voiced," to consider but one feature. Features are formally represented by listing the relevant and nonredundant ones for each phoneme in square brackets.

As we saw above, the main objective of generative analysis is to identify the underlying representation of the surface forms and induce the rules by which the surface forms can be derived from the underlying representation in the most straightforward and efficient manner. The most basic form of writing a rule is this: $a \rightarrow b/$ ___ . This means that an underlying representation a becomes realized phonetically as b when it is in the environment described to the right of the slash. The underline signifies the location of a in the environment. Sometimes a and b are best represented not by a particular phoneme but by a set of distinctive features because in that way a number of phonemes can be grouped to express a more general process.

Here is an illustration. A short /a/ in a closed and unstressed syllable raises to *i*, but not if the following consonant is a guttural. Thus, *yišmór* 'he watches', but *yaḥtóm* 'he seals'. Characterizing gutturals as [+back], [+low], and [−vocalic], I write the rule as follows ("str" = "stressed"):

(New York: Garland, 1985); and idem, "OCP Effects: Gemination and Antigemination," *Linguistic Inquiry* 17 (1986) 207–63, esp. 234–38. See the critical discussion in J. L. Malone, "Messrs McCarthy and Prince and the Problem of Hebrew Vowel Color" (ms., 1980). This is not the place to delineate my differences from Prince and McCarthy, but suffice it to say that they extend beyond defining vowel quality and rules governing *šĕwā*ʾ reduction and deletion.

$$a \rightarrow i / \underline{\quad} \; C$$
$$\text{[-str] [-back]}$$

Noting that /a/ is the lowest and only back vowel in Hebrew, one may incorporate a greater degree of explanation into the rule by labeling *a* as [+low] (and coincidentally [+back]). In other words, /a/ is not attenuated to *i* when the immediately following consonant is articulated in a position similar to it. This yields (# = word boundary):

$$\begin{array}{c} V \\ \text{[+low]} \end{array} \rightarrow i / \underline{\quad} \begin{array}{c} C \\ \text{[-str] [-back]} \end{array} \left\{ \begin{array}{c} C \\ \# \end{array} \right\}$$

I could go further and describe /i/ as [-flat]—to distinguish it from /u/—and as [+high]—to distinguish it from /e/—but that is not germane to my purpose.

What is even more interesting is that Tiberian Hebrew not only raises /a/ to *i* in certain circumstances; in similar circumstances it lowers an underlying /i/ to *a*. There is something of an inverse, or flip-flop, relationship between the two processes. Generative analysis seeks a single formulation to express both processes in the same rule. Malone has formulated such a rule of lowering-raising.[25] Here I present a slightly simpler version of the rule and illustrate. The rule reads ("voc" = "vocalic," i.e., a vowel):

$$[\alpha \text{ high}] \rightarrow [-\alpha \text{ high}] / \underline{\quad} \begin{array}{c} C \\ \text{[+voc]} \\ \text{[} \alpha \text{ str]} \end{array} \left\{ \begin{array}{c} C \\ \# \end{array} \right\}$$

This means a vowel that is plus-or-minus "high" (α represents a variable feature) will become the opposite value of "high" when it is plus-or-minus (i.e., the same value for) stressed and is in a closed syllable. This rule accounts for the second vowel of the underlying singular construct form /kabid/ 'heavy' becoming *a* in *kəvàḏ* and the first vowel of the underlying plural construct /kabiday/ becoming *i* in *kivd*ẽ.

For my concluding illustration in this introduction, let us see how rules apply beneath the surface and in regulated sequences. One of the most salient rules of Tiberian Hebrew phonology is spirantization. A stop consonant is spirantized following a vowel at any level of derivation. Thus, in the absolute form of the plural for 'kings', *məlɔk̲ím*, the /k/ spirantizes to *k̲* following a vowel. The derivation is more or less as follows:

25. J. L. Malone, "A Hebrew Flip-Flop Rule and Its Historical Origins," *Lingua* 30 (1972) 422–48. For another Hebrew variable rule, cf. low shortening in Malone, "Textually Deviant Forms," 73 n. 8.

/malakīm/
malak̲īm   spirantization
malak̍im   stress assignment
malāk̲ím   pretonic lengthening
məlāk̲ím   vowel reduction
[məlɔ̄k̲ím]   rounding

Note that stress assignment must precede pretonic lengthening and vowel reduction, and that pretonic lengthening must precede rounding.

What is clear from the following case is that spirantization applies at
every opportunity in the derivation of surface structure from deep structure.[26] Consider the derivation of the corresponding construct form:

/malakay/
malak̲ay   spirantization
malak̲ày   stress assignment
malk̲ày   vowel deletion
[malk̲ḕ]   diphthong contraction

Spirantization of /k/ must occur early in the derivation because if stress
assignment and the succeeding vowel deletion had preceded it, the context
for spirantization would no longer exist.

Generative analysis, then, does not stop after positing underlying bases
and formulating rules. It proceeds to study relations among rules and overriding constraints that dominate the rules. It begins on the top, or surface,
and works its way down to the deep structure, the level that is closer to cognition itself. Its value to biblicists is (at least) twofold. On the one hand, it
seeks to provide more adequate explanations for the phenomena of Hebrew
than what we find in existing grammars. It accounts for the spirantization of
/k/ in *malk̲ē*, for example, without making up an ad hoc rule or a phantom
"*šĕwā³ mobile*." On the other, it explains how the language works and, more
fundamentally, to the degree it is successful, how language works.

26. Cf. Malone, "Flip-Flop Rule," 441–42.

[February, 1989]

Gregory Enos

Phonological Considerations in the Study of Hebrew Phonetics: An Introductory Discussion

The philologist who wishes to investigate the phonetics of Biblical Hebrew plainly must have some acquaintance with modern linguistics. No one familiar with articulatory phonetics, for instance, can be satisfied with the older descriptions of the Hebrew gutturals, as exemplified in Kautzsch's treatment of ᶜ*ayin*: "ע is related to א, but is a much stronger guttural. Its strongest sound is a rattled, guttural *g* . . . ; elsewhere, a weaker sound of the same kind. . . . In the mouth of the Arabs one hears in the former case a sort of guttural *r*, in the latter a sound peculiar to themselves formed in the back of the throat" (GKC §6e / p. 32). Among other questions, we ask, What is meant here by "stronger"? By "rattled"? Is the "guttural" point of articulation velar, uvular, pharyngeal, laryngeal?[1]

Of course, it is not Kautzsch (still less Gesenius) himself who is to be faulted here, but the limited linguistic resources at his disposal; whether or not he had any clear notion of the character of the sounds he was describing, he had no clear way to discuss them. Again, one could wish for more science and less local color in Joüon's characterization of ᶜ*ayin*: It is like the Arabic ᶜ*ayn*, and is "une gutturale sonore qui n'existe pas dans nos langues. . . . On a comparé ce son à 'l'articulation gutturale du chameau que l'on charge de son bât' (Joüon §51 / p. 15).

Certain matters which lie at the border between phonetics and phonology are also of immediate interest to the student of Hebrew phonetics. Linguists

---

1. Kautzsch's discussion of the pronunciation of *ḥêt* (GKC §6f / p. 33) is similarly unsatisfactory.

recognize, for example, that there is no strict division between such major sound categories as vowel versus consonant and segment versus sequence. Certain sounds, such as [y], [i], [w], [u], may be treated either as consonants or vowels, depending upon whether a particular language employs them at positions within the word where vowels belong, or where consonants are to be expected. A sound like [dʒ] will be a single segment in one language (as in English *Jill*, *jay*), but a sequence of two segments in another. Thus, we must find implausible Joüon's argument that *ṣādê* cannot have been pronounced as [ts] because in that case "un mot pourrait commencer, en fait, par deux consonnes, ce qui répugne au sémitique" (Joüon §5m / p. 16). The rarity of consonant sequences at the beginning of words in Hebrew and other Semitic languages means merely that if *ṣādê* is found to have been pronounced as [ts], it should be analyzed as a single affricate segment (as in Modern Hebrew and in the French *tsar* 'czar,' *tzigane* 'gypsy,' etc.), rather than as a sequence of plosive followed by spirant.

Again, we may be skeptical regarding Kahle's and Sperber's hypothesis that by Jerome's time the Hebrew gutturals had become vowels.[2] It is true that Jerome himself identifies each of these sounds as a vowel,[3] but it is also clear that he regards them as very peculiar and difficult-to-pronounce vowels.[4] Since the gutturals lie near the border between vowel and consonant, it is only to be expected that their consonantal pronunciations would count as vowels to a speaker of Vulgar Latin, which possessed no similar consonants. Jerome's Latin did not have [h], but he knew it from traditional grammar as an *adspiratio*, a modification of the following vowel.[5] Thus, he terms the Hebrew letter *hēʾ* a vowel and an *adspiratio*. The pharyngeal spirant *ḥêt*, then, would quite reasonably be seen by Jerome as a *duplex adspiratio*, a strengthened *hēʾ*, and thus another vowel. The glottal stop *ʾālep* would scarcely qualify as a "sound" in Latin, any more than it does in English; but in terms of Latin phonology it is obviously another vowel modification. Perhaps the most interesting of Jerome's "vowels" is *ʿayin*. It is widely held that this guttural was given a "weak" pronunciation in Jerome's time. If so, it quite likely fell squarely on the border between vowel and consonant and could be interpreted as either a lenis voiced pharyngeal spirant or a pharyngealized vowel, with the phonological structure of the language determining the issue. The syllable structure of Hebrew certainly demands that such a

---

2. P. Kahle, *The Cairo Geniza* (2d ed.; New York: Praeger, 1959) 164–71; A. Sperber, *A Historical Grammar of Biblical Hebrew: A Presentation of Problems with Suggestions to Their Solution* (Leiden: Brill, 1966) 109–10, 171.
3. J. Barr, "St Jerome and the Sounds of Hebrew," *JSS* 12 (1967) 23.
4. Ibid., 14–23.
5. Phonetically, the consonant [h] generally is a voiceless version of the adjacent vowels.

borderline sound be analyzed as a consonant, but in Latin, it would almost as certainly have to be a (rather peculiar-sounding) vowel.[6]

It is not only where they border on phonetics, however, that phonological theory and analysis are relevant to the investigation of Hebrew phonetics. Though phonological patterning has long been recognized as possessing implications for our understanding of phonetic contrasts in Hebrew,[7] recent work by J. Barr and others has demonstrated that broader phonological considerations are of central importance in the study of Hebrew phonetics.[8] The present essay illustrates this point by exploring the application of one twentieth-century school of phonology—generative phonology—to questions of Hebrew phonetics, particularly Tiberian phonetics. It builds upon E. Greenstein's essay in this volume (pp. 29–40) and loosely parallels his essay in organization.

SYNCHRONIC AND DIACHRONIC

Kahle and Sperber maintained that, since the gutturals had lost their consonantal pronunciation by the time of Jerome, their presence as consonants in Tiberian Hebrew must be reckoned as a language reform imposed by the Masoretes themselves, largely on the model of the Arabic gutturals.[9] They seem to have assumed that linguistic forms can somehow be remembered after they have disappeared from speech, a view whose popularity in traditional philology is attested by such idiosyncrasies as Robertson's assignment of eight cases to the Koine Greek noun.[10] Even granting the probable influence of Arabic upon Tiberian pronunciation, their hypothesis appears quite

6. See E. Y. Kutscher, *A History of the Hebrew Language* (Jerusalem: Magnes/Leiden: Brill, 1982) 18–19, on the "weak" pronunciation of ᶜ*ayin*. On the strange and even unpleasant impact of certain Hebrew sounds upon Latin ears, note Barr, "St Jerome," esp. 16–17, 23. The discussion in this paragraph is dependent upon Barr's treatment of the same issue. On the ambiguous position of the gutturals at the borderline between vowel and consonant, note M. M. Bravmann, "Concerning the Border-Line between Consonant and Vowel," in *Studies in Semitic Philology* (Leiden: Brill, 1977) 160–64.

7. Cf., for instance, J. Cantineau, "Essai d'une phonologie de l'hébreu biblique," *Bulletin de la Société de Linguistique de Paris* 46 (1950) 82–122.

8. Barr, "St Jerome"; U. Ornan, "The Tiberian Vocalization System and the Principles of Linguistics," *Journal of Jewish Studies* 15 (1964) 109–23; J. Malone, "Systematic vs. Autonomous Phonemics and the Hebrew Grapheme *Dagesh*," *AAL* 2 (1975) 113–29; P. Wernberg-Møller, "Aspects of Masoretic Vocalization," in *International Organization for Masoretic Studies: Proceedings and Papers of 1972 and 1973 Meetings* (ed. H. M. Orlinsky; New York: Ktav, 1974) 121–30.

9. Kahle, *Cairo Geniza*, 164–71; Sperber, *Historical Grammar*, 122–24.

10. A. T. Robertson, *A Grammar of the Greek New Testament in the Light of Historical Research* (Nashville: Broadman, 1934) 446–543.

incredible apart from such a belief in linguistic ghosts, as Bergsträsser's response to Kahle's initial presentation of this view may indicate: the attested Tiberian forms cannot have been Masoretic creations unless they "wenigstens den kleinen Brockelmann studiert haben."[11] But generative phonology, in common with most modern linguistic perspectives, makes a definite, if not necessarily absolute, distinction between synchronic and diachronic linguistics.[12] Since language learners are not generally historical linguists, Z. Harris's maxim would appear to be self-evident: "Phonemes are not remembered once they cease to exist [i.e., to be pronounced] in a dialect."[13] Scholars who suppose that a lost pronunciation of the Hebrew gutturals suddenly reappeared with the Masoretes must also suggest mechanisms whereby the lost sounds might maintain, for several centuries, some spectral presence within the language. Otherwise, they are exercising faith in the occurrence of an implausible linguistic phenomenon. One such mechanism may be the retention of the gutturals in the Hebrew script; but this possibility immediately raises the question why the guttural graphemes did not prevent the loss of the guttural pronunciations in the first place.

TWO LEVELS OF STRUCTURE

Another possible mechanism whereby a language might "remember" lost pronunciations is suggested by the generative-phonological distinction between a language's phonetic surface structure and its abstract underlying phonological structure. Granted certain rather extreme assumptions about permissible underlying representations, one could hypothesize that underlying consonantal gutturals were in the pre-Masoretic period subject to a rule which deleted them or transformed them into vowels, possibly quite late in the derivational process, so that such reflexes of the (consonantal) gutturals as the furtive *pataḥ* might be retained.[14] It is far more reasonable to assume that the furtive *pataḥ* and other phonetic phenomena governed by the gutturals were present in pre-Masoretic Hebrew because the consonantal pronunciation of the gutturals was also present. But the evidence for the furtive *pataḥ* in pre-Masoretic Hebrew is not quite as decisive against the Kahle–Sperber

11. J. Hempel, "Chronik," *ZAW* 61 (1945–48) 251 (citing oral communication from Bergsträsser).
12. On the possibility of some mixture of diachronic with synchronic explanation in generative linguistics, see J. Greenberg, "Rethinking Linguistics Diachronically," *Lg.* 55 (1979) 275–90.
13. Z. Harris, *Development of the Canaanite Dialects: An Investigation in Linguistic History* (AOS 16; New Haven: American Oriental Society, 1939) 63.
14. G. Janssens, *Studies in Hebrew Historical Linguistics Based on Origen's Secunda* (Leuven: Peeters, 1982), 42, finds evidence in Jerome for the furtive *pataḥ*. But Sperber, *Historical Grammar*, 429, understands data of this sort as proving not the existence of the furtive *pataḥ* but the pronunciation of the guttural itself as a vowel.

position as it initially seems, if this extreme generative-phonological stance be permitted. Indeed, if the Kahle–Sperber hypothesis should ever be proven, an analysis of the guttural vowels as derived from underlying guttural consonants would be the only way to avoid a hopeless muddle in the description of Hebrew morphophonemics.

THE PROBLEM OF SPOKEN LANGUAGE

In actuality, however, the legitimacy of attempting a detailed generative-phonological analysis of Tiberian Hebrew is questionable, since this method is applicable only to natural languages. A more traditional structuralist treatment, accounting for the actually attested forms of Tiberian Hebrew without reconstructing the phonological knowledge of a native speaker who actually does not seem to have existed, would seem safer. There are two features of natural language, however, which Tiberian Hebrew appears to have exhibited with unusual intensity, precisely because it was a dead language: a tendency toward simplifying sound change, and pedagogical prescriptivism. In a language largely restricted to written and liturgical uses, simplification of the phonological structure would not be countered by the necessity to maintain the comprehensibility of the spoken language. The strong conservatism and prescriptivism in the traditional liturgical reading of the Hebrew Scriptures certainly was a countervailing force, but it did not apply with equal force in every place and at every time. Thus, Kahle's and Sperber's hypothesized loss of the consonantal pronunciation of the gutturals does not seem to have occurred once and have endured for centuries, but to have taken place repeatedly and repeatedly to have been reversed by prescriptivist zeal. A goodly portion of the evidence for loss of the consonantal pronunciation of the gutturals comes from denunciations of those who do not pronounce the gutturals "properly" or "carefully" by prescriptivists who do pronounce them as consonants.[15] It is, then, quite probable that the ancient pronunciation of the gutturals was indeed lost and subsequently recovered—but within the course of a single generation, or through the prescriptive influence of neighboring communities.

MASORETIC VOCALIZATION AND PHONETIC ANALYSIS

Even if the marginal linguistic status of Tiberian Hebrew makes a systematic generative-phonological analysis of the language somewhat problematical,

---

15. A typical example is the prohibition in *y. Ber.* 4:4 against men from certain towns leading congregational prayers, because of their confusion of *ḥêt* with *hēʾ* and of *ʿayin* with *ʾālep*.

the Tiberian Masoretes were nonetheless native speakers of *some* natural language: Aramaic. It is therefore quite permissible to consider the relevance of the generative-phonological perspective to the Masoretes' own phonological analyses of Hebrew. Recent studies by J. L. Malone and me, for instance, have proposed interpretations of the phonetic values of the emphatic consonants *ṣādê*, *ṭêt*, and *qôp* based on the assumption that the Masoretic term *emphatic* designates a natural class of sounds which can be expressed in terms of generative-phonological distinctive features.[16] Malone suggests that *qôp* may be an uvular plosive and the other emphatics uvularized consonants, so that the class of emphatics would be specified by $\begin{bmatrix} -\text{high} \\ +\text{back} \end{bmatrix}$. My hypothesis is that all three emphatics are glottalized. Again, the recognition in the Masoretic grammarians that *rêš*, as well as the *begadkepat* letters, possessed a hard and a soft pronunciation suggests that the difference was one of [+continuant] versus [−continuant], as in the plosive/spirant series.[17] A soft uvular or alveolar trill and a hard tap [r], interpreted as—quite possibly pronounced as—a tongue flap [D] by the Masoretes, seems most likely.[18]

These considerations suggest an answer to a question that has long troubled philologists: Just what sort of linguistic analysis of Hebrew phonetics were the Tiberians attempting? The Masoretic focus upon exactitude in cantillation makes it implausible to suppose that the Tiberians would very frequently exhibit the naïve generative-phonological analysis implied in most traditional spelling systems (e.g., in the English spelling of schwa as the underlying vowel from which it is derived). Indeed, Malone has argued that the distribution of the grapheme *dāgēš* cannot be adequately described within the generative-phonological model, but can be accounted for within the ·older "autonomous phonemic" analysis.[19] The Masoretic notation and analysis, then, are best regarded as reflecting rather directly the actual pronunciation of Hebrew as they knew it. The question of how exact this reflection is, and whether the Masoretic analysis is basically phonetic, basically

16. J. L. Malone, "Messrs Sampson, Chomsky and Halle, and Hebrew Phonology," *Foundations of Language* 14 (1976) 251–56; G. Enos, "Generative Phonology and Tiberian Phonetics," in *Society of Biblical Literature 1983 Seminar Papers* (ed. K. H. Richards; Chico: Scholars, 1983) 309–13.

17. Cf. G. Schramm, *The Graphemes of Tiberian Hebrew* (University of California Publications, Near Eastern Studies 2; Berkeley and Los Angeles: University of California Press, 1964), 18–19.

18. An alveolar point of articulation for at least one of the allophones of the Tiberian *rêš* seems most probable in view of the fact that the grammatical tradition classes *rêš* with the "dental" series *zayin*, *sāmek*, *šîn*, and *ṣādê*. On the similarity (identity?) of tap [r] and tongue flap [D], note N. Chomsky and M. Halle, *The Sound Pattern of English* (New York: Harper & Row, 1968) 318.

19. Malone, "Systematic vs. Autonomous Phonemics."

phonemic, or stands at some intermediate level of analysis, is far more difficult to answer. Views have ranged from U. Ornan's confidence that the Masoretes "noted graphically everything their ears heard; it was, then, basically
a *phonetic* marking, not a phonemic one"[20] to Barr's warning that "information about the sound of Hebrew must be carefully sorted out in order to dis-
criminate between phonemic and phonetic realities. It is not to be expected
that the transcriptions will furnish one level of information which can then
be taken to be the 'pronunciation' of Hebrew."[21]

It is probable that both these views are essentially correct: the Masoretes
did note—though not necessarily graphically, in their pointing system—
"everything their ears heard," but they would not hear many minor allophonic
variations, any more than speakers of English hear the difference between $[t^h]$
of *top* and $[t]$ of *stop*. The task set for us by Barr, of separating the phonetic
from the phonemic features in Tiberian vocalization and phonetic analysis, remains. If the Masoretes really were attempting a more-or-less-complete phonetic analysis of Hebrew, then it is relatively easy to suggest where they are
likely to have succeeded in this, and where their work reflects only the phonemic reality. In a word, it is most likely that the Masoretic analysis of Tiberian
phonetics approximates the phonetic transcription that a modern phonetician
would make, if Hebrew were the world's only language. A phonetic transcription makes no attempt to represent all features of an utterance, but only those
features which are linguistically significant—that is, preeminently, those features which sometimes distinguish phonemes from one another in one or another of the world's languages. But for the Masoretic phoneticians, it is only
the features which distinguish Hebrew phonemes from one another which
would naturally come under consideration. Thus, since the plosive/spirant distinction distinguishes between the phonemes *ʾālep* and *hēʾ* in Tiberian Hebrew, the Masoretes could be expected to note this contrast in the case of the
begadkepat phonemes as well, even if the contrast there is not phonemic.
Knowing that the plosive/ spirant contrast has phonemic significance in Hebrew, we may suspect that the Masoretes' analysis is consistently phonetic with
regard to this contrast. It is unlikely in the extreme that there were any spirant
allophones of plosive phonemes (or vice versa) which are unknown to us from
the Masoretic tradition. Thus, it seems conceivable that the level of abstraction
of the Masoretic analysis of Hebrew may eventually be ascertained with considerable confidence, despite the fact that this level of analysis is, in terms of
modern linguistic method, an arbitrary mixture of levels.

20. Ornan, "Tiberian Vocalization," 111.
21. Barr, "St Jerome," 2.

[November, 1986]

W. Randall Garr

The Linguistic Study of Morphology

The word *morphology* owes its existence to Goethe.[1] In 1817, Goethe introduced the word to denote the study of biological unity in organic form.[2]
Augustin de Saint-Hilaire later popularized the term and, in 1840, extended
its domain to include botanical forms.[3] Thereafter, morphology represented
a branch of biology which studies form.

While morphology began with form, it did not end there. Morphology, as
portrayed at the turn of the century,[4] *analyzes* the forms of organic structure,
classifies these forms, and *assesses* the developmental relation among like
forms. This discipline was concerned with the components of biological

Author's note: I thank Laura Kalman and Charles Li for critiquing an earlier draft of this paper.
The following symbols are used in this study:

{ }	morpheme
[ ]	phonetic realization
| |	underlying form; base form
/ /	allomorph; derived form
. . .	interdigitated slots
X+ +X	discontinuous morpheme
:	gemination (in morphophonemic representation)
#	word boundary
≠	construct boundary
+	morphemic boundary
[superscript x][ ]	nonexistent outcome
~	alternation; alternating forms
"	pausal accent

1. P. Geddes and P. C. Mitchell, "Morphology," in *Encyclopaedia Britannica* (11th ed., 1911)
   18:864.
2. J. W. Goethe, *Zur Morphologie*, 1/1. Already in the mid-1790s, Goethe had begun to develop
   his views on morphology; see "Betrachtung über Morphologie überhaupt," in *Hamburger
   Ausgabe* (ed. E. Trunz; 3d ed.; Hamburg: Wegner, 1960) 13:123–24.
3. A. de Saint-Hilaire, *Leçons de botanique, comprenant principalement la morphologie
   végétale, la terminologie, la botanique comparée, l'examen de la valeur des caractères dans
   les diverses familles naturelles* (Paris: Loss, 1840).
4. Geddes and Mitchell, "Morphology," 868.

structures and their arrangement into taxonomical categories. Further, the forms were not seen as discrete items but as the result of process and change; the scientist could then inquire about the relation of forms to one another, as well as the morphological processes which account for their development and outcome.

The study of linguistic morphology is akin to its biological ancestor. One goal is the analysis of structure and its taxonomy. In linguistic study, though, "organic form" is replaced by "word."[5] Morphology studies word structure and analyzes this structure into its component elements (*morphemes*).[6] The second goal also follows the biological model: the relation among forms. Morphology seeks the relation among different representations of forms (*allomorphs*)[7] and the processes which account for alternation (*morphophonemics*).[8] The study of linguistic relation is also applied to word-building; morphology uncovers the relation among constituent elements which, in their proper arrangement (*tactics*),[9] form words. Linguistic morphology, then, proceeds from morphemes, to their relations, and their ultimate construction into words.[10]

WORD COMPONENTS

The *morpheme* is the most elemental word component. It is a linguistic abstraction[11] denoting a "linguistic form which bears no partial phonetic-

5. On this term, and its definitional difficulties, see C. F. Hockett, Review of Nida, *Morphology*, *Lg.* 23 (1947) 275–79; J. H. Greenberg, "A Quantitative Approach to the Morphological Typology of Language," *International Journal of American Linguistics* 26 (1960) 191–92; E. A. Nida, *Morphology: The Descriptive Analysis of Words* (2d ed.; Ann Arbor: University of Michigan Press, 1963) 102–3; P. H. Matthews, *Morphology: An Introduction to the Theory of Word-Structure* (Cambridge Textbooks in Linguistics; Cambridge: Cambridge University Press, 1974) 31–33; S. R. Anderson, "Typological Distinctions in Word Formation," in *Language Typology and Syntactic Description*, vol. 3: *Grammatical Categories and the Lexicon* (ed. T. Shopen; Cambridge: Cambridge University Press, 1985) 4; and idem, "Inflectional Morphology," 150–58 in the same work.

6. Z. S. Harris, "The Linguistic Structure of Hebrew," *JAOS* 61 (1941) 143; Hockett, in *Lg.* 23 (1947) 284; idem, "Problems of Morphemic Analysis," *Lg.* 23 (1947) 321; idem, *A Course in Modern Linguistics* (New York: MacMillan, 1958) 177; Nida, *Morphology*, 1; and J. L. Bybee, *Morphology: A Study of the Relation between Meaning and Form* (Typological Studies in Language 9; Amsterdam and Philadelphia: Benjamins, 1985) v.

7. Hockett, *Modern Linguistics*, 272.

8. See especially Hockett, in *Lg.* 23 (1947) 274, 281; and Bybee, *Morphology*, v.

9. Hockett, in *Lg.* 23 (1947) 274; idem, "Morphemic Analysis," 321. See also Harris, "Structure of Hebrew," 143; and Nida, *Morphology*, 1.

10. In actual practice, the reverse procedure is used, moving from the sentence, to the word, to the immediate constituent, to the morpheme. See A. N. Chomsky, *Morphophonemics of Modern Hebrew* (M.A. thesis, University of Pennsylvania, 1951; repr. New York: Garland, 1979) 3, 9.

11. C. F. Hockett, "Linguistic Elements and their Relations," *Lg.* 37 (1961) 42. Cf. Nida, *Morphology*, 58–59.

semantic resemblance to any other form."[12] The morpheme is therefore a minimal, irreducible unit.[13] For example, English *schoolbus* and *blackbird* do not constitute single morphemes; both words contain two elements, each of which recurs[14] in other utterances. *Schoolbus* consists of *school + bus*, and these parts may appear in detached form: *I went to <u>school</u>*, and *I took the <u>bus</u>*. Similarly, *blackbird* is analyzable as *black + bird*, occurring in different phrases like *a <u>black</u> hat* and *the pretty <u>bird</u>*.[15] Yet these constituent elements cannot be further reduced into component elements which themselves recur in the language. Thus, four morphemes—{school}, {bus}, {black}, and {bird}—have been isolated.

Semantically, the morpheme carries only one meaning.[16] If two or more forms are homophonous, they do not constitute a single morpheme unless they have the same meaning.[17] For example, English [mirərz] can be analyzed into two components—[mirər] + [z]—each of which recurs in different utterances (though not necessarily in isolation). Yet the meaning of the form, and of its parts, changes with different contexts. Thus [mirərz] = noun + {PLURAL} in *the polished <u>mirrors</u>*; noun + {POSSESSIVE} in *the <u>mirror's</u> reflection*; verb + {be} in *the <u>mirror's</u> polished*; or verb + {THIRD PERSON SINGULAR PRESENT} in *he <u>mirrors</u> my opinion*. Despite a single surface representation, the final element [z] corresponds to four different morphemes.

When, however, a minimal form recurs in different words and bears one meaning, the form is one morpheme. Thus Hebrew [yɔ̄d̄] 'hand', [yɔ̄dī] 'my hand', and [yɔ̄d̄ay] 'my hands' share the morpheme {hand}, which is represented by |yad|. The form and meaning of this element correspond in all occurrences and therefore constitute one morpheme.

Implicit in Bloomfield's definition of the morpheme is the concept of phonemic representation.[18] On the one hand, the morpheme carries meaning. This meaning can be abstract, as in {PL} or {POSS}; or it can be concrete, as

---

12. L. Bloomfield, *Language* (New York: Holt, Rinehart & Winston, 1933) 161. See also B. Elson and V. Pickett, *An Introduction to Morphology and Syntax* (Santa Ana: Summer Institute of Linguistics, 1968) 19. See S. Saporta, "Morph, Morpheme, Archimorpheme," *Word* 12 (1956) 13–14.

13. Harris, "Structure of Hebrew," 152 n. 42; idem, "Morpheme Alternants in Linguistic Analysis," *Lg.* 18 (1942) 169; Hockett, *Modern Linguistics*, 123; and Matthews, *Morphology*, 12.

14. On the use of recurrence in morphology, see Hockett, "Morphemic Analysis," 322.

15. There are diachronic processes involved in these compound formations which complicate a strictly formal analysis. See, e.g., Anderson, "Typological Distinctions," 40–43, on the accent.

16. See Nida, *Morphology*, 7.

17. See E. A. Nida, "The Identification of Morphemes," *Lg.* 24 (1948) 434–36; and idem, *Morphology*, 7, 55–56.

18. See Hockett, *Modern Linguistics*, 135.

in {bus} or {black}. On the other hand, the morpheme is represented by language-specific phonemes which particularize the morpheme for a given language.[19] The morpheme, then, is actualized by a phonemic string.

The phonemes which represent a morpheme occur in various sequences. Most commonly, they assume a successive, linear arrangement. For example, {1 SING PERFECT} is represented by |tī|, whose two phonemes—*t and *ī—appear in strictly sequential order. Similarly, {and} is represented by |wa| (*w and *a), {FEM SING NOUN} = |at|, and {2 MASC PL PF} = |timm|.[20] The constituent phonemes follow one another in linear succession. The resultant forms are *continuous*.[21]

Not all underlying (or surface) forms conform to this pattern, however. Whereas {2 MASC PL PF} is represented by the continuous |timm|, its imperfect counterpart surrounds[22] the verbal stem—[tizkərū] 'you will remember' (Num 15:40, Jer 23:36) and [tišmərū] 'you protect'. The underlying form would appear to be |tV+ +ū|. {2 FEM SING IMPF} is similar; the attested [tizkərī] 'you will remember' (Ezek 16:63, 23:27) and [taᵓargī] 'you weave' (Judg 16:13) point to an underlying |tV+ +ī|. Neither part, moreover, can occur in isolation and still represent the same morpheme.[23] One element requires the presence of the other.[24] Under these circumstances—when the morpheme is represented by phonemes which are interrupted by intervening elements, yet whose parts comprise a single, irreducible unit—the form is *discontinuous*.[25]

Roots and *patterns*, too, are continuous or discontinuous. Continuous sequences, however, are rare in the Semitic languages. For example, [bēn] 'son' and [šēm] 'name' are generally considered to represent |bn| and | šm|, respectively. The root—reflecting individual phenomena[26]—consists of two contiguous consonantal radicals, unmodified by any vowel (or other) pattern. The root is therefore continuous.

---

19. See Anderson, "Inflectional Morphology," 159.

20. For the latter, see Meyer § 30.2b, 3c/pp. 2:8–9, 11.

21. Z. S. Harris, "Discontinuous Morphemes," *Lg.* 21 (1945) 121, 122; and Nida, "Identification of Morphemes," 439.

22. See Greenberg, "Quantitative Approach," 186.

23. For example, |tV+| recurs throughout the second-person imperfects, and |+ī| may form part of the 2 FEM SING PF [+tī+] (before objective suffixes) and POSSESSIVE [+k̲ī] 'your' (e.g., Jer 11:15, Ps 103:3–4). Nevertheless, these forms are morphemically distinct from {2 FEM SING IMPF} = |tV+ +ī|.

24. Nida, *Morphology*, 84–85.

25. Harris, "Discontinuous Morphemes," 121–27; Nida, "Identification of Morphemes," 439; and idem, *Morphology*, 84–85.

26. Harris, "Structure of Hebrew," 152; Greenberg, "Quantitative Approach," 191; and A. F. L. Beeston, *The Arabic Language Today* (London: Hutchinson University Library, 1970) 31. See J. Barr, *Comparative Philology and the Text of the Old Testament* (Oxford: Oxford University Press, 1968; repr. Winona Lake, IN: Eisenbrauns, 1987) 197.

Most roots and most[27] patterns are discontinuous.[28] [zɔ̄kar] 'he remembered', for example, consists of the root |z.k.r| {remember} and vowel pattern |.a.a.| representing {QAL ACTIVE PF}.[29] The pattern modifies the root, conveying the phenomenon and its relation or particular character.[30] The pattern, interdigitated among the root radicals, therefore creates two discontinuous underlying forms. Each is interrupted by the other.

Roots rarely occur in isolation. Patterns never occur without an accompanying root. For the most part, then, roots and patterns are interdependent.[31] Together, this intertwined (compound of) root + pattern constitutes a *stem*.[32] Thus {steal} + {AGENT} > |g.n.b| + |.a.:a.| > [gannɔ̄b] 'thief', or {write} + {QAL PASSIVE ADJECTIVE} > |k.t.b| + |.a.ū.| > [kɔ̄tūb] 'written'. The stem functions as a single, inseparable entity within the language.[33] The stem is, in effect, an interdigitated morphemic compound.

Not only can sequences vary, but the surface representation of morphemes may vary as well. A morpheme may be represented uniformly, by one fixed shape in all occurrences. Or, it may have multiple shapes (governed by a variety of conditions). The surface representation is therefore either *invariant* or *variant*.

Invariant shapes in Hebrew contain unchangeable syllables. For example, {voice} is represented by the superheavy[34] |qōl| in all constructions—[qōl#] 'voice', [qōl≠] 'voice of', [qōlī] 'my voice' < |qōl| + |ī|, and [qōlōt] 'voices' (Exod 9:23, 28; 19:16; 1 Sam 12:17–18; Job 28:26, 38:25) < |qōl| + |ōt|. Similarly, {warrior} is consistently represented by |gibbōr|— [gibbōr#] 'warrior', [gibbōr≠] 'warrior of', [gibbōrɔ̄m] 'their warrior' (1 Sam 17:51), [gibbōrīm] 'warriors', and [gibbōrē≠] 'warriors of'. The surface representation of these morphemes is invariant.[35]

---

27. A continuous pattern may be |hit| {reflexive}, if it is to be separated from the root-internal pattern. See Harris, "Structure of Hebrew," 157.
28. R. S. Wells, "Immediate Constituents," *Lg.* 23 (1947) 110 n. 52; and Chomsky, *Modern Hebrew*, 19.
29. {PRONOMINAL SUBJECT} is not significant for present purposes. In this case, however, {PRON SUBJ} is represented by |∅|; see Bybee, *Morphology*, 4; and, more generally, H. M. Hoenigswald, *Language Change and Linguistic Reconstruction* (Chicago: University of Chicago Press, 1960) 35–36.
30. See Harris, "Structure of Hebrew," 152.
31. See Beeston, *Arabic Language*, 31.
32. See Nida, *Morphology*, 83; and Elson and Pickett, *Morphology and Syntax*, 79–80, 97.
33. See Barr, *Comparative Philology*, 197.
34. A superheavy syllable has four segments, either *$C\bar{V}C$ (*CVVC) or *CVCC.
35. Hockett, *Modern Linguistics*, 271, 272. See also J. Kilbury, *The Development of Morphophonemic Theory* (Studies in the History of Linguistics 10; Philadelphia and Amsterdam: Benjamins, 1976) 80.

ALTERNATION PROCESSES

Representation may also vary. If the variants are noncontrastive and semantically alike, as well as complementarily distributed, these variants (*allomorphs*) constitute one morpheme.[36] The variants, then, must be governed by statable conditions.[37]

Alternation among allomorphs may be phonemically conditioned. Affecting all phonemes, it follows rules of regular sound change. For example, the change in |k.t.b| > /k.t̪.b̪/ (as in [kɔ̄t̪ab̪] 'he wrote') and /k̪t̪.b̪/ (as in [yik̪t̪ob̪] 'he will write' [Isa 44:5]) follow the Biblical Hebrew rule of postvocalic spirantization: a nonemphatic stop is spirantized when immediately following a vowel.[38] The rule is almost exceptionless[39] and affects all words alike. Or, {QAL PASS ADJ} is represented by |.a.ū.|, whose allomorphs are /.ō.ū./ (as in [kɔ̄t̪ūb̪] 'written') and /.ə.ū./ (as in [kət̪ūb̪īm] 'written' [MASC PL] and [kət̪ūb̪ɔ̄] 'written' [FEM SING] [Josh 10:13, 2 Sam 1:18, Isa 65:6, Jer 17:1, Ezek 2:10, Dan 9:11]). These variants, too, conform to regular sound patterns: the former reflects pretonic vowel lengthening,[40] and the latter exhibits propretonic vowel reduction.[41] When variants reflect regular, phonemically conditioned rules, the alternation is *automatic*.[42]

Since automatic alternation is predictable by rules of regular sound change, *zero alternation* is automatic as well. For in zero alternation, a phonemic shape is invariant—that is, all allomorphs are identical, according to regular sound patterns. |qōl| is always replaced by /qōl/, whose outcome is [qōl], regardless of environment or construction; in Biblical Hebrew, this invariance (self-replacement)[43] is fully predictable. The same is true for |gibbōr| > /gibbōr/ > [gibbor ̯#]. Since the patterning is phonologically pre-

36. Harris, "Structure of Hebrew," 152–53; Hockett, "Morphemic Analysis," 322; idem, *Modern Linguistics*, 274–75; Nida, "Identification of Morphemes," 419–37; idem, *Morphology*, 14; Greenberg, "Quantitative Approach," 190; Elson and Pickett, *Morphology and Syntax*, 27; Matthews, *Morphology*, 82–83; and Kilbury, *Morphophonemic Theory*, 80–81. See P. Garvin, "On the Relative Tractability of Morphological Data," *Word* 13 (1957) 18–20.
37. Elson and Pickett, *Morphology and Syntax*, 39.
38. E.g., BL § 19a–b, e/pp. 209–10; GKC § 21a, e/pp. 75–76.
39. For exceptions, see BL § 19d, f/pp. 209, 210; Joüon § 19f/p. 59.
40. For the rules, see W. R. Garr, "Pretonic Vowels in Hebrew," *VT* 37 (1987) 129–53.
41. Joüon § 30e/p. 76.
42. Hockett, in *Lg.* 23 (1947) 284; idem, *Modern Linguistics*, 279–80; Greenberg, "Quantitative Approach," 185, 190; and W. U. Dressler, *Morphonology: The Dynamics of Derivation* (Ann Arbor: Karoma, 1985) 3. See also Harris, "Structure of Hebrew," 153; and Elson and Pickett, *Morphology and Syntax*, 31.
43. Hoenigswald, *Language Change*, 28.

dictable, affecting all words without exception, this zero alternation is a part of automatic alternation.[44]

Nonautomatic alternation, however, is irregular[45] and phonologically unpredictable.[46] Nonautomatic alternation affects some morphemes in some conditions, not others, and to different degrees. Unlike automatic alternants, nonautomatic alternants are individually learned—either grammatically or lexically.[47]

Grammatically (*morphemically*) conditioned alternation is governed by morphological rules. The sound change affecting the form or word is not panlexical, but is conditioned by grammatical environment.[48] For example, the monovocalic noun |qVtl|—as in |malk| {king}, |sipr| {document}, and |qudš| {holiness}—is replaced by bivocalic /qVtal/ before plural suffixes;[49] in the plural, the contiguous final radicals are separated by an *a vowel. This vowel is not phonologically predictable: Hebrew anaptyctic vowels are *i grade, not *a grade;[50] and in suffixing there is no phonological reason for vowel insertion, since the original consonant cluster now falls into separate syllables—|malk| + |īm| > ˣ[malkīm] 'kings' (see [malkī] 'my king' [2 Sam 19:44; Ps 2:6, 5:3, 44:5, 68:25, 74:12, 84:4]) or |malk| + |ōt| > ˣ[malkōt] 'queens' (see [malkɔ̄] 'queen'). Rather, the factor conditioning this change is grammatical: plurality. |qVtl| > /qVtal/ before the plural morpheme. Schematically, |.V..| > /.V.a./ /_____ + {PL}.

Lexically conditioned alternation, or suppletion, is the complete replacement of one underlying form by another.[51] The resultant allomorphs are neither patterned by phonology or morphology, nor are they cognate; they are phonemically dissimilar. For example, Aramaic {give} is |y.h.b| in the perfect, imperative, and participle, while |n.t.n| performs this function in the imperfect and infinitive. These roots are therefore alternating representations

---

44. Greenberg, "Quantitative Approach," 185.

45. See Hockett, *Modern Linguistics*, 280.

46. On the background, see J. L. Bybee and C. L. Moder, "Morphological Classes as Natural Categories," *Lg.* 59 (1983) 251.

47. Matthews, *Morphology*, 91–92.

48. Harris, "Morpheme Alternants," 177; Hockett, *Modern Linguistics*, 281; Matthews, *Morphology*, 91–92; Elson and Pickett, *Morphology and Syntax*, 37–38; and Dressler, *Morphonology*, 12. See also Bloomfield, *Language*, 212–14.

49. Z. S. Harris, *Development of the Canaanite Dialects* (AOS 16; New Haven: American Oriental Society, 1939) 9.

50. The anaptyctic wedge was, in all probability, an original šĕwāʾ (see, e.g., BL §20/pp. 210–14). On the various replacements of šĕwāʾ in Biblical Hebrew, see R. Hetzron, "Third Person Singular Pronoun Suffixes in Proto-Semitic," *Orientalia Suecana* 18 (1969) 121–122.

51. Bloomfield, *Language*, 215; Harris, "Morpheme Alternants," 177; and Hockett, *Modern Linguistics*, 280. See also Bybee, *Morphology*, 83, 91–96, for the background.

of {give} (/y.h.b̲/ ~ /n.t̲.n/). The variant shapes of the near demonstrative pronoun are another example. The Semitic languages represent {this} by |d̲|, yet {this} + {PL}[52] is represented by |ʾil(l)|,[53] that is, /d̲/ ~ /ʾil(l)/. In neither case are the two components of the paradigm phonemically related: |d̲| and |ʾil(l)| are not cognate, nor are |y.h.b| and |n.t.n|. And in neither case does the particular relationship between components extend beyond the single morpheme. The allomorphs, then, are suppletive.

Zero allomorphs are likewise suppletive. In certain cases, a morpheme is represented by no phonemes, or zero. In English, for example, {PL} surfaces as a sibilant—*books* ([s]), *roses* ([əz]), *forms* ([z]); or as a nasal—*oxen* ([ən]). Sometimes, however, noun + {PL} is represented by noun + |∅|, for example, *fish, deer,* or *sheep.*[54] In Hebrew, too, {PL} may assume the form of zero. Thus, {sheep} + {PL} = [ṣōn], as in Gen 30:39 [wattēladnɔ haṣṣōn] 'the sheep bore' (cf. Jer 29:6 [nɔšīm ... wətēladnɔ] 'that [the] women may bear'); so too {cattle} + {PL} in Job 1:14 [habbɔqɔr hɔyū ḥōrəšōt̲] 'the cattle were plowing'.[55] In these English and Hebrew examples, then, {PL} can be represented by the suppletive zero allomorph.

While suppletion differs from automatic and morphemically conditioned nonautomatic alternation in scope, it differs in compositional function as well. Suppletion, being replacive, does not bind morphemes together, but substitutes one for another. The constituents are not joined together more closely; there is no intermeshing of morphemes. |X| is replaced by |Y|.

FUSION

The other alternation processes, however, facilitate sandhi, or *fusion.*[56] The constituent parts of a word are bound in closer union by interlocking (morpho)phonemic changes. In this way, the boundary between morphemes is obscured.

Assimilation is a common fusional process.[57] By spirantization, for example, the root |k.t.b| is fused to both the subjective prefix |yV| > [yi] and interdigitated *qal* imperfect pattern |..u.| > [..o.]; thus [yik̲tob̲] 'he writes'.

52. This analysis is comparable to that of the plural formation on all other adjectives, regardless of final outcome. See, e.g., Nida, *Morphology*, 44, 54, for the tactics.

53. J. Barth, *Die Pronominalbildung in den semitischen Sprachen* (Leipzig: Hinrichs, 1913) §48/pp. 118–19. Ugaritic and Akkadian, however, are exceptions.

54. Bloomfield, *Language*, 215; Nida, *Morphology*, 42, 46; and Elson and Pickett, *Morphology and Syntax*, 49.

55. GKC § 145c/pp. 462–63.

56. See, in general, Hockett, *Modern Linguistics*, 277; Matthews, *Morphology*, 111–13; and, somewhat differently, Bybee, *Morphology*, 4, 46, 96–98, 211.

57. Nida, *Morphology*, 21–22; and Matthews, *Morphology*, 101.

The postvocalic context engenders spirantization, which in turn assimilates the stop to the vowel.[58] The root, then, is fused to the other word parts.

Assimilation can also be morphologically conditioned. The numeral {one}, for example, is [ʔɛḥɔ̄d̲] (MASC SING) and [ʔaḥat] (FEM SING). The feminine form, according to consensus, developed from *ʔaḥad+t > ʔaḥadt > ʔaḥatt > ʔaḥat > [ʔaḥat]; the final root letter assimilated to the feminine marker and was lost altogether.[59] Similarly, [ʕēt] 'time' developed from *ʕid+t.[60] This assimilation, however, is not general; for the sequence *-dt- may be preserved in Biblical Hebrew, for example, [yōlad̲t] 'you have borne' (Judg 13:3) and [wəyōlad̲t] 'and you will bear' (Gen 16:11; Judg 13:5, 7). Assimilation, then, occurs in nouns;[61] verbs are exempt.[62] The sound change *-dt- > [tt] is therefore morphemically conditioned and, when it does occur, serves to unite the stem and feminine suffix.

Like assimilation, *dissimilation* can interlock morphemes.[63] The Barth-Ginsberg law is a classic example.[64] In G stem imperfects, *u verbs have /a/ in the subjective prefix, *i verbs have /a/ too, and *a imperfects use prefix /i/; in other words, |yV| + |qtVl| > /yaqtul/, /yaqtil/, and /yiqtal/. The vowel of the prefix therefore responds to that of the verbal stem: a high thematic vowel takes a low prefix vowel; and a low thematic vowel is coupled with a high prefix vowel. The underlying neutral prefix vowel surfaces as a dissimilated (inverse) counterpart of the thematic vowel. In Hebrew, this relationship is preserved when |yV| lies in a pretonic open syllable: for example, [yōqūm] 'he arises', [yōšīr] 'he sang' (Exod 15:1, Num 21:17), [yōbō] 'he comes', and [yērak̲] 'may it (not) be soft' (Deut 20:3, Isa 7:4, Jer 51:46).

Another fusional device is *metathesis*, whereby one morpheme is intercalated by another.[65] In Hebrew, *t* stems ({REFLEXIVE-PASSIVE}) are generally prefixed, for example, [yitpɔ̄rəd̲ū] 'they are scattered' (Ps 92:10) and [yitgaddel] 'it magnifies itself' (Isa 10:15). Yet when the first radical is a sibilant, *t metathesizes with the sibilant and becomes infixed.[66] Thus *hitsappeaḥ > [(mē)his-tappeaḥ] 'from having a share' (1 Sam 26:19), *titšappek > [tištappek̲] 'it runs

---

58. See Harris, *Canaanite Dialects*, 66; and L. M. Hyman, *Phonology: Theory and Analysis* (New York: Holt, Rinehart & Winston, 1975) 157.
59. E.g., BL § 15h/p. 198; GKC § 19d/p. 69; and Joüon § 17g/p. 52.
60. See *HALAT* (3d ed.) 851.
61. [lat̲] 'to give birth' (1 Sam 4:19) < *lid+t probably arose by extension. See [lɛd̲ɛt] 'to give birth' < *lid+t.
62. See BL § 15i/p. 198; GB pt. 1 § 19c/p. 109.
63. Nida, *Morphology*, 23; and Dressler, *Morphonology*, 46.
64. See R. Hetzron, "The Vocalization of Prefixes in Semitic Active and Passive Verbs," *Mélanges de l'Université Saint-Joseph* 48 (1973–74) 38–39.
65. Nida, *Morphology*, 16–17; Elson and Pickett, *Morphology and Syntax*, 44; and Dressler, *Morphonology*, 45.
66. E.g., BL § 23a/p. 217; GB pt. 1 § 20d/pp. 111–12.

out' (Job 30:16), and, with assimilation, [niṣtaddå̄q] 'we can prove ourselves innocent' (Gen 44:16).[67] Yet since metathesis does not occur in [təsōb̲eb̲] 'she surrounds(?)' (Jer 31:22) or [təšabber] 'you will smash, have smashed' (Exod 23:24, Ps 48:8), the alternation is, on the descriptive-synchronic level, morphologically restricted to the *t* prefix. By metathesis, then, {REFL-PASS} and stem partially overlap.[68]

Even greater overlapping can occur. Like [ʾaḥaṯ], < *ʾaḥad+t, a boundary may be completely obscured by assimilation, whereby a phoneme is lost. Similarly, the boundary in |ma| + |qtal| nouns—for example, [maʾăk̲ōl] 'food' or [mōsōk̲] 'screen'—is not transparent in I-*wāw* roots. Thus, |ma| + |qtal| > /ma/ + /wᶜid/ > *mawᶜid* > [mōᶜēd̲] 'appointed time, place'; /ma/ + /wṣaʾ/ > *mawṣaʾ* > [mōṣō] 'exit'; or /ma/ + /wšab/ > [mōšōb̲] 'seat'. In monophthongization, the boundary between prefix and stem is blurred, and part of each morpheme merges into a new, ambivalent phone.[69]

WORD FORMATION

Fusion, however, does not apply to contiguous word elements alone. The same processes applied to two adjacent constituents also extend to word composition. Words, then, are formed by various fusional processes whose effect reigns over the entire word unit.

All constituent word elements are either *bound* or *free*.[70] A free form may potentially occur in isolation. For example, English *school* is actually free in the phrase *a free school*. Yet in the compound *schoolbus*, it is only potentially free. In Hebrew too, [bəlī] 'without' is both actually and potentially free.[71] Or, |qōl| is a free form as well (> [qōl#] vs. [qōl≠]/[qōl+]).

A bound form, however, does not occur in isolation but only as part of a larger complex.[72] The English negative prefix *un-* and adverbial suffix *-ly*, which never appear as independent words,[73] are bound to their nucleus. Similarly, the Hebrew pattern never occurs independently, but is always intertwined with a root. A word, then, consists of bound and/or free forms.

Just as bound and free forms represent compositional types, languages themselves can be categorized by compositional processes.[74] Chinese repre-

---

67. See Akkadian, in W. von Soden, *Grundriss der akkadischen Grammatik* (2d ed.; Analecta Orientalia 33/47; Rome: Pontifical Biblical Institute, 1969) §36a/p. 35.
68. See interdigitation, above.
69. Garvin, "Relative Tractability," 14–15.
70. See Bloomfield, *Language*, 207, 210; Nida, *Morphology*, 81; Elson and Pickett, *Morphology and Syntax*, 11; and Matthews, *Morphology*, 160. Cf. Hockett, in *Lg*. 23 (1947) 282.
71. On the latter, see [bəlīmō] 'nothing' and [bəlīyaᶜal] 'wicked(ness)'.
72. Therefore the *status constructus* and *status pronominalis* are bound forms.
73. Except in phrases like *the ly and un affixes are bound to their nucleus*.
74. See Hockett, *Modern Linguistics*, 181.

sents one extreme: it has few bound forms; each constituent element therefore forms an independent word; and elements show little or no fusion.[75] Chinese is an *isolating* language. Latin represents the other extreme: it has many bound forms; and bound forms may represent several morphemes simultaneously (e.g., |us| = {MASC}, {SING}, {NOMINATIVE}.[76] Such a language is *fusional*. The intermediate language-type is *agglutinative*. Represented by Turkish, it consists of bound forms joined to each other with little or no modification;[77] and bound elements are strung together in a particular order.[78] While no language represents one language-type exclusively, these categories form the parameters of classification.[79]

Hebrew falls within the agglutinative-fusional camp. Within this continuum, it favors the fusional.[80] {voice} + {PL}, for example, consists of the free |qōl| + bound |ōt| which, as [qōlōt], shows no intermorphemic modification. In {thing} + {PL}, |dabar| + |īm| > [dəḇārīm], two bound forms are fused, but with only slight modification. These agglutinative traits, however, are not preponderant.

Fusional features, on the contrary, are more plentiful. Like Latin, Hebrew has bound forms which represent several morphemes. For example, the suffix [+ō] specifies {GENDER}, {NUMBER}, and {SYNTACTIC VALENCE}, that is, {FEM SING ABSOLUTE}. Hebrew also exhibits allomorphy and other fusional processes, like interdigitation, which weld constituent elements together. In this way, Hebrew behaves like most world languages.[81]

Hebrew utilizes other word-forming devices too, yet ones which facilitate development from base > derivative forms. For example, new forms can be generated by *addition*, the expansion of a stem by adding elements (prefixes, suffixes, infixes, etc.).[82] *Subtraction* is the opposite process, the production of new forms by removing one or more compositional elements.[83] And finally, *replacement* substitutes a new element for part of the stem.[84] Of these processes, addition is best attested in Biblical Hebrew.

---

75. Bloomfield, *Language*, 207–8; Greenberg, "Quantitative Approach," 180; R. H. Robins, *General Linguistics: An Introductory Survey* (Bloomington: Indiana University Press, 1964) 333; and Bybee, *Morphology*, 44.

76. Bloomfield, *Language*, 208; Robins, *General Linguistics*, 333–34; and Bybee, *Morphology*, 45. See also Anderson, "Inflectional Morphology," 160–62.

77. Bloomfield, *Language*, 208; and Greenberg, "Quantitative Approach," 185.

78. R. A. Hall Jr., *Introductory Linguistics* (Philadelphia: Chilton, 1964) 149.

79. See Greenberg, "Quantitative Approach," 178–94.

80. Bybee, *Morphology*, 45.

81. Ibid., 45.

82. Nida, "Identification of Morphemes," 440; and idem, *Morphology*, 69.

83. Bloomfield, *Language*, 217; Nida, *Morphology*, 75–76; and Elson and Pickett, *Morphology and Syntax*, 48–49.

84. Nida, *Morphology*, 71–72; and Elson and Pickett, *Morphology and Syntax*, 47–48.

Addition itself, however, is an umbrella term which includes two well-known word-forming phenomena, *derivation* and *inflection*.[85] A derivational additive is restricted in application and nonobligatory.[86] In other words, it is not predictable. For example, {FEM SING ABS} surfaces not only as [+ɔ̄] (and its allophones), but also as [+∅]. In contrast to [ʔiššɔ̄] 'woman' and [malkɔ̄] 'queen', there occur [ʔem] 'mother', [ʔɔ̄tōn] 'she-ass', as well as many other grammatically feminine nouns, for example, [ʔɛrɛṣ] 'land' and [yɔ̄ḏ] 'hand'. The derivational suffix, then, is not a requirement.

Nor do derivational additives have full generality within a given class. It is not possible, for example, to convert any noun into an abstract by suffixing |+ōn|. Whereas this process applies in [šabbɔ̄t] 'Sabbath' > [šabbɔ̄tōn] 'Sabbatical' and [yɛtɛr] 'remainder' > [yitrōn] 'advantage', ˣ[malkōn] 'royal sovereignty' < [mɛlɛk] 'king' (cf. [mamlɔ̄kɔ̄] 'royal sovereignty') and ˣ[kōhănōn] 'priesthood' < [kōhēn] 'priest' (cf. [kəhunnɔ̄] 'priesthood') do not exist. Derivational elements therefore have circumscribed application.

Derivational affixes may also change the semantic or grammatical class of a word.[87] For example, [yɛtɛr] and [yitrōn] are nouns, despite morphological differences, and are mutually substitutable in certain environments. Yet the suffix |+ōn| alters semantic categories; the base noun becomes abstract. Or, the affix may change the word's grammatical class, as when the homophonous |+ōn| {ADJECTIVE} converts nouns to adjectives: [qɛḏɛm] 'East' > [qaḏmōn] 'eastern', or perhaps [riʔšōn] 'first' < |riʔš| {head} + |ōn| {ADJ}. For the most part, then, derivational affixes produce a change of class membership.[88]

Inflectional elements, however, do not change class membership, are obligatory, and have predictable meaning.[89] Markers of the pronominal subject on verbs typify inflection. For in a finite clause, the marker is obligatory and semantically predictable by the subject. Thus, {1 SING INDEPENDENT PRON} stem + {PRON SUBJ} must be realized as {I}[90] stem + |tī| with a perfect verb, or {I} |ʔV|[91] + stem with an imperfect; |+tī| and |ʔV+| are required by construction. Similarly, gender/number agreement on adjectives is inflectional, since the adjective must match the natural sex/number and/or grammatical gender/number of the governing noun.[92] For example, {one} {woman} >

85. On the nonabsolute dichotomy between derivation and inflection, see Bybee, *Morphology*, 5, 87.
86. Ibid., 12, 81.
87. Nida, *Morphology*, 99.
88. See Greenberg, "Quantitative Approach," 191; and Anderson, "Inflectional Morphology," 162.
89. Nida, *Morphology*, 99; and Bybee, *Morphology*, 5, 11, 27, 81, 99. See also Greenberg, "Quantitative Approach," 191.
90. Abbreviated for convenience.
91. Revised below.
92. See Kuryłowicz, cited in Bybee, *Morphology*, 98–99. See Harris, "Discontinuous Morphemes," 122–23.

[ˀiššɔ̄ ˀaḥat] (Zech 5:7); {many} {woman} + {PL} > [nɔ̄šīm rabbōt] (Judg 8:30); {many} {sheep} + {PL} > [ṣōn∅ rabbōt] (Gen 30:43); and {good} {rumor} > [šəmūᶜɔ̄ ṭōbɔ̄] (Prov 15:30). And in neither the verbal nor the adjectival inflections does the additive alter class membership; verbs remain verbal, and adjectives adjectival.

These examples illustrate another aspect of inflectional elements: they are fully general in application, within a given class.[93] All perfect verbs, for example, whose subject is "1 SING" end in |+tī|; all corresponding imperfects prefix |ˀV+|. Similarly, all FEM PL adjectives end in [+ōt], regardless of the form of the governing noun; and all FEM SING adjectives append [+ɔ̄]. Inflectional elements, then, are predictable in meaning as well as scope.

Whereas addition—whether derivational or inflectional—expands an existing stem, subtraction truncates the base form. Masculine singular French adjectives, for example, develop by subtraction; the shorter masculine form is derived from the longer feminine form by removing the feminine marker: *bonne* > *bonne̸* > *bon* 'good', or *blanche* > *blanche̸* > *blanc* 'white'.[94] The imperative in Hidatsa (a Siouan language of Native America) is derived from the past tense by subtracting final segments: [cixīc] 'he jumped' > [cix] 'jump!' or [ikāc] 'he looked' > [ika] 'look!'[95] Similarly, the Hebrew imperative is subtractive, formed by removing the pronominal prefix of the imperfect: for example, [tiškab] 'you (will) lie down' (Lev 18:22, Deut 24:12, Ezek 4:4, 31:18; Prov 3:24) > *t̸iškab* > *škab* > *šəkab* > [šəkab] 'lie down!' (2 Sam 13:5, Ezek 4:4). By basing the imperative on the imperfect, the alternation between [k] and [k] can be explained; after removal of the prefix, the once syllable-initial, postconsonantal stop is spirantized following a mobile šĕwāˀ.[96] Certain Biblical Hebrew masculine forms are subtractive as well. For example, [mɛlɛk] 'king' may be derived from [malkɔ̄] 'queen': *malkȥ > *malk* > *malək*[97] > [mɛlɛk]. In this way, the different outcomes of *k > [k] ~ [k] are attributable to regular sound change.

Replacement is a third compositional device whereby one word element is substituted for another within a stem.[98] Unlike addition and subtraction, replacement exchanges one element for another. For example, English {PL}

93. Bybee, *Morphology*, 5, 16–19, 99.
94. Bloomfield, *Language*, 217–18. Cf. Matthews, *Morphology*, 134.
95. Harris, "Morpheme Alternants," 171.
96. The only exception is the numeral 'two' [šətayim]. More difficult is [kətob] 'write!' (Exod 17:14, Hab 2:2) < [tiktob] '(you) write' (Num 17:17–18, Ezek 37:20, Job 13:26). Having developed from [tiktob] > *t̸iktob* > *ktob* > *kətob* > *kətob* > [kətob], the second radical is spirantized after the mobile šĕwāˀ (see [tiškab] > [šəkab]). Also, the first radical is despirantized in word-initial position since, according to regular sound rules, word-initial nonemphatic stops are hard (GKC §21b/p. 75).
97. On the anaptyctic šĕwāˀ, see n. 50 above.
98. See n. 84 above.

is usually additive, as in *clock-s*, *table-s*, and *ox-en*. Other words, however, form the plural by internal modification, or replacement. Thus, the new vowel in *men* < *man*, *geese* < *goose*, and *feet* < *foot* is a replacive {PL} element.[99] The Arabic broken plural[100] may also represent replacement, for example, {eye} [ᶜaynun] > {eye} + {PL} [ᶜuyūnun], or {man} [rajulun] > {man} + {PL} [rijālun].[101] Part of the stem is replaced to form the plural. Hebrew has only a vestige of replacive plurals, when |qVtl| nouns are reshaped as /qVtal/ before the plural ending.[102] Yet since the form also carries an additive element denoting {PL}, the stem-internal modification is not replacement, in the strict sense, but rather morphemically conditioned alternation.

WORD STRUCTURE

Word composition, however, consists not only of these three processes and different degrees of alternation; it also concerns the overall structure of words. Morphemes are arranged in a certain order which, in its sum, forms words. This hierarchical arrangement is called *tactics*.[103]

Whereas phrasal arrangement is flexible (to a certain degree), a word's tactical arrangement of morphemes is fixed.[104] For example, English sentences like *John loves Jane* and *Jane loves John* both make sense, despite the syntactical rearrangement, albeit with different meanings. Or in Hebrew, the orders Verb + Subject + Object [wayyōḇē yōsēp ʾɛt-dibbɔ̄ṯɔ̄m] 'Joseph brought (bad) reports of them' (Gen 37:2), S + V + O [umalkī-ṣɛdɛq . . . hōṣī lɛḥɛm] 'Malkizedek brought out bread' (Gen 14:18), O + V + S [ʾim-ᶜɛḇɛd yiggaḥ haššōr] 'if the bull gores a slave' (Exod 21:32), and other combinations all make sense.[105]

Tactical arrangements, however, are immutable. In English, the past tense of {help} is actualized as |help| + |ed| > *helped*; the reverse order, |ed| + |help|, does not exist and is impossible. Hebrew enclitic pronominal objects, too, are always suffixed and follow the verb + {PRON SUBJ}: for example, [ləqɔ̄ḥánī] 'he took me' (Gen 24:7) < {take} + {QAL ACTIVE PF} + {PRON SUBJ} + {PRON OBJ}, [wayyiqqɔ̄ḥúhū] 'they took him' (Gen 37:24,

---

99. See Bloomfield, *Language*, 216.
100. On the whole issue, see F. Corriente, *Problematica de la pluralidad en semitico el plural fracto* (Madrid: Instituto "Benito Arias Montano," 1971).
101. G. Bergsträsser, *Einführung in die semitischen Sprachen* (Munich: Hueber, 1928) 141.
102. See p. 55 above.
103. Hockett, in *Lg.* 23 (1947) 274; idem, "Morphemic Analysis," 321.
104. Bloomfield, *Language*, 207; Nida, *Morphology*, 78, 102; and Matthews, *Morphology*, 162. Cf. Garvin, "Relative Tractability," 21.
105. See C. Brockelmann, *Hebräische Syntax* (Neukirchen: Neukirchener Verlag, 1956) § 122/ pp. 119–21.

1 Sam 10:23) < {take} + {QAL NARRATIVE} + {PRON SUBJ} + {PRON OBJ}, and [šəmɔ́ᶜū́nī] 'hear me!' (Gen 23:8; 1 Chr 28:2; 2 Chr 13:4, 15:2, 20:20, 28:11, 29:5) < {hear} + {QAL IMPV} + {PRON SUBJ} + {PRON OBJ}. Each morpheme, then, occupies a specific slot which, in relation to other constituent morphemes, is fixed. Tactics, then, signifies a fixed, relative hierarchy.[106]

Yet some morphemes occupy multiple slots, although complementarily distributed. The pronominal subjects of Hebrew verbs illustrate this point. {I} occurs as either |+tī| or |ᵓV+|, depending upon verbal stem. Similarly {they} is |+ū| with perfects, and |yV+ +ū| with imperfects. Since the choice of subjective pronouns is morphologically conditioned, and the pronouns never overlap,[107] they represent single morphemes whose allomorphs assume different tactical positions.

When a tactical slot is occupied by several, mutually substitutable elements, these elements form a tactical *class*.[108] The pronominal subjects |+t| {you}, |timm| {you}, and |+ū| {they} are substitutable subjective pronouns on perfect verbs. They form the class PF PRON SUBJ and occupy one tactical slot. Similarly, |tV+ +ī| {you}, |tV+ +ū| {you}, and |yV+ +ū| {they} form a second class, IMPF PRON SUBJ. Zero-ending pronominal subjects, as in |ᵓV+ +∅| {I}, |tV+ +∅| {you}, and |yV+ +∅| {he} are tactically identical, except that their final segment is -∅. Thus within each class, whether PF PRON SUBJ or IMPF PRON SUBJ, all elements are mutually substitutable.

A class may be more complex than single substitutable elements. Verbal patterns, for example, constitute a class. Thus |..u.| {QAL·ACTIVE IMPF}, |n.a.i.| {NIPHAL MEDIO-PASSIVE IMPF}, |ha..ī.| {HIPHIL CAUSATIVE IMPF}, and |hit.a.:i.| {HITHPAEL REFL-PASS IMPF} are mutually substitutable and occupy the same tactical position relative to the pronominal subject: [yišmərū] 'they guard' < |ya| + |ṧm.r ..u.| + |ū|, [yillɔ̄ḵḗḏū] 'they are caught' (Prov 11:6) < |yi| + |.1.m.d n.a. i.| + |ū|, [yašmíḏū] 'may they (not) destroy' (2 Sam 14:11) < |yV| + |..ṧm.d ha.. i.| + |ū|, and [yitpɔ̄rəḏū] 'they are scattered' (Ps 92:10) < |yV| + |...p.r.d hit.a.:i.| + |ū|. Although these patterns do not occupy the identical tactical slot, they are mutually substitutable, make sense, and therefore constitute one class.

Just as a class may occupy several complementarily distributed tactical slots, so too one slot may be filled by multiple morphemes.[109] In this characteristic of fusional languages, two or more morphemes merge into a single

---

106. See Harris, "Structure of Hebrew," 159–61.

107. See M. Lambert, *Traité de grammaire hébraïque* (Paris: Presses Universitaires de France, 1946) 291 n. 1. For a different opinion, see C. R. Krahmalkov, "The Enclitic Particle *ta/i* in Hebrew," *JBL* 89 (1970) 218–19.

108. Harris, "Structure of Hebrew," 143; idem, "From Morpheme to Utterance," *Lg.* 22 (1946) 163; and Elson and Pickett, *Morphology and Syntax*, 57. See also Wells, "Immediate Constituents," 81; and Greenberg, "Quantitative Approach," 190.

109. I. J. Gelb, *Sequential Reconstruction of Proto-Akkadian* (Assyriological Studies 18; Chicago: University of Chicago Press, 1969) 25 (cf. 13–14).

element. For example, Latin {NOM} + {MASC} + {SING} > |us| and occupies
the same slot as {GENITIVE} + {FEM} + {PL} > |ārum|. Or, Hebrew |at| > [+ɔ̄]
{FEM} + {SING} + {ABS} is tactically identical to |ay| > [+ē] {MASC} + {PL} +
{CONSTRUCT} since they are mutually substitutable ([šɔ̄nɔ̄] 'year' : [šənē]
'years of'; see also [šənɔ̄t̲ō] 'his year', and [šɔ̄nɔw] 'its, his years' [Lev 25:52,
Job 36:26, Qoh 6:3] < |šan| + |ay| + |hū|). Thus one tactical slot may be occu-
pied by one class, whether that class is morphemically singular or multiple.

Tactics, the overall arrangement of morphemes into words, has been formalized as a descriptive method portraying word construction.[110] This
method, called "item-and-arrangement," describes a word in terms of constituent morphemes which are arranged in a given, relative order. Alternation is accommodated by environmental, that is, structural, conditions
occurring within and between slots. Tactically, item-and-arrangement results
in morpheme lists and the positions (slots) they occupy.[111]

While item-and-arrangement successfully isolates elements and their tactical order, it ignores compositional processes operative in word formation.
For example, addition, subtraction, and replacement find no place in item-
and-arrangement. But an alternative method, item-and-process, highlights the
dynamics of construction. A word consists of elements (items) and the processes they undergo. A form, then, is either basic or derived by certain processes. Or, in tactical terms, a word contains elements, arranged in certain
positions relative to other elements, and influencing processes. Whereas, for
example, *men* and *books* would be interpreted as different plural formations
by item-and-arrangement, in item-and-process they participate in the same
{PL} process whose surface representations differ. Item-and-process thus as-
sembles identical processes under one rubric, as well as separates process
from outcome.

In sum, morphology is analysis and construction. Words are analyzed into
their most simple components (morphemes). Where different representations of
components occur (allomorphs), these representations are associated with
governing conditions (morphophonemics). Components are studied in relation to
neighboring components to reveal the processes which bind elements together
(fusion). Components are also studied in their hierarchical arrangement (tactics),
whereby components are strung together to form words. Morphology therefore
treats all stages of word formation.

110. For this and the following discussion, see C. F. Hockett, "Two Methods of Grammatical
     Description," *Word* 10 (1954) 210–34.
111. See the item-and-arrangement study of Akkadian in Gelb, *Sequential Reconstruction*, esp.
     17.

[September, 1986]

Gary A. Rendsburg

Morphological Evidence for Regional Dialects in Ancient Hebrew

To all who have ever undertaken the linguistic study of the Hebrew Bible, it is abundantly clear that the text bristles with an inordinate number of grammatical peculiarities. Although I have no empirical evidence to substantiate the following statement, my sense is that on a relative scale one encounters more such difficulties in the Hebrew Bible than in comparable corpora, for example, Homer's *Iliad* and *Odyssey*, the Qurᵓān, the Avesta, Assyrian annals, etc. In the past, scholars have ascribed this situation to the unusual history of the Bible's textual transmission, which purportedly has led to all sorts of scribal errors being inadvertently introduced into the text. The response of scholars who are responsible for our standard reference grammars and for our standard editions of the Bible has been to emend the text in innumerable instances in order to restore it to its presumed autographed version.[1] Often this is done with the support of other manuscript traditions (Qumran, Samaritan, etc.) and/or the versions (Septuagint, Targum, Vulgate, etc.), but just as often these emendations are executed ad hoc.

Author's note: I take this opportunity to gratefully acknowledge a grant from the National Endowment for the Humanities Fellowship for College Teachers program, which enabled me to spend a good portion of the academic year 1986–87 in Jerusalem. Research for the present article was conducted there at the Jewish University and National Library of the Hebrew University and at the École Biblique. I am indebted to the staffs of both institutions for many privileges extended to me. I have benefited greatly from the good counsel of a number of faculty members of the Hebrew University, who kindly discussed with me many aspects of my investigation into regional dialects of ancient Hebrew. In particular I offer my thanks to Joshua Blau, Jonas Greenfield, Avi Hurvitz, Shelomo Morag, and Shalom Paul. An oral version of this paper was presented to the annual meeting of the American Oriental Society, March 1988, in Chicago.

1. I have in mind here, of course, such volumes as GKC and *BHS*.

In recent years, at least in some circles, the practices just outlined have lessened. Instead of simply emending the text when a difficulty presents itself, there has been a growing trend toward seeking to explain the peculiarity. This has resulted in an increased respect for the MT, or at least its consonantal skeleton. David Noel Freedman's recent opinion on the subject is emblematic of this new approach. The following lines were written in regard to the Book of Job, but they are equally cogent for all of the MT:

> Traditional approaches and methods have not proved notably successful, and neither has the radical surgery attempted by many more recent scholars. Most such conjectural emendations have proven ephemeral or evanescent and have failed to convince any stable majority of scholars. . . . Some commonly accepted rules of the road can help in the assessment of procedures and products in this field. (a) It is better to stay with the existing text than to change it. . . . (d) Emendation of the text, while sometimes inevitable and unavoidable in view of the present and ongoing state of research, is often little better than a counsel of despair. . . . For books like Job, there is little choice among texts and versions. Some help can be gained from the newly published Targum, as well as the versions, but for the most part we are bound to the MT.[2]

Often this defense of the MT has been sparked by the discovery of cognate forms in other Semitic languages. For example, before the recognition of enclitic *mēm* in Ugaritic and thence in Hebrew, rare was the scholar who would defend *mtnym qmyw* in Deut 33:11. Now, with our increased knowledge of ancient Hebrew morphology, rare is the scholar who would not defend the consonantal text of the MT at Deut 33:11.[3] Or another example more recently advanced: virtually all scholars who have dealt with *wmpᵓt* in Ezek 48:16 have proposed deleting the *mēm*. Now, however, with the discovery that enclitic *mēm* may be attached to conjunctive *ù* in Eblaite, a number of such constructions have been isolated in the Bible and thus we may defend the otherwise peculiar *wm-* in Ezek 48:16 and various other passages.[4]

In the two preceding paragraphs, I have spoken mainly of the consonantal text. But the rules against emendation are also valid for the vocalization of the Masoretes. Many if not most scholars, and here I include even those who do respect the consonantal text, have little regard for the pointing of the text. They consider it a relatively unreliable guide to the pronunciation of ancient Hebrew, and peculiarities are typically considered corrupt and then altered to conform to the standard Masoretic vocalization. However, several

2. D. N. Freedman, Review of A. R. Ceresko, *Job 29–31 in the Light of Northwest Semitic, JBL* 102 (1983) 138–39.

3. See W. L. Moran, "The Hebrew Language in Its Northwest Semitic Background," in *The Bible and the Ancient Near East: Essays in Honor of William Foxwell Albright* (ed. G. E. Wright; Garden City: Doubleday, 1961) 60.

4. G. A. Rendsburg, "Eblaite *ù-ma* and Hebrew *wm-*," *Eblaitica* 1 (1987) 34–41.

important investigations into the subject have shown that the vocalization is historically valid and that unusual forms can be explained when the factor of linguistic diversity is taken into consideration.

Here I take the opportunity only to cite the summary statements penned by J. Barr and S. Morag on the subject. The former wrote as follows:

> Firstly, no one doubts that the traditional vocalization is subject to error and may deserve emendation by scholars under the safeguard of proper consideration of the factors involved. There is no evidence, however, that entitles us to carry this so far that we begin to regard the vocalization as entirely arbitrary or chaotic and therefore subject to alteration on no greater basis than the liking of the modern scholar. The vocalization is historical evidence just as other aspects of the text are; it has to be explained and not merely altered.[5]

Morag wrote an extremely important article on the subject and concluded thus:

> To sum up, it appears that the vocalization peculiarities we have attempted to elucidate in the present paper are evidently not to be considered whims of the Massoretes. The vocalization is definitely of historical value, and even those of its features that look strange should be examined seriously, and must not be labeled as "errors" of the vocalizers. This point cannot be stressed too far.[6]

Another development which has led to a greater respect for the MT has been the application of linguistic methods associated with dialectology. (As will become evident, I use this term in its broadest sense.) Most biblicists have sheepishly accepted the belief that "historical differences have for the most part been obliterated by the harmonizing activity of the Masoretes" (GKC, vii). Recent studies, however, have shown that just the opposite is true. Far from having harmonized Biblical Hebrew into one standard language, the Masoretes clearly preserved what had been transmitted, dialectal differences and all. A. Hurvitz has emphasized the existence of features of Late versus Early Biblical Hebrew in his research,[7] and I have dealt extensively with the issue of diglossia in ancient Hebrew, that is, the existence of separate written and spoken dialects of the language.[8] These studies have

---

5. J. Barr, *Comparative Philology and the Text of the Old Testament* (Oxford: Clarendon, 1968; repr. Winona Lake, IN: Eisenbrauns, 1987) 221.
6. S. Morag, "On the Historical Validity of the Vocalization of the Hebrew Bible," *JAOS* 94 (1974) 307–15, esp. 315.
7. See most importantly A. Hurvitz, *Ben Lašon le-Lašon* (Jerusalem: Bialik, 1972); "The Evidence of Language in Dating the Priestly Code—A Linguistic Study in Technical Idioms and Terminology," *Revue biblique* 81 (1974) 24–56; and *A Linguistic Study of the Relationship between the Priestly Source and the Book of Ezekiel* (Paris: Gabalda, 1982).
8. G. A. Rendsburg, "*Laqṭîl* Infinitives: Yiphᶜil or Hiphᶜil?" *Orientalia* 51 (1982) 231–38; and *Diglossia in Ancient Hebrew* (AOS 72; New Haven: American Oriental Society, 1990).

compiled numerous examples of grammatical forms which are to be labeled post-classicisms (in the case of Hurvitz's work) or colloquialisms (in the case of my own work), but which in no way are to be considered textually corrupt, as many scholars of the past have opined.

In light of the foregoing, in the present article I propose to present evidence for the existence of regional varieties of Hebrew in antiquity. Based on the above conclusions that in the main the MT is a reliable textual witness and that it preserves dialectal differences, I hope to demonstrate that atypical grammatical forms often are characteristic of regional variation. With most scholars, I assume that the vast majority of the Bible was written in Judah, in Jerusalem in particular, and/or by exiles from Judah. This holds presumably for most, if not 99 percent, of the Pentateuch; the material in Samuel and Kings concerning David, Solomon, and the succeeding kings of Judah; the prophets Isaiah, Ezekiel, Micah, Zephaniah, Habakkuk, Second Isaiah, etc.; most of Psalms; the books of Ruth, Lamentations, Chronicles, etc. But naturally there are portions of the Bible which demonstrably are non-Judahite in origin, namely the stories in Judges dealing with the northern and Transjordanian heroes, the material in Kings presenting the history of the northern kingdom of Israel, the prophet Hosea, some Psalms, etc.[9]

An investigation into these latter sections of the Bible reveals that it is specifically in these texts where one finds a larger concentration of the aforementioned atypical grammatical forms. This will become clear in the treatment of the individual morphemes below. Most of these forms also appear in other non-Judahite dialects of Canaanite (e.g., Phoenician, Ammonite, Moabite, Deir ʿAlla)[10] and/or in Aramaic. The conclusion to be reached is that in regions of Israelite settlement away from Jerusalem and Judah there was a distinct dialect (or dialects) of Hebrew with isoglosses connecting this speech to other Canaanite and Aramaic dialects. This has been theorized be-

---

9. Selected pericopes elsewhere as well, e.g., Nehemiah 9, as demonstrated by A. C. Welch, "The Source of Nehemiah IX," *ZAW* 47 (1929) 130–37; see G. A. Rendsburg, "The Northern Origin of Nehemiah 9," in *Biblica* (forthcoming); and 2 Sam 23:1–7, for which see G. A. Rendsburg, "The Northern Origin of 'The Last Words of David' (2 Sam 23,1–7)," *Biblica* 69 (1988) 113–21.

10. I accept the conclusion of J. A. Hackett, *The Balaam Text from Deir ʿAllā* (Harvard Semitic Monographs 31; Chico: Scholars Press, 1984), that the Deir ʿAlla texts are written in a dialect of Canaanite. See now the very important article by B. Halpern, "Dialect Distribution in Canaan and the Deir Alla Inscriptions," in *"Working with No Data": Semitic and Egyptian Studies Presented to Thomas O. Lambdin* (ed. D. M. Golomb; Winona Lake, IN: Eisenbrauns, 1987) 119–39. This article came to my attention too late for its results to be incorporated into the present paper in any meaningful manner. But its overall conclusion that "Canaan was linguistically cantonized even in the latest Israelite periods" (139) is consistent with my own approach.

fore, most prominently by C. Rabin;[11] and already early in the twentieth century C. F. Burney made an important contribution in identifying various characteristic features of northern Hebrew.[12] The present article puts forward many more examples of such features, and it also benefits from recent work on geographical variation, especially W. R. Garr's very important and exceedingly useful volume on the subject.[13]

I also go beyond previous work in this area in the following regard. In several instances, I show that a particular feature which I suspect is non-Judahite, based on its appearance in stories dealing with the north and/or in other dialects of Canaanite or in Aramaic, occurs sporadically elsewhere. Occasionally these elements appear in the speeches of the prophets (even those active in Jerusalem) addressed to the foreign nations. In these cases I assume that code-switching is present, that is, non-Judahite forms are intentionally used to color the language in a manner reflecting the speech of Judah's neighbors.[14] In other cases, these elements will bunch in a work whose provenance is not *a priori* southern or northern. When this occurs, I conclude that this section of the Bible is also of non-Judahite authorship. This methodology will become clearer as I proceed to the data.

An additional matter which needs to be discussed is what to call this non-Judahite variety of Hebrew. The term *Northern Hebrew* is not perfectly acceptable because it may imply that we are dealing only with the area in the far north, such as the tribal territories of Dan, Asher, Naphtali, etc. As I show, however, the evidence for non-Judahite Hebrew includes grammatical forms which occur in stories presumably emanating from central regions such as the territory of Ephraim and from a territory such as Reuben's which is essentially on the same latitude as Judah. Accordingly, I opt for the term *Israelian*, which was introduced by H. L. Ginsberg to refer to the northern

---

11. C. Rabin, "The Emergence of Classical Hebrew," in *The Age of the Monarchies: Culture and Society* (ed. A. Malamat; World History of the Jewish People 4/2; Jerusalem: Massada, 1979) 71–78, 293–95; and "Lešonam šel ᶜAmos we-Hošeaᶜ," in ᶜ*Iyyunim be-Seper Tre-*ᶜ*Aśar* (ed. B. Z. Luria; Jerusalem: Kiryath Sepher, 1981) 117–36.

12. C. F. Burney, *Notes on the Hebrew Text of the Books of Kings* (Oxford: Clarendon, 1903) 208–9; and *The Book of Judges* (London: Rivingtons, 1918) 171–76. These two books have been reprinted in one volume with a prolegomenon by W. F. Albright (New York: Ktav, 1970).

13. W. R. Garr, *Dialect Geography of Syria-Palestine, 1000–586 B.C.E.* (Philadelphia: University of Pennsylvania Press, 1985).

14. On this phenomenon see S. A. Kaufman, "The Classification of the North West Semitic Dialects of the Biblical Period and Some Implications Thereof," in *Proceedings of the Ninth World Congress of Jewish Studies* (*Panel Sessions: Hebrew and Aramaic Languages*) (Jerusalem: World Union of Jewish Studies, 1988) 55. See also N. H. Tur-Sinai, "ᵓAuramit: Hašpaᶜat ha-ᵓAuramit ᶜal ha-ᶜIbrit šel ha-Miqra," *Enṣiqlopediya Miqraᵓit* 1 (1965) 593–94; and G. A. Rendsburg, "Bilingual Wordplay in the Bible," *VT* 38 (1988) 354–57.

kingdom.[15] As I noted above parenthetically, it is possible if not probable that we are dealing with more than one Israelian dialect. There is no reason to assume, for example, that the people of Reuben, Ephraim, and Dan all spoke the same brand of Hebrew. With perhaps two exceptions (the third-person masculine singular pronominal suffix -ôhî and the third-person masculine plural objective pronoun hēm, on which see below) it is doubtful whether there is enough evidence to posit, let us say, a Transjordanian dialect of Hebrew versus an extreme northern dialect of Hebrew. Of course, it may be assumed that the former is closer to Deir ꜥAlla, Ammonite, and Moabite, and the latter closer to Phoenician and Aramaic, but lack of sufficient information prevents us from drawing any unequivocal conclusions. Therefore, I use the term *Israelian Hebrew*, keeping in mind that it may be an umbrella for a series of subdialects. Collectively it stands in contrast to what I call *Judahite Hebrew*, a term already inherent in the oft-cited yĕhûdît in 2 Kgs 18:26, 28 = Isa 36:11, 13 = 2 Chr 32:18; Neh 13:24.

As the title of this article implies, the evidence presented is all in the realm of morphology (embracing morphophonemic and morphosyntactic material). Phonological differences between Israelian and Judahite Hebrew no doubt existed,[16] and it would not be surprising to find syntactic distinctions as well.[17] But for the purposes of linguistic classification, the morphological evidence remains primary. I. J. Gelb's dictum for linguistic classification is most apt: "We must recognize that certain levels have precedence over others: grammar over lexicon, and within grammar, morphology over phonology and, even more, over syntax. These are not spur-of-the-moment conclusions; they reflect my thinking on these matters over the years of life-long experience."[18] With all this in mind, let us proceed to the evidence.

15. H. L. Ginsberg, *The Israelian Heritage of Judaism* (New York: Jewish Theological Seminary, 1982).

16. The paradigm example for phonological variation in ancient Israel is of course the shibboleth incident in Judg 12:6; see now G. A. Rendsburg, "More on Hebrew *šibbōlet*," *JSS* 33 (1988) 255–58; and "The Ammonite Phoneme /Ṯ/," *BASOR* 269 (1988) 73–79. On the representation of proto-Semitic /ḍ/ by qôp and of proto-Semitic /θ/ by tāw in Judges 5, see Rabin, "Emergence of Classical Hebrew," 293 n. 4; and "Lešonam šel ꜥAmos we-Hošeaꜥ," 120. On the monophthongization of aw and ay in Israelian Hebrew, see Garr, *Dialect Geography*, 38–39. For another case of phonological variations among the local dialects of ancient Hebrew, see S. Morag, "Mēšaꜥ," *ErIsr* 5 (1958) 138–44.

17. S. Gevirtz, "Asher in the Blessing of Jacob (Genesis XLIX 20)," *VT* 37 (1987) 160, proposed one such example, the "double plural" in the construct state, e.g., baꜥălê hiṣṣîm 'archers' (literally 'masters of the arrows') in Gen 49:23. For a more detailed treatment, see idem, "Of Syntax and Style in the 'Late Biblical Hebrew'—'Old Canaanite' Connection," *JANESCU* 18 (1986) 28–29. A complete study of syntactic differences between Israelian and Judahite Hebrew remains a desideratum.

18. I. J. Gelb, "Thoughts about Ibla: A Preliminary Evaluation," *Syro-Mesopotamian Studies* 1 (1977) 17.

Meh before Nonlaryngeal Consonants

The standard form of the interrogative pronoun for inanimate objects is *mah*. Before laryngeals, changes occur, including the shift to *meh* before *ḥêt* and *ᶜayin* normally. However, in more than a dozen instances the form *meh* occurs before nonlaryngeal consonants: 1 Sam 4:6, 4:14, 15:14; 2 Kgs 1:7, 4:13, 4:14; Isa 1:5; Jer 8:9, 16:10; Hag 1:9; Ps 4:3, 10:13; Job 7:21; Prov 31:2. In addition, instead of the standard forms *lammāh, kammāh, bammāh,* we also encounter the variants *lāmeh* in 1 Sam 1:8*tris, kammeh* in 1 Kgs 22:16, and *bammeh* in Exod 22:26, 33:16; Judg 16:5*bis*, 16:6*bis*, 16:10, 16:13, 16:15; 1 Sam 6:2, 29:4; Isa 2:22; Mal 1:6, 1:7, 3:7, 3:8; Ps 119:9; Prov 4:19.

An investigation of these passages reveals that a disproportionate number occur in non-Judahite contexts. All seven attestations in Judges 16 are spoken by either the Philistine lords or Delilah; in 1 Sam 1:8 the speaker is Elkanah of Ephraim; in 1 Sam 4:6, 6:2, 29:4 once more the Philistines are the speakers; in 1 Sam 4:14 it is Eli, priest of Shiloh, speaking; in 1 Sam 15:14 it is Samuel of Ephraim;[19] in 1 Kgs 22:16 it is the Israelian king Ahab; in 2 Kgs 1:7 it is his son Ahaziah; in 2 Kgs 4:13, 4:14 it is the northern (or Transjordanian)[20] prophet Elisha; and in Prov 31:2 the speaker is the mother of Lemuel king of Massa.[21] In addition, the example in Prov 4:19 occurs in a section of the Bible with many Phoenician affinities,[22] and the example in Ps 10:13 occurs in a chapter which witnesses several other Israelian Hebrew elements (see below). I have not explained all of these attestations of *meh*, but a sizable majority are in non-Judahite contexts. Moreover, I have accounted for all the attestations of *meh* before nonlaryngeal consonants in narrative prose. On the basis of this evidence, one may postulate an isogloss stretching from Philistia[23] in the southwest through central and northern Israel to Massa in the northeast.

19. From several scholars (orally) I have heard the suggestion that the use of *meh* here is an intentional imitation of the sound that sheep make. This is very clever, and I would have no objection to this explanation were this the only example of *meh* before a nonlaryngeal consonant in the Bible. But I prefer to explain the *meh* of 1 Sam 15:14 with the other attestations of the form in Biblical Hebrew and not as a singular phenomenon.
20. See G. A. Rendsburg, "A Reconstruction of Moabite-Israelite History," *JANESCU* 13 (1981) 67–73, esp. 71.
21. Most authorities place Massa in the Syrian Desert; see I. Ephᶜal, *The Ancient Arabs* (Jerusalem: Magnes/Leiden: Brill, 1982) 218–19.
22. Ginsberg, *Israelian Heritage*, 36; and W. F. Albright, "Some Canaanite-Phoenician Sources of Hebrew Wisdom," in *Wisdom in Israel and in the Ancient Near East: Presented to Professor Harold Henry Rowley* (ed. M. Noth and D. W. Thomas; Vetus Testamentum Supplement 3; Leiden: Brill, 1960) 1–15.
23. Regardless of what language the Philistines spoke before they arrived in Canaan, it is abundantly clear from the biblical record that once in Canaan they spoke a Canaanite dialect.

2fsg Pronominal Suffix -kî

The standard Hebrew second-person feminine singular pronominal suffix is
-k preceded by a vowel (ē with verbs and nouns, ā after uniconsonantal
prepositions, etc.). However, in the following instances the suffix -kî appears, retaining the proto-Semitic form:[24] 2 Kgs 4:2 Kethiv, 4:3 Kethiv,
4:7bis Kethiv; Jer 11:15; Ps 103:3bis, 103:4bis, 103:5, 116:7bis, 116:19,
135:9, 137:6; Song 2:13 Kethiv. The form -ky also appears in Aramaic,[25]
which leads me to suggest that its occasional presence in Biblical Hebrew is
due to geographical variation. This conclusion is bolstered by the following
considerations: (a) four of the attestations of -kî, from 2 Kings 4, are placed
in the mouth of Elisha; (b) five occurrences of -kî are in Psalm 103, which
witnesses an additional northernism;[26] (c) three instances of -kî appear in
Psalm 116, which is another chapter which evinces a concentration of
northernisms (see below); and (d) the example from Song of Songs dove-
tails with other linguistic evidence in this poem which points to a northern
provenance.[27] Again, I have not accounted for all sixteen examples of -kî in
the MT, but since thirteen of them occur in texts which include additional
Israelian Hebrew elements, there is every reason to conclude that this
second-person feminine singular suffix was at home in northern Israel.

3msg Pronominal Suffix -ôhî

Standard Hebrew utilizes several third-person masculine singular pronominal suffixes, -ô, -hû, -w, etc., depending on the phonetic environment. In one
instance a unique form occurs: -ôhî in the word tagmûlôhî 'his good deeds'

Note that never is communication a problem between Israelites and Philistines; see C. H.
Gordon, "The Rôle of the Philistines," *Antiquity* 30 (1956) 22 n. 2.

24. This reconstruction is based mainly on the Akkadian, Arabic, and Ethiopic forms, which are
all -kī (the vowel is apparently anceps). See S. Moscati, *An Introduction to the Comparative
Grammar of the Semitic Languages* (Wiesbaden: Harrassowitz, 1964) 106, 109; J. H. Kram-
ers, *De semietische Talen* (Leiden: Brill, 1949) 122; and Meyer §30.3c/p. 2:10.

25. S. Segert, *Altaramäische Grammatik* (Leipzig: VEB, 1975) 169.

26. I refer to the use of nṭr 'guard' (instead of standard Hebrew nṣr) in Ps 103:9. See further the
following note.

27. I have in mind such usages as the relative particle še-, the use of the root nṭr 'guard' (compare standard Hebrew nṣr), the word bĕrôtîm 'cypresses' (compare standard Hebrew bĕrôš),
etc. See M. H. Pope, *Song of Songs* (Anchor Bible 7c; Garden City: Doubleday, 1977) 33–
34, 362; S. R. Driver, *An Introduction to the Literature of the Old Testament* (New York:
Scribner, 1906) 448–49; Y. Avishur, "Le-Ziqa ha-Signonit ben Šir ha-Širim we-Siprut
ʾUgarit," *Beth Mikra* 59 (1974) 508–25; and idem, *Stylistic Studies of Word-Pairs in Biblical and Ancient Semitic Languages* (Alter Orient und Altes Testament 210; Neukirchen-
Vluyn: Neukirchener Verlag/Kevelaer: Butzon & Bercker, 1984) 367–68. Additional items
are noted below.

in Ps 116:12. This usage is almost always characterized as an Aramaism, but new evidence forces us to evaluate -ôhî afresh. It is true that -wh is the Aramaic third-person masculine singular pronominal suffix attached to plural nouns,[28] but the same form is now attested at Deir ʿAlla.[29] In addition, Moabite -h probably was vocalized somewhat similarly.[30] Accordingly, the sole use of -ôhî in Ps 116:12 should be understood as a non-Judahite form.[31] It may, moreover, even be further localized to Transjordan. As I have already mentioned, Psalm 116 also includes the second-person feminine singular pronominal suffix -kî, which is uttered by the Transjordanian prophet Elisha four times in 2 Kings 4. It also includes another feature which may be characterized as a feature of Israelian Hebrew (see the discussion below on the non-elision of hēʾ in *Hiphil/Hophal* imperfects and participles).

3mpl Pronominal Suffix -ham

In 2 Sam 23:6 we encounter the unusual form kullāham 'all of them'. Standard Hebrew calls for the elision of hēʾ after consonants (thus the expected form is kullām). In Aramaic, on the other hand, the third-person masculine plural pronominal suffix is normally -hm or -hwm. The very form klhm is attested in line 2 of the Kandahar inscription and the feminine counterpart klhn is attested in the Arsama correspondence, fragment 26, line 1.[32] It is true that the Fekherye inscription now presents us with something unique, the forms klm in line 4*bis* and kln in line 3,[33] but the overall picture is not greatly affected.[34] Thus, I would argue that the use of -ham in 2 Sam 23:6 represents an isogloss between a northern variety of Hebrew and neighboring Aramaic.

28. Segert, *Altaramäische Grammatik*, 169–70; and R. Degen, *Altaramäische Grammatik* (Abhandlungen für die Kunde des Morgenlandes 38/3; Wiesbaden: Steiner, 1969) 57.

29. Hackett, *Balaam Text*, 115–16; and Garr, *Dialect Geography*, 108.

30. J. Naveh, Review of J. Hoftijzer and G. van der Kooij, *Aramaic Texts from Deir ʿAlla*, *Israel Exploration Journal* 29 (1979) 136; J. C. Greenfield, Review of J. Hoftijzer and G. van der Kooij, *Aramaic Texts from Deir ʿAlla*, *JSS* 25 (1980) 250; and Garr, *Dialect Geography*, 108.

31. Regardless of how this form is judged, Hackett, *Balaam Text*, 115–16, is wrong in stating that -wh appears "in Aramaic and never in Canaanite" or that it does not occur "in previously known Canaanite texts." It patently does occur in Ps 116:12. Ironically, Hackett referred to the presence of -wh in Deir ʿAlla as "the strongest argument for the Aramaic classification of the text." Had Hackett cited this unique occurrence in the Bible, she would have removed the sole nexus with Aramaic and further bolstered her argument that the language of the Deir ʿAlla texts is Canaanite.

32. Segert, *Altaramäische Grammatik*, 170, 173, 222; and Degen, *Altaramäische Grammatik*, 55–56.

33. See T. Muraoka, "The Tell-Fekherye Bilingual Inscription and Early Aramaic," *Abr-Nahrain* 22 (1983–84) 92.

34. Garr, *Dialect Geography*, 105–6.

This is further borne out by the presence of other links with Aramaic in this pericope.[35]

3mpl Objective Pronoun hem

Another unique third-person masculine plural pronominal suffix occurs in 2 Kgs 9:18 in the expression *ᶜad hēm* 'unto them'. The typical reaction of exegetes to this usage has been emendation to the expected form *ᶜādêhem*.[36] Again, however, an apparent anomaly in Biblical Hebrew is paralleled in another Canaanite dialect. In the Mesha Stele, line 18, we read *wᵓshb.hm* 'I dragged them', with a very clear word divider separating the two words. Garr commented that "the objective suffix was probably a form of the independent pronoun in Moabite; the plural suffix had not yet been fused to the verb."[37] This is exactly what appears in *ᶜad hēm* in 2 Kgs 9:18. Furthermore, as J. C. L. Gibson astutely noted,[38] in later dialects of Aramaic the third-person masculine plural independent pronoun is similarly used.[39]

In light of this evidence there is no reason to emend the MT at 2 Kgs 9:18. Rather, we are dealing with a dialectal variation presumably native to Transjordan. The context of 2 Kings 9 places us once more in that region. Although the specific words *ᶜad hēm* are spoken by a watchman from Jezreel, the central character of this pericope is Jehu. And although we do not know exactly whence Jehu hailed, it is clear that he has Transjordanian connections. For example, in 1 Kgs 19:16 the Gileadite prophet Elijah is instructed by God to anoint Jehu; and in 2 Kgs 9:1–6 Jehu is eventually anointed king by Elisha in Ramoth-gilead. In short, it is not coincidental that *ᶜad hēm* occurs in an Israelian story and that it is most closely paralleled by Moabite usage. The two passages mutually elucidate each other and confirm that we are dealing with a non-Judahite construction.

Non-elision of hēᵓ after Prefixed Prepositions

As is well known, when the definite article *ha-/hā-/he* follows the uniconsonantal prefixed prepositions *bě, lě, kě*, "the ה is elided, and its vowel is thrown back to the prefix, in the place of the Šᵉwâ" (GKC §35n/p. 112). However, in the following instances this process does not occur: 1 Sam

---

35. See my detailed study, "'The Last Words of David'."
36. Thus, e.g., GKC §32n/p. 108; Burney, *Books of Kings*, 299; *BHS*, ad loc.; and J. Gray, *I and II Kings* (Old Testament Library; Philadelphia: Westminster, 1970) 545.
37. Garr, *Dialect Geography*, 112.
38. J. C. L. Gibson, *Textbook of Syrian Semitic Inscriptions* (Oxford: Clarendon, 1971–75) 1:81.
39. See, e.g., F. Rosenthal, *A Grammar of Biblical Aramaic* (Wiesbaden: Harrassowitz, 1974) 54; and C. Brockelmann, *Syrische Grammatik* (Leipzig: VEB, 1960) 49.

13:21; 2 Kgs 7:12 *Kethiv*; Ezek 40:25, 47:22; Ps 36:6; Qoh 8:1; Neh 9:19, 12:38; 2 Chr 10:7, 25:10, 29:27.[40] The only parallel usage to the non-elision of *hē²* in this environment within the Canaanite sphere is its eightfold appearance in Punic.[41] Now it is true that this phenomenon does not occur in any standard Phoenician texts, but nevertheless it may be suspected that it was native to some north Canaanite dialects. There are indications of this in at least some of the aforementioned biblical attestations.

In 1 Sam 13:21 the action occurs in the territory of Benjamin and the story concerns the kingship of Saul. 2 Kgs 7:12 *Kethiv* is in the mouth of an Israelian king (which king is referred to is not altogether certain). Psalm 36 has other grammatical peculiarities which I have analyzed as Israelian Hebrew elements in a previous study.[42] Qoh 8:1 appears in a book where considerable northern influence has been demonstrated.[43] Neh 9:19 appears in a pericope which also originated in the northern kingdom.[44]

I have only placed five of the eleven occurrences of this usage in northern texts, but proportionately this is sufficient to label this phenomenon a characteristic of Israelian Hebrew. The remaining six passages are all in exilic or postexilic compositions. At first this may seem to present an insurmountable problem for identifying this feature as characteristic of Israelian Hebrew. However, I appeal to the attractive hypothesis of C. H. Gordon that postexilic literature evinces northern grammatical and stylistic features due to the reunion of Israelian exiles and Judahite exiles in Mesopotamia in the sixth century B.C.E.[45] The non-elision of *hē²* following the prefixed prepositions would be another example of this phenomenon.[46] I return to this discussion on several occasions below.

40. I exclude from consideration 2 Sam 21:20, 22 *lĕhārāpāh* = 1 Chr 20:6, 8 *lĕhārāpā²*, where *hē²* is apparently considered part of the title; Dan 8:16 *lĕhallāz*, where *hē²* is an essential part of the demonstrative pronoun; and the eight cases of *kĕhayyôm* 'on this particular day', which is used to distinguish it from *kayyôm* 'now'.

41. J. Friedrich and W. Röllig, *Phönizisch-punische Grammatik* (2d ed.; Analecta Orientalia 46; Rome: Pontifical Biblical Institute, 1970) 53 §119.

42. Rendsburg, "'The Last Words of David'," 4.

43. See M. J. Dahood, "Canaanite-Phoenician Influences in Qoheleth," *Biblica* 33 (1952) 30–52, 191–221. Dahood already referred to the non-elision of *hē²* after the prefixed prepositions in his study (see 45–46). Although Dahood may have pressed some of the evidence too far (as he often did, especially in his later research), I accept his overall conclusion concerning Qoheleth. See also J. R. Davila, "Qoheleth and Northern Hebrew," *Maarav* 5–6 (1990) 69–87.

44. Welch, "Source of Nehemiah IX."

45. C. H. Gordon, "North Israelite Influence on Postexilic Hebrew," *Israel Exploration Journal* 5 (1955) 85–88.

46. Alternatively, I would explain these instances as hypercorrections (on this aspect of language see J. Blau, *On Pseudo-Corrections in Some Semitic Languages* [Jerusalem: Israel Academy of Sciences and Humanities, 1970]). Given the tendency for *hē²* to be syncopated

Non-elision of hē³ in Hiphil/Hophal Verbs

Another place where *hē³* is typically elided is after the preformatives of the *Hiphil/Hophal* imperfect and participle (*yaqṭîl, maqṭîl*, etc.; GKC §53q/ p. 148). In about ten instances, however, *hē³* is retained. The same is true of the corresponding Aramaic *Haphel*,[47] a fact which led P. Joüon to suggest that the biblical examples were "peut-être en partie sous l'influence de l'araméen" (Joüon §54b/p. 121). To some extent Joüon was correct, but some refinement of his opinion is necessary.

In several instances *Hiphil/Hophal* imperfects which retain *hē³* are found in northern compositions. Ps 45:18 *yĕhôdûkâ* 'they praise you' occurs in a poem which has long been recognized as a northern psalm, probably a Tyrian epithalamium in origin.[48] Ps 116:6 *yĕhôšîaᶜ* 'he will save' occurs in a poem in which other Israelian Hebrew elements appear (see the discussions on the second-person feminine singular pronominal suffix *-kî* and the third-person masculine singular pronominal suffix *-ôhî* above). The proper name *yĕhôsēp* 'Joseph' in Ps 81:6 is a third instance. This psalm is part of the Asaph collection, in which previous scholars have already detected northern affinities.[49]

The remaining cases of the non-elision of *hē³* in *Hiphil/Hophal* imperfects and participles occur in unexplained contexts (1 Sam 17:47 [in the mouth of David], Ps 28:7 [a chapter which does not evidence other Israelian Hebrew elements]), or in books from the time of Jeremiah to the time of

---

in *Hiphil* and *Niphal* infinitive constructs with *lĕ, bĕ, kĕ*, which itself was a characteristic of spoken Hebrew (see Rendsburg, "*Laqṭîl* Infinitives"), authors went beyond the norm and occasionally reintroduced *hē³* where it did not properly belong.

47. Segert, *Altaramäische Grammatik*, 264, 269; Degen, *Altaramäische Grammatik*, 66, 70; and Rosenthal, *Biblical Aramaic*, 44, 60.

48. See most recently M. D. Goulder, *The Psalms of the Sons of Korah* (Journal for the Study of the Old Testament Supplement Series 20; Sheffield: JSOT Press, 1982) 134–35. For the identification of northern grammatical elements in this chapter see already C. A. Briggs, *A Critical and Exegetical Commentary on the Book of Psalms* (2 vols.; International Critical Commentary; New York: Scribner, 1906–7) 1:384. In an extremely illuminating study, T. H. Gaster, "Psalm 45," *JBL* 74 (1955) 239–51, pointed out "that in the Near East, as elsewhere, it is common convention to treat a bridal couple as royalty" (239); thus it may be unnecessary to have to posit a particular royal couple as the subject of our poem. Gaster is correct, yet I would still argue for a northern provenience, based on the linguistic evidence and on the reference to the bride as *bat ṣōr* 'daughter of Tyre' in v. 13.

49. See M. J. Buss, "The Psalms of Asaph and Korah," *JBL* 82 (1963) 382–92, esp. 384–85; Ginsberg, *Israelian Heritage*, 31–33; and Goulder, *Sons of Korah*, 220. An additional northern element in Psalm 81 is the word *keseh* 'full moon' in v. 4. This lexeme appears elsewhere only in Prov 7:20 (where it is spelled *kese³*) in a section of the Bible with numerous Phoenicianisms (see n. 22 above), and it has cognates in Phoenician and Ugaritic; see M. Dahood, *Psalms II* (Anchor Bible 17; Garden City: Doubleday, 1968) 264.

Nehemiah (Isa 52:5; Jer 9:4, 37:3; Ezek 46:22; Job 13:9; Neh 11:17). For the latter set we may again appeal to Gordon's hypothesis concerning Israelian Hebrew elements in postexilic works, or we may merely consider them Aramaisms (*pace* Joüon). Regardless of these cases, I view the non-elision of $h\bar{e}^{\jmath}$ in *Hiphil/Hophal* imperfects and participles as another isogloss uniting Israelian Hebrew and Aramaic.

Retention of Feminine Singular Nominal Ending -at

All the Canaanite dialects for which we have sufficient evidence retain the feminine singular nominal ending -*at* in the absolute state. This may be demonstrated in Phoenician, Ammonite, Moabite, and Deir ʿAlla,[50] and probably in Edomite as well.[51] The sole exception is Hebrew, where normally this ending shifts to -*āh* (Meyer §42.3b/pp. 2:41–42). Nevertheless, there are isolated instances in Biblical Hebrew where the dominant Canaanite form appears, vocalized either -*at* (with *pataḥ*) or -*āt* (with *qāmeṣ*).[52] These examples may be explained in a variety of ways, for example, the vocables *māhŏrāt* 'morrow' (25x) and *rabbat* 'much' (7x) are adverbs where the ending -*at*/-*āt* was felt to have an adverbial function and thus did not shift to -*āh*;[53] the forms *pōrāt* (Gen 49:22*bis*) and *zimrāt* (Exod 15:2) appear in early poetry, so they presumably stem from a time before the shift of -*at* > -*āh* and/or they reflect archaic diction, as poetry often does;[54] and the noun *qĕṣāt*, which appears only in Daniel and Nehemiah, is a borrowing from Aramaic.[55]

For many of the remaining cases of -*at* in the MT, it is apparent that once more regional variation is the best explanation. Two nouns, *mĕnāt* 'portion' (Ps 16:5) and *naḥălāt* 'heritage' (Ps 16:6), appear in a psalm with other indications of northern provenience.[56] The same is true of *šĕnāt* (Ps 132:4); this

---

50. Garr, *Dialect Geography*, 93–94.

51. F. Israel, "Miscellanea idumea," *Rivista Biblica Italiana* 27 (1979) 183.

52. When the latter appears in construct state, this will also be considered an example of the retention of -*at*, since the expected vocalization would be with *pataḥ*, not *qāmeṣ*. The question of the different *a* vowels in this ending is an issue which requires further discussion.

53. J. Blau, "The Parallel Development of the Feminine Ending -*at* in Semitic Languages," *HUCA* 51 (1980) 18.

54. The word *zimrāt* also appears in Isa 12:2 and Ps 118:14 in the expression ʿozzî wĕzimrāt yāh, but one can surmise that it is merely a fossilized form in the three-word phrase which apparently had become a byword in ancient Israel.

55. For the Aramaic form and its development see Segert, *Altaramäische Grammatik*, 111, 207.

56. For example, the negative particle *bal*, whose closest cognates appear in Phoenician and Ugaritic especially, appears five times in Psalm 16; and the consonantal writing ʾmrt lyhwh in v. 2 reflects Phoenician orthography and is to be translated as 'I said'. On the former note that H. L. Ginsberg, "The Northwest Semitic Languages," in *Patriarchs* (ed. B. Mazar;

composition also exhibits several Israelian Hebrew elements.[57] The form *šipᶜat* 'multitude' in 2 Kgs 9:17 appears in a story about the northern kings Jehoram and Jehu and is actually placed in the mouth of an Israelian scout. Jeremiah utilizes the words *yitrat* 'abundance' (48:36) and *těhillat* 'praise' (49:25 *Qere*) in speeches addressed to Moab and Damascus respectively, and thus has colored his native Anathoth dialect with non-Judahite Hebrew forms. The musical instruments *maḥălat* (Ps 53:1, 88:1) and *něgînat* (Ps 61:1) may have been borrowed from a Canaanite dialect which preserved the *-at* suffix. Finally, *měʾat* 'hundred' in Qoh 8:12 is further evidence on the northern origin of this book.

Furthermore, a survey of those toponyms which end in *-at/-āt* reveals that the vast majority of them are located in northern Israel (Anaharath in Issachar; Daberath in Zebulun; Helkath and [Shihor-]libnath in Asher; Hammath, [Beth-]anath, and Rakkath in Naphtali; etc.) or in non-Israelite territory (Elath in Edom; Zephath [=Hormah] in the Negeb; Kenath and Tabbath in Transjordan; Hammath and Tibhath in Aram; Zarepath in Phoenicia; etc.) It is true that proper names often fossilize earlier linguistic features. In the present case, however, the geographical distribution of these cities may be regarded as confirmation of the fact that retention of the feminine singular nominal ending *-at* in the absolute state was an element of Israelian Hebrew.

World History of the Jewish People 2; New Brunswick: Rutgers University Press, 1970) 109, lists *bl* as one of the discriminants distinguishing his Phoenic group from his Hebraic group. On the latter see M. Dahood, *Psalms I* (Anchor Bible 16; Garden City: Doubleday, 1965) 87. Most of the ancient versions (for a convenient survey see Briggs, *Psalms*, 1:122) and most modern translations also render 'I said'. On *šěmāḥôt* in v. 11 see below. On Psalm 16 in general, see also Avishur, *Stylistic Studies of Word-Pairs*, 461. In G. A. Rendsburg, *Linguistic Evidence for the Northern Origin of Selected Psalms* (Society of Biblical Literature Monograph Series 43; Atlanta: Scholars Press, 1990), I devote chapters to the following individual psalms: 9–10, 16, 29, 36, 45, 53, 58, 74, 116, 132, 133, 140, 141; and there are also two chapters on the Korah collection and on the Asaph collection. All these poems, I conclude, are of Israelian provenience.

57. Most importantly, note the feminine singular demonstrative pronoun *zô* in v. 12. With this spelling it occurs again only in the northern prophet Hos 7:16. With the spelling *zōh* it occurs in an Israelian story in 2 Kgs 6:19 and in Qoh 2:2, 24; 5:15, 18; 7:23; 9:13. In three additional instances we encounter the idiomatic expression *kāzōh wěkāzeh* 'thus and thus'. Of these, Judg 18:4 occurs in the story of the Danite migration northward, and 1 Kgs 14:5 appears in a story about the Israelian king Jeroboam I. Accordingly, of all the occurrences of *zô/zōh* in Biblical Hebrew only Ezek 40:45 and 2 Sam 11:25 are in typically Judahite contexts. These data conform with the fact that in Phoenician the feminine singular demonstrative pronoun is *z(ʾ)*; see Friedrich and Röllig, *Phönizisch-punische Grammatik*, 50; and Garr, *Dialect Geography*, 83. The northern home of *zô/zōh* is generally recognized; see E. Y. Kutscher, *A History of the Hebrew Language* (Jerusalem: Magnes/Leiden: Brill, 1982) 31. On the form *ᶜēdōtî* in Ps 132:12, see below.

Use of the Alternative Feminine Singular Nominal Ending -ôt

In the preceding section I stated that in most if not all Canaanite dialects (Judahite Hebrew excepted) the feminine singular nominal ending is -*at*. This statement can now be refined by noting that in Phoenician the ending is -*ot*.[58] Accordingly, the few examples of feminine singular nouns in Hebrew which end in -*ôt* are to be classified as northernisms. It needs only to be demonstrated that these nouns are indeed singular and not feminine plural.

The forms *ḥokmôt* 'wisdom' (Prov 1:20, 9:1) and *ḥakmôt* 'wise lady' (Judg 5:29, Prov 14:1) bear feminine singular verbs and are the antecedents of feminine singular pronominal suffixes. They appear in an unmistakably northern poem[59] and in a book with many Phoenician influences.[60] From both the suffix -*î* and the feminine singular demonstrative pronoun which follows, it can be shown that *ʿēdōt* 'testimony' in Ps 132:12 is a feminine singular noun. It too occurs in a poem with other northern characteristics (see above).

As noted above, Psalm 45 has long been recognized as a northern composition. Thus we may propose that *yĕdîdōt* in v. 1 is feminine singular and means 'love' and that *śĕmāḥôt* in v. 16 means 'joy'. The latter is linked with *gîl* in a hendiadys;[61] in such a construction there is usually number accord between the two components,[62] as in *ḥesed weʾĕmet, ḥōq ûmišpāṭ, śar wĕśōpēṭ*, but *ḥuqqîm ûmišpāṭîm*.[63] Since *gîl* is singular, then *śĕmāḥōt* must also be singular.[64] By comparison, note Isa 16:10, where the expression *śimḥâ wāgîl* occurs. Moreover, the only other occurrence of *śĕmāḥōt* in the Bible is in Ps 16:11, a composition with northern affinities as well. From the context of Ps 16:11 it cannot be decided whether the form *śĕmāḥôt* is feminine singular or plural, but I would lean toward interpreting it as a singular based on the total picture.[65] Using the same logic, I am also inclined to view *hôlēlôt*

58. Friedrich and Röllig, *Phönizisch-punische Grammatik*, 29–30 §78, 106–7 §227–28. The length of the *o* vowel is unclear. For full discussion of all the pertinent data, notwithstanding a contrary conclusion, see A. Dotan, "Stress Position and Vowel Shift in Phoenician and Punic," *IOS* 6 (1976) 71–121.

59. See already Burney, *Book of Judges*, 171–76.

60. Ginsberg, *Israelian Heritage*, 36.

61. See M. Buttenweiser, *The Psalms* (Chicago: University of Chicago Press, 1938) 92.

62. This point has been made by E. Z. Melamed, "Šnayim šehem ʾeḥad (*hen dia duoin*) ba-Miqraʾ," *Tarbiẓ* 16 (1944–45) 173–89, esp. 177. This article has been reprinted in *Miqraʾa be-Ḥeqer Lešon ha-Miqraʾ* (ed. A. Hurvitz; *Liqqûṭe Tarbiẓ* 3; Jerusalem: Magnes, 1982–83) 37–53.

63. The same is true of English hendiadys constructions: *by hook or by crook*, *jot and tittle*, etc., vs. *odds and ends*, *bits and pieces*, etc.

64. Many scholars, e.g., Gaster, "Psalm 45," 251, translate the word as singular.

65. Buttenweiser, *Psalms*, 512, opined similarly, translating the word as 'joy' and calling it an "intensive plural, intensifying the idea expressed—a nicety which is lost in the translation."

'madness' in Qoh 1:17, 2:12, 7:25, 9:3 as a feminine singular noun. It too is linked solely with singular nouns. Finally, if we accept the position that Psalm 53 is a northern version of Psalm 14,[66] then *yĕšū̆cȏt* 'salvation' in 53:7 (corresponding to *yĕšûcat* in 14:7) would be another feminine singular noun ending in *-ȏt*.[67]

Use of b and l for 'from'

The interchange of the prefixed prepositions *b*, *l*, and *m(n)* is considered a standard feature of Biblical Hebrew by many scholars.[68] In a very important article which has still gone unanswered, Z. Zevit raised some serious objections to this view.[69] Moreover, his call for a complete detailed study of the subject has also gone unheeded.[70] I also have no intentions of conducting such a study—at least not in the present article—yet I would like to underscore one of Zevit's points and posit a working hypothesis. Zevit noted that in Phoenician not until the fourth century B.C.E. do we have the first appearance of ablative *m(n)*,[71] suggesting that *b* and *l* served to express 'from' in this language prior to this time.[72] If this is the case, it would not be too great a step to suggest the same for Israelian Hebrew.

66. Dahood, *Psalms II*, 19.
67. Ibid. I do not, however, concur with the long list of such examples presented by Dahood. For the most comprehensive statement see M. Dahood, *Psalms III* (AB 17A; Garden City: Doubleday, 1970) 379–80.
68. The most important article on the subject remains N. M. Sarna, "The Interchange of the Prepositions *Beth* and *Min* in Biblical Hebrew," *JBL* 78 (1959) 310–16.
69. Z. Zevit, "The So-Called Interchangeability of the Prepositions *b*, *l*, and *m(n)* in Northwest Semitic," *JANESCU* 7 (1975) 103–11.
70. Ibid., 111: "What is desired is an inner Hebrew study. . . . All verbs which are coordinated with at least two proclitic prepositions should be isolated and their semantic and syntactic contexts described, catalogued, and compared. . . . Once collected, the data should be analyzed with an eye to the synchronic and diachronic distribution of the phenomena insofar as this is possible."
71. Ibid., 107–9: "Thus it seems that Phoenician, or minimally Phoenician up to the fourth century B.C., like Ugaritic, functioned with only *b* and *l/lm* (and *lmb*) as separative, directive, and limiting prepositions in contexts where Hebrew would usually employ *min* and English 'from.'"
72. As Zevit, ibid., 109, noted, the situation in Phoenician is similar to that in Ugaritic. The Ugaritic poetic texts, presumably composed in a more archaic idiom, use only *b* and *l*. The prose texts, where innovative usages are likely to appear first, include the one attestation of *m*. See M. Liverani, "Elementi innovativi nell'ugaritico non letterario," *Atti della Accademia nazionale dei Lincei, Rendiconti della Classe di scienze morali, storiche e filologiche*, 8th ser., 19/5–6 (1964) 173–91, esp. 188. Should this be used as another point to bolster the classification system of Ginsberg ("Northwest Semitic Languages"), with a Phoenic group distinguished from a Hebraic group? I am content merely to raise the issue without entering further discussion.

This conclusion is bolstered by the following examples from the Bible where *b* and *l* clearly do mean 'from':

Josh 3:16 Kethiv *harḥēq mĕʾōd bĕʾādām* [Qere: *mēʾādām*]
very far from Adam

2 Kgs 4:24 *ʾal taʿăṣor lî lirkōb*
do not prevent me from riding

2 Kgs 14:13 *bĕšaʿar ʾeprayim ʿad šaʿar happinnāh*
from the gate of Ephraim unto the corner gate

2 Kgs 14:28 *hēšîb ʾet dammeśeq wĕʾet ḥămāt lîhûdāh bĕyiśrāʾēl*
he retrieved Damascus and Hamath from Yehuda [=Samʾal] for Israel[73]

Ps 10:1 *lāmāh yhwh taʿămōd bĕrāḥôq*
why, O Yahweh, do you stand from afar?

Ps 29:10 *yhwh lammabbûl yāšāb*
Yahweh has reigned from [=since] the flood

In these examples there is evidence for northern composition. The first concerns a city in the territory of Manasseh; the second appears in a story of the northern prophet Elisha; the third and fourth occur in the records of Israelian kings (Jehoash and Jeroboam II, respectively); and the last two occur in psalms with northern affinities. In Psalm 10 we may note the fivefold use of *bal*, the occurrence of *meh* in v. 13 (see above), and the periphrastic perfect *hāyîtâ ʿôzēr* 'you were helping' in v. 14 (a usage which occurs commonly in Aramaic). Psalm 29, as is well known, refers to northern locales such as Lebanon, Sirion, and Kadesh, and mentions northern flora such as cedars and forests.

In light of this evidence, I am inclined to include the ablative sense of *b* and *l* in my list of Israelian Hebrew features. I repeat that this proposal is but a working hypothesis, and I agree that it merits further study along the lines called for by Zevit, but for the nonce I believe the conclusion is defensible.

Retention of yôd in III-y Verbs

In standard Biblical Hebrew, the *yôd* of III-*y* verbs is elided, as in **yiglayu > yiglû* (Meyer §82.1b/pp. 2:156–57). In a number of instances, however, *yôd* is retained, both in perfect and in imperfect forms.[74] Many of these occur

---

73. For the proper understanding of this verse, see C. H. Gordon, *Ugaritic Textbook* (Analecta Orientalia 38; Rome: Pontifical Biblical Institute, 1967) 92; and idem, *The Ancient Near East* (New York: Norton, 1965) 219.

74. For a complete list and discussion see D. A. Robertson, *Linguistic Evidence in Dating Early Hebrew Poetry* (Society of Biblical Literature Dissertation Series 3; Missoula: Scholars Press, 1972) 57–62.

in sections of the Bible where northern origin may be detected or where code-switching is at work. Furthermore, the retention of *yôd* in III-*y* verbs is also a characteristic of Aramaic;[75] thus we may recognize another isogloss linking Israelian Hebrew and Aramaic.

The biblical forms which occur in northern compositions are Deut 32:37 *ḥāsāyû* 'seek refuge', Ps 36:8 *yeḥĕsāyûn* 'seek refuge', Ps 36:9 *yirwĕyûn* 'overflowing', Ps 77:4 *ʾehĕmāyāh* 'moan', Ps 78:44 *yištāyûn* 'drink', and Ps 83:3 *yehĕmāyûn* 'moan'. O. Eissfeldt has argued on nonlinguistic grounds for a non-Judahite provenience of Deuteronomy 32,[76] and his conclusion is generally accepted. As noted above, Psalm 36 is a poem with other elements of Israelian Hebrew. The last three examples occur in the psalms of Asaph, which, as noted above, demonstrate northern connections. Psalms 77 and 78, for example, refer several times to Joseph and Ephraim. Psalm 83 invokes the memories of the battle against Sisera and Jabin and the exploits of Gideon. An additional linguistic marker of Israelian Hebrew is found in Ps 77:18: the plural form *ḥăṣāṣekâ* (see below).

Code-switching is present in many other cases where *yôd* of III-*y* verbs is retained, namely, Num 24:6 *nittāyû* 'stretch out', Isa 17:12 *yehĕmāyûn* 'roar', and Isa 21:12 *tibʿāyûn* 'inquire', *bĕʿāyû* 'inquire', *ʾētāyû* 'come'. The first occurs in the Balaam oracles,[77] the second appears in Isaiah's address to Damascus, and the last three examples appear in Isaiah's reproduction of the speech of a watchman of Dumah.[78] In addition, we should probably add the six examples from Job (3:25, 12:6, 16:22, 19:2, 30:14, 31:38), all of which are placed in the mouth of the protagonist.

Use of Inflected Participles

Eight times in the Bible, participles (both active and passive) are inflected with the suffixes normally attached to perfect verbs. Most scholars subsume this usage under the phenomenon known as the *ḥîreq compaginis*.[79] I am in-

---

75. See, e.g., *yḥywn* 'they will live' in line 8 of the inscription published by A. Caquot, "Une inscription araméene d'époque assyrienne," in *Hommages à André Dupont-Sommer* (Paris: Maisonneuve, 1971) 9–16. For the *yôd* retaining consonantal force in some forms in Biblical Aramaic, see Rosenthal, *Biblical Aramaic*, 51, 66.

76. O. Eissfeldt, *Das Lied Moses Deuteronomium 32,1–43 und das Lehrgedicht Asaphs Psalm 78 samt einer Analyse der Umgebung des Mose-Leides* (Berichte über die Verhandlungen der Sächsischen Akademie der Wissenschaften zu Leipzig, Philologisch-historische Klasse 104/5; Berlin: Akademie Verlag, 1958) 41–43.

77. For additional Aramaizing elements in the Balaam oracles, see Rendsburg, "'The Last Words of David'," 115–16.

78. See Kaufman, "Classification of the North West Semitic Dialects," 55; and Tur-Sinai, "ʾAramit," 593–94.

79. GKC §90l–n/pp. 253–54; and Robertson, *Linguistic Evidence*, 69–76.

clined, however, to separate these eight instances and treat them as a distinct phenomenon.

Before proceeding to the biblical evidence, it should be noted that this usage is paralleled in certain dialects of Aramaic.[80] In his grammar of Galilean Aramaic,[81] G. Dalman presented about a dozen examples, of which I cite three for purposes of illustration: *Tg. Ps.-J.* Gen 15:12 *mtrmyyt* 'sie wurde geworfen'; Num 22:30 *mthnyyty* 'ich wurde benutzt'; and *t. Ketub.* 11:5 *mytznt* 'du wirst ernährt'.[82] In his monograph on the language of the Babylonian Talmud, M. Margolis noted that although the masculine plural participle is paradigmatically *yhby(n)*, the form *yhbw* also appears, with "the ending imported from the perf."[83]

In view of the Aramaic evidence, we can explain the eight examples of inflected participles in the Bible. Gen 31:39*bis genūbĕtî* 'I was robbed', uttered by Jacob to Laban, appears in an Aramaic-speaking environment.[84] 2 Kgs 4:23 *Kethiv hlkty* (presumably to be vocalized *hōlāktî*) 'you [fem. sing.] are going' is spoken by the man from Shunem in the territory of Issachar. The remaining examples occur in books written ca. 586 B.C.E. when Aramaic influence began to exert itself upon Hebrew: Jer 10:17 *Kethiv*, 22:23*bis Kethiv*, 51:13 *Kethiv*; Ezek 27:3 *Kethiv*; Lam 4:21. Moreover, all but one of these passages may evidence code-switching. Although Jer 22:23 occurs in a speech addressed to Jehoiakim in Jerusalem, the prophet evokes the imagery of far northern Israel ("Lebanon" and "cedars"). Jer 51:13 occurs in the famous address to Babylon, a country which at this time was already speaking Aramaic. Ezek 27:3 is in a context concerning Tyre, and although we have no evidence for inflected participles in Phoenician, we are once again in a northern setting. Finally, Lam 4:21 refers to Edom and Uz. We know precious little

---

80. The use of inflected participles is not to be confused with another, quite widespread, phenomenon in Aramaic, namely, the attachment of the independent pronouns (or shortened forms thereof) to the participle. This is an altogether different feature. See T. Nöldeke, *Mandäische Grammatik* (Halle: Waisenhaus, 1875) 230–33; idem, *Compendious Syriac Grammar* (London: Williams & Norgate, 1904) 45; and C. Brockelmann, *Grundriss der vergleichenden Grammatik der semitischen Sprachen* (Berlin: Reuther & Reichard, 1908–13) 1:582.

81. For the use of this term see E. Y. Kutscher, *Meḥqarim ba-ʾAramit ha-Gelilit* (Jerusalem: Hebrew University, 1952); and idem, *Studies in Galilean Aramaic* (Ramat-Gan: Bar-Ilan University Press, 1976).

82. G. Dalman, *Grammatik des jüdisch-palästinischen Aramäisch* (Leipzig: Hinrichs, 1905) 284.

83. M. Margolis, *A Manual of the Aramaic Language of the Babylonian Talmud* (Munich: Beck, 1910). For many examples see J. N. Epstein, *Diqduq ʾAramit Bablit* (Jerusalem: Magnes, 1960) 39.

84. For additional Aramaisms in the chapters narrating the dealings of Jacob and Laban, see J. C. Greenfield, "Aramaic Studies and the Bible," in *Congress Volume Vienna 1980* (ed. J. A. Emerton; Vetus Testamentum Supplement 32; Leiden: Brill, 1981) 129–30.

about Edomite and of course nothing about the language of Uz (save for what may be inferred from our knowledge of North Arabian dialects such as Thamudic, Lihyanic, and Safaitic). However, the Aramaic coloring of the Book of Job, set in the land of Uz, is substantial. It is possible and maybe even probable that Aramaic or Aramaic-type dialects were spoken over a wide area of the Syrian Desert.[85]

The total picture, then, allows us to conclude that the use of inflected participles was another isogloss linking Israelian Hebrew and Aramaic. Whether other dialects (Phoenician? Edomite?) also incorporated this feature cannot be determined given the present state of our knowledge.

Reduplicatory Plural of Nouns Based on Geminate Stems

The term *reduplicatory plural* refers to the repeating of the final consonant of a singular noun based on a geminate stem. Normally, Hebrew resorts to gemination in such cases, for example $^c\bar{a}m$ 'people', pl. $^c amm\hat{\imath}m$. But in a considerable number of instances the reduplicatory type appears, for example $^c\check{a}m\bar{a}m\hat{\imath}m$.[86] This latter method of forming the plural is standard in Aramaic, as in $^c mmy^{\jmath}$ 'peoples', $kddn$ 'pitchers', $tlly^{\jmath}$ 'shades'.[87] Accordingly, it will not be surprising to learn that a goodly number of the reduplicatory plurals in the Bible appear in texts where northern origin may be detected.

Judges 5 is a good place to start the survey. The northern affinities of this poem are well established. Two reduplicatory plurals of nouns based on geminate stems appear therein: $^c\check{a}m\bar{a}mek\hat{a}$ 'your peoples' (v. 14) and $hiq\check{e}q\hat{e}$ 'decisions of' (v. 15). Num 23:7 $har\check{e}r\hat{e}$ 'mountains of' is in the mouth of Balaam, the Aramean prophet. Nehemiah 9, whose northern provenience was mentioned earlier,[88] includes two such plurals: $^c\check{a}m\bar{a}m\hat{\imath}m$ 'peoples' (v. 22) and $^c am\check{e}m\hat{e}$ 'peoples of' (v. 24). Ps 36:7 $har\check{e}r\hat{e}$ 'mountains of' occurs in a poem with a plethora of northernisms (see above). Ps 50:10 $har\check{e}r\hat{e}$ 'mountains of', Ps 76:5 $har\check{e}r\hat{e}$ 'mountains of', and Ps 77:18 $h\check{a}s\bar{a}sek\hat{a}$ 'your arrows' all appear

---

85. The linguistic evidence from Isa 21:11–15 would suggest this; see Kaufman, "Classification of the North West Semitic Dialects," 55–56.

86. For the term *reduplicatory* and for the Afroasiatic background of this formation, see J. H. Greenberg, "Internal *a*-Plurals in Afroasiatic (Hamito-Semitic)," in *Afrikanistische Studien* (ed. J. Lukas; Berlin: Akademie Verlag, 1955) 198–204. In light of Greenberg's penetrating study, it is best to view the reduplicatory plurals of geminate nouns in Hebrew as internal or broken plurals with the *-îm* ending added secondarily due to *Analogiebildung*. Note the similarity between the Hebrew forms under discussion and such Afar-Saho (Cushitic) lexemes as *il* 'eye', pl. *ilal*; *bo·r* 'cloth', pl. *bo·rar*.

87. Segert, *Altaramäische Grammatik*, 537, 546; and M. Jastrow, *A Dictionary of the Targumim, the Talmud Babli and Yerushalmi, and the Midrashic Literature* (London: Luzac, 1903), 1:537.

88. Welch, "Source of Nehemiah IX."

in the Asaph collection, whose northern provenience was commented upon above. Ps 133:3 *harĕrê* 'mountains of' occurs in a poem which evokes Mt. Hermon (v. 3) and in which the relative pronoun *še-* appears (vv. 2 and 3).[89] Prov 29:13 *tekākîm* 'oppressions' places us in a book with considerable northern influence.[90] Song 2:17, 4:6 *ṣelālîm* 'shadows' and Song 4:8 *harĕrê* 'mountains of' may be advanced as additional examples of the northern affinities of this book. Analogous to the discussion in the previous section, Jer 6:4 *ṣilĕlê* 'shadows of' and Ezek 4:12, 4:15 *gelĕlê* 'pellets of' appear in prophetic books where Aramaic influence may be increasingly seen. There thus remain only a handful of occurrences which do not fit this interpretation: Deut 33:15; Hab 3:6; Ps 87:1.[91] In short, I have isolated another isogloss linking Israelian Hebrew and Aramaic.[92]

The Plural *ʾîšîm* 'Men'

The standard plural of Hebrew *ʾîš* 'man' is *ʾănāšîm* 'men', built from a different root. Three times, however, Biblical Hebrew admits the "expected" plural *ʾîšîm*: Isa 53:3, Ps 141:4, Prov 8:4. Since Phoenician utilizes *ʾšm* 'men' as the plural of *ʾš* 'man',[93] there is reason to believe that the biblical form was at home in northern Israel. This conclusion is borne out by two of the attestations listed above.

Psalm 141 includes several indications of northern origin. Dahood has already noted that this poem uses *dal* 'door' (v. 3) and *man^cammêhem* 'their delicacies' (v. 4), hapax legomena with analogs only in Phoenician, as well as the negative particle *bal* (v. 4).[94] In addition, I have already pointed out that the use of *lḥm* 'to eat' (v. 4) is a northern feature.[95] Furthermore, it is more than likely that the very enigmatic *yānî* (v. 5) is 'my wine', reflecting monophthongization of the diphthong *ay*.[96] Note that this vocable is parallel

---

89. For the northern origin of *še-*, see Kutscher, *History of the Hebrew Language*, 32.

90. Furthermore, nearby in Prov 29:10 we encounter the expression *ʾanšê dāmîm* with both members of the construct chain in plural. For the northern origin of this syntagma, see Gevirtz, "Asher in the Blessing of Jacob," 160; and see above n. 17.

91. For Ps 87:1, however, note that Goulder, *Sons of Korah*, has argued for a Danite origin for the Korah collection.

92. After I completed the research for this section, I was happy to discover that I was anticipated in my conclusion by E. Y. Kutscher, "Ha-Šapa ha-ʿIbrit u-Benot Libyata be-Mešek ha-Dorot," *Hadoar* 47 (1968–69) 507–9. This article has been reprinted in E. Y. Kutscher, *Hebrew and Aramaic Studies* (Jerusalem: Magnes, 1977) שזה-שׁטו, see esp. שו.

93. R. S. Tomback, *A Comparative Semitic Lexicon of the Phoenician and Punic Languages* (Society of Biblical Literature Dissertation Series 32; Missoula: Scholars Press, 1978) 33.

94. Dahood, *Psalms III*, 309–11.

95. Rendsburg, "'The Last Words of David'," 117 n. 32.

96. On monophthongization of *aw/ay* as an Israelian Hebrew feature, see Garr, *Dialect Geography*, 38. Moreover, the vocalization *yānî* (as opposed to *yênî*) is probably correct; see G. A.

to *šemen* 'oil' in Ps 141:5, as is also the case in Amos 6:6; Mic 6:15; Ps 104:15; Song 1:2–3, 4:10.[97]

Little need be said about the use of *ʾîšîm* in Prov 8:4. After all the evidence adduced in this article, it is patently clear that Proverbs in general and chapters 1–9 in particular exhibit numerous traits of Phoenician and Israelian Hebrew. As far as Isa 53:3 is concerned, I again advance Gordon's theory concerning the influence of Israelian Hebrew on exilic and postexilic literature.

CONCLUSION

The work of scholars such as Burney, Albright, Ginsberg, Kutscher, and Rabin has provided a basis for the conclusion that the Hebrew of northern Israel differed in a variety of ways from the Hebrew of Judah in the south. Rabin has been somewhat cautious in his statement: "The geographical separation of Judah and its non-participation in the political events affecting the North must also have led to a certain amount of linguistic separatism. How large this gap was, we cannot properly gauge. . . ."[98]

In the foregoing presentation I have adduced fourteen additional features of Biblical Hebrew which may be considered characteristic of Israelian but not of Judahite Hebrew. In light of this material, I believe we may now better assess the situation described by Rabin. We still, unfortunately, do not possess sufficient data to conduct a thorough investigation of the problem, but the picture is becoming clearer. There were, in fact, considerable differences between the Hebrew of the north and the Hebrew of the south. Obviously, there was no communication problem between, let us say, Naphtalites and Judahites. But the differences between Israelian and Judahite Hebrew during the Iron Age were probably along the lines known to us from such modern examples as English in the northern and southern regions of the United States, German in northern Germany versus Bavaria and Austria, Arabic as represented by the various colloquials spread from Morocco to Iraq, etc.

Rendsburg, "Monophthongization of *aw/ay* > *ā* in Eblaite and in Northwest Semitic," in *Eblaitica* 2 (1990) 91–126; also BL §171/p. 202; and see C. H. Gordon, "Eblaitica," *Eblaitica* 1 (1987) 24.

97. As a syndetic parataxis the nouns *yayin* and *šemen* appear in Prov 21:17 and 2 Chr 11:11, and they are also collocated in Deut 28:39–40. In Ugaritic poetry they are parallel in Gordon, *Ugaritic Textbook*, 126:iii:15–16, 128:iv:4–5, 128:iv:15–16. For discussion see M. Dahood, "Ugaritic-Hebrew Parallel Pairs," in *Ras Shamra Parallels* (ed. L. R. Fisher and S. Rummel; Analecta Orientalia 49; Rome: Pontifical Biblical Institute, 1972) 210; and Avishur, *Stylistic Studies of Word-Pairs*, 367–68.

98. Rabin, "Emergence of Classical Hebrew," 71.

Moreover, the relatively small geographic area covered by ancient Israel (in contrast to the aforementioned English-, German-, and Arabic-speaking areas) is no reason not to assume regional dialects. The United Kingdom, for example, is one thirty-fifth the size of the United States, and yet the former has far more regional varieties of English than the latter.[99]

This article has utilized Aramaic and Phoenician parallels to a great extent. Does this mean that Israelian Hebrew more closely resembled these two varieties of Northwest Semitic speech than it did Judahite Hebrew? To answer this question, I turn once again to Rabin (who treated only Aramaic, but the discussion is equally appropriate for the case of Phoenician):

> It is an acknowledged fact in modern linguistics that dialect features are not distributed in sharply defined areas, but rather each single feature, and in fact every single word in a certain dialect form, has its own distinct area of distribution; the lines drawn around such areas, called "isoglosses," cross and recross each other. Sharp divisions are generally brought about by political events which obliterate the dialects of intermediate areas. There is thus nothing unusual in thinking that certain [features of Aramaic] extended over part of the northern dialects of Hebrew, as well as over the area of Damascus. . . . Some such isoglosses may well have run along the northern edge of the Canaanite corridor of Jerusalem, thus marking off Judah from the northern tribes, but linking the latter to the plain of Damascus.[100]

In other words, Israelian Hebrew shared many isoglosses with Phoenician and Aramaic. Nevertheless, based on such texts as Judges 5; Deuteronomy 32; Psalms 10, 36, 45, 103, and 116; Proverbs 1–9; etc., it is clear that the language of the northern tribes is still Hebrew. Again a modern analogy will be helpful. The language spoken by rural Dutchmen on the Dutch-German border shares many isoglosses with that of their German counterparts across the border, and such speech communities have little difficulty communicating with each other. The speech of these Dutchmen may even have more in common with the German spoken across the border than it does with the Dutch spoken in Amsterdam. Similarly, the German spoken along the Dutch border may have more in common with the Dutch spoken across the border than it does with the German spoken in Frankfurt. And yet, due mainly to political reasons (see Rabin's statement above), we still must label the language of these rural Hollanders "Dutch" and the language of their German counterparts "German." Similar situations are found elsewhere in the world, as in the French and Italian spoken respectively along the French–Italian border. Accordingly, we must still reckon Israelian Hebrew as Hebrew, albeit a regional variety thereof sharing many isoglosses with Phoenician and Aramaic. A

99. R. McCrum, W. Cran, and R. MacNeil, *The Story of English* (New York: Viking, 1986) 238.
100. Rabin, "Emergence of Classical Hebrew," 72.

glance at the map indicates that Dan, Naphtali, Asher, and other northern tribes were closer to Tyre and Damascus than they were to Jerusalem. It is not surprising, therefore, to be able to isolate northern dialectal features in Hebrew paralleling usages better known from Phoenician and Aramaic.

As far as the presence of northernisms in exilic and postexilic literature is concerned, the evidence adduced herein confirms Gordon's position.[101] Gordon's article only discussed a few features; I have now added several additional items (non-elision of $h\bar{e}^{\,\jmath}$ following prefixed prepositions, and non-elision of $h\bar{e}^{\,\jmath}$ in *Hiphil/Hophal* imperfects and participles). Accordingly, I affirm the view that northern tribes reunited with Judahites during the Exile in Babylonia, at which time Israelian Hebrew elements returned to Hebrew idiom.

Finally, let me respond to an obvious criticism which may be leveled against the methodology used in this article. There is a danger, in some of the treatments above, of circular reasoning. That is to say, grammatical feature *X* is considered a northernism on the basis of its parallel in Phoenician or Aramaic; it is then located in text *A* which is now considered a northern composition. When grammatical feature *Y* is isolated and it too appears in text *A*, this is considered confirmation both of the identification of *Y* as an Israelian Hebrew characteristic and of the northern provenience of text *A*. As I remark above, I recognize the difficulties with this kind of argumentation. However, I should note the following. In almost every case, the texts in which northernisms have been found have previously been theorized as being Israelian compositions based on other, nonlinguistic criteria. This is true of such diverse compositions as Deuteronomy 32; the stories of the northern judges; the material concerning the northern kingdom of Israel; Psalms 29, 45, and 77; Nehemiah 9; etc. Accordingly, the linguistic evidence adduced herein confirms the views already expressed by Eissfeldt, Welch, Ginsberg, Goulder, etc., concerning the non-Judahite origin of such sections of the Bible as the aforementioned chapters.[102]

---

101. See n. 45 above.
102. On the other hand, although we are dealing with an argument *ex silentio*, the lack of any northernisms in the so-called E source and in the core of Deuteronomy mitigates against proposals to view these documents as Israelian. See O. Procksch, *Das nordhebräische Sagenbuch, Die Elohimquelle* (Leipzig: Hinrichs, 1906); and Ginsberg, *Israelian Heritage*. On efforts to locate "E" in the north, see the cogent remarks of O. Eissfeldt, *Einleitung in das Alte Testament* (Tübingen: Mohr, 1964) 269–71 = *The Old Testament: An Introduction* (New York: Harper & Row, 1965) 203–4.

Note added in proof: Since the present article was authored, I have turned my attention to the northern Psalms in great detail. The result is the book cited above in n. 56. I was able to incorporate mention of my newer study into the footnote, but I have made no substantive changes in the text of the article itself. I append this one suggestion: that Psalm 87:1 is not a northern text (though see n. 91). In light of further research, I am now able to demonstrate that the Korah collection of Psalms is also of northern origin. See *Linguistic Evidence for the Northern Origin of Selected Psalms*, 51–60.

Walter R. Bodine

How Linguists Study Syntax

The preparation of a brief survey of how syntax is studied by linguists has been both a frustrating and a revealing experience. Frustration was inevitable because of the relative weakness in past study of the syntax of Biblical Hebrew[1] and Semitics generally,[2] with which weakness I was already familiar. I did hold the hope at the outset of this venture, however, that the reason for this weakness might have been a gap between the achievements of linguists

Author's note: At various stages in the preparation of this essay, I have benefited from the insights and suggestions of Donald Burquest, Jerold Edmondson, John Huehnergard, Robert Longacre, and Michael O'Connor.

1. Brockelmann's work on Hebrew syntax is usually regarded as below the level of his other writings; *Hebräische Syntax* (Neukirchen: Neukirchener Verlag, 1956). Perhaps the most highly regarded study of the subject is still F. E. König, *Historisch-kritisches Lehrgebäude der hebräischen Sprache*, vol. 2/2: *Historisch-komparative Syntax der hebräischen Sprache* (Leipzig: Hinrichs, 1897).

2. An example of the lack of adequate research into syntax in ancient Semitic is Moscati's decision to confine his survey to phonology and morphology: S. Moscati et al., *An Introduction to the Comparative Grammar of the Semitic Languages: Phonology and Morphology* (Wiesbaden: Harrassowitz, 1964). S. J. Lieberman speaks of a "near silence" on questions of historical syntactic reconstruction in comparative Semitic studies and a "near void" even of synchronic syntactic treatments; "Word Order in the Afro-Asiatic Languages," in *Proceedings of the Ninth World Congress of Jewish Studies* (Jerusalem: World Union of Jewish Studies, 1986) D 1:7. It is probably true that syntactic reconstruction is less feasible than phonological and morphological reconstruction, whether or not it is fundamentally different, as W. Winter claims; "Reconstructional Comparative Linguistics and the Reconstruction of the Syntax of Undocumented Stages in the Development of Languages and Language Families," in *Historical Syntax* (ed. J. Fisiak; Trends in Linguistics, Studies and Monographs 23; Berlin: Mouton, 1984) 613–25. This does not, however, explain the silence in Moscati, *Comparative Grammar*, since a number of the other topics covered therein are only dealt with in the specific languages without a proposed reconstruction of Proto-Semitic. G. Khan, *Studies in Semitic Syntax* (London Oriental Series 38; Oxford: Oxford University Press, 1989) appeared after the present work was completed.

and the application of their work to Biblical Hebrew and other ancient Semitic languages. That such a gap does exist is clear.[3] That it represents inadequacy only in the readiness of Hebraists and Semitists to incorporate the results achieved by linguists is not the case. It will, hopefully, be clear by the conclusion of this essay that syntax is yet to fully come into its own in modern, general linguistics. Significant developments, however, have taken place; and others are presently in process. The plan of the following overview is to set forth some outlines of a definition of the field, to trace briefly the study of syntax among linguists, and to suggest some initial thoughts as to how I am inclined to approach the study of syntax.

A DEFINITION OF SYNTAX

It has been common among linguists to recognize *syntax* as a second phase of the study of *grammar*, *morphology* being the first.[4] These, together with *phonology* and *semantics*,[5] constitute the major components of a language. It can, and probably should, be argued that the given situation in life (or, context of situation) at the time of communication is also indispensable for adequate linguistic analysis. In any case, syntax has usually been seen in a closer relationship with morphology, so much so that even as long ago as de Saussure the distinction between the two was said to be "illusory."[6] Lyons has pointed out that the opposition of syntax and morphology is as recent as the origin of

---

3. Cf. W. R. Bodine, "Linguistics and Philology in the Study of Ancient Near Eastern Languages," in *"Working with No Data": Semitic and Egyptian Studies Presented to Thomas O. Lambdin* (ed. D. M. Golomb and S. T. Hollis; Winona Lake, IN: Eisenbrauns, 1987) 39–54, together with the references cited therein; as well as O. Grether, "Erwagungen zum hebräischen Sprachunterricht," in *Festschrift Alfred Bertholet* (ed. W. Baumgartner et al.; Tübingen: Mohr, 1950) 192–207; H. A. Gleason Jr., "Linguistics in the Service of the Church," *Hartford Quarterly* 1 (1960) 7–27; P. Fronzaroli, "Statistical Methods in the Study of Ancient Near Eastern Languages," in *Approaches to the Study of the Ancient Near East* (ed. G. Buccellati; Los Angeles: Undena, 1973) 97–113; R. Kieffer, "Die Bedeutung der modernen Linguistik für die Auslegung biblischer Texte," *Theologische Zeitschrift* 30 (1974) 223–33; R. J. Erickson, "Linguistics and Biblical Language: A Wide-Open Field," *Journal of the Evangelical Theological Society* 26 (1983) 257–63.
4. L. Bloomfield, *Language* (New York: Holt, Rinehart & Winston, 1933) 184.
5. I believe a strong case can be made that meaning (semantics) is not a separate component of language, but rather that every other component should be analyzed in relation to it; cf. P. L. Garvin, "An Empiricist Epistemology for Linguistics," in *The Fourth LACUS Forum 1977* (ed. M. Paradis; Columbia: Hornbeam, 1978) 339. An adequate theoretical and methodological framework for this purpose, however, has yet to be elaborated.
6. F. de Saussure, *Course in General Linguistics* (ed. C. Bally, A. Sechehaye, and A. Riedlinger; Lausanne: Payot, 1916; trans. W. Baskin; New York: McGraw-Hill, 1959) 135.

the understanding of the morpheme in general linguistics and that in earlier traditional grammar the opposition was, rather, between syntax and inflection.[7] While the distinction between syntax and morphology still needs clear definition, some distinction, together with their close relationship, continues to be commonly recognized among linguists.[8]

The primary unit under consideration in the study of syntax has usually been the *word* and continues to be for many linguists.[9] Others, however, have preferred to leave the unit of syntactic study more vague. For Hockett, syntax is the arrangement of words and suprasegmental morphemes.[10] For Gleason the basic units of syntax are the combinations described under morphology, "roughly what are familiarly called 'words.'"[11] One reason for the hesitancy is the difficulty in defining the word for linguistic purposes.[12] Therefore, others prefer to regard the morpheme as the basic unit of syntax.[13]

Matthews is of the opinion that the choice between words and morphemes must be made before syntactic analysis can proceed, for regarding either as fundamental will result in discovering constructional relations which vitiate the other for syntactic purposes.[14] Granted that this may be the case within a given language (and Matthews has illustrated his point well), it might still be maintained that a larger view of syntax could allow for flexibility in this regard when the languages under study indicate such.[15] The disadvantage of a variable approach would become apparent when comparative work among languages becomes desirable. Since the more common preference among linguists would still seem to be the word,[16] and since the word would appear to serve as the best starting point for syntactic analysis

---

7. J. Lyons, *Language and Linguistics: An Introduction* (Cambridge: Cambridge University Press, 1981) 100–103.
8. Although the term *grammar* has taken on a wider sense in the usage of the many linguists since the advent of transformational-generative linguistics, the distinction between morphology and syntax continues to be recognized; see, e.g., R. H. Robins, *General Linguistics: An Introductory Survey* (London: Longman, 1980) 142; V. Fromkin and R. Rodman, *An Introduction to Language* (New York: Holt, Rinehart & Winston, 1983) 126, 200.
9. Robins, *General Linguistics*, 146; idem, "Syntactic Analysis," in *Readings in Linguistics* (ed. E. P. Hamp et al.; Chicago: University of Chicago Press, 1966) 2:386.
10. C. F. Hockett, *A Course in Modern Linguistics* (New York: Macmillan, 1958) 177.
11. H. A. Gleason Jr., *An Introduction to Descriptive Linguistics* (New York: Holt, Rinehart & Winston, 1961) 58.
12. L. M. Hyman, "Word Demarcation," *Universals of Human Language* (ed. J. H. Greenberg; Stanford: Stanford University Press, 1978) 2:443–70; and the references cited above by Garr (p. 50, n. 5).
13. W. P. Lehmann, *Language: An Introduction* (New York: Random, 1983) 7.
14. P. H. Matthews, *Syntax* (Cambridge Textbooks in Linguistics; Cambridge: Cambridge University Press, 1981) 50–53.
15. This seems to be suggested in Robins, "Syntactic Analysis," 386.
16. This is Matthews's decision (*Syntax*, 53–70).

in Biblical Hebrew and other ancient Semitic languages,[17] the matter can be left at that for the purposes of this discussion.

Concerning the extent of linguistic material encompassed by syntax, it has generally been thought that the sentence was the largest unit.[18] Thus, in the study of syntax, one would investigate grammatical relationships among morphemes or words, as well as phrases and clauses. The limitation of syntactic analysis to the sentence is still widely espoused by practicing linguists.[19] In spite of its radical departure otherwise from traditional perspectives, early transformational-generative grammar also retained this boundary,[20] although some more recent offshoots have gone beyond it.[21]

The urgency of this question is underscored by the rapidly developing field of discourse analysis.[22] Whereas the study of discourse comprehends all phases of traditional linguistic investigation,[23] it impinges most concertedly, I believe, on the kinds of questions which have been raised in the past in the field of syntax. The issue now to be decided is that of the relationship of discourse analysis, or textlinguistics (as it is known in Europe), to other areas of general linguistics as previously known. At the very least, it must be acknowledged that discourse study is making itself indispensable by raising new questions, producing new tools for analysis, and yielding new insights into the nature of language and the meaning of texts. Whether one decides to preserve the older limitation of syntax to the sentence and regard discourse as a separate branch of linguistic investigation,[24] or to integrate

17. Space does not permit an elaboration of this point. It can simply be noted that the difficulties in identifying word boundaries which exist in some languages do not appear to be present, for the most part, in Semitic.

18. It will be necessary, in the interest of space, to simply bypass the difficulties in defining the sentence from a linguistic perspective: "But of all linguistic units this is the most problematic, and the one whose nature has been most debated" (Matthews, *Syntax*, 26). For studies of the sentence, see A. DeGroot, "Structural Linguistics and Syntactic Laws," *Word* 5 (1949) 2 and n. 3; F. Daneš, "A Three-Level Approach to Syntax," *Travaux Linguistiques de Prague* 1 (1964) 229, and the references cited therein.

19. Robins, *General Linguistics*, 169; Fromkin and Rodman, *Introduction to Language*, 126, 200.

20. N. Chomsky, *Syntactic Structures* (Janua Linguarum Series Minor 4; The Hague: Mouton, 1957) 13; idem, *Aspects of the Theory of Syntax* (Cambridge: MIT Press, 1965) 4–5.

21. For example, the work in discourse from the perspective of generative semantics by J. E. Grimes, *The Thread of Discourse* (Janua Linguarum Series Minor 207; The Hague: Mouton, 1975), and references in S. Kuno, "Generative Discourse Analysis in America," in *Current Trends in Text Linguistics* (ed. W. Dressler; New York: de Gruyter, 1978) 275–95.

22. See the essay by P. J. MacDonald in this volume (pp. 151–74) for an introduction to discourse analysis.

23. Cf., e.g., the discourse vistas even on phonology in M. K. Meyers and J. W. Park, *Discourse Phonology: A Manual for Field Linguistics* (Dallas: Summer Institute of Linguistics, 1978).

24. As was done, e.g., by Matthew, *Syntax*, xix.

the two,[25] the necessity for students of syntax to draw upon the store of new insights emerging from discourse analysis is clear. I believe that integration will eventually appear as the only viable alternative. Discourse investigation is already beginning to directly inform every phase of linguistic analysis, and especially syntax.

THE HISTORY OF THE STUDY OF SYNTAX

Questions of a syntactic nature have been discussed as long as language has been studied. The Greek philosopher Protagoras attempted to classify sentences in the fifth century B.C.E.[26] Later, the Latin grammarian Priscian wrote of the "concordant ordering of words" in an "utterance" [*oratio*].[27] The direction of medieval linguistics was established by Helias with his commentary on Priscian. Medieval speculative grammar was set within a rationalistic framework based on Aristotelian logic. Discussion of such matters as *case* and *parts of speech* took place, but came under this limitation.[28]

In the Renaissance, language study was extended to contemporary national tongues as well as Latin, Greek, and Hebrew. The study of syntax did not notably advance, however. Ramus, a transitional figure between medieval and modern times, shifted attention from case inflection to number as the principal category for grammatical classification[29] and discussed syntax in terms of concord and government, basing this on medieval grammatical theory.[30]

Nor was understanding of syntax significantly advanced from the sixteenth to the eighteenth centuries, during which the study of language reflected philosophical movements. The French grammarians of Port Royal attempted to construct a rational system that would explain the varieties of natural languages.[31] By the eighteenth century, English and American writers were working to establish correct norms in pronunciation and usage. Bishop Lowth, known to students of Biblical Hebrew poetry, published *A Short Introduction to English Grammar* in 1762, in which he formulated

---

25. Some interaction between syntax and textlinguistics may be found in R. A. de Beaugrande and W. Dressler, *Introduction to Text Linguistics* (London: Longman, 1981) 48–83. A number of particular topics are discussed in T. Givón, ed., *Discourse and Syntax* (Syntax and Semantics 12; New York: Academic Press, 1979).
26. Matthews, *Syntax*, 27–28.
27. Ibid., 27. Priscian wrote about 500 C.E..
28. F. P. Dinneen, *An Introduction to General Linguistics* (Washington, DC: Georgetown University Press, 1967) 126–50.
29. R. H. Robins, *A Short History of Linguistics* (London: Longman, 1979) 102.
30. Ibid., 103.
31. J. Lyons, *Introduction to Theoretical Linguistics* (Cambridge: Cambridge University Press, 1968) 17.

many rules of correct usage. That two negatives make an affirmative, for example, was set forth by Lowth.[32]

The major developments in the linguistics of the nineteenth century were in the fields of historical and comparative study. The discovery of the relationship of Sanskrit to Greek, Latin, and other European languages inaugurated this movement.[33] The discovery of several systematic sound correspondences between the classical languages and the Germanic languages by Grimm was followed with refinements by Grassmann, Verner, and others.[34] In the last quarter of the century, the Neogrammarians (*Junggrammatiker*), in accord with prevailing positivistic and evolutionary views of the natural sciences, proposed that all language change proceeds in accord with fixed and invariable laws, a notion that has not survived in such rigid form.[35] During the nineteenth century, major language families were distinguished, and a general theory was developed for tracing language change and relationship. Unfortunately for the present topic, the focus of attention was on phonetics and dialectology; virtually no attention was given to syntax as such.[36]

The beginning of the modern phase of linguistics, perhaps best referred to as *general linguistics*,[37] is usually traced to de Saussure (1857–1913). Although his immediate recognition came from an early contribution to Indo-European comparative linguistics,[38] his teaching, made available through the publication of his lecture notes by several of his students two years after his death, set a new direction for the study of linguistics.[39] Some of the most

---

32. Dinneen, *General Linguistics*, 161.

33. Whereas the discovery was made independently by several scholars, its most famous proponent was Sir William Jones in 1786 (Lyons, *Theoretical Linguistics*, 24).

34. Dinneen, *General Linguistics*, 184–86.

35. Robins, *Short History of Linguistics*, 182–92.

36. W. F. Twaddell, "The Study of Syntax: Past, Present, Future," in *Essays in Honor of Charles F. Hockett* (ed. F. B. Agard et al.; Leiden: Brill, 1983) 36.

37. This modern phase could be spoken of, up to the advent of transformational-generative theory, as descriptive linguistics (Robins, *Short History of Linguistics*, 199). Lyons, however, prefers the term *structural*, regarding *descriptive* as a term better reserved for American linguistics in the Bloomfieldian tradition (*Theoretical Linguistics*, 38, 50–51; and especially *Language and Linguistics*, 217–23.) All these designations are employed in the literature. Because of the varied uses of the term *structuralism* in other disciplines and its recent usage on the part of biblical scholars, I prefer the designation *general linguistics*. This allows for the inclusion of transformational-generative theories and offshoots, which are a prominent part of the modern period and which do have continuities with de Saussure, although they must be distinguished (sharply, Chomsky would insist) from linguistic theories that may be called descriptive.

38. Paradoxical features of this work of de Saussure are discussed in Lyons, *Language and Linguistics*, 219–20.

39. See the reference in n. 6 above. In this brief survey an effort is made only to cite one or more of the best known publications of certain prominent linguists as representative of the individuals and movements discussed.

significant distinctions established by de Saussure include those between diachronic and synchronic analysis, *langue* and *parole*, the syntagmatic and the paradigmatic (for de Saussure the associative),[40] and the signified and the signifier, this latter distinction involving his famous principle of the arbitrariness of the linguistic sign.[41] While his discussion of syntagmatic and associative relations is fundamental to any approach to syntax, he did not develop it significantly or explore the field of syntax at length otherwise.

The principal figures who shaped the direction of American descriptive linguistics following the seminal work of de Saussure were Boas, Sapir, and Bloomfield. Boas concentrated his work on American Indian languages.[42] Sapir explored broad relationships of linguistics to related fields.[43] Bloomfield viewed the regularity of sound change as the cornerstone of linguistic science and restated the findings of Grimm and the Neogrammarians in terms of rigorous scientific description.[44]

Somewhat greater attention was devoted to syntax in this phase. Sapir discussed word order and stress as the primary means of expressing syntactic relations, together with concord.[45] Bloomfield devoted one of twenty-eight chapters to syntax.[46] Significantly, he separated that chapter from meaning and even from his discussion of sentences, which is semantically based in part, as well as from morphology.[47] At one point he acknowledged that the "details of syntax are often complicated and hard to describe."[48] Overall, the emphasis of this period was on phonology and, secondarily, morphology.

The same can be said in general of the American linguists who followed in this descriptive tradition, whose work came to be known as *post-Bloomfieldian*.[49] The linguists of this group (such as Bloch, Trager, Hockett, Hill, and Harris) went beyond the search for relationships of units and categories, and operations that exhibit those relationships, to press for mechanical operations. This involved for some of them an attempt to describe

---

40. The replacement of "associative" with "paradigmatic" is to be credited to Hjelmslev (Dinneen, *General Linguistics*, 305).
41. This principle did not originate with de Saussure. Rather, he derived it from W. D. Whitney (W. Baskin, "Translator's Introduction," in de Saussure, *General Linguistics*, xi).
42. F. Boas, *Handbook of American Indian Languages* (Washington, DC: Smithsonian Institution, 1911).
43. E. Sapir, *Language: An Introduction to the Study of Speech* (New York: Harcourt, Brace & World, 1921).
44. Bloomfield, *Language*.
45. Sapir, *Language*, 110–19.
46. Bloomfield, *Language*, chap. 12.
47. Meaning received three chapters (9–11), and morphology four (13–16).
48. Bloomfield, *Language*, 201.
49. P. W. Davis, *Modern Theories of Language* (Englewood Cliffs: Prentice-Hall, 1973) 129–72. Another designation is *neo-Bloomfieldian*; C. T. Hodge, "Morphology and Syntax," in *Linguistics Today* (ed. A. Hill; New York: Basic Books, 1969) 37.

language without reference to meaning.[50] The linguist who represents the high point in this development, Harris, attempted in his later work to expand his efforts at exhaustive analysis in the direction of transformations and the analysis of discourse.[51] He was a transitional figure in several respects. What is significant here is his recognition of the need to move beyond phonology and morphology[52] to the description of larger units of language.

Major developments in this century outside the United States have included the following. The theory known as *glossematics*, developed by Hjelmslev of Copenhagen, is highly formal in orientation.[53] Hjelmslev's primary concern was, following de Saussure, to elaborate a theory of the form of language rather than its substance. His goal was to analyze a text so as to recognize behind it a system of categories from which could be derived the units of the language. The result would be neither phonetics nor semantics, but a linguistic algebra which would provide the formal basis for deductions.[54] Syntax was given attention only within the context of Hjelmslev's larger project.

The Prague school, represented by the work of Trubetzkoy[55] and Jakobson,[56] developed a viewpoint which came to be known as *functionalism*.[57] Their work in phonology, especially pioneered by Trubetzkoy, was developed by Jakobson and Halle into distinctive feature analysis.[58] Together with the distinctive function of phonetic material, they also examined the demarcative function (marking boundaries) and the expressive function (indicating the speaker's feelings and attitudes). In this latter interest the Prague school was at odds with the positivism of the Neogrammarians and of some American descriptivists. Arising within the Prague school, the approach

50. W. Haas, "Linguistics 1930–80," *Journal of Linguistics* 14 (1978) 294. I address this point in the following section.

51. Many of Harris's important essays are collected in Z. S. Harris, *Papers in Structural and Transformational Linguistics* (Dordrecht: Reidel, 1970).

52. Phonology and morphology, however, constitute the limits of his major work, *Methods in Structural Linguistics* (Chicago: University of Chicago Press, 1951).

53. L. Hjelmslev, *Prolegomena to a Theory of Language* (trans. F. J. Whitfield; Madison: University of Wisconsin Press, 1961).

54. Dinneen, *General Linguistics*, 348.

55. N. Trubetzkoy, *Principles of Phonology* (trans. C. A. M. Beltaxe; Berkeley and Los Angeles: University of California Press, 1969).

56. R. Jakobson, *Selected Writings I* (The Hague: Mouton, 1962).

57. The term has been used by many linguistic theorists, as is evident from the rest of this section. On some broad uses of the term, see M. A. K. Halliday, "Language as Social Semiotic: Towards a General Sociolinguistic Theory," in *Linguistics at the Crossroads* (ed. A. Makkai; Padua: Liviana, 1977) 16–17.

58. R. Jakobson, G. Fant, and M. Halle, *Preliminaries to Speech Analysis* (Cambridge: MIT Press, 1951); R. Jacobson and M. Halle, *Fundamentals of Language* (Janua Linguarum Series Minor 1; The Hague: Mouton, 1956).

known as *functional sentence perspective* has emphasized natural word order in sentences and developed the theme/rheme distinction in analyzing sentence structure.[59]

J. R. Firth was the first professor to hold a title in linguistics in England. Starting from the idea of the "context of situation," which arose out of the work of anthropologist B. Malinowski in the South Seas, Firth developed a contextual theory of language.[60] Building on the Saussurean distinction between the syntagmatic and the paradigmatic, he called for analysis at the phonetic, lexical, grammatical, and situational levels with a view to understanding language in actual use.[61] His insistence that phonetics had meaning led him to elaborate his approach known as *prosodic analysis*. His work with the grammatical level is less explicitly developed and has exerted less lasting influence.[62]

An explicit theory of language based on ideas of Malinowski, Firth, Whorf, Hjelmslev, and the Prague school and known as *systemic-functional linguistics* has been developed by Halliday.[63] His concern is heavily sociolinguistic, having to do with the function of language. His grammar is paradigmatic with roots in rhetoric and ethnology, as over against transformational-generative and American structuralist theories, both of which are syntagmatic with roots in logic and philosophy.[64] Considerable attention is given to syntax.

In the Netherlands a theory called *functional grammar* has been elaborated by Dik.[65] Dik views language primarily as an instrument of social communication. Thus, his priority is on pragmatics, with semantics and syntax being subservient in that order. Again, syntax has a significant place in the research being carried out within this framework.

Arising out of earlier American descriptivism, but with distinctiveness, is the theory of *tagmemics* developed especially by Pike and Longacre.[66]

59. Daneš, "Three-Level Approach"; Jan Firbas, "On Defining the Theme in Functional Sentence Analysis," *Travaux Linguistiques de Prague* 1 (1964) 267–80.

60. J. R. Firth, *Papers in Linguistics 1934–51* (Oxford: Oxford University Press, 1957); idem, *Selected Papers of J. R. Firth, 1952–59* (ed. F. R. Palmer; Bloomington: Indiana University Press, 1968). Firth was professor of general linguistics in the University of London from 1944 to 1956 (Robins, *Short History of Linguistics*, 213).

61. Dinneen, *General Linguistics*, 302–10.

62. J. C. Catford, "J. R. Firth and British Linguistics," in *Linguistics Today*, 228.

63. M. A. K. Halliday, *An Introduction to Functional Grammar* (London: Arnold, 1985).

64. Halliday believes, in fact, that the distinction between paradigmatic and syntagmatic grammars is more fundamental than that between structuralist and transformational-generative grammars, which has been so visible in the United States (ibid., xxviii).

65. S. Dik, *Functional Grammar* (Publications in Language Sciences 7; Dordrecht: Foris, 1981).

66. K. L. Pike, *Language in Relation to a Unified Theory of the Structure of Human Behavior* (The Hague: Mouton, 1967); K. L. Pike and E. G. Pike, *Grammatical Analysis* (Summer

Here language is viewed as similar to other patterns of human behavior. It is seen in terms of discrete units, continuity and change, and relatedness.[67] Analysis is carried out via the tagmeme, which consists, in Pike's theory, of four parts: slot (syntagmatic relation), class (paradigmatic filler), role (pragmatic relevance), and cohesion (agreement of items). These are to be discerned within the hierarchies of grammar, sound, and the referential realm.[68] A noteworthy aspect of Pike's view is his insistence that components of a language, such as the phonological or the syntactic, cannot be analyzed satisfactorily in isolation, but must be studied in relation to other components. For example, he argues that form and meaning should not be separated in linguistic inquiry.[69] A way of doing syntactic analysis from this perspective that is readily accessible to philologians and others who are not primarily linguists is that of Elson and Pickett.[70]

Under the influence of the glossematics of Hjelmslev, the theory of *stratificational grammar* has been pioneered by Lamb,[71] with a more extended introduction by Lockwood.[72] Stratificational theory is in continuity with American descriptivism in that it deals with surface structure. It is distinctive, however, in its approach. The data of language are seen in several strata which are to be studied both horizontally (the tactics of given strata) and vertically (the relationships among strata in terms of realizations). In his original statement Lamb recognized six strata: the phonetic, phonemic, morphemic, lexemic, sememic, and semantic.[73] These have been and are being revised. It is said that the lexemic stratum is the primary focus of syntax.[74] I feel that there is significant potential in stratificational grammar for the development of a more comprehensive and satisfactory linguistic theory, but it has yet to be sufficiently elaborated. In a fairly recent effort to set forth a stratificational approach to syntax, Sullivan found it necessary to devote a good deal of

---

Institute of Linguistics Papers in Linguistics 53; Dallas: Summer Institute of Linguistics, 1977); R. E. Longacre, *Grammar Discovery Procedures* (Janua Linguarum Series Minor 33; The Hague: Mouton, 1973); idem, "Tagmemics," *Word* 36 (1985) 137–77.

67. K. L. Pike, "Language as Particle, Wave, and Field," in *Kenneth L. Pike: Selected Writings* (ed. R. M. Brend; The Hague: Mouton, 1972) 129–43.

68. K. L. Pike, *Linguistic Concepts: An Introduction to Tagmemics* (Lincoln: University of Nebraska Press, 1982) 70–106.

69. Ibid., 111–17.

70. B. F. Elson and V. B. Pickett, *Beginning Morphology and Syntax* (Dallas: Summer Institute of Linguistics, 1983).

71. S. M. Lamb, *Outline of Stratificational Grammar* (Washington, DC: Georgetown University Press, 1966).

72. D. G. Lockwood, *Introduction to Stratificational Linguistics* (New York: Harcourt Brace Jovanovich, 1972).

73. Lamb, *Stratificational Grammar*, 18.

74. Ibid., 21.

space to preliminary matters such as the definition of language, a comparison of stratificational theory with other linguistic theories, and especially arguments for the superiority of stratificational linguistics.[75]

The most radical break with earlier descriptive linguistics has been that of the *transformational-generative*[76] *grammar* of Chomsky. His theory has developed from its early phase[77] through stages which have been called the *standard theory*,[78] the *extended standard theory*,[79] the *revised extended standard theory* or *trace theory*,[80] and *government and binding*.[81]

The main outlines of Chomsky's views, especially in the earlier phases, are as follows. He distinguishes between the competence and performance of a native speaker (roughly equivalent to de Saussure's *langue* and *parole*). The first represents the internalized ability acquired as a child to produce grammatical, that is, acceptable or well-formed, sentences in the language. The task of a grammar is to describe this ability. The goal of linguistic theory, in turn, becomes that of supplying an evaluation procedure whereby proposed grammars of a language may be judged and the better one(s) acknowledged. To this is added the goal of supplementing particular grammar with universal grammar, which would express universal regularities and explicate the creative aspect of language use.

It can be seen, even from this grievously simplified account, that the primary focus of transformational-generative theory is on the production of well-formed sentences and, in this sense, on syntax. In the generation following the publication of *Syntactic Structures*, transformational-generative grammar became widely influential among American linguists; and many felt that "the scalp of syntax" was now being added "to those of phonology and morphology."[82] For Dinneen, "Chomsky is the one author who has

75. W. J. Sullivan, "Syntax and Linguistic Semantics in Stratificational Theory," in *Current Approaches to Syntax* (ed. E. A. Moravcsik and J. R. Wirth; Syntax and Semantics 13; New York: Academic Press, 1980) 301–27.
76. While transformations are less prominent in Chomsky's more recent work, it seems best to retain the term in a descriptive label in order to draw a distinction from other, quite different linguistic theories that also claim to be generative.
77. Chomsky, *Syntactic Structures*.
78. Chomsky, *Aspects of the Theory of Syntax*.
79. Chomsky, *Language and Mind* (New York: Harcourt Brace Jovanovich, 1972); idem, "Remarks on Nominalization," in *Readings in English Transformational Grammar* (ed. R. A. Jacobs and P. S. Rosenbaum; Waltham: Ginn, 1970) 184–221.
80. N. Chomsky and H. Lasnik, "Filters and Control," *Linguistic Inquiry* 8 (1977) 425–504.
81. Chomsky, *Rules and Representations* (New York: Columbia University Press, 1980); idem, *Some Concepts and Consequences of the Theory of Government and Binding* (Linguistic Inquiry Monograph 6; Cambridge: MIT Press, 1982); idem, *Barriers* (Linguistic Inquiry Monograph 13; Cambridge: MIT Press, 1986).
82. Twaddell, "Study of Syntax," 44.

made explicit his concept of what grammar is and what it is not, and why he prefers his approach to other alternatives."[83] For Gragg, Chomsky "had provided a whole generation of linguists with a handle on syntax."[84]

It must be acknowledged that, given the transformational-generative theoretical framework, what is viewed as syntax is handled explicitly. But is this the syntax which has so long eluded other linguistic methods? Some linguists are not satisfied that it is. Reichling is uneasy because of the divorce of transformational-generative syntax from meaning and from the communication situation.[85] Likewise expressing concern over the understanding of the nature of language in transformational-generative theory, specifically over Chomsky's insistence that the primary interest of linguistics is in the internal structure of language and that this exists independent of communicative settings and the native speaker's knowledge of the world, is Oller.[86] Matthews is troubled over the increasingly unconstrained use of deep structure in transformational-generative theory and notes a growing tendency toward wholesale abandonment of transformations in linguistic literature.[87] Twaddell traces the evolution of his initial enthusiasm to final despair over transformational-generative theory.[88]

In the present climate of opinion, an increasing number of linguists find themselves somewhere between these two extremes of wholesale endorsement or repudiation of transformational-generative theory. It is clear, in any case, that since the second phase, signaled by the publication of *Aspects of the Theory of Syntax*, such dramatic recasting has gone on within and in response to the transformational-generative paradigm that readers familiar only with the standard theory would be disoriented in the later literature. Theories such as *generative semantics, case grammar, Montague grammar, relational grammar, context-free grammar,* and *daughter-dependency grammar* are a

83. Dinneen, *General Linguistics*, 416.
84. G. Gragg, "Linguistics, Method, and Extinct Languages: The Case of Sumerian," *Orientalia* 42 (1973) 83. For comment on Chomsky's positive contributions from a non-Chomskyian, see R. E. Longacre, "Why We Need a Vertical Revolution in Linguistics," in *The Fifth LACUS Forum 1978* (ed. W. Wolek and P. L. Garvin; Columbia: Hornbeam, 1979), 247.
85. A. Reichling, "Principles and Methods of Syntax: Cryptanalytic Formalism," *Lingua* 10 (1961) 8–17. The latter point is taken farther in A. Reichling and E. M. Uhlenbeck, "Fundamentals of Syntax," in *Proceedings of the Ninth International Congress of Linguists, 1962* (ed. H. G. Lunt; The Hague: Mouton, 1964) 166–75. A strong statement of the necessity of considering nonsyntactic factors in evaluating the acceptability of certain structures within a perspective that is generally favorable to transformational-generative theory is given in S. Kuno, *Functional Syntax: Anaphora, Discourse and Empathy* (Chicago: University of Chicago Press, 1989).
86. J. W. Oller Jr., "On the Relation between Syntax, Semantics and Pragmatics," in *Linguistics at the Crossroads*, 43–45.
87. Matthews, *Syntax*, 283–91. These criticisms are not so relevant to more recent developments in Chomsky's work.
88. Twaddell, "Study of Syntax," 35–49.

part of this proliferation.[89] It is too soon to attempt an evaluation of their respective degrees of success in dealing with syntax. Indeed, one's view of the current state of syntactic understanding would appear to depend, in large part, on one's theoretical commitment.

Yet the future of the study of syntax seems bright from any perspective. Transformational-generative work has produced valuable insights and is spawning an extensive and substantial literature. At the same time, linguistic models are being developed from other starting points which provide an explicit account of syntax, including *stratificational grammar, role and reference grammar,*[90] *systemic-functional linguistics, functional grammar,* and *functional-typological linguistics.*[91] There are linguists who are comfortable moving from one paradigm to another, depending on the task at hand.[92] Among those who deem it necessary to adhere to one theoretical framework, communication and understanding are improving.[93] Regardless of the degree of progress one may be comfortable acknowledging to date, prospects are positive.

---

89. Essays showing how syntax is approached within some of these theories may be found in Moravcsik and Wirth, *Current Approaches.* To even begin to update the bibliography and thinking of these and other important linguistic theoreticians would expand this essay into a book and be quite impractical. Several more recent approaches are included in F. G. Droste and J. E. Joseph, eds., *Linguistic Theory and Grammatical Description* (Current Issues in Linguistic Theory 75; Amsterdam: Benjamins, 1991).

90. W. A. Foley and R. D. Van Valin Jr., *Functional Syntax and Universal Grammar* (Cambridge Studies in Linguistics 38; Cambridge: Cambridge University Press, 1984).

91. T. Givón, *Syntax: A Functional-Typological Introduction* (2 vols.; Amsterdam: Benjamins, 1984, 1991). Closely related to the work of Givón is that of B. Comrie: *Language Universals and Linguistic Typology: Syntax and Morphology* (2d ed.; Chicago: University of Chicago Press, 1989).

92. Cf. J. L. Malone, "Systematic vs. Autonomous Phonemics and the Hebrew Grapheme *dagesh,*" *AAL* 2 (1975) 113–29, in which neo-Bloomfieldian autonomous phonemics, transformational-generative systematic phonemics, and stratificational phonemics are all entertained in the explication of an issue in Tiberian Hebrew. E. A. Moravcsik speaks of doing syntax "atheoretically"; see "Introduction: On Synthetic Approaches," in *Current Approaches to Syntax,* 1. I am aware of the integral relationship of theory and analysis and the probable impossibility of doing research without a theoretical commitment, implicit if not explicit. Yet I believe that the genuinely manifold diversity of theoretical starting points (i.e., not reducible to one or only a few discrete options) among current working linguists is adequate justification for flexibility and charity among those who disagree with one another about their choice of models, those who are not yet sure of their choice, those who have worked within a model but now want out and are looking around, and those who feel that the model they would envision has not yet seen the light of day.

93. Halliday believes that the transcending of the polemical atmosphere of the 1960s owes much to preoccupation with discourse in the 1970s (*Functional Grammar,* xxix). An example of improved communication is the conference which produced *Current Approaches to Syntax.*

STUDYING SYNTAX

The following remarks conclude this essay, but only introduce the study of syntax. I am not yet prepared to commit myself to a specific model and thus be able to set forth how syntax may be approached from within it. I fall within the last category of those mentioned above at the close of n. 92, those who are still waiting for their model to emerge. If I had to make a choice at this time, I would probably work within a stratificational model; but this would be due more to exposure than to studied preference. My preference would be for a model which would somehow combine a rock-hard empiricism like that of a Garvin;[94] an overall coherence and an integration of semantics as in the stratificational model, especially as it has been developed by Fleming;[95] an understanding of the inseparable union of the synchronic and the diachronic such as is inherent in the functional-typological approach of Givón; a solid grounding in sociolinguistic reality as is present in the systemic-functional framework of Halliday; and a recognition of grammatical phenomena at the discourse level as developed by Longacre.[96]

I think it is no more than an issue of terminology as to whether one restricts the term *syntax* to phenomena of units no larger than the sentence, or employs it more broadly for phenomena of discourse. That there are grammatical phenomena that operate beyond the sentence within the paragraph[97] and within discourse[98] can now be confidently affirmed.

I would employ methodologies that analyze language with reference to meaning, though I am eager to learn from those that exclude meaning from their database.[99] A research agenda of this sort seems to me like a study of arteries, veins, and capillaries without reference to blood. Such a study could

---

94. P. L. Garvin, *On Linguistic Method* (Janua Linguarum Series Minor 30; The Hague: Mouton, 1972); idem, "Aspects of Linguistic Discovery," *Foundations of Language* 11 (1978) 189–218; idem, "Empiricist Epistemology." His volume *Discovery Procedure: Theory and Practice. An Empiricist Epistemology for Linguistics and Its Application to the Writing of a Grammar,* cited for so long as "in preparation," has never appeared, to my knowledge.
95. I. Fleming, *Communication Analysis: A Stratificational Approach,* vol. 2 (Dallas: Summer Institute of Linguistics, 1988). The first volume of this set is presently in preparation.
96. R. E. Longacre, *The Grammar of Discourse* (New York: Plenum, 1983).
97. See R. E. Longacre, "The Paragraph as a Grammatical Unit," in *Discourse and Syntax,* 115–34.
98. See G. Sankoff and P. Brown, "The Origins of Syntax in Discourse: A Case Study of Tok Pisin Relatives," *Lg.* 52 (1975) 631–66; Longacre, *Grammar of Discourse.*
99. It may be necessary to trace this unnatural bifurcation all the way back to Petrus Ramus (1515–1572), who was fundamentally influential in the development of other features of Western thought as well; O. Funke, "On the System of Grammar," *Anthropological Linguistics* 6 (1954) 2–3. On the place of Ramus in the history of western thought, see W. J. Ong, *Ramus, Method, and the Decay of Dialogue* (Cambridge: Harvard University Press, 1958).

indeed be carried out, and certain things could be learned, though the danger of misinterpretation would be high and the scope of conclusions limited and superficial. The very preparation of the data would involve the removal of blood from the vessels, probably filling them with some other fluid, and their isolation from their natural setting in a living organism. Though some aspects of the analysis of blood vessels might call for this isolation, others would be gravely distorted by it; and a wholistic analysis would surely be precluded. So it is, I believe, in the study of language. The isolation of language forms from their meaning and context is probably even more unnatural than the study of blood vessels apart from blood and the body.

Language is a medium of meaningful communication and will never be correctly understood, either in the particulars of a given language or the universals of language as language, apart from its use in conveying meaning. This entails not only semantics (the study of meaning), but also pragmatics (the study of the speaker's knowledge of the world and his or her situational context at the time of speaking).[100]

Perhaps the reason syntax has been, and continues to be, such a challenge to linguists is that it protrudes most obviously into the semantic dimension (to borrow Longacre's term, which he uses in a slightly different sense, the "soft underbelly of language")[101] and sits squarely on the hazy border between linguistic form and function. It may, for these reasons, prove to be the watershed in the development of a linguistic theory which will prove able to endure ongoing scrutiny.

Such an admission immediately involves the linguist in a dilemma. Language use is a part of human social behavior, and the patterns of human behavior are not neat and tidy. Thus, a linguist confronts the tension between the desire to construct a highly formalized theory and the reality of sets of data which will not readily yield themselves to a high degree of formalization. I believe what is needed in the face of this situation is a commitment to data over theory (so that the latter is continually called back to the former to

---

100. Oller, "Syntax, Semantics and Pragmatics"; S. C. Levinson, *Pragmatics* (Cambridge Textbooks in Linguistics; Cambridge: Cambridge University Press, 1983) 54, 186–91, 212–15, 276–83; F. C. C. Peng, "On the Context of Situation," *International Journal of the Sociology of Language* 58 (1986) 91–105. The conviction is growing in strength that the situational context of communication must be drawn into linguistic analysis for that analysis to be adequate. Witness the many theoretical perspectives that agree on this point, including the models of Dik, Firth, Fleming, Foley and Van Valin, Givón, Halliday, and even the generative approach of Kuno (*Functional Syntax*). Linguists are more ready to acknowledge the necessity of their dealing with the "open-ended, contingent and less-than-categorical nature of language" (Givón, *Syntax*, 1:9); the "indeterminacies, intricacies, 'fuzzy edges' and general complexity of naturally occurring human behavior" (Garvin, "Empiricist Epistemology," 332).

101. Longacre, *Grammar of Discourse*, 5.

give account), to inductive method which includes discovery procedures,[102] and to open-minded interaction with linguists of other viewpoints and interested persons in other fields.[103]

The study of syntax involves formal features which signal syntactic patterns. These include *grammatical morphemes, suprasegmentals, word order,* and *juncture.* Grammatical morphemes would include the various modifications of nouns, verbs, and adjectives (in languages in which these modifications occur) which are usually called inflection, prepositions, pronouns, deictics, determiners, etc.[104] "Suprasegmental" is a term often used to refer to features of pitch, stress, and duration.[105] Pitch occurs in the word (tone) and in units larger than the word (intonation). Intonation is recognized as a syntactic marker.[106] Stress should be as well,[107] especially within the sen-

---

102. Chomsky's rejection of discovery procedures (*Syntactic Structures*, 49–60) has never been reversed, to my knowledge. His critique of the absolutist use of discovery procedures by his immediate predecessors can be appreciated. Also, it is his prerogative to define the goals he wishes to pursue. The simple question that must be answered is: Whence the grammars that are to be evaluated? To say that their discovery is not within the pale of linguistic theory is hardly helpful. It is surely as essential that the procedures followed in the discovery process be consonant with a valid view of language as it is that the evaluation process be so grounded (even if the former is a stronger requirement on a theory, and that may yet be open to question). Of course, such inductive procedures should not be applied in a mechanical way, nor should their results be expected to follow automatically. Neither, however, can they be dispensed with in any model which purports to elucidate the nature of language wholistically.

103. This is an appropriate place for an appeal to linguistic theoreticians that they make a more concerted attempt to distill the essentials of their views and communicate them more simply to a wider audience—a priority to which linguists, especially of the last half of this century thus far, have not displayed strong commitment. See H. A. Gleason Jr., "Linguistics and Philology," in *On Language, Culture, and Religion: In Honor of Eugene A. Nida* (ed. M. Black and W. A. Smalley; The Hague: Mouton, 1974) 210–12, for a similar appeal from a working linguist to his colleagues.

104. The Biblical Hebrew definite object marker *ʾet* and relative clause marker *ʾăšer* are best regarded as grammatical morphemes. The distinction between grammatical morphemes and lexical words is sometimes unclear (Lyons, *Theoretical Linguistics*, 438). For some distinctions, see Givón, *Syntax*, 1:48–50 (where lexical words are distinguished from inflectional grammatical morphemes, which are further distinguished from derivational grammatical morphemes).

105. L. M. Hyman, *Phonology: Theory and Analysis* (New York: Holt, Rinehart & Winston, 1975) 186–238.

106. F. Daneš, "Order of Elements and Sentence Intonation," in *To Honor Roman Jakobson: Essays on the Occasion of His Seventieth Birthday* (The Hague: Mouton, 1967) 1:499–512; D. Bolinger, ed., *Intonation* (Baltimore: Penguin, 1972).

107. Gleason, *Descriptive Linguistics*, 167–69. D. L. Bolinger suggests using the term *accent* in syntactic and *stress* in morphological discussion; "Stress and Information," *American Speech* 33 (1958) 20.

tence.[108] The variability of word order in a given language is relative, depending on its interplay with other formal syntactic indicators; but it is probably not ever completely free, no matter how rich the other factors may be.[109] Greenberg's seminal essay of 1966 on word-order universals has provoked an extensive literature and served as a catalyst for a new, typological approach to word-order studies. Clear-cut typological distinctions can be identified between languages with an order of S (subject) O (object) V (verb), VSO, and SVO which strongly affect syntax and discourse.[110] Juncture also serves as a syntactic signal.[111]

It might be useful to think of kinds of relationships at the syntactic level which are signaled by these markers. Bloomfield spoke of *concord, government*, and *cross reference* as types of syntactic agreement.[112] Concord has to do with syntactic units appearing in forms which correspond in specific ways with other syntactic units, such as the agreement of the attributive adjective in Biblical Hebrew with its noun in gender, number, and definiteness. Government exists when one syntactic unit determines the form to be taken by another, but does not exhibit that form itself, as in the construct form of the noun in Biblical Hebrew which is governed by its following noun. Cross-reference refers to an appositional relationship in which certain units restrict

---

108. I know of no study of duration in relation to syntax, but I suspect that a relationship could be shown. Duration intersects with juncture, which is mentioned below.

109. Matthews, *Syntax*, 256. Matthews points to a "variable balance between economy and redundancy" in language as it reflects a varying relationship between fixity of word order and richness of inflection (259).

110. J. H. Greenberg, "Some Universals of Grammar with Particular Reference to the Order of Meaningful Elements," in *Universals of Language* (ed. J. H. Greenberg; Cambridge: MIT Press, 1966) 73–113; C. Li, ed., *Word Order and Word Order Change* (Austin: University of Texas Press, 1975); J. A. Hawkins, "On Implicational and Distributional Universals of Word Order," *Journal of Linguistics* 16 (1980) 193–235; J. Fisiak, ed., *Historical Syntax* (Trends in Linguistics, Studies and Monographs 23: Berlin: Mouton, 1984), esp. the essays by Harris and Vennemann; T. Shopen, ed., *Language Typology and Syntactic Description* (3 vols.; Cambridge: Cambridge University Press, 1985); W. Croft, *Typology and Universals* (Cambridge Textbooks in Linguistics; Cambridge: Cambridge University Press, 1990).

111. Haiim B. Rosén, "An Outline of a General Theory of Junction," *Studies in Egyptology and Linguistics* (Jerusalem: Israel Exploration Society, 1964) 153–89.

112. Bloomfield, *Language*, 191–94. For E. A. Nida they are secondary class restrictions; *Syntax: A Descriptive Analysis* (Glendale: Summer Institute of Linguistics, 1946) 27–35. For Hockett, these are kinds of linkage indicated by inflection; and he adds a fourth category, *governmental concord* (*Modern Linguistics*, 214–18). For Gleason, they are syntactic devices used to indicate structure, though he sees cross-reference as a type of government; and he once speaks of concord as a relationship (*Descriptive Linguistics*, 165). For Robins, they are types of control exercised by certain syntactic groupings over the forms of variable words; and he includes only concord and government (*General Linguistics*, 186–89). I am suggesting that these could be analyzed as types of relationships that are signaled by the kinds of markers already discussed and that function at the syntactic level.

others, but do not necessarily exhibit the same form, as in the agreement of the implicit subject indicated by the inflection of the Biblical Hebrew finite verb with the expressed subject.

I believe this list can best be seen as an early attempt to discern syntactic relationships. When enlarged and made adequate, it could specify such relationships as they are expressed at the intraclausal level (a predicate calculus), the interclausal level (a statement calculus), and the discourse level (which may or may not involve relationships different from the statement calculus).[113] Case grammar has elaborated a predicate calculus.[114] In Longacre's proposal of a statement calculus, there are basic and elaborative deep structures, including conjoining, alternation, temporal, and implication as basic devices and paraphrase, illustration, deixis, and attribution as elaborative features.[115]

The study of syntax has been the focal point, especially of American linguistics, since shortly after the middle of the twentieth century. While descriptive work had made great progress in phonology and considerable advance in morphology, it was stymied by syntax. As mentioned before, I believe this was due, in part at least, to the attempt to separate language from meaning and situational context. The transformational-generative movement, pioneered by Chomsky, brought syntax front-and-center and offered a highly formalized model that could explicitly account for it. Together with any number of specific insights, the movement must be credited with underscoring the necessity of adequate linguistic theory and establishing the notion of relative degrees of depth in the structure of language.[116] Nevertheless, the transformational-generative paradigm has not proven to be the final stage in the quest for a satisfying understanding of syntax,[117] as witnessed by the increasing diversification among linguistic models.

---

113. I have found significant help in my thinking at this point from Longacre, both in personal conversation and from his *Grammar of Discourse.*
114. A chronicle of work up through 1977 may be found in ibid., 158–59.
115. Ibid., chap. 3. Antecedent bibliography is given on p. 87. Cf. also R. E. Longacre, "Sentences as Combinations of Clauses," in *Language Typology and Syntactic Description*, 2:235–51.
116. This is true, I believe, whether or not one accepts the existence of deep structure in the earlier transformational-generative sense. Linguists who do not work within a transformational-generative framework frequently speak in similar terms, e.g., "I group the notions of the expanded statement calculus under two main heads: basic and elaborative *deep structures*" (emphasis added; Longacre, *Grammar of Discourse*, 87). The notion of transformations is also employed in non–transformational-generative frameworks, e.g., the uses of transformations as rules which are "structure sensitive," while not structure changing, in functional grammar (Dik, *Functional Grammar*, 10).
117. Twaddell's conclusion in 1983 was that "syntax is still one of the largely unmapped areas of linguistics" ("Study of Syntax," 48).

Perhaps our brightest hope may be for an eventual merging of some theories which are now in process. That this process may be underway could be suggested, for instance, by the growing acceptance from many perspectives of the need to reckon with the sociolinguistic context of given language data.[118] Of course such a process would be expedited by the more immediate appearance of a theoretical formulation that would command general assent. In either case, the pathway to this long-sought formulation will likely emerge along a number of stopping points at which further inductive work in the hard data of specific languages will be necessary. At these points students of Biblical Hebrew and other ancient Near Eastern languages can contribute to, as well as learn from, their interaction with specialists in the field of general linguistics.

118. See n. 100 above.

[December, 1987]

Barry L. Bandstra

Word Order and Emphasis in Biblical Hebrew Narrative: Syntactic Observations on Genesis 22 from a Discourse Perspective

What motivates a writer of Biblical Hebrew at one time to order his clause with subject preceding predicate, as in Gen 22:1:

    wh²lhym nsh ²t-²brhm
    S   V   O
    And God tested Abraham

and at another time to order his clause with subject following predicate, as in Gen 22:3:

    wyškm ²brhm bbqr
    V   S   M
    And got-up Abraham in the morning?

What factors determine the linear sequencing of words in Biblical Hebrew? Are there any linguistic tendencies, or perhaps even rules, in evidence when it comes to word order?

Word order, when it is treated at all in grammars of Biblical Hebrew, is viewed primarily as a matter of authorial style. This is the case especially when it comes to Biblical Hebrew poetry. Except for certain situations which demand an obligatory order of the core constituents (e.g., negative commands), word order is considered to be subject to free variation. Any strange or unexpected word order is generally attributed to the author's desire to emphasize a certain clause constituent.

Author's note: Abbreviations used in the syntactic parsing of clauses are as follows: S = subject; V = verb; WP = *wāw*-prefix verb; O = object; IO = indirect object; M = margin, i.e., any other nonnuclear constituents, such as adverbs and prepositional phrases.

Modern studies in text linguistics and discourse analysis suggest that word order may be motivated beyond authorial whim. In fact, modern linguistic studies of word order in various natural languages suggest that word order is one of the devices which code how a speaker or writer intends the communication to be received.[1] It turns out to be one of the most important devices for maintaining comprehensibility on the part of the reader or hearer. This paper seeks to provide a framework for understanding the principles of word order and word-order variation in Biblical Hebrew. It is the premise of this study that it is possible to account for word order in terms of functional principles and identifiable linguistic processes. Because emphasis is largely a function of word order, the study will also give some definition to our commonly intuited but vaguely understood notions of emphasis in Biblical Hebrew discourse.

PREVIOUS WORD-ORDER STUDIES OF BIBLICAL HEBREW

Word order in Biblical Hebrew has been the subject of only a very few extended studies. Albrecht was the first to apply any kind of controlled method.[2] He investigated the Biblical Hebrew nominal clause by categorizing clause types based on how the predicate is realized, whether as adjective, participle, adverb, etc., eight categories in all. He concluded that the natural order of elements is subject-predicate. The frequent P–S deviations from this norm result either from emphasis on the predicate which places it first, or from what he claims are certain obligatory orderings, such as when the clause is interrogative.

In spite of certain serious inadequacies in Albrecht's study,[3] it should be noted that he was the first to attempt to give quantitative evidence for word-order regularities. His conclusions became the basis for the claim in *Gesenius' Hebrew Grammar* (GKC § 141l–n/pp. 454–55) and in Brockelmann's

---

1. See C. N. Li, ed., *Word Order and Word Order Change* (Austin: University of Texas Press, 1975); T. Givón, ed., *Topic Continuity in Discourse: A Quantitative Cross-Language Study* (Amsterdam and Philadelphia: Benjamins, 1983); R. S. Tomlin, *Basic Word Order: Functional Principles* (London: Croom Helm, 1986). The studies of T. Givón deal thoroughly with the issue of word order and the notion of topicality. He is to be noted by Hebraists because of the pioneering work he has done in the discourse grammar of Biblical Hebrew. In addition to the above-cited volume, which includes a chapter by A. Fox entitled "Topic Continuity in Biblical Hebrew Narrative," see T. Givón, "The Drift from VSO to SVO in Biblical Hebrew: The Pragmatics of Tense-Aspect" in *Mechanisms of Syntactic Change* (ed. C. N. Li; Austin: University of Texas Press, 1977).
2. C. Albrecht, "Die Wortstellung im hebräischen Nominalsatze," *ZAW* 7 (1887) 218–24, 8 (1888) 249–63.
3. F. I. Andersen, *The Hebrew Verbless Clause in the Pentateuch* (Nashville: Abingdon, 1970) 20–24.

Hebräische Syntax[4] that nominal-clause word order is normally S–P. Both Kautzsch and Brockelmann claim that the natural order of words in the verbal clause is V–S–O. Kautzsch says the verb comes first because "the principal emphasis rests upon the action which proceeds from (or is experienced by) the subject" (GKC § 142a / p. 455). However, if any other member of the clause is to be emphasized, it takes the primary position in the clause. Joüon departs from most other studies and posits an S–P order for both nominal and verbal clauses (Joüon § 155k / p. 474). But the order is reversed, he says, if the nominal or verbal predicate is emphasized. The P–S order will also be found if the clause is introduced with a particle such as *ky*, *ʾm*, *lʾ*, or *hnh* because in such cases the predicate is emphasized (Joüon § 155m / p. 475).

Only recently have statistical studies been done on selected text samples in an attempt to establish a reliable empirical base for statements about basic word order. The first such study is the Hebrew University doctoral dissertation of Muraoka on emphasis in Biblical Hebrew.[5] He demonstrates that S–P word order cannot be posited as the "normal" order in the nominal clause. Both S–P and P–S serial orders are significantly attested in his text sample, 69 percent and 31 percent respectively. He suggests that the order of constituents in nominal clauses is determined by the semantic nature of the clause. In a clause with P–S order, the predicate is descriptive of the subject. In a clause with the S–P order, the predicate is either descriptive or identifying, depending on the nature of the predicate. As for verbal clauses, the normal order of constituents is V–S. The predominance of the V–S order is due largely to the narrative use of the *wāw*-conversive. He claims that with the V–S order neither subject nor predicate is marked for emphasis. And even in those clauses where the verb does not come first, the order is not necessarily due to the emphasis of the nonverbal preposed element. Other factors may be at work, such as deliberate contrast resulting in chiasmus, or the introduction of a circumstantial clause, or a deliberate break in narrative continuity.[6]

Andersen's study of the verbless clause in the Pentateuch is perhaps better known than Muraoka's, and it attains many of the same results.[7] Andersen classifies each nominal clause on formal as well as semantic criteria. He attempts to demonstrate that nominal clauses which are functionally different have different syntactic structures. His summary conclusion is that nominal clauses manifest two different semantic functions depending on the order of

---

4. C. Brockelmann, *Hebräische Syntax* (Neukirchen: Neukirchener Verlag, 1956) 24–25 §27 and 188 §121.

5. T. Muraoka, *Emphasis in Biblical Hebrew* (Ph.D. diss., Hebrew University, 1969). This work is now available in a version only slightly revised from the original: *Emphatic Words and Structures in Biblical Hebrew* (Jerusalem: Magnes/Leiden: Brill, 1985).

6. Muraoka, *Emphasis in Biblical Hebrew*, 15–31.

7. Andersen, *Hebrew Verbless Clause.*

constituents. When the predicate is definite, the S–P sequence is preferred. Such a clause functions to supply the identity of the subject. A simple clause of this type is Exod 6:2 *ᵓny yhwh* 'I am Yahweh'. This is a very nice case in point. Here Yahweh is identifying himself as such and equating himself as Yahweh with the El-Shaddai the patriarchs knew. On the other hand, when the predicate is indefinite, the sequence P–S is preferred. This type of clause functions to classify the subject, that is, to specify the general class to which the subject belongs. As an example he cites Gen 42:9 *mrglym ᵓtm* 'Spies you are'. In effect what Joseph is saying to his brothers is, 'I know you and you are the type of guys who are spies'.

This survey suggests that the earliest studies of word order tended to posit a base order, and deviations from this base were explained using an intuitive notion of emphasis. The working assumption was that first position in the clause is the location of emphasis. The studies of Muraoka and Andersen go beyond the earlier studies by factoring in the semantic function of the clause. In so doing they begin to look at the clause as it functions within the larger discourse.

THE NOTION OF EMPHASIS

Emphasis has tended to become "the great explanation" of syntactic irregularities in many commentaries and grammatical studies. Examples could be multiplied, and the following is cited not because it is particularly errant, but because it is wholly typical in its resort to a notion of emphasis. J. Mac-Donald, in an article on "The Distinctive Characteristics of Israelite Spoken Hebrew,"[8] does a commendable job of detailing the peculiar features of direct discourse in 1 Samuel. He examines inverted word order, the use of the independent personal pronoun with a finite verb, the infinitive absolute, and other features. His amassing of data is impressive, but his explanation for the presence of many of the features, especially inverted word order, is simply "emphasis" without specifying what is meant.

If some particle, word, or construction is difficult to explain, the notion of emphasis is invoked and the problem is considered solved. The presence of emphasis is somehow assumed to be transparent. It is true that we all intuitively know what emphasis is. But I suspect the emphasis we know or imagine we know is the emphasis realized in the performance of a discourse, effected by stress or intonation. Such emphasis is not a feature of texts as such. Somehow our perception of presumed emphasis in the text is skewed by an imagined oral performance of the text—how it could be creatively and expressively read. This imagined emphasis lends credibility to a resort to

8. *BO* 32 (1975) 162–75.

emphasis as an explanation of a textual feature, because we can sense how it could be emphatically rendered in an oral interpretation.

Furthermore, the attempted explanation of syntactic phenomena by means of emphasis is really a non-explanation, at least until the notion is given empirical linguistic definition. After all, who can say a claim for the presence of emphasis is wrong? How can you either prove or disprove it? For, an emphatic construction is generally considered to reflect some disposition of the mind of the speaker/writer, and we have no access to that anymore, given only the written text. This is what Muraoka says about the use of emphasis as an explanation:

> The term "emphasis" is often too lightly and rashly called in, like a pinch hitter in [a] baseball game, by those who want to get rid of a certain grammatical or philological difficulty, without giving much thought to precisely what they themselves mean by the term, nor, more important, to the question why the writer or the speaker possibly felt the need for an emphatic form of construction.[9]

While the claim for the presence of emphasis is easy to make, it is difficult either to refute or to substantiate. Perhaps any measure of the imprecision of the notion of emphasis is the large number of adjectives and nouns which have been used as virtual synonyms of "emphasis" and "emphatic": *affirmative, asseverative, demonstrative, deictic, intensive,* and *corroborative*; and in German one finds *bekräftigend, hinweisend, hervorhebend,* and *betonend*.

By these remarks the suggestion is not being made that there is no such thing as emphasis in Biblical Hebrew discourse. Rather, what is claimed is that we need a more refined and linguistically grounded approach in order to give definition to what easily remains just a psychological notion. The claim presented here is that emphasis, when it is present, is a function of word order. It must be understood in terms of the information structure of the clause.

INFORMATION STRUCTURE

Every text has a mixture of already-known information and new information.[10] The already-known information may be known from a variety of sources. It may be known because it has already been mentioned in the text, or it may be known from the general situation of communication, or it may

9. Muraoka, *Emphasis in Biblical Hebrew*, i.
10. For an introduction to the notion of information structure as well as to the study of discourse analysis in general, see G. Brown and G. Yule, *Discourse Analysis* (Cambridge Textbooks in Linguistics; Cambridge: Cambridge University Press, 1983). See also J. Grimes, *The Thread of Discourse* (The Hague: Mouton, 1975); W. Chafe, "Givenness, Contrastiveness, Definiteness, Subjects, Topics, and Point of View," in *Subject and Topic* (ed. C. N. Li; New York: Academic Press, 1976); T. van Dijk, *Text and Context* (London: Longman,

be information which is assumed to be known by anyone living in a particular culture. This already-known information has also been called "old" or "given information" and is frequently referred to as "topic." The already-known information enables us to process new information by providing a peg to hang it on.

"New information" or the "comment," on the other hand, does not have to be totally unknown or come out of the blue. Some have suggested that it is perhaps better to refer to it as information that has not been activated in this particular communicative situation, whereas given information is information that has recently been activated. It is the new information which has communicative value or saliency.

In a text, the normal movement is from what is known to what is unknown. This has even been formalized in linguistics as Behagel's second law:

> The sentence element that is the subject of discussion, the topic of that part of the discourse—either because it has been mentioned previously or because it is conspicuous in the environment—tends to come first and to be destressed (downgraded by intonation or even reduced to some substitute form such as pronoun) in subsequent references to it, whereas the new information, the comment, tends to come near the end and to be highlighted by intonation.[11]

This principle has its effects on the clause. First, it is transparent that each clause normally must have some given information and some new information. Clauses with only new information would be incoherent, and clauses with only old information would be redundant. Furthermore, the given-new distinction has implications for text information structure as well. Because given material is frequently material that has already been given in the discourse at hand, the designations *given* and *new* are text-dependent notions, at least to a degree.[12]

Given elements are contextually and textually bound. As a result, they are usually referred to anaphorically or by some other means of cross reference. And they are grammatically definite, presupposing identifiability in the mind of the reader. New information, on the other hand, is usually indefinite and must be spelled out in full.

The structuring of clauses and texts in terms of types of information, whether given or new, has implications for understanding principles of word order. The expected or unmarked order of constituents in the clause is *given* information (or information in continuity with the preceding textual context) preceding *new* information. These general principles of information structure

1977); R. de Beaugrande and W. Dressler, *Introduction to Text Linguistics* (London: Longman, 1980).

11. R. Stockwell, *Foundations of Syntactic Theory* (Englewood Cliffs: Prentice-Hall, 1977) 68.

12. Chafe, "Givenness, Contrastiveness," 30–33; van Dijk, *Text and Context*, 117.

are both intuitive and demonstrable in terms of natural language. What is needed at this point is the application of these principles to an understanding of Biblical Hebrew.

INFORMATION STRUCTURE AND THE BIBLICAL HEBREW CLAUSE

Biblical Hebrew is a verb-first language. When an explicit subject is present, the expected and most frequent order of constituents in narrative verbal clauses is V–S–O. When the subject is implicit in the verbal form, the order is V–O. The form of the V constituent in narrative is typically a prefix verb with *wāw*-conversive (WP).

It would be incorrect simply to map given information onto the V constituent and new information onto the S constituent for the V–S–O clause structure. As suggested above, determinations of given and new are based on discourse and cannot be determined for any clause as it stands isolated from text and context. The primary utility of the given-new distinction is that it will enable the interpreter to understand why a particular order out of the range of possible constituent orders occurs at a particular place in the text. The given-new textual dynamic will primarily serve to explain deviations from the V–(S)–O order. What follows is a treatment of the basic word-order options, with illustration from Gen 22:1–19.

V–S–O, V–S–M, V–S

Orders where the subject must be made explicit typically occur at the beginning of a paragraph unit. The subject has to be made explicit because it is either a new subject or a subject resumed after a break in attention.

> 3a   *wyšqm*   *ʾbrhm*   *bbqr*
>   V   S   M
>   and Abraham got up early in the morning
> 6a   *wyqḥ*   *ʾbrhm*   *ʾt-ʿsy hʿlh*
>   V   S   O
>   and Abraham took the wood of the sacrifice

See also vv. 7a, 15a, and 19a (V–S–IO); 8a and 13d (V–S); 10a, 13a, and 14a (V–S–O); and 19d (V–S–M).

V–O, V–M, V

Orders with subject implicit by form in the verb assume the recoverability of the subject from the preceding text (given information) and carry the argument or narrative forward. Such clauses typically continue the action or event line of the preceding narrative in a natural or, at least, not unexpected way.

> 3b   *wyḥbš   ²t-ḥmrw*
>   V   O
>   and he saddled his donkey
> 6b   *wyśm   ᶜl-yṣḥq bnw*
>   V   M
>   and he placed them on Isaac his son

See also vv. 3d, 9c, 9d, and 13e (V–O); 1c (V–IO); 3c (V–O–IO); 3e, 9a, and 19c (V–M); 4b and 9e (V–O–M)

> 1a   *wyhy   ²ḥr hdbrym h²lh*
>   V   M
>   and after these things

While this is a verb-first pattern, it is not typical of V–S–O or V–O functions. The WP of *hyh* is a special case. While it does not narrate action, it still functions to maintain continuity with the preceding textual unit. This is further indicated by *hdbrym h²lh* 'these things', vaguely referring to the preceding events.

S–V–O, O–V–S

Non-verb-first clause shapes, as well as verbless clauses, are informationally marked. They typically signal informational discontinuity or discourse transition from one unit to another. These types of clauses are found more frequently in spoken discourse than in narrative discourse. What follows is a treatment of those clauses in Gen 22:1–19 which are not V–S–O or V–O.

Marked Orders in Narrative Discourse

> 1b   *wh²lhym   nsh   ²t-²brhm*
>   S   V   O
>   and God tested Abraham

This marked order is typical of discourse-initial position. When anything other than a WP verb form is found in initial position, it signals that new or unexpected information is being introduced. This clause establishes the theme for the unit (Gen 22:1–19) as a whole.[13]

---

13. C. Westermann, *Genesis 12–36* (Minneapolis: Augsburg, 1985) 354: "A heading or statement of theme which synthesizes what follows in a pregnant expression: God is testing Abraham."

4a *bywm hšlyšy wyś᾿ ᾿brhm ᾿t-ʿynyw*
    M   V   S   O
    on the third day raised Abraham his eyes

The fronting of the temporal prepositional phrase, and that without a conjunction, indicates a new stage in the action. In this case, the episode here introduced is where the main action of the story begins.[14]

6c *wyqh bydw ᾿t-h᾿š w᾿t-hm᾿klt*
    V   M   O
    and he took in his hand the fire and the knife

The prepositional phrase *in his hand* would normally follow the direct object. Here it is placed in primary postverbal position to effect contrast with *ʿl-yṣḥq* in v. 6b. In other words, while Isaac carried wood, Abraham *with his own hand* carried the fire and the knife.

9b *wybn šm ᾿brhm ᾿t-hmzbḥ*
    V   M   S   O
    and built there Abraham the altar

The adverb *there* is placed in primary postverbal position. The subject of this clause, namely Abraham, represents subject shift from the preceding clause, which has a plural subject. Furthermore, v. 9b begins a new paragraph. *Šm* functions anaphorically and deictically with *᾿l-hmqwm ᾿šr ᾿mr-lw h᾿lhym* in v. 9a. *Šm* thus effects the continuity of the two clauses across the discontinuity of the paragraph boundary.

11a *wyqr᾿ ᾿lyw ml᾿k yhwh mn-hšmym*
     V   IO   S   M
     and called to him the angel of the Lord from heaven

The indirect object prepositional phrase *to him*, that is, to Abraham, maintains continuity with the preceding, where Abraham is the grammatical subject (vv. 9b–10b). Certainly *ml᾿k yhwh* is a new subject/topic, but by placing *᾿lyw* in primary postverbal position the intrusiveness of this new player is lessened, with the result that overall narrative continuity, and especially action continuity, is maintained. If instead this clause had been ordered **wyqr᾿ ml᾿k yhwh ᾿lyw mn-hšmym*, then a break between vv. 10b and 11a would be more evident. The swift sequencing of Abraham raising the knife to slaughter Isaac, and then being stopped in the nick of time, was the primary motivation of the writer as he ordered the constituents of this clause. Compare

---

14. The lack of a conjunction is quite unusual. See F. I. Andersen, *The Sentence in Biblical Hebrew* (Janua Linguarum Series Practica 231; The Hague: Mouton, 1974) 37: They are "rare instances when a new paragraph begins without conjunction."

v. 15a, where this latter construction is in fact found and where the need for immediacy in temporal sequencing was not a factor.

13c *whnh-ʾyl ʾḥr* [read *ʾḥd*] *nʾḥz   bsbk   bqrnyw*
        S   V   M   M
        and behold a ram was caught in the thicket by its horns

This clause is the complement of v. 13b *wyrᶜ*. The unexpected nature of this sight is indicated first of all by complementation with *hnh* rather than with *ky*. What would normally be a complement phrase is raised from subordinate status to "independent" status and made a clause in its own right. Normally a subordinate *ky* clause follows *rʾh*, but here a coordinate *hnh* clause is the complement of *rʾh*. The construction *hnh* + noun phrase introduces a highly discontinuous element into the narrative. Indeed, the ram is a new and highly unexpected participant in the story. Characteristic of such new topics, this phrase is indefinite when here first introduced, *ʾyl ʾḥd* 'a certain ram'. When referred to in v. 13e, it is definite.

Some remarks are called for. First, narrative is characterized by the use of the WP form in first position. In the present text, forty-four of forty-seven narrative clauses (including those clauses in direct discourse which are narrative) begin with WP. When it is not so found, as in vv. 1b, 4a, and 13c, this is first of all a signal of narrative discontinuity. Narrative discontinuity means the introduction of a new, unexpected participant, or major narrative break. Second, primary post-WP position is a position of informational significance. A nonsubject constituent found here is marked. It can do one of two things. In a situation of discontinuity when the clause undergoes subject switch, it can serve to reestablish continuity, as in vv. 9b and 11a, or it can effect contrast or contra-expectation (new topic), as in vv. 6c and 13c.

Marked Orders in Spoken Discourse

2d *whᶜlhw   šm   lᶜlh   ᶜl ʾḥd hhrym ʾšr ʾmr ʾlyk*
        V   M   C   M
        and offer him there as an offering on one of the mountains which
        I will tell you

The adverb *šm* is anaphoric to *ʾl-ʾrṣ hmryh* of the preceding clause. As such it is old information and precedes the other nonverbal constituents.

3c *wyqh   ʾt-šny nᶜryw   ʾtw   wʾt yṣḥq bnw*
        V   O   M   O
        and he took his two servants with him and Isaac his son

This clause has the expected order of WP first followed by direct object and margin. The noteworthy element is the final phrase *wʾt yṣḥq bnw*, which is part of the direct object but is separated from it by *ʾtw*. This is a deliberate technique, called back-shifting, which establishes a constituent as significant to the discourse. Not only is clause-initial position significant in regard to information status, so is clause-final position.

> 5c *wʾny whnᶜr nlkh ᶜd-kh*
>   S   V   M
>   and I and the boy, we will go there

The subject noun phrase *I and the boy* signals that this clause stands in binary contrast with the preceding: 'You servants stay here with the donkey, I and the lad will go there'. The contrast is further indicated by the *ph-kh* pair.

> 8b *ʾlhym yrʾh-lw hśh lᶜlh bny*
>   S   V   IO   O
>   God will himself see a lamb for the offering my son

The fronted subject *ʾlhym* is a new topic, and so is informationally discontinuous with the preceding context.

> 16b *by nšbᶜty*
>   M V
>   by myself I swear

Preposing of the prepositional phrase *by* implies that 'not by something or someone else, but only by myself do I swear'. This is fronting to effect contrast.

> 18a *whtbrkw bzrᶜk kl gwyy hʾrṣ*
>   V   M   S
>   and will bless themselves by your seed will all the nations of the earth

The phrase *bzrᶜk* is an instrumental prepositional phrase. Even though the grammatical subject of this clause is new (*kl gwyy hʾrṣ*), the *topic* remains the same (i.e., Abraham's seed). So *bzrᶜk* is placed in primary postverbal position to maintain continuity with this already established topic.

In spoken discourse, verb-first clause structure still predominates. But compared to narrative discourse, it allows greater flexibility. Nonverbal clauses are more frequent, as well as single words or fragmentary dialogue (v. 1: *ʾbrhm . . . hnny*; v. 7: *ʾby . . . hnny bny . . . hnh hʾš . . .* , etc.). The position immediately after the verb appears to be especially significant in spoken discourse. It is crucial in determining the informational continuity of that clause with the preceding discourse context. In verbal clauses where the verb is not first (vv. 5c, 8b, 16b), the fronted element effects contrast or discontinuity.

TOPICALIZATION TRANSFORMATIONS IN
BIBLICAL HEBREW

What previously has been termed "emphasis" now can be understood more profitably as the discourse effect of placing new information in the position where given information is typically found. Thus, the presumption that first position in the clause is always the place of emphasis is not correct. But when something other than a WP is found in first position, something significant has taken place. Perhaps a better term to apply to this fronting transformation is *topicalization*. Topicalization is the process whereby a writer brings into prominence new information and places it into the given information slot or the topic position.

The following are examples of some identifiable patterns of topicalization in Biblical Hebrew. These marked word orders and other syntactic devices signal what others have been calling emphasis. The following is a preliminary catalog of such devices, including some examples from Genesis 22 as well as from other texts.

Word-Order Topicalization

The device of fronting a clause constituent other than that expected to be in topic position for that particular genre is known as "word-order topicalization." For narrative, including direct discourse in narrative, this would be virtually anything other than the WP *wayyiqtol*.

1. *Subject fronting.* Gen 22:1b *whʾlhym nsh ʾt-ʾbrhm* 'and God tested Abraham'. This S–V–O order introduces the discourse topic of the Genesis 22 Aqedah passage, as stated above. This marked order is typical for discourse initial topic clauses (cf. Gen 3:1, 4:1, etc.).

2. *Object fronting.* Gen 31:42 *ʾt-ᶜnyy wʾt-ygyᶜ kpy rʾh ʾlhym* 'my affliction and the toil of my hands saw God'. This O–V–S order effects a contrast between Laban, who would send Jacob away empty-handed (*ryqm*), and God, who saw the toil of Jacob's hands.

3. *Adverb fronting.* Gen 49:31 *šmh qbrw ʾt-ʾbrhm* 'there buried they Abraham'. The M–V–O order, with the fronting of *šmh* 'there', provides continuity with vv. 29–30. *Šmh* refers anaphorically to the cave of Machpelah recalled in those verses. In this case the fronted element is not new information, but is the clause constituent which provides smooth transition and continuity to v. 31. In Deut 31:29 the temporal-adverbial phrase *ʾhry mwty* 'after my death' is fronted before the *ky* complement clause which it modifies: *ydᶜty ʾhry mwty ky hšht tšhtwn* 'I know after my death that you will surely become corrupt' → 'I know that you will become corrupt after my death'. The adverb does not condition 'know' but 'become corrupt', yet it is topicalized, the motivation being to foreground the impending death of Moses, which is in turn the occasion for the Song of Moses, which this verse introduces.

4. *Verb complement fronting.* Gen 42:9 *lr°wt °t-°rwt h°rṣ b°tm* 'to see the nakedness of the land you came'. The verb complement is fronted to highlight the claim that Jacob's brothers are spies. This again establishes continuity with the preceding discourse.

5. *Subject of embedded clause fronting.* Exod 9:30 *w°th w°bdyk yd°ty ky ṭrm tyr°wn mpny yhwh °lhym* 'you and your servants, I know that you do not yet fear the Lord God'. The fronting of the phrase *w°th °bdyk* 'and as for you and your servants' is intended to contrast Pharaoh (and his servants), who do not acknowledge the Lord, with the earth in v. 29, which is the Lord's.

6. *Object of preposition fronting.* Exod 32:1 *ky-zh | mšh . . . l° yd°nw mh-hyh lw* 'this Moses . . . we do not know what happened to him'. Again, the fronting of 'Moses' effects contrast with Aaron, mentioned earlier in the verse. The people say in effect, 'Aaron, do something, because this Moses is nowhere to be found'. The topicalization of clause constituents can even displace conjunctive and subordinating particles which would normally be found in clause initial position.

7. *Waw displacement.* Ps 77:2 *qwly °l-°lhym w°ṣ°qh // qwly °l-°lhym wh°zyn °ly* 'my voice to God I cry out // my voice to God, and may he give ear to me'. The conjunctive *waw* on *°ṣ°qh* is postpositive. I would suggest that postposition of the conjunction is the explanation as well of Exod 15:2 *zh °ly w°nwhw // °lhy °by w°rmmnhw* 'and I shall praise him who is my God, and I shall exalt him who is my father's God'. In other words, we are to read the first stichos not as two coordinate clauses, 'this is my God and I will exalt him', but as one clause with topicalization of 'this my God' and with suffixed pronoun reprise on the verb.

8. *Ky displacement.* Gen 18:20–21 *z°qt sdm w°mrh ky-rbh wḥṭ°tm ky kbdh m°d: °rdh-n°* 'the cry against Sodom and Gomorrah because it is great, and their sin because it is so very grievous, I will descend . . . '. This verse has been taken as a primary case in support of an emphatic *ky*—in fact a notion without any linguistic support.[15] The construction is one of topicalization of the phrase *cry against Sodom and Gomorrah* parallel to the topicalization of *their sin*, resulting in two cases of displaced and postposed particle *ky*. There is certainly some kind of emphasis going on here, but it is not due to a lexicalized emphatic *ky*. The marked order consisting of the topicalization of the two phrases *cry of Sodom and Gomorrah* and *their sin* is where the emphasis lies.

9. *Mh/my displacement.* Gen 23:15 *°rṣ °rb° m°h šql-ksp byny wbynk mh-hw°* 'a land of four hundred silver shekels between me and you, what is it?' The topic of debate between Ephron and Abraham is the property worth four hundred shekels. So it is topicalized, resulting in postposing of the interrogative particle. For an example of postposing of *my* see Prov 24:22.

10. *H-/hl° displacement.* Gen 34:23 *mqnhm wqnynm wkl-bhmtm hlw° lnw hm* 'their livestock and their property and all their animals, will they not become ours?' The topicalization of 'livestock and property' with pronoun reprise (*hm*) perhaps reflects what is the most powerful argument Hamor and Shechem can make to convince their townspeople to agree to the circumcision.

15. See B. Bandstra, *The Syntax of Particle ky in Biblical Hebrew and Ugaritic* (Ph.D. diss., Yale University, 1982).

11. *Hnh displacement.* Gen 42:22 *wgm-dmw hnh ndrš* 'and his blood, now it is
    avenged'.
12. *Trm displacement.* Gen 2:5 *wkl śyḥ hśdh ṭrm yhyh bᵓrṣ wkl-ᶜśb hśdh ṭrm yṣmḥ*
    'every shrub of the field, before it was on the earth, and every grass of the field,
    before it sprouted . . .'.

Independent Pronoun Topicalization

"Redundant" Pronoun.   The independent personal pronoun can be used
redundantly with a finite verb, which is inflectionally already marked for
subject. The pronoun can be found in contexts where the referent is unambiguous, such as in Gen 3:15 *hwᵓ yšwpk rᵓš wᵓth tšwpnw ᶜqb* 'he will strike
you on the head, but you will strike him on the heel'. The pronouns are used
to effect contrast even while the same verbal root is used in the two clauses.
The pronoun can be used redundantly with the imperative, Num 1:50 *wᵓth
hpqd ᵓt-hlwym* 'but you, appoint the Levites'. Again, the pronoun is used to
effect contrast, in this case between the tribe of Levi and Moses, the referent
of *ᵓth.* The independent personal pronoun (presumably nominative in case)
can be used "pleonastically" to topicalize a clause constituent which may in
fact be a constituent other than the grammatical subject. The independent
pronoun can be used to so topicalize a direct object, as in Gen 24:27 *ᵓnky
bdrk nḥny yhwh byt ᵓḥy ᵓdny* 'I, on the way led-me the Lord to the house of
my lord's brothers'. This leads to what appears at first to be a patently un-
grammatical situation, where a presumably nominative subject pronoun has
cataphoric reference to an accusative verbal object. Grammarians have
termed this phenomenon *casus pendens* (Joüon § 156a / p. 477). But what we
witness is not a grammatical slip so much as a discourse device whereby the
writer uses a nominative element to topicalize a clause component, perhaps
because the nominative subject rather than an oblique noun phrase would be
the more likely element to be found in topic/given position.

Reprise Pronoun.   Reprise is effected when a noun phrase which is
found at the beginning of the clause is later resumed at its normal place in the
clause by the independent or suffixed pronoun. This type of construction has
been called the copular use of the pronoun.[16] But this is not the correct construction to put on it. In so reading it one would miss the topicalization device which in fact is being employed. The use of the independent pronoun
following the noun phrase which is its referent has the effect of isolating the
noun phrase by placing it in clause initial position. The device has the effect
on the level of thematic structure of establishing the theme of the clause.

Subject reprise.   Gen 34:21 *hᵓnšym hᵓlh šlmym hm ᵓtnw* 'these men,
friendly they are to us'. It is interesting to note in this and like cases how the

---

16. See Muraoka, *Emphasis in Biblical Hebrew*, chap. 4.

Muraoka-Andersen classification of nominal clauses is upheld. Clauses with an indefinite predicate (*šlmym* in this case) should realize the order P–S, and this is in fact what we have. The noun phrase *hᵓnšym hᵓlh* is the subject which is topicalized and resumed at its expected place by the personal pronoun *hm*. The opposite S–P order in a nominal clause with pronoun reprise is found, for example, in Gen 9:18 *whm hwᵓ ᵓby knᶜn* 'and Ham, he is the father of Canaan'.

Object reprise. Lev 2:11 *ky kl-śᵓr wkl-dbš lᵓ-tqtyrw mmnw ᵓšh lyhwh* 'for, any yeast or any honey, you must not any of it offer by fire to the LORD'. Gen 2:17 *wmᶜṣ hdᶜt twb wrᶜ lᵓ tᵓkl mmnw* 'but from the tree of the knowledge of good and evil, you must not eat from it'. In both cases the topicalized phrase is resumed by the pronoun suffix on *mn*. And in both cases, in addition to topicalized nonsubject noun phrases, the topicalization picks up previously mentioned discourse elements and reintroduces them into the narrative, namely, yeast and the tree of the knowledge of good and evil respectively. Perhaps, then, such topicalization can function on the level of information structure to maintain or reestablish discourse continuity.

CONCLUSION

Word order in Biblical Hebrew narrative must first be defined in terms of an unmarked constituent order, namely V–S–O and V–O. Presence and absence of an explicit noun phrase subject primarily reflect actor discontinuity and continuity respectively. Nonsubject or nonobject constituents in immediate postverbal position have marked informational status. In effect the nonsubject constituent which is put in what is normally the subject position becomes the topic of the clause.

What has been perceived by students of the text and termed *emphasis* can now be given linguistic definition. Emphasis is a function of non-V–(S)–O word order and can better be termed *topicalization*. Topicalization takes what is normally nonsalient information, fronts that constituent, and places it in a position of informational prominence.

Word order is thus seen to be one of the most significant syntactic factors which are responsible for maintaining continuity between clauses as well as indicating thematic breaks between paragraphs. The function of word order cannot be understood by examining clauses in isolation from discourse. Rather, an examination of discourse reveals the function of word order.

[December, 1986]

Harold P. Scanlin

The Study of Semantics in General Linguistics

"Colorless green ideas sleep furiously." This sentence has been devised to remind linguists that a sentence can be completely "grammatical" but nevertheless be total nonsense.[1] For many years, linguists generally focused on the traditional aspects of phonetics, morphology, and syntax, believing that semantics was not a subject that could be described or analyzed linguistically.

There was, of course, a vague recognition among linguists that semantics (or "meaning") is ultimately what linguistics is all about. Earlier agendas of linguistics understandably focused on phonetics, etc. Once the groundwork was established, the focus shifted to higher levels. Any communication event must involve meaning, whether partial or complete, whether the communication of "authorial intent" is successful or unsuccessful. Yet semantics as a subdiscipline of linguistics was largely a neglected area of study until relatively recently.

This neglect, one could even say avoidance, was grounded in the nature of linguistic inquiry of earlier generations.[2] Among some linguists (especially Neogrammarians) there was a residue of a type of Platonic thinking that identified words and things. A word, in and of itself, referred to an "ideal" or object in the spectrum of reality.

In the behaviorist school (exemplified by L. Bloomfield), the linguistic event was the focus of inquiry, never considering semantics as a component of this approach except as it may relate to semantic change. Thus, Bloomfield's famous treatment devotes only a few pages to semantics, concentrating entirely in this chapter on a diachronic description of semantic change.[3]

1. N. Chomsky, *Syntactic Structures* (Janua Linguarum Series Minor 4; The Hague; Mouton, 1957) 15.
2. W. L. Chafe, *Meaning and the Structure of Language* (Chicago: University of Chicago Press, 1970) 73.
3. L. Bloomfield, *Language* (New York: Holt, Rinehart & Winston, 1933) chap. 24; cf. chap. 9.

Another popular linguistic theory, known as the Sapir–Whorf hypothesis, also tended to distract from a rigorous consideration of semantics. This hypothesis also influenced some theological thinking. "Sapir–Whorf" is defined by its principal advocate as follows: "We see and hear and otherwise experience very largely as we do because the language habits of our community predispose certain choices of interpretation."[4]

But the notion that differences in worldview are somehow imposed by the "linguistic systems in our minds" has largely been discredited both by the failure to support this idea with actual language evidence and the regrettable consequences of assuming that intellectual superiority is achieved by an ethnocentric language system.

It was sometimes argued that Jewish philosophical thinking was hampered by the limitations of Hebrew as a language for speculative thought. But Arabic, and ultimately Hebrew, philosophy flourished, adapting syntax and vocabulary to meet their needs. J. Barr's well-known criticism of the assumed contrast between Greek speculative and Hebrew concrete-image thought has countered, for example, the conclusions of T. Boman in his *Hebrew Thought Compared with Greek.*[5]

THE MEANING OF MEANING

Humpty Dumpty, in commenting on the relative merits of birthdays and unbirthdays, laments to Alice that there's

> " . . . only *one* [day] for birthday presents, you know. There's glory for you!"
>
> "I don't know what you mean by 'glory,'" Alice said.
>
> Humpty Dumpty smiled contemptuously. "Of course you don't—till I tell you. I meant 'there's a nice knock-down argument for you!'"
>
> "But 'glory' doesn't mean 'a nice knock-down argument,'" Alice objected.
>
> "When *I* use a word," Humpty Dumpty said in rather a scornful tone, "it means just what I choose it to mean—neither more nor less."
>
> "The question is," said Alice, "whether you *can* make words mean different things."
>
> "The question is," said Humpty Dumpty, "which is to be master—that's all."[6]

This famous little encounter points up two important issues in semantics—meaning involves communication; if communication does not take

---

4. B. L. Whorf, "The Relation of Habitual Thought and Behavior to Language," in *Language, Thought, and Reality: Selected Writings of Benjamin Lee Whorf* (ed. J. B. Carroll; Cambridge: MIT Press, 1956) 134, quoting E. Sapir without attribution.

5. J. Barr, *The Semantics of Biblical Language* (Oxford: Oxford University Press, 1961).

6. L. Carroll, *Alice Through the Looking Glass and What Alice Found There* (1871), chap. 6.

place, does meaning really matter? And, who decides what a word really means? Does an English dictionary such as Webster's *Third International* or the *Oxford English Dictionary (OED)* prescribe meanings of words, or does it merely report on the consensus view of English speakers? In fact, the *OED* gained its well-deserved reputation largely because it provides a diachronic catalog of contextual quotations.

Alice, and the linguist, should ask not only, "What do words mean?" but, "How do words mean?" The fundamental question, then, is, "What is meaning?"

Although it may be acknowledged that meaning is a set of relations for which a verbal symbol is a sign, the notion that this relationship is to some entity in the practical world still persists. The meaning of verbal symbols has traditionally been regarded as some kind of attribute or inherent property belonging to words. In large measure this opinion may be due to such expressions as "the word has this meaning . . . " or "this word's meaning is. . . . " But meaning is not a possession; it is a set of relations for which a verbal symbol is a sign.

Although many people recognize that meaning is essentially a relation, they tend to view it as a relation to some entity in the practical world. The meaning of the word *chair* is thus considered to be the relation of the symbol to the thing called "chair," and the meaning of *house* is the relation of the word to some particular dwelling which can be referred to by this symbol. In reality, however, the referent of a verbal symbol is not an object in the practical world; rather, it is a concept or a set of concepts which people may have about objects, events, abstracts, and relations.[7]

When, however, one speaks of concepts as the true referents of words, people generally conclude that one is not speaking about "mental images." Rather, the concepts the semanticist talks about are sets of features defined by contrasts. In fact, meaning exists only where systematic sets of contrasts exist. The meaning of *father*, in its most common sense, depends on certain contrasts with the meanings of other words within the same domain of kinship.[8]

The meaning of *father* contrasts with that of *mother* in terms of sex.

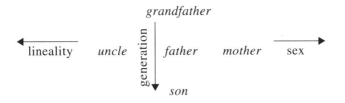

7. E. A. Nida, *Exploring Semantic Structures* (Munich: Fink, 1975) 14.
8. Ibid., 14–15.

The meaning of a word consists of a set or bundle of distinctive features that makes possible reference; thus, meaning makes reference possible. It is from observing the range of reference of a symbol that we normally determine its meaning. But before pursuing the specifics of "how words mean," we should further clarify a few methodological issues.

D. Crystal said, "Semantics, for the linguist, must be primarily concerned with problems of how the semantic system hypothesized for a language is organized, and what kind of model might most usefully be constructed in order to facilitate analysis."[9] This raises the crucial question of the existence of linguistic universals. Linguistic universals are described as "formal" and "substantive." The term *substantive universals* is not necessarily used by linguists to mean that all languages have a category X, but that there exists a universal set of semantic features of which every language has a subset.[10] But this definition may be too broad unless it can be demonstrated that natural languages do share the same categories.

The analysis of certain referents has been used to explore the possibility of semantic universals. The classic study of Berlin and Kay, *Basic Color Terms*,[11] could examine a semantic domain of color terms for which the "referents" would be some definable wavelength in the light spectrum. If all languages followed some similar pattern, it would suggest that at least in this domain language universals exist. Based on an examination of color terms in almost a hundred languages, Berlin and Kay hypothesized that there are eleven basic color categories which are ordered as follows: if a language contains only two color terms, they are "black" and "white"; if it has three, the additional term will be "red." The next level language will have "green" and/or "yellow," in addition to black, white, and red. As the number of terms increase in a given language, the same relationship holds.

But if Berlin and Kay are essentially correct, in which sense does this demonstrate semantic universals? Certainly not in the sense that all languages use a specific color term for a definable wavelength spectrum. The contrary is true. The range of colors referred to as "red" in English does not correspond to Hebrew *ʾādōm*, which included colors that we would call "brown."

Universality, to Berlin and Kay, would be the categorizing and ordering of color distinctions in (almost all) languages. We must, therefore, be more precise in saying what we mean by "semantic universals." Chomsky distinguishes between "formal" and "substantive" universals.[12] *Formal universals*

9. D. Crystal, *Linguistics* (Harmondsworth: Penguin, 1971) 234.

10. G. Leech, *Semantics* (Harmondsworth: Penguin, 1974) 233.

11. B. Berlin and P. Kay, *Basic Color Terms: Their Universality and Evolution* (Berkeley and Los Angeles: University of California Press, 1969).

12. N. Chomsky, *Aspects of the Theory of Syntax* (Cambridge: MIT Press, 1965) 27–30.

are general characteristics or rules of language construction (grammar) required in order for them to be able to operate. On the other hand, *substantive universals* are constructs, identifiable by linguistic theory, that are capable of general application, enabling cross-language generalizations. It should be remembered that all categories need not be, and in fact are not, present in every language.

The notion of formal universals, the base components of linguistic universals, has been especially influential in the development of recent semantic thought. W. Chafe, in his groundbreaking *Meaning and the Structure of Language*, analyzes the relationship of syntax and meaning in a structural environment.[13] For example, noun–noun relationships may be described in terms of patient–agent, experiencer, beneficiary, instrument, etc. All of these relationships, which are, of course, syntactic, have obvious relationships to semantics. Chafe goes on to discuss the relationships of other language structures to semantics/meaning. Inflection, new and old information, and post-semantic processes are other fruitful structural relationships that bear meaning.

C. Fillmore introduces the notion of "case" grammar.[14] (He is not referring to "case" in noun inflection, but to judgment universals—who did what to whom with what consequences?)

Thus, the notion of semantic universals is not a simplistic or primitive notion of the relationship of words to ideas or objects, but the fundamental basis for the communication event.

Let us now look at several proposals for describing the ways in which words mean. According to Nida, languages have three types of variability in the relation of form to meaning, namely: referential, grammatical, and emotive meanings.[15] Referent(ial) meaning is the entity (object, state of affairs, etc.) in the external world to which a linguistic expression refers, e.g., *table* referent ⌗. But this "referent" is communicated only when other factors are operative. Many words, especially those whose referent is a discrete entity in the physical world, have a generally recognized referent, when otherwise unmarked. Thus, the referent of *chair* will generally be understood as ♗. But if one says, "In the absence of the president, the vice-president took the chair," it would not be interpreted as an act of theft, but of parliamentary procedure. Likewise, "The murderer got the chair" would not be misunderstood as a gift of furniture to a convicted criminal.

---

13. Chafe, *Meaning and the Structure of Language.*
14. C. J. Fillmore, "The Case for Case," in *Universals in Linguistic Theory* (ed. E. Bach and R. Harms; New York: Holt, Rinehart & Winston, 1968) 1–88.
15. Nida, *Exploring Semantic Structures*, 20.

Table 1 outlines the seven types of meaning as analyzed by Leech. Other analyses are added: to the left for componential analysis; and to the right for referential semantics.[16]

Important differences exist between referential, grammatical, and emotive meanings; but referential meanings are undoubtedly the most arbitrary and conventional of the three. Except for a few onomatopoeic expressions (and even these are largely arbitrary and differ greatly from one language to another), there is simply no logical relation between the sounds employed and the referent that a particular series of sounds designates. Grammatical meaning, on the other hand, is more closely related to experience. For example, the grammatical meanings of actor–action constructions closely parallel the participation of people in events. The ways in which adjectives qualify the meanings of nouns also have close parallels to the ways in which people perceive differences in entities. Emotive meanings are even more closely related to experience; in fact, they depend primarily on the act of communication, and not on language as a structure. Thus, they are much more closely related to performance and much less associated with competence—though the expectations of appropriateness are certainly a part of competence.[17]

THE SEMANTIC RELATIONS BETWEEN
RELATED SETS OF MEANINGS

Any description of the semantic relations between related sets of meanings must take into consideration two quite different types of relations: (1) those which exist between related meanings of different lexical units (morphemes, words, and idioms), and (2) those which exist between related meanings of the same lexical units. In general, the former are much closer together in semantic space (that is, they are more alike) than the latter. For example, the related meanings of *chair, stool, bench,* and *sofa* are more alike than are the diverse meanings of *chair* in such contexts as 'he sat in the chair', 'the chair of philosophy' (a post in a university), and 'to chair a meeting'; or of *stool* in such meanings as 'a piece of furniture', 'a specimen of fecal matter', 'a cluster of shoots or stems springing up from a single root', and 'the sill of a window'.

To a certain extent, this statement about degrees of semantic difference reflects the principles we employ in setting up different meanings of single lexical units. These meanings of single lexical units are defined on the basis of their belonging to different semantic domains, while the related meanings

16. Leech, *Semantics*, 26.
17. Nida, *Exploring Semantic Structures*, 20.

Table 1. Types of Meaning

Compo-nential:	Leech: SEVEN TYPES OF MEANING			Referential:
Denote	1. CONCEPTUAL MEANING or *Sense*		Logical, cognitive, or denotative content.	referential
Connote	ASSOCIATIVE MEANING	2. CONNOTATIVE MEANING	What is communicated by virtue of what language refers to.	paradigmatic
		3. STYLISTIC MEANING	What is communicated of the social circumstances of language use.	
		4. AFFECTIVE MEANING	What is communicated of the feelings and attitudes of the speaker/writer.	
		5. REFLECTED MEANING	What is communicated through association with another sense of the same expression.	syntagmatic
		6. COLLOCATIVE MEANING	What is communicated through association with words which tend to occur in the environment of another word.	
	7. THEMATIC MEANING		What is communicated by the way in which the message is organized in terms of order and emphasis.	

Source: Geoffrey Leech, *Semantics* (Harmondsworth: Penguin, 1974), p. 26.

of different lexical units are combined on the basis of their belonging to the same semantic domain. In addition, there is a structural and communicational basis for this significant difference. If the different meanings of the same lexical units were not relatively dissimilar, communication would be extremely difficult, since the identity of form and the proximity of meaning would cause numerous ambiguities and obscurities. But since the different meanings of the same forms are relatively dissimilar, an identity of form can be tolerated in the communication system. In most contexts it is quite clear which of the diverse meanings is intended.

LOGICAL CLASSIFICATION OF SEMANTIC CHANGE

Semantic change is the area of semantic study that has traditionally been of primary interest to biblical scholars, especially in the study of Hebrew.[18] This is probably true because of the influence of the Neogrammarians as well as the problems imposed on semantic analysis because we are dealing with a fixed corpus of an ancient language with little synchronic evidence outside the corpus and no native-speaker informants.

The failure to recognize the difference between "unmarked" and "marked" meaning has also led to a reliance on semantic change as a means of discovering "meaning." Unmarked meaning, which is approximately equivalent to "general meaning," is the meaning that would generally be applied by a receptor in a minimum context, that is, where there is little or no help to determine the meaning. Thus, the unmarked meaning of *dog* is '*Canis familiaris*' and of *turkey*, a bird in the family of fowl. Choice may be determined by a host of factors which may or may not be consciously perceived (cf. the relationship of meaning to semiotics as well). Unmarked meaning is a matter of frequency, not "root" or "basic" meaning. Marked meaning is marked by morphosyntax, collocation ("fixed phrases"), context, and semiotics.

A SEMANTIC DOMAIN APPROACH TO HEBREW LEXICOGRAPHY

The scientific study of Hebrew grammar has benefited greatly in recent years from the work of linguists. Advances have been made in the fields of phonology, morphology, and morphosyntax, with a great deal of published material available. Yet in the area of semantics, and especially lexicography, the advances have been much more modest. This is due in part to the limitations in Biblical Hebrew data mentioned above. These factors are especially crucial in the area of semantics. The proper assimilation of data from the expanding evidence of cognate languages continues to be the subject of methodological debate.

A Colloquium on Semitic Lexicography was convened in Florence, Italy, in 1972 to assess the state of lexicographical research in the major ancient Semitic languages. In that volume, J. Barr summed up the situation in Hebrew from his perspective. His evaluation of the current state of Hebrew lexicography is worth quoting in full:

---

18. Bloomfield's classification system (*Language*, chap. 24) is still useful.

The average dictionary of Hebrew, or of most languages, offers a brief verbal indication in the language in which the dictionary is written: thus an English-language dictionary of Hebrew will register the Hebrew word *dabar* and set against it the legend "word, matter, thing", or something of the sort. It is probably the popular impression of the dictionary that in furnishing this brief indication the lexicographer is "telling us the meaning". This however is hardly so. These simple equivalents can hardly be dignified with the term "meanings"; they are rather *glosses*, rough indications, sufficient to furnish an approximate impression of what word it is and how it functions. They are useful in a number of ways: in a learning situation, they enable the learner to assimilate the new words more easily; in cases of homonymy and other ambiguities, they provide convenient labels, so that we refer to *gil* "rejoice" in contrast to *gil* "age"; conversely, with a polysemous word, they may (as in the case of *dabar* just cited) indicate a rough classification of distinguishable senses or functions. But they are not themselves meanings nor do they tell us the meanings; the meanings reside in the actual Hebrew usage, and for real semantic analysis the glosses have no greater value than that of indicators or labels for a meaning which resides in the Hebrew itself and which depends on the prior experience of the scholar (or, in ancient times, of the actual speaker of Hebrew).[19]

The traditional criteria for arraying student Hebrew lexicons such as BDB and KB and classifying meanings are usually (1) etymology, (2) diachronic analysis, (3) a structural semantic analysis usually proceeding from a perceived "direct" or "basic" sense to indirect or derivative meanings even when the latter are statistically dominant, (4) identification of syntagmatic relations, and (5) occasionally encyclopedic information. Useful as this information may be, this type of presentation has frequently been misleading, especially to the user at the student or popular level. It is also likely that traditional approaches to lexicography have encouraged the etymological fallacy as well as a variety of other semantic errors in Hebrew exegesis.[20]

In an effort to overcome the inherent difficulties in traditional approaches to lexicography, the insights of modern semantic analysis have been called upon by the United Bible Societies to develop a new kind of dictionary of the Greek New Testament.[21] In a sense it is an experimental, pioneering work, since no other dictionary of its type has ever been published. We believe that it will be useful to Hebrew scholarship to consider the application of this new approach to Hebrew lexicography. In fact, preliminary work is already under way. We look to readers for comments and criticisms.

19. J. Barr, "Hebrew Lexicography," in *Studies on Semitic Lexicography* (ed. P. Fronzaroli; Quaderni di Semitistica 2; Florence: University of Florence, 1973) 119–20.
20. D. Carson has a chapter on semantic fallacies in *Exegetical Fallacies* (Grand Rapids: Baker, 1984), with examples drawn from Greek. His general classification is useful.
21. J. P. Louw and E. A. Nida, *Greek-English Lexicon of the New Testament Based on Semantic Domains* (2 vols.; New York: United Bible Societies, 1988).

A semantic-domains dictionary is based on several important linguistic principles which are crucial to its development. First, in the words of a famous cliché, "Words don't have meanings; meanings have words." Since one can assign meaning to the vast majority of words, it has been assumed that meaning must be an inherent feature of a word form. And since words usually have more than one meaning for a particular word form, it was also assumed that one word form must have one basic meaning and that the multiple meanings are merely variations of that one central idea. This assumption was considered axiomatic for many centuries. Whenever two or more meanings of the same word form seemed to be so far apart that no linkage could be determined, it was generally explained as a matter of two distinct words having incidentally the same form. Thus dictionaries list words such as *hail* meaning 'pellets of ice' or 'to salute' as hail[1] and hail[2], that is, as homonyms.

Though F. de Saussure had radically changed the direction of linguistics at the beginning of the twentieth century by arguing for the arbitrary relationship between words and meanings, the etymological approach still maintained its supremacy in many language studies. It was only after another radical change in linguistic approach brought about by N. Chomsky in the 1950s that semantics emerged in the 1960s as a scientific discipline. At present one may confidently say that linguists generally no longer uphold the etymological approach for dealing with the relationship between words and meanings or, for that matter, any aspect of the field of lexicography.

It is important to distinguish between meaning and translational equivalents, or "glosses." The problem alluded to by Barr suggests another truism: "The last place to look for the meaning of a word is in the dictionary." By this I mean, first, that the meaning of a semantic unit (generally a word) is composed of referential meaning and associative meaning. The former can only be determined by knowing the relation of one lexeme to others in the same semantic domain. The latter is determined by the context—grammatical at the level of syntax and discourse, and emotional (sometimes described as "connotative meaning"). Second, when a lexicon offers glosses, receptor language equivalents that apply to a specific context, the user can mistakenly assume that the gloss is the meaning of the word.

Therefore, definitions should be given in terms of componential features, rather than glosses. The componential analysis of meaning is a useful means for determining meaning and not merely usage. For example, Greek *dōron* "means" 'gift', yet it is used frequently to describe a 'sacrifice'.

The Greek word *pneuma* is glossed 'spirit', but its meaning appears in four different semantic domains: physical events, 'wind'; physiological events, 'breath'; features of personality, 'spirit' (of a person); supernatural beings, 'evil spirit', 'Holy Spirit'. The final step is the development of semantic domains.

A semantic domain consists essentially of a group of meanings (by no means restricted to those reflected in single words) which share certain semantic components.[22] The organization is emic, rather than etic. For example, it is structured according to the world view of the particular language, rather than a modern world view. This would place Greek *pyr* 'fire' in the domain of "natural substances," rather than events. The componential analysis of referential meaning enables each semantic unit to find its proper domain. While it may not be possible to isolate every possible component, the necessary and sufficient features that distinguish the meaning of any one form from every other can be determined in most cases. Where evidence may be insufficient, the options and degree of probability can be recorded. In the case of Biblical Hebrew, these cases are likely to be more frequent than in New Testament Greek, due to the nature of the corpus and the limited extra-biblical evidence.

BASIC ANNOTATED BIBLIOGRAPHY ON SEMANTICS

Barr, James. *The Semantics of Biblical Language*. London: Oxford University Press, 1961. [The well-known book that introduced biblical scholars to the importance of a sound linguistic approach to semantics.]

Bloomfield, Leonard. *Language*. New York: Henry Holt, 1933. [Bloomfield's only treatment of semantics dealt with the diachronic mechanics of semantic change, pp. 425–43.]

Chafe, Wallace L. *Meaning and the Structure of Language*. Chicago: University of Chicago Press, 1970. [Chafe (structural) and Katz (generative), perhaps more than any others, established semantics as a legitimate topic in modern linguistics.]

Cruse, D. A. *Lexical Semantics*. Cambridge Textbooks in Linguistics. Cambridge: Cambridge University Press, 1986.

Eco, Umberto. *A Theory of Semiotics*. Bloomington: Indiana University Press, 1976. [Eco's scholarly reputation was established long before *The Name of the Rose*.]

Katz, Jerrold. *Semantic Theory*. New York: Harper & Row, 1972.

Kempson, R. M. *Semantic Theory*. Cambridge Textbooks in Linguistics. Cambridge: Cambridge University Press, 1977.

Lakoff, George. *Women, Fire, and Dangerous Things*. Chicago: University of Chicago Press, 1987. [A psycholinguistic perspective on cognition.]

22. A discussion of the process of establishing the domains employed in the United Bible Societies' New Testament lexicon may be found in J. P. Louw, "A Semantic Domain Approach to Lexicography," in *Lexicography and Translation* (ed. J. P. Louw; Cape Town: Bible Society of South Africa, 1985) 157–97.

Leech, Geoffrey. *Semantics*. Harmondsworth: Penguin, 1974. [A useful general introduction to the subject.]

Lehrer, Adrienne. *Semantic Fields and Lexical Structure*. Amsterdam: North-Holland, 1974.

Lyons, John. *Semantics*. 2 vols. Cambridge: Cambridge University Press, 1977. [Lyons also has useful introductory chapters (9 and 10) in his *Introduction to Theoretical Linguistics* (Cambridge: Cambridge University Press, 1968).]

Nida, Eugene A. *Exploring Semantic Structures*. Munich: Fink, 1975. [Includes original material and eight essays previously published; provides the theoretical framework for componential analysis and semantic-domain approach to lexicography.]

Ogden, C. K., and I. A. Richards. *The Meaning of Meaning*. 8th edition. New York: Harcourt, Brace & World, 1946. [An influential pioneering study.]

Steinberg, Danny D., and Leon A. Jakobovits, eds. *Semantics*. Cambridge: Cambridge University Press, 1971. [Seminal essays in philosophical, linguistic, and psychological aspects of semantics.]

Ullmann, Stephen. *The Principles of Semantics*. 2d edition. New York: Philosophical Library, 1957. [A presentation of the role of semantics in linguistic study before the changed outlook emerging in the late 1960s.]

Weinreich, Uriel. *On Semantics*. Philadelphia: University of Pennsylvania Press, 1980. [Collected essays of an innovative semanticist; includes his important "Explorations in Semantic Theory," first published in 1966.]

[June, 1989]

James Barr

Hebrew Lexicography:
Informal Thoughts

If one is to talk about the state of Hebrew lexicography as it stands today, the first obligation is to express admiration for the work of earlier scholars in this field. When I was editor of the Oxford Hebrew Lexicon, a project that was never completed, I remember the growing sense of admiration in my soul as I looked back on Baumgartner; on Buhl; on Brown, Driver and Briggs; and of course on Gesenius. We in the modern world may set out to surpass them, but we shall be fortunate in the end if we succeed in equaling them. In an American overview of Hebrew linguistics, moreover, one cannot omit calling attention to the very significant achievement of American scholars within this distinguished tradition: we think of C. A. Briggs, still more of Francis Brown, who did the largest proportion of the articles in BDB, and earlier of Moses Stuart, of Josiah W. Gibbs, and of Edward Robinson.[1] They had no computers or word processors and they wrote out the lengthy texts of their volumes by hand; in the case of BDB two of the editors were on one side of the Atlantic and the third on the other; but the post was fast and efficient. They commanded the mass of complicated and minute detail with commendable accuracy.

This reference to the past is more than just a debt of admiration: it has a practical side to it. Many of the main scholarly dictionaries of Hebrew have been in effect revisions of existing dictionaries. The Oxford Hebrew Lexicon (henceforth OHL) was at one stage planned to be a revision of BDB; but at the time when I was editor the policy was to make a completely new dictionary from the ground up, built upon the texts themselves and not upon the

1. The important influence of Gibbs upon E. B. Pusey in Oxford has been interestingly traced by A. Livesley in his survey of Pusey's Hebrew scholarship, in *Pusey Rediscovered* (ed. P. Butler; London: SPCK, 1983) 71–118; on Pusey more generally see also H. C. G. Matthew, "Edward Bouverie Pusey: From Scholar to Tractarian," *JTS* 32 (1981) 101–24.

analysis inherited from previous lexicographers. Academically, I think that this was the right decision; but, practically speaking, it was also one major reason why the project did not come to completion: starting afresh from the raw material meant that the writing of entries on most words was taking too long. Particularly is this true of the semantic analysis: the lexicographer has to have perhaps two hundred cases of a word under the eye, with perhaps three or four departments of meaning, and has to think how these meanings are to be classified, arranged, ordered, and provided with English glosses. This is the most difficult of the tasks because it requires the most thought, and in this respect it is quite the opposite of the listing, compiling, annotating, and other more empirical work that also falls to the lexicographer. And in many words the semantic analysis must be rethought: the revision of older dictionary editions tended to perpetuate old and unsuitable classifications and descriptions of meanings.

PRELIMINARIES

Before we go farther, however, some words about the limits assumed for the purpose of this paper. I take it that we are thinking of a dictionary of classical Hebrew or Biblical and Biblical-type Hebrew: that is, basically it would register the Hebrew of the Bible, of inscriptions of biblical times, of Ben Sira of course, and of such Dead Sea Scrolls as are more or less in a Late Biblical stage of the language. In other words, it would be a dictionary that would not seek to include Mishnaic or Middle Hebrew. It would of course indicate appropriate connections with Mishnaic Hebrew, but would not be a dictionary of that stage of the language. Even so, the importance of providing adequate connections with Mishnaic Hebrew was always very much in my mind, and I think that biblical lexicography needs to be improved in this regard.[2] Nevertheless the corpus of text taken as the basis for the dictionary remains, for present purposes, the Bible plus Hebrew inscriptions, Ben Sira, and Qumran materials.

Second, I take it that we are talking about a dictionary in the form of a printed book. In other words, the time might come when all this sort of information would be stored electronically and retrieved through a computer. This would have certain enormous advantages. There would be almost infinite extensibility: new words, newly found occurrences, new cognates discovered, new ideas about meanings, possible emendations of the text, could

---

2. Baumgartner's procedure, of obtaining the help of E. Y. Kutscher and introducing such distinctions as that between Mhe.[1] and Mhe.[2], marked a slight step forward, but the total resultant effect on the dictionary remained slight and much more requires to be done in this direction.

all be added without disturbing what is already there. Future Hebrew lexicographers will probably have that sort of mechanism at their disposal. They may have the text itself on tape and have an electronic concordance system which will give automatic verification of numbers and occurrences and save the enormous time spent on checking and rechecking what has been prepared. Such electronically stored information could be made available also to other scholars who wanted to have access to it. The very idea opens up all sorts of new prospects. Nevertheless I assume that for present and practical purposes we are talking about a basic dictionary for publication as a bound volume of so many pages.

Third, I assume that the center of our thinking concerns a full-sized academic dictionary, one of roughly the size or format of BDB or of Gesenius-Buhl, and one that would seek to provide guidance and information on roughly the same level. This is of practical significance, for there could be sense in aiming at a smaller work, say half the size of BDB, which would not offer the same completeness, would therefore as a matter of policy omit certain areas or functions, and would thereby be able to be produced more quickly and with less complication. One might, for instance, omit such elements as the listing of forms actually found (inflected, suffixed, variously spelled, etc.) except when they are specially notable; the cognate forms in other Semitic languages and, indeed, the entirety of the etymological and comparative material; and the listing of divergent views and interpretations. (Some of these points are mentioned again below.) Practically speaking, then, it could be that the next stage in Hebrew lexicography would be the production of a somewhat shorter and less comprehensive dictionary. Nevertheless for the discussion of the main problems I proceed from the assumption of a full-sized lexicon, probably one large volume of over a thousand pages.

PROPOSED WORDS AND MEANINGS

With this as preamble, I turn to some of the key questions that engaged us, and I state what the policy of the OHL was to have been; not that that policy is necessarily the right one or the only possible one, but it gives us a definition of the question to start with. One of the primary questions is this: Is the dictionary to include the registration of all the many proposals about identification of words and their meanings that have come forth in the last half-century or so? Especially since work on Ugaritic became so influential has this posed an organizational problem for the Hebrew lexicographer. If one thinks of the later work of M. Dahood alone, for instance, in the Psalms alone there are hundreds and even thousands of words that, according to his judgment, have to be reclassed as forms from a word other than that to which they have customarily been considered to belong;[3] and similarly with the work of G. R. Driver, much of which came to be represented in the New English Bible. Or take the many idiosyncratic identifications of words and meanings in Tur-Sinai's commentary on Job.[4] Faced with this accumulation of multiple and often contradictory philological solutions, our decision in OHL was to omit them all. In other words, the dictionary would furnish only the identification and the meaning which the editor of the dictionary considered to be the right one. If he could not make up his mind, then he might mention two or more; but none would be listed simply because they had been made, even if by distinguished people. In other words, the dictionary would turn its back upon the idea of acting as a list or providing a registration of modern philological proposals. This is not to say that such proposals should be ignored or forgotten, but only that the dictionary is not the place for them to be registered. The number of them is now very large and may well increase even faster in the future; the best way to publish them will be in some sort of rolling list with supplements added every two or three years, or of course they could be stored electronically. But within a printed dictionary of conventional type their presence and their number can, in the present stage of scholarly opinion, only be confusing, and will in any case cause the work to go rapidly out of date.

So we decided to take the bull by the horns and say what we thought to be the right identification and meaning, and leave it at that. But for this to work one has to provide another desideratum: the lexicographer has to be a central scholar with an understanding of, and an appreciation for, the main currents of opinion within biblical scholarship. Otherwise the strong-minded policy which I have outlined will produce a lot of idiosyncratic decisions, which will leave many users at a loss to understand the grounds upon which decisions were made.[5] In all matters involving works of reference we should be careful to avoid persons, however brilliant, who have bees in their bonnet, *idées fixes*, and the like.

COMPARATIVE AND ETYMOLOGICAL MATERIAL

A second difficult question to decide is the place to be accorded to the comparative philological material. The traditional practice has been, of course, to

---

3. See E. R. Martinez, *Hebrew-Ugaritic Index to the Writings of Mitchell J. Dahood* (Rome: Pontifical Biblical Institute, 1967); and *Hebrew-Ugaritic Index II with an Eblaite Index to the Writings of Mitchell J. Dahood* (Subsidia Biblica 4; Rome: Pontifical Biblical Institute, 1981).
4. N. H. Tur-Sinai, *The Book of Job: A New Commentary* (Jerusalem: Kiryath Sepher, 1954).
5. This was a problem particularly with the Old Testament of the New English Bible; see J. Barr, "After Five Years: A Retrospect on Two Major Translations of the Bible," *Heythrop Journal* 15 (1974) 381–405.

put in a selection of this material early in most entries; usually it is the first section of the entry after the lemma itself and the basic English gloss. In the case of words adopted from outside Semitic, for instance from Egyptian, it has been customary to indicate here that it is a loanword and to give some explanation of it; and if it is of Semitic origin it has been customary to cite some relevant cognates along with their meanings in their respective languages (as, for instance, under *hlk* 'walk' BDB cites some Aramaic forms, the Akkadian *alāku*, and Arabic *halaka* with the sense 'perish').

About this material, modern trends of opinion tend to pull in opposite directions. On the one hand, the practice of making new identifications of Hebrew words and/or their meanings on the basis of cognates within Semitic has enormously increased in the last fifty years or so, as every scholar in the field is aware. The more central this is to Hebrew studies, the more essential it would seem to be that students and scholars, and dictionary users of all kinds, should be informed and trained in the known facts of these cognate relations. On the other hand, modern linguistic ideas have tended to set limits to the importance of etymology and to stress the distortion of semantic information that can follow from etymological explanation even when it is factually correct. A word has meaning only within its own language and its own period of usage. According to this view, the stress on cognate relationships customary within Hebrew studies may mean that the Hebrew dictionary is dominated by etymological relationships to an extent not to be found in other comparable lexical works. Thus, for instance, the impressive *Chicago Assyrian Dictionary*, in spite of its great length, avoids almost entirely the presentation of comparative philological information, considering that meanings should be determined from the Akkadian texts themselves and the Mesopotamian context. At the most, brief notes of a comparative nature are permitted, and these come at the end of the entry in order to avoid prejudicing judgments about the actual senses in Akkadian. And some go farther and say that etymology is interesting but the dictionary is not the place for it. Thus, the *Sabaic Dictionary* contains numerous words and meanings which are highly suggestive for etymological explanations in Hebrew, but no such connections are mentioned.[6]

Another possibility is that the comparative and etymological material should all be concentrated together in a separate work, as is commonly done with many languages (e.g., English). For Hebrew, however, this is perhaps not a practical possibility at the present time. Another possibility is that all the comparative material should be assembled in a comparative dictionary of all the Semitic languages, leaving the dictionary of Hebrew to deal with the

---

6. A. F. L. Beeston, M. A. Ghul, W. W. Müller, and J. Ryckmans, *Sabaic Dictionary (English-French-Arabic)* (Louvain: Peeters / Beirut: Librairie du Liban, 1982).

Hebrew itself alone. Moreover, if comparative material is to be included, there are questions about the extent to which it is to be quoted. Existing dictionaries may be faulty through either over-quotation or under-quotation. Sometimes there is quite extensive quotation of cognate relations that are in fact very obvious, as in a word like *ʾēm* 'mother', where the existence of forms in numerous languages and dialects really tells us nothing significant. In other places an entry may cite some examples and meanings that seem favorable, in the sense of coming close to what is taken to be the meaning of the Hebrew, but may in so doing conceal the fact that most Semitic languages either do not have the word or else have a cognate but only with a very different meaning.[7]

In the OHL we decided to continue including comparative philological material, as the tradition of dictionaries has done. We felt that in the present state of scholarship in Hebrew there was no alternative. We do not have the sort of knowledge of many terms in Biblical Hebrew that can stand on its own as a purely intra-Hebraic matter, to be taken in total indifference to other Semitic languages. We have to accept that, for us in our situation, our perception of Hebrew words and their meanings is linked with comparative-philological and historical-philological perceptions; and this fact is no modern innovation arising from the purely historical approach, but goes back into the Middle Ages and even earlier times and is thus built into the indigenous tradition of language meanings itself. But, to give a simple example: the identification of the separate verb *ʿnh* IV 'sing' (numbering of BDB), though very suitable for Hebrew and convincing when perceived there, is nevertheless almost entirely dependent on our awareness of the Arabic *ġannā* and other possible cognates. Left to itself and treated in separation from this information, the term would be naturally taken as a form from *ʿnh* 'answer', and that assumption would then also generate false etymological/semantic connections, for example, through the idea that the sense was 'respond' and hence 'sing responsively'. The existence of a separate entry for *ʿnh* IV in a dictionary would not be intelligible if no reference to the cognate were given.

On grounds of this kind, we thought that we must continue on the traditional path and provide comparative philological information within the dictionary. The presentation of it, however, ought to be done in a more systematic way. The reader should be able to rely on the dictionary to give some brief mention of each of the main branches of the Semitic languages, which would normally be represented by Akkadian, Arabic, Aramaic/Syriac, Ethiopic/South Arabian, Ugaritic and other Canaanite, and to try to give one clear example for each, while avoiding useless duplication and repetition,

---

7. On this see, in more detail, J. Barr, "Limitations of Etymology as a Lexicographic Instrument in Biblical Hebrew," *Transactions of the Philological Society* 1983: 41–65.

and also, where required, to give a negative statement, such as "absent from Akkadian" or "found in Arabic but not with relatable meaning"; for the absence of negative registration, commonly ignored in the existing dictionaries, creates a distortion of the comparative information and leads readers to expect a higher degree of etymological overlap between the languages than is justified by the facts of their vocabularies when taken as a whole. Through such a plan we thought that we would give a more balanced picture of the total Semitic material and avoid giving the impression that cognates in Semitic are always to be expected, which happens sometimes in the existing dictionaries, when they give too much cognate evidence where it is obvious anyway, but in case there is very little or none, they fail to make it clear that there in fact is little or none. Given the present state of Hebrew studies, it seems that a balanced reference to the comparative philological material will be more salutary, and more in tune with the mode in which most Hebrew scholarship is conducted, than would be the more radical policy of simply omitting all this material, which might just—among other things—open the gates to a lot of popular etymology, which we are in any case beginning to suffer more than before.

The investigation and verification of the comparative material is, moreover, a very time-consuming task. As is well known, many of the meanings for words that have been cited from the Arabic dictionaries, or quoted from modern discoveries such as Ugaritic, are very uncertain or are in some way secondary or marginal, in such a manner that they could not be taken as reliable evidence of a common Semitic anterior to Hebrew usage. For, it should be remembered, the correlation of comparative philological evidence is not a purely empirical matter; rather, it requires the perceptive projection of plausible semantic relationships and developments. And this brings us back to semantics, which forms the next major section of my paper.

SEMANTIC ANALYSIS

As I said, the semantic analysis of the older dictionaries seems often to be defective and needs to be rethought. If one takes a look at articles such as *lēb*, *lēbāb* in BDB it will quickly be seen what I mean. The categories used were those of Victorian psychology and religion: "conscience," "specific reference to moral character," etc. One cannot say that these are necessarily wrong and misleading, but they have to be reconsidered, perhaps reformulated. But what a task it is, with something like 850 cases in the Bible alone! One of the amusing things, incidentally, is that although these words are usually glossed as 'heart' and commonly so translated, they never seem to mean the physical organ 'heart' at all, and this is no doubt why BDB begin with glosses such as 'inner man', 'mind', 'will', before adding 'heart'.

The problem with the semantic analysis and description, as stated above, was that it proved to take a long time. It is not something that is simply evident, that can be established by making simple lists or counting statistics. Each word required something like a dissertation, or the amount of study that would have produced a dissertation. In most cases I found that one had to make a very thorough investigation, working through a mass of examples and considering the wider exegetical problems; and if one did this properly, it seemed that one needed a complete journal article of twenty or twenty-five pages to go over all this ground. But this would take perhaps a month to do, for just one word. Sometimes I did publish such an article: I did, for instance, with *bên* 'between' or with *migrāš*.[8] And this leads on to another of the fundamental points about dictionary writing: lexicographers commonly cannot explain their reasons; they cannot tell the user just why they have analyzed semantically in this way rather than in that, because discussion of semantic analysis commonly takes up too much space to be displayed on the pages of the lexicon. A simple example: under *hêkāl* one would certainly have one department of meaning as 'main room of temple' or the like, one would also have 'palace', one might also have something like '[God's] heavenly sanctuary'; and within these various possibilities one might list certain cases as clearly belonging to one or another, but one would not be likely to have space to explain on exactly what grounds each case was classified as one more than another.

Another aspect of semantic description is as follows: Should one seek to group words under semantic "fields"? The traditional dictionary concentrated mainly on explaining and describing the individual word: occasionally it would mention antonyms and the like, as in easy cases like *ṭm²* / *ṭhwr* or *qdš* / *ḥl*. But it can be argued that the real meaning of a word has to be expressed paradigmatically, that is, in terms of the difference that it makes to choose this word rather than some other word, in a related field, that might have been in the same place: for instance, what does it mean when the text says *bārā²* rather than *ᶜāśâ* or *geber* rather than *²îš* or *²ādām*? One way of dealing with this would be, at the end of each entry on an individual word, to add a note listing related or comparable words. We experimented with this, but it proved to be too complicated to carry out; and the chief reason was that each department of meaning in a word placed it in a somewhat different semantic field. If we take *bêt* 'house', it sometimes means 'family' and then it belongs with terms like *mišpāḥâ*; when it means 'temple' it belongs with *hykl*, *mqdš*, etc.; when it means 'inside' it should be conjoined with the antonym *ḥwṣ* 'outside', etc. We found it impracticable to diagram all these relations

---

8. "Some Notes on *ben* 'between' in Classical Hebrew," *JSS* 23 (1978) 1–22; and "*Migraš* in the Old Testament," *JSS* 29 (1984) 15–31.

within each department of every article. Another possibility is to use the "Roget's Thesaurus" method: at the end of the dictionary one would put sections with headings for various concepts, such as "nation" or "house," and list under these the words that are apparently relevant; or one could put "colors" and list under this the spectrum of all Hebrew color terms. The simplest method, however, and one that can easily be done by mechanical means, is to provide a reverse index: at the end of the dictionary, under the English words, you simply list all the Hebrew words that are glossed with each English term: thus under "hide" one would list the six or seven verbs 'to hide', under "lion" the five or so 'lion' terms. This is easy to do and the result is helpful in many ways; all it means is that the volume becomes larger and somewhat more expensive.

Another point that touches upon this and belongs rather to the philosophy of lexicography than to the practice of dictionary-making: the dictionary does not provide "definitions," although that term is often erroneously used, deriving perhaps from the way in which people in modern English consult a dictionary in order to find a "definition" of a term. In a case like ancient Hebrew the dictionary provides not definitions (for who could "define" what a *śār* or a *šaḥal* was, or the action indicated by the verb *kḥd*?), but glosses, that is, English words that sufficiently indicate the sort of area in which the Hebrew meaning must lie. The meaning itself, for the user of the dictionary, must remain within the Hebrew. One does not suppose that these glosses are perfect translations, or even the best renderings that can be produced; in this respect the lexicographer does not have to worry about the renderings as much as one has to worry about them when a translation of the Bible is being made. The dictionary says: this word belongs in the area approximately indicated by the English gloss 'cattle' or 'lion' or 'hide' or whatever it may be; and, if the user wants to know more exactly what it means, he or she must study the Hebrew of the passages as quoted.

EDITORIAL RESPONSIBILITY

The most serious practical question in lexicography, I found, lay in the matter of responsibility. If I was editor, I did not want to publish anything that I did not know, by my own knowledge, to be right. But this created a problem in teamwork. For dictionary-writing is very different from writing any other book or article. In essence this is because you cannot retain the material in the mind. One can, as editor of a journal, look at an article and say, "Yes, that's an excellent article, we'll go ahead and publish it." With a dictionary it does not work like that. If someone else writes an entry, unless it is an unusually clear or simple case, you can't just look at it and approve it: in order to assess it, you have to do all the work yourself again. There seems to be no methodological principle that one can simply lay down and then leave alone with the assurance that it will generate correct and satisfactory entries for every word, with all exceptions and anomalies properly mentioned and accounted for. It's the same if you do the work yourself: if you write half of the article on *midbār* and then go off for the weekend, when you come back you find that you have to do all that work again before you write the second half. And the dictionary does not get written except by writing it: in a conceptual problem, as in biblical theology, or even in exegesis, you can have ideas of real value when you are away from the actual writing, and all you have to do is to come back and write down what you have thought out. With a dictionary, this doesn't work: except when you are actually writing, nothing gets done.

This means that the possession of teams of colleagues or assistants does not help so very much. The more there are of them, the more you worry whether their work is right or not, the more you have to do in checking and rechecking. What if an important example has been omitted? What if this or that case has been assigned to the wrong semantic department? It seems to me, therefore, that the task of lexicography, in a field like ancient Hebrew, cannot really be much alleviated by having a large force of people on the job. What one can do is to have several equal editors and make it clear which words each of them is responsible for: one thus has a common general plan, but each editor is in final charge of perhaps a third or a quarter of the entries. This is, of course, how BDB was done: Driver did pronouns, particles, prepositions, etc.; Briggs did mainly "terms important to Old Testament Religion, Theology and Psychology," all of which are listed; and Brown did the rest, which must have been by far the greatest portion.[9] But, even allowing for this kind of cooperation and division of the work, writing a dictionary takes a very long time. I found it often took me a month to write the entry on one word of average frequency. The lexicographer has to be a person who starts writing at 8:00 A.M. and works on till 8:00 P.M. or later, 365 days a year, and who has no other interests in anything. I found my own rate of progress to be such that it would have taken forty years or so to reach a finish, even if I had not had wide interests in other aspects of biblical study.

TEXTUAL BASIS

One other question may be posed, in this era of canonical consciousness: On what temporal stage of the text does the dictionary focus? Is it on the "original" meaning, or is it perhaps on the meaning as it was understood in the final stage of the text? We took it to mean the meaning that was involved

---

9. These details are set out in the preface to BDB, ix–x.

in the coming to be of the text. This is not identical with the "original" meaning but could involve a temporal spectrum: if there is a shift in understanding,
one may have to record more than one stage in meaning. Take an easy example: the first word in the Bible, *bĕrēʾšît*. Does the dictionary record this as
absolute or as construct, with corresponding differences of syntax and of
meaning? There is quite strong comparative evidence, as we all know, for a
sense like 'in the beginning of God's creating'. Perhaps this was the "original"
meaning, that is, the meaning in an earlier stage of the text. But it could be
argued that it is extremely probable that, even if this was so, the meaning in
the text as we have it is 'in the beginning God created. . . . ' It is true that a
host of commentators, from Rashi on, have said or implied that *rēʾšît* here is
a construct. This I think to be quite mistaken. In form the absolute and the
construct are identical. The only sign, therefore, that points toward the construct is the absence of the definite article. But, in words for remotest time it
is common practice that the article is not used, as the lexicographer will have
to register under other entries: in particular *mērōʾš*, which cannot be other
than 'from the beginning' (Isa 40:21; 41:4, 26; 48:16; Prov 8:23; Qoh 3:11).
Similarly, as seen in *ʿôlām* and *hāʿôlām* over many cases, the presence or absence of the article makes no difference. It may be therefore that we have a
spectrum within which we have to record that *rēʾšît* at Gen 1:1 may have been
construct in the earlier stages of the biblical tradition and its formation, but
in the final form of the text should be considered as absolute. That is the sort
of spectrum that a dictionary could be expected to cover. But it would not
cover, within the same operation, those who say that *rēʾšît* means the Torah,
or that it means Israel or its teachers, because these exegetical ideas are not
parts of the coming to be of the text and because they are meanings that are
formed by radical decontextualization and extraction from the actual linguistic web of the text. This is only one illustration, but one sufficient to give an
idea of how one might approach such problems.

LEXICAL ORDERING

It is now usually thought that a dictionary should be ordered in the alphabetical
order of words, and not of roots as BDB did it. And in OHL we followed this
modern trend, which of course was already followed in the German-language
tradition of dictionaries. But the alphabetical principle of ordering is far from
being as simple as it sounds. If you order according to the actual spelling of
the word, you come up against the problem of the many words that have more
than one spelling through having vowels that may or may not be marked with
vowel letters. If (say) *soper* 'scribe' is spelled with *wāw*, it will appear ten
pages earlier in the dictionary than if it is spelt without *wāw*. Well, you may
say, one must follow the majority spelling. But that is not so simple either.

Does it mean the majority spelling of the singular absolute, or the majority spelling of all forms found? I spent months and years on this problem, and indeed the attempt to master it became one of my biggest pieces of research over many years.[10] Among the various familiar dictionaries, BDB was much the best in paying attention to this question and providing data about the proportions of spelling; but even so its coverage was very unequal. In any case all these data had to be redone because we were working from the Leningrad Codex, the spellings of which, in this respect, often diverged from those of the texts used by BDB and other older dictionaries. It is remarkable, incidentally, that these older works commonly gave no indication in their prefaces or introductions which form of Hebrew text they took as definitive for their work; and indeed they provided as a rule very little in the nature of prefatory matter which would both explain how they had themselves worked and also give guidance to the user of their work when complete.

CRITICAL QUESTIONS

Another question of a practical type is this: How far does one take account of critical concepts such as P and J, Deutero-Isaiah, etc.? BDB did so in considerable measure, though unevenly. It makes a practical difference in that one can order instances simply sequentially, from the front of the Bible to the back, as it were, or historically, placing earlier instances first and later ones later. Historical ordering leads straight into the critical question. In the earlier work on OHL much of the critical implications used by BDB had been cut out, on the ground, I think, that it was not certain. I myself tended to put it back again, though in limited scope and quantity. Of course these things are not certain, but it seemed to be easier for those who disliked the critical analysis to ignore it, than for those who found it helpful to have to insert it into a dictionary entry that disregarded it. In fact it needs to be done only in a very simple, rough, and tentative way; but it meant, for instance, that in words where some sort of historical shift in usage or meaning could be discerned we would take it that a citation from the Song of Deborah was earlier than one from Deuteronomy. One can of course refuse to do any of this, but if so it has to be admitted that the dictionary provides no guidance at all in matters of diachronic change within the Bible except for the obviously late works like Esther or Ben Sira.

We took *BHS* as our textual basis; it has of course its faults and weaknesses, but one can hardly doubt that it will remain the standard academic

---

10. This research culminated in my Schweich Lectures, delivered before the British Academy in May 1986, published as *The Variable Spellings of the Hebrew Bible* (Oxford: Oxford University Press, 1989); cf. at the same time F. I. Andersen and A. Dean Forbes, *Spelling in the Hebrew Bible* (Rome: Pontifical Biblical Institute, 1986), and my review in *JSS* 33 (1988) 122–31.

text of the Hebrew Bible for some decades to come. Its critical apparatus has been much criticized, but that, of course, could be and should be rethought and redone as a way to achieve a massive improvement of the edition without requiring the resetting of the whole. But in any case, whatever our evaluation of *BHS* or of any other academic edition, the mere mention of the *apparatus criticus* leads us to another question that is a serious practical one for the lexicographer: What is to be done about the registration of possible textual emendations, or, conversely, what is to be done about the registration of the MT where it is considered to be textually faulty?

EMENDATIONS

The tendency today is to deplore the many corrections of the text that have been proposed by scholars, and the faultiness of the apparatus of *BHS* may have strengthened that tendency. Yet the opposition against the correction of the text has also often been exaggerated and hysterical. After all, the general practice has been to print the MT as the text of the edition, and to cite proposed corrections, and alternative text forms, only in the margin as possibilities, as suggestions which are reported, with more or less support from the editor.[11] This falls far short of the accepted practice with other ancient texts, where the editor prints as the base text the text considered to have been the linguistic form of the original, corrections and all. At least in certain books, Qumran evidence makes it more and more likely that the MT is only one among the several textual possibilities we have to consider.

The only course for the lexicographer, therefore, is to take account of both the MT and the convincing corrections of it which have been proposed, whether with support of the LXX (and other versions) or on the basis of the integrity of our picture of the Hebrew language itself. Clearly not all textual corrections cited by *BHS*, or by any other edition, must be taken seriously; but it would be equally mistaken to take none of them seriously, to act as if, from the lexical point of view, none of these possibilities existed at all. It would be perverse, I suggest, if the dictionary registered the MT plural *babĕqārîm* at Amos 6:12 without at the same time giving a line of space to the rather probable *babbāqār yām*, even if the latter has no actual manuscript or versional support. Concinnity of usage over numerous examples, and considerations such as poetic parallelism and other exegetical factors, make this particular correction into one that has to be taken very seriously indeed.

---

11. See my review of *BHS* in *JTS* 30 (1979) 212–16. On recent trends that appear to oppose even the mere mention of emendations of the text, see B. Albrektson, "Difficilior lectio probabilior," *Oudtestamentische Studiën* 21 (1981) 5–18; and my review of the report of the textual project of the United Bible Societies, *JTS* 37 (1986) 445–50.

What I am saying here is, in a sense, nothing new; what I propose is just what the major dictionaries have already been doing over most of a century, if not more. But I am supporting it with a more comprehensive reasoning. The dictionary has to give account of the lexis of a language as it was. If a particular text contains forms that were not part of the usage of the language, or that were not used in the same proportion, then the dictionary would distort the realities of the language if it did not point out that the text might require correction. Conversely, the integrity of the grammar and lexis of the language is a powerful and significant reason why the text should deserve to be corrected, even where no textual evidence in favor of a correction can be cited.[12]

Proposals for text emendations have often been criticized on the ground that they rested on no evidence. This, though often justified in individual cases, is in principle a superficial opinion. The evidence behind textual proposals lies ultimately, in many cases, in our view of the consistency and coherence of the lexis, the grammar, the syntax, and the semantics of the Hebrew language as we understand it to have worked in ancient times. The task of the dictionary is to present in classified format the lexical element of all this. In doing so it has to be open to the possibility that occasional words found in the text do not represent genuine elements of the actual lexical usage of the language. The dictionary is not a mere registration of the signs found on paper in the traditional text; it is a registration of the lexical elements that functioned in the language. It must certainly register all elements of the MT and give what account of them it can; but for the sake of its own linguistic functioning it ought to give due consideration to possibilities of an alternative text. Certainly it should not register text corrections simply because they have been proposed; and there is no automatic or objective criterion which can decide for us which ones deserve to be noticed. The matter must be left to the decision of the editors, who will include what they think to be worthy of inclusion—just as was the case with philological identifications and suggestions about meaning.

Considering the complexity of all these questions, it is remarkable, within the tradition of dictionaries of Biblical Hebrew, how little discussion of them is provided in the prefaces or introductions that they contain. In the Oxford project our plan was to produce a full statement of the principles involved in all of them; such a statement might take twenty or thirty pages of print. It would serve a dual role: On the one hand it would be a guide for the lexicographers in their work, and on the other hand it would be printed in the eventual volume as a preface and would thus act as a guide to readers. It is

---

12. In this respect see my review of the Sample Edition of the Hebrew University Bible Project, *Book of Isaiah*, in *JSS* 12 (1967) 113–22.

hoped that the present short and simplified paper may stimulate further such discussions of principle which will affect the dictionaries of the future.

Note: in addition to the material listed in the preceding notes, other relevant contributions of my own include:

1. "Hebrew Lexicography," in *Studies on Semitic Lexicography* (ed. P. Fronzaroli; Quaderni di Semitistica 2; Florence, 1973) 103–26.

2. "Philology and Exegesis: Some General Remarks, with Illustrations from Job iii," in *Questions disputées d'Ancien Testament* (2d ed., ed. C. Brekelmans and M. Vervenne; Bibliotheca Ephemeridum Theologicarum Lovaniensium 33; Louvain, 1989) 39–61, 209–10.

3. Reviews of *HALAT*, 1st fascicle in *JSS* 13 (1968) 260–67; 2d fascicle in *JSS* 20 (1975) 236–41.

4. "Semitic Philology and the Interpretation of the Old Testament," in *Tradition and Interpretation* (ed. G. W. Anderson; Oxford: Clarendon, 1979) 31–64.

[October, 1987]

Peter J. MacDonald

Discourse Analysis and Biblical Interpretation

It was an early goal of generative-transformational grammarians to produce syntactic descriptions of sentences without taking sentence meaning into consideration. Few linguists were ever able to achieve that goal, and those who did found their analyses restricted to limited realms of syntax. Without recourse to meaning and function it was difficult to account for syntactic phenomena such as variations of word order, tenses, and pronoun usage. Today, however, linguists interested in semantics are no longer relegated to the fringes of the discipline. In fact, there are new approaches to syntactic analysis that are specifically designed to accommodate meaning (i.e., semantics and pragmatics), and some of the practitioners even deny that it can be done in any other way.[1]

The attempts to place meaning at the center of attention in linguistics have enriched the discipline with fresh insights from sociology, psychology, and philosophy. In these disciplines, methods and vocabularies have been developed to help us understand the social, cultural, and mental contexts that form the matrix of meaning for language. It is not uncommon any more to find articles in even the well-established linguistic periodicals on the relation of syntactic form to conversational etiquette, presupposition, intentions, cognitive

---

1. Such approaches are often called "functional" approaches to syntax and are represented by S. C. Dik, *Functional Grammar* (3d ed.; Dordrecht: Foris, 1981); T. Givón, *On Understanding Grammar* (New York: Academic Press, 1979); idem, *Syntax: A Functional-Typological Introduction* (2 vols.; Amsterdam: Benjamins, 1984–1991); W. A. Foley and R. D. van Valin Jr., *Functional Syntax and Universal Grammar* (Cambridge Studies in Linguistics 38; Cambridge: Cambridge University Press, 1984); and M. A. K. Halliday, *An Introduction to Functional Grammar* (London: Arnold, 1985).

processes, world views, and even personal values. Such contextual approaches are often grouped under the rubric of *discourse analysis*, which is a term that in current linguistic circles has become nearly synonymous with contextual studies of almost any kind.[2] The code words in linguistics today are no longer the *transformation* and the *deep structure*, but rather the *context* and the *function*.

My first task in this paper is to survey several of the kinds of discourse analysis that are currently being discussed in the linguistic literature and to summarize their distinctive goals, methods, and especially their treatment of the notion of context. My second task is to consider the usefulness of some of those views of context to the act of interpreting a discourse.

Terminology

Two key words require some initial definition: *discourse* and *context*.

I use the term *discourse* in a general sense to refer to any unit of speech that is considered by native speakers to be a complete and interpretable act

2. Reviews of discourse analysis reflecting its interdisciplinary nature can be found in R. A. de Beaugrande, *Text, Discourse, and Process: Toward a Multidisciplinary Science of Texts* (Norwood, NJ: Ablex, 1980); R. A. de Beaugrande and W. U. Dressler, *Introduction to Text Linguistics* (London: Longman, 1981); and G. Brown and G. Yule, *Discourse Analysis* (Cambridge Textbooks in Linguistics; Cambridge: Cambridge University Press, 1983). See also the two-volume collection edited by J. S. Petöfi, *Text vs. Sentence: Basic Questions of Text Linguistics* (2 vols.; Hamburg: Buske, 1979–1981).

The most ambitious collection of articles on discourse analysis to date is T. A. van Dijk, ed., *Handbook of Discourse Analysis*. vol. 1: *Disciplines of Discourse Analysis*; vol. 2: *Dimensions of Discourse*; vol. 3: *Discourse and Dialogue*; vol. 4: *Discourse Analysis in Society* (New York: Academic Press, 1985).

Bibliographical works dedicated to various types of discourse analysis and context are the following: On discourse grammar, see W. U. Dressler and S. J. Schmidt, eds., *Textlinguistik: Kommentierte Bibliographie* (Munich: Fink, 1973); and H. Jelitte, "Kommentierte Bibliographie zur Sovetrussischen Textlinguistik," *Linguistische Berichte* 28 (1973) 83–100, 29 (1974) 74–92. On pragmatics, see J. Verschueren, *Pragmatics: An Annotated Bibliography with Particular Reference to Speech Act Theory* (Library and Information Sources in Linguistics 4; Amsterdam: Benjamins, 1978). On presupposition, see I. A. Sag and E. F. Prince, "Bibliography of Works Dealing with Presupposition," in *Presupposition* (ed. C.-K. Oh and D. Dineen; Syntax and Semantics 11; New York: Academic Press, 1979) 389–402. On stylistics, see J. R. Bennett, *Bibliography of Stylistics and Related Criticism, 1967–83* (New York: Modern Language Association of America, 1986).

Several periodicals have been established to promote work on discourse analysis of the types discussed in this paper: *Language in Society* (Cambridge: Cambridge University Press, from 1972); *Journal of Pragmatics* (Amsterdam: North-Holland, from 1977); *Discourse Processes* (Norwood, NJ: Ablex, from 1978); and *Text* (The Hague: Mouton, from 1981).

Some monographic series to be aware of are Papiere zur Textlinguistik (Hamburg: Buske); Advances in Discourse Processes (Norwood, NJ: Ablex); and Pragmatics and Beyond (Amsterdam: Benjamins).

of communication.[3] It may be a simple conversational exchange or an extended turn of one of the participants. It may be a letter, an essay, a song, or a novel. To make distinctions between types of discourses, the term *discourse* can be modified by such adjectives as "conversational," "expository," "historical," "poetic," "narrative," etc.[4] The written (or otherwise recorded) version of a discourse is called the "text."

The *context* of a discourse has features that are linguistic, social, cultural, cognitive, and even personal. The meaning of context in this paper varies as the discussion moves vertically from smaller to larger units of discourse and horizontally from one disciplinary approach to another. In general, the context of a unit of language is the larger framework of entities of which it is a functional part. For example, the context of a word is the phrase, the clause, and the sentence. The context of a sentence is the paragraph (i.e., the sequence of sentences). The context of an event is its event sequence or plot line, and the context of a form of address is the social situation.

VARIETIES OF DISCOURSE ANALYSIS

Although studies that resemble discourse analysis are undertaken by researchers who are not linguists, in this paper I discuss only research in which the author has attempted to characterize the way the average speaker and hearer[5] produce and comprehend everyday language.[6]

---

3. A word or a sentence may be a discourse, but only on the condition that in its context it counts as a complete act of speech. Discourse analysts are less interested in describing sentences than they are in describing functional acts of speech—sometimes simply called "utterances."

4. The use of *discourse* in the opposition "narration vs. discourse," which has been used by some linguists and literary critics, in which *discourse* refers to dialog, has not caught on among discourse analysts in general. Nor is it popular to use *discourse* as it is used by S. Chatman in the oppositions of "story vs. discourse," in which *story* is the content and *discourse* the form; *Story and Discourse: Narrative Structure in Fiction and Film* (Ithaca: Cornell University Press, 1978). The terminology of "histoire vs. discours" of É. Benveniste has enjoyed no popularity either; *Problems in General Linguistics* (Coral Gables: University of Miami Press, 1971; French orig., 1966).

5. The terms *speaker* and *hearer* are used throughout to refer respectively to the transmitter of the discourse, whether speaker, writer, or editor, and to the receiver of the discourse, whether hearer or reader. Members of the unique class of receivers that includes the linguist, critic, and biblical interpreter are distinguished from the "normal" hearer by their respective designations.

6. This eliminates from discussion the work by researchers who are not concerned with the role of linguistic forms in the structure and meaning of discourse, or who are not interested in generalizing their ideas and formulating them into testable hypotheses, or who do not at all interact with the linguistic literature in the field of discourse analysis.

Grammarians who do discourse analysis look at discourses as grammatical structures with internal cohesion created by the rule-governed use of
grammatical structures, such as tenses, pro-forms, deictic terms, lexical collocation patterns, conjunctions, sentence types, etc.[7] They describe the grammatical features of a discourse in terms of their function in the organization
of the larger linguistic context.[8] They identify each grammatical level of discourse—the phrase, the sentence, the paragraph, and the discourse—by its
collection of functional parts. When discourse grammarians speak of
"context," they refer to the matrix of linguistic entities that makes up the discourse itself.[9]

7. One grammatical structure that has received wide attention by discourse grammarians is
   tenses. On the function of tenses in discourse see H. Weinrich, *Tempus: Besprochene und
   erzählte Welt* (Stuttgart: Kohlhammar, 1964; 2d ed., 1971; 3d ed., 1977); and N. Wolfson,
   CHP, the Conversational Historical Present in American English Narrative (Dordrecht:
   Foris, 1982). For articles on both tenses and aspects in discourse see P. J. Hopper, ed., *Tense-
   Aspect: Between Semantics and Pragmatics* (Amsterdam: Benjamins, 1982). Other grammatical features that have been widely discussed are deixis, anaphora, and coordination.
8. Articles that question the need to introduce factors of discourse such as social and linguistic
   context into syntactic analysis are these: M. Dascal and A. Margalit, "A New 'Revolution' in
   Linguistics—'Text Grammars' versus 'Sentence Grammars,'" *Theoretical Linguistics* 1
   (1974) 195–213; J. L. Morgan, "Discourse Theory and the Independence of Sentence
   Grammar," in *Analyzing Discourse* (ed. D. Tannen; Washington, DC: Georgetown University
   Press, 1982) 196–204; and numerous articles in Petöfi, *Text vs. Sentence.*
9. Some of the main monographs on discourse grammar to date are J. E. Grimes, *The Thread of
   Discourse* (The Hague: Mouton, 1975); M. A. K. Halliday and R. Hasan, *Cohesion in English*
   (London: Longman, 1976); E. Werlich, *A Text Grammar of English* (Heidelberg: Quelle &
   Meyer, 1976); T. A. van Dijk, *Text and Context: Some Explorations in the Semantics and
   Pragmatics of Discourse* (London: Longman, 1977); W. Pickering, *A Framework for Dis-
   course Analysis* (Dallas: Summer Institute of Linguistics and University of Texas at Arling-
   ton, 1978); K. L. Pike, *Tagmemics, Discourse, and Verbal Art* (Ann Arbor: Michigan Studies
   in the Humanities, 1981); K. L. Pike and E. G. Pike, *Text and Tagmeme* (Norwood, NJ:
   Ablex, 1983); R. E. Longacre, *The Grammar of Discourse* (New York: Plenum, 1983); and
   P. Werth, *Focus, Coherence and Emphasis* (London: Croom Helm, 1984).
       Some important collections of articles on discourse grammar are F. Daneš, ed., *Papers on
   Functional Sentence Perspective* (The Hague: Mouton, 1974); N. E. Enkvist and V. Kohonen,
   eds., *Approaches to Word Order: Reports on Text Linguistics* (2d ed.; Åbo: Åbo Akademi,
   1982 [1976]); J. E. Grimes, ed., *Papers on Discourse* (Dallas: Summer Institute of Linguistics
   and University of Texas at Austin, 1978); T. Givón, ed., *Discourse and Syntax* (Syntax and
   Semantics 12; New York: Academic Press, 1979); T. Givón, ed., *Topic Continuity in Dis-
   course: A Quantitative Cross-Language Study* (Amsterdam: Benjamins, 1983); R. E. Long-
   acre and F. Woods, eds., *Discourse Grammar: Studies in Indigenous Languages of Columbia,
   Panama, and Ecuador* (2 vols.; Dallas: Summer Institute of Linguistics and University of
   Texas at Arlington, 1977); J.-O. Östman, ed., *Reports on Text Linguistics: Cohesion and
   Semantics* (Åbo: Åbo Akademi, 1978); J. V. Hinds, ed., *Anaphora in Discourse* (Alberta, BC:
   Linguistic Research, 1978); L. Jones and R. E. Longacre, eds., *Discourse in Mesoamerican
   Languages*, vol. 1: *Discussion* (Dallas: Summer Institute of Linguistics and University of

Sociolinguists do a form of discourse analysis that is less formal than that of the grammarians and is often called "conversational analysis" because it focuses on everyday interactive speech.[10] Context in conversational analysis includes the shifting social settings in which speakers and hearers find themselves.[11] A change in social context involves changes in the relations between speakers and hearers, which in turn causes changes in the selection and function of the linguistic forms. The analyst of conversational discourse might study anything from topical coherence of an entire discourse to the function of filler words like *uh* and *you know*.[12] Some have studied the

Texas at Arlington, 1979); W. L. Chafe, ed., *The Pear Stories: Cognitive, Cultural and Linguistic Aspects of Narrative Production* (Norwood, NJ: Ablex, 1980); F. Klein-Andreu, ed., *Discourse: Perspectives on Syntax* (New York: Academic Press, 1983); F. Neubauer, ed., *Coherence in Natural-Language Texts* (Hamburg: Buske, 1983); J. S. Petöfi and E. Sözer, eds., *Micro and Macro Connexitivity of Texts* (Hamburg: Buske, 1983); D. Tannen, ed., *Coherence in Spoken and Written Discourse* (Norwood, NJ: Ablex, 1984); J. R. Wirth, ed., *Beyond the Sentence: Discourse and Sentential Form* (Ann Arbor: Karoma, 1985); and J. D. Benson and W. S. Greaves, eds., *Systemic Perspectives on Discourse* (2 vols.; Norwood, NJ: Ablex, 1985).

10. Sociolinguists have investigated a variety of interactions: Between patients and doctors: W. Labov and D. Fanshel, *Therapeutic Discourse: Psychotherapy as Conversation* (New York: Academic Press, 1977); and S. Fisher and A. Todd, eds., *The Social Organization of Doctor–Patient Communication* (Washington, DC: Center for Applied Linguistics, 1983). Between children and adults: E. Ochs and B. B. Shieffelin, eds., *Developmental Pragmatics* (New York: Academic Press, 1979). Between students and teachers: J. M. Sinclair and R. M. Coulthard, *Towards an Analysis of Discourse: The English Used by Teachers and Pupils* (London: Oxford University Press, 1975). Between customers and salesmen: A. Tsuda, *Sales Talk in Japan and the United States: An Ethnographic Analysis of Contrastive Speech Events* (Washington, DC: Georgetown University Press, 1984). Between lawyers and juries: T. Liebes-Plesner, "Rhetoric in the Service of Justice: The Sociolinguistic Construction of Stereotypes in an Israeli Trial," *Text* 4 (1984) 373–92; and S. Fisher and A. Todd, eds., *Discourse and Institutional Authority: Medicine, Education, and Law* (Norwood, NJ: Ablex, 1986). Between members of interaction groups: J. J. Gumperz, *Discourse Strategies* (Cambridge: Cambridge University Press, 1982). Between peers: D. Tannen, *Conversational Style: Analyzing Talk among Friends* (Norwood, NJ: Ablex, 1984).

11. For an account of the major social factors influencing discourse form, see M. Gregory and S. Carroll, *Language and Situation: Language Varieties and Their Social Contexts* (London: Routledge & Kegan Paul, 1978); and M. A. K. Halliday, *Language as Social Semiotic: The Social Interpretation of Language and Meaning* (London: Arnold, 1978).

12. For overviews of conversational analysis see M. Stubbs, *Discourse Analysis* (Chicago: University of Chicago Press, 1983); and W. A. Corsaro, "Sociological Approaches to Discourse Analysis," in *Handbook of Discourse Analysis*, vol. 1: *Disciplines of Discourse* (ed. T. van Dijk; New York: Academic Press, 1985) 167–92. Some important monographs on conversational analysis are E. Goffman, *Frame Analysis: An Essay on the Organization of Experience* (New York: Harper & Row, 1974); idem, *Forms of Talk* (Philadelphia: University of Pennsylvania Press, 1981); D. Burton, *Dialogue and Discourse: A Sociolinguistic Approach to Modern Drama Dialogue and Naturally Occurring Conversation* (London: Routledge & Kegan Paul, 1981); and W. Edmondson, *Spoken Discourse: A Model for Analysis* (London:

rules for sequencing of turns in conversation, and others have concentrated on the suprasegmental features of oral discourse, such as voice quality, pitch, and intonation.[13]

In the field called "ethnography of speaking," analysts study the speech of a homogeneous group of people as a reflection of their unifying sociocultural knowledge, values, and attitudes. The sociocultural context of a discourse is the worldview behind the discourse that is shared by a large segment of the cultural community to which the speaker and hearer belong.[14]

The pragmatic approach to discourse is taken by linguists under the influence of the work done by philosophers on speech act theory, in which discourse is considered a form of action that is motivated by the speaker's intentions or beliefs about the situation.[15] Speech act theory has provided linguists and discourse analysts of diverse backgrounds with a common inven-

---

Longman, 1981). Important collections are P. P. Giglioli, ed., *Language and Social Context* (Harmondsworth: Penguin, 1972); J. Schenkein, ed., *Studies in the Organization of Conversational Interaction* (New York: Academic Press, 1978); D. Tannen, ed., *Analyzing Discourse: Text and Talk* (Washington, DC: Georgetown University Press, 1981); and T. A. van Dijk, ed., *Handbook of Discourse Analysis*, vol. 3: *Discourse and Dialogue* (New York: Academic Press, 1985).

13. On discourse intonation, see D. Brazil, "Phonology: Intonation in Discourse," in *Handbook of Discourse Analysis*, vol. 2: *Dimensions of Discourse* (ed. T. van Dijk; New York: Academic Press, 1985) 57–76; and D. Gibbon and H. Richter, eds., *Intonation, Accent, and Rhythm: Studies in Discourse Phonology* (New York: de Gruyter, 1984).

14. On the ethnographic approach to discourse analysis see J. J. Gumperz and D. Hymes, eds., *Directions in Sociolinguistics: The Ethnography of Communication* (New York: Holt, Rinehart & Winston, 1972); A. Cicourel, "Language and Society: Cognitive, Cultural and Linguistic Aspects of Language Use," *Sozialwissenschaftliche Annalen* 2 (1978) B25–B58; M. Agar and J. Hobbs, "Interpreting Discourse: Coherence and the Analysis of Ethnographic Interviews," *Discourse Processes* 5 (1982) 1–32; M. Saville-Troike, *The Ethnography of Communication: An Introduction* (Oxford: Blackwell, 1982); L. Polanyi, *Telling the American Story: From the Structure of Linguistic Texts to the Grammar of a Culture* (Norwood, NJ: Ablex, 1984); C. Linde, *The Creation of Coherence in Life Stories* (Norwood, NJ: Ablex, 1984); and T. A. van Dijk, *Prejudice in Discourse* (Amsterdam: Benjamins, 1984). An early influential collection of articles along these lines was R. Bauman and J. Sherzer, *Explorations in the Ethnography of Speaking* (Cambridge: Cambridge University Press, 1974).

15. On speech act theory see J. L. Austin, *How to Do Things with Words* (Cambridge: Harvard University Press, 1962); J. Searle, *Expression and Meaning: Studies in the Theory of Speech Acts* (Cambridge: Cambridge University Press, 1979); K. Bach and R. M. Harnish, *Linguistic Communication and Speech Acts* (Cambridge: MIT Press, 1979); and J. Verschueren, *On Speech Act Verbs* (Amsterdam: Benjamins, 1980). For an overview of the pragmatics of language, see especially S. C. Levinson, *Pragmatics* (Cambridge Textbooks in Linguistics; Cambridge: Cambridge University Press, 1983); and C. Ferrara, "Pragmatics," in *Handbook of Discourse Analysis*, vol. 2: *Dimensions of Discourse*, 137–58. For a bibliography of works on speech acts by linguists see Verschueren, *Pragmatics: An Annotated Bibliography*.

tory of basic acts that are performed by speakers. When people speak, they do so to accomplish something, whether it be to inform, scold, impress, encourage, or to deceive. The pragmatic context of a discourse is a broad notion that encompasses the beliefs, attitudes, and commitments of the speaker that shape the purpose and meaning of his or her utterance.[16]

Psycholinguists who study discourse focus on the mental processes controlling the reception or perception of discourse. Psycholinguists have performed detailed experiments to determine how well subjects can recall information from a discourse under varying conditions.[17] From these experiments some researchers have modeled the mental processes that operate during one's encounter with discourse.[18] They have also hypothesized about how the information is stored in short-term and long-term memories.[19] Others have studied the effects that certain syntactic structures and lexical choices have on the response of the reader.[20] The psycholinguistic context of a discourse involves the hearer's mental processes, abilities, and habits.[21]

16. For attempts to integrate speech act theory into discourse studies, see especially these works: M. L. Pratt, *Toward a Speech Act Theory of Literary Discourse* (Bloomington: Indiana University Press, 1977); W. Labov and D. Fanshel, *Therapeutic Discourse: Psychotherapy as Conversation*; T. A. van Dijk, *Text and Context: Some Explorations in the Semantics and Pragmatics of Discourse*; idem, *Macro-structures: An Interdisciplinary Study of Global Structures in Discourse, Interaction and Cognition* (Hillsdale, NJ: Erlbaum, 1980); and idem, *Studies in the Pragmatics of Discourse* (The Hague: Mouton, 1981).

17. See B. Meyer, *The Organization of Prose and Its Effects on Memory* (Amsterdam: North-Holland, 1975); N. L. Stein and T. Nezworski, "The Effects of Organization and Instructional Set on Story Memory," *Discourse Processes* 1 (1978) 177–94; and E. Tulving, *Elements of Episodic Memory* (Oxford: Clarendon, 1983).

18. See W. Kintsch and T. A. van Dijk, "Toward a Model of Text Comprehension and Production," *Psychological Review* 85 (1978) 363–94; W. Kintsch, "On Modeling Comprehension," *Educational Psychologist* 14 (1979) 3–14; and P. N. Johnson-Laird, "Mental Models of Meaning," in *Elements of Discourse Understanding* (ed. A. Joshi et al.; Cambridge: Cambridge University Press, 1981) 106–27.

19. See W. Kintsch, "On Comprehending Stories," in *Cognitive Processes in Comprehension* (ed. M. Just and P. Carpenter; New York: Wiley, 1977) 33–62; and W. Kintsch and J. M. Keenan, "Reading Rate and Retention as a Function of the Number of Propositions in the Base Structure of Sentences," *Cognitive Psychology* 5 (1973) 257–74.

20. See T. K. Tyler and W. D. Marslen-Wilson, "The On-line Effects of Semantic Context on Syntactic Processing," *Journal of Verbal Learning and Verbal Behavior* 16 (1977) 683–89; and C. H. Sider III, *Some Effects of Syntax on Comprehension: A Psycholinguistic Study* (Ph.D. diss., University of Massachusetts, 1981).

21. Important collections of articles using the psycholinguistic approach to discourse are J. B. Carroll and R. O. Freedle, eds., *Language Comprehension and the Acquisition of Knowledge* (Washington, DC: Winston, 1972); Just and Carpenter, *Cognitive Processes in Comprehension*; D. L. Laberge and S. J. Samuels, eds., *Basic Processes in Reading: Perception and Comprehension* (Hillsdale, NJ: Erlbaum, 1977); R. O. Freedle, ed., *Discourse Production*

Cognitive linguists attempt to model the mental processes involved in the production and reception of discourse. The essential cognitive context for communication is a mental representation of information known variously as "scripts," "schemata," or "frames."[22] These represent the knowledge of everyday events that both the speaker and hearer have acquired through experience. During the production and reception of discourse, certain knowledge is activated by the social circumstances and the content of the discourse. These scripts allow the hearer to make sense of discourse even when the discourse itself is elliptical, imprecise, and loaded with presuppositions. Some computer scientists have used these cognitive notions to develop computer programs that can understand natural language input.[23] To do so, they have had to determine just what background knowledge would be necessary for a hearer to have in order to understand a given natural discourse. For communication to be successful, speakers and hearers must share the same scripts. The cognitive context of a discourse is the realm of knowledge possessed by the speaker and hearer that is being activated by the discourse.[24]

Other types of discourse analysis practiced today could be discussed as well, such as stylistics, poetics, and hermeneutics, but in this paper I discuss

---

and Comprehension (Norwood, NJ: Ablex, 1977); R. O. Freedle, ed., *New Directions in Discourse Processing* (Norwood, NJ: Ablex, 1979); T. A. van Dijk, ed., *Poetics 9: Story Comprehension* (no. 1–3; Amsterdam: North-Holland, 1980); and A. K. Joshi, B. L. Webber, and I. A. Sag, eds., *Elements of Discourse Understanding* (Cambridge: Cambridge University Press, 1981).

22. These are not synonymous notions, but for our purposes the differences may be ignored. On scripts see R. Schank and R. P. Abelson, *Scripts, Plans, Goals and Understanding: An Inquiry into Human Knowledge Structures* (Hillsdale, NJ: Erlbaum, 1977). On frames see D. Metzing, ed., *Frame Conceptions and Text Understanding* (New York: de Gruyter, 1980). On schemata see D. E. Rumelhart, "Notes on a Schema for Stories," in *Representation and Understanding* (ed. D. Bobrow and A. Collins; New York: Academic Press, 1975) 211–36.

23. See T. Winograd, *Language as a Cognitive Process* (Reading, MA: Addison-Wesley, 1983); J. E. Fahlman, *NETL: A System for Representing and Using Real-World Knowledge* (Cambridge: MIT Press, 1979); and D. G. Bobrow, R. M. Kaplan, D. A. Norman, H. Thompson, and T. Winograd, "GUS, a Frame-driven Dialog System," *Artificial Intelligence* 8 (1977) 155–73. For a study that discusses a computer program to generate discourse, see K. R. McKeown, *Text Generation: Using Discourse Strategies and Focus Constraints to Generate Natural Language Text* (Cambridge: Cambridge University Press, 1985).

24. For additional work on the cognitive approach to discourse analysis, see especially de Beaugrande, *Text, Discourse, and Process*; and J. Andor, *Frame Semantics and the Typology of Actions* (Amsterdam: Benjamins, 1985). A few of the important collections in the cognitive and computational approach to discourse are D. G. Bobrow and A. M. Collins, eds., *Representation and Understanding: Studies in Cognitive Science* (New York: Academic Press, 1975); R. Schank, N. Goldman, C. Rieger, and C. Riesbeck, eds., *Conceptual Information Processing* (Amsterdam: North-Holland/Elsevier, 1975); and R. O. Freedle, ed., *New Directions in Discourse Processing* (Norwood, NJ: Ablex, 1979).

only approaches to discourse that can be identified as explicitly linguistic in their methods and goals.[25] The approaches to discourse are so many because the object of analysis—human discourse—is so complex. Speaking draws upon all the senses and mental capacities of the participants and must be versatile enough to operate efficiently in many different social contexts. Consequently, analysts who limit themselves to only one kind of discourse analysis have little hope of understanding the workings of even the simplest of human communication. In the following pages I draw upon each of the approaches discussed above in the investigation of how humans go about making sense of discourse.

INTERPRETATION AND DISCOURSE ANALYSIS

Discourse analysts usually study discourses that were uttered in their own native language and in a familiar and well-defined context. Such discourses are usually easier for them to understand. Consequently, discourse analysts rarely ask the question, "*What* does the discourse mean?" They are more likely to ask, "*How* does the discourse mean what it does?" Biblical scholars, on the other hand, and other scholars who study texts written in languages other than their own, do not always clearly understand the meaning of a discourse. Consequently, the analyst of biblical texts is often concerned with *what* the discourse means. However, in this paper, I approach the problem of interpretation by first asking the following question: "*Why* does the hearer perceive the meanings she or he does in the discourse?" I conclude with an examination of textual devices that may tell us something about the author.

I discuss several of the concepts under development in the current linguistic literature that appear to be sufficiently well developed today to be

---

25. On stylistics, see N. E. Enkvist, *Linguistic Stylistics* (The Hague: Mouton, 1973); Z. Szábò, "Stylistics within the Interdisciplinary Framework of Text Linguistics," in *Text vs. Sentence* (ed. J. Petöfi; Hamburg: Buske, 1981) 2:433–49; and G. N. Leech and M. H. Short, *Style in Fiction: A Linguistic Introduction to English Fictional Prose* (London: Longman, 1981). The work in literary stylistics undertaken up through the early 1970s had an important influence on much of early discourse analysis—especially on the European varieties. For evidence of this one can scan the bibliography in W. U. Dressler, *Einführung in die Textlinguistik* (Tübingen: Niemeyer, 1972); or in Dressler and Schmidt, *Textlinguistik: Kommentierte Bibliographie*. On poetics, see T. Todorov, *The Poetics of Prose* (Ithaca: Cornell University Press, 1977 [French orig., 1971]); and G. Genette, *Narrative Discourse: An Essay in Method* (Ithaca: Cornell University Press, 1980 [French orig., 1972]). On hermeneutics, see P. Ricoeur, *Interpretation Theory: Discourse and the Surplus of Meaning* (Fort Worth: Texas Christian University Press, 1976); and H.-G. Gadamer, *Truth and Method* (New York: Continuum, 1975 [2d German ed., 1965]).

worthy of consideration by biblical scholars interested in how readers understand biblical discourse. The discussion focuses on the notions of discourse types, scripts, cohesion and coherence, co-text, topic, and evaluative devices.

More Terminology

"Semantics," in current linguistics, is the study of the information provided by an utterance due to its distinctive combination of grammatical and lexical patterns. The semantic features of a sentence are more or less fixed meaningful references that do not change from speaker to speaker or social setting to social setting.

"Pragmatics," on the other hand, is the study of the information transmitted by an utterance that goes beyond the information that is carried by the grammatical and lexical patterns. It concerns such information as the speaker's beliefs, knowledge, commitments, social status, purpose for speaking, etc. These factors are part of the psychosocial context of the discourse and give the utterance meanings that are not always clear in the semantics of the forms themselves.

Basically, then, *semantics* is the study of the variations of meaning that occur in a language when the grammatical and lexical forms change; *pragmatics* is the study of the variation of meanings of an utterance that are caused by shifts in the conditions of its utterance. This simplified contrast does not do justice to the multitude of issues covered by each approach, but it is one of the distinctions popularly made between them. Since the interpretation of discourse simultaneously involves them both, semantics and pragmatics cannot always be kept distinct, nor should one try to do so, but it is sometimes useful to discuss them separately because they sometimes require distinctive methods of description.

By "interpretation" I do not have in mind the intentional act of *explication de texte* as performed by a professional critic in examining the style, metaphors, and author biography of a discourse with the goal of understanding what it was that the author really meant by what is said. Nor am I interested in discovering any profound insights into human nature, literary allusions, or secret meanings of the discourse. Rather, by "interpretation" I am referring to the involuntary act of the common hearer who, by using normal cognitive abilities, infers meanings from the forms of a discourse with the help of its multilayered contexts. For the analyst who may not be the intended reader or hearer of a discourse, interpretation involves the study not only of the formal linguistic properties of the discourse and of the semantic and rhetorical structure of the discourse, but also of the pragmatic (i.e., psychosocial) context in which the discourse was/is to be used and the mental processes involved in the production and comprehension of discourse in general.

Discourse Types

One factor that controls what meanings a hearer perceives in a discourse is the type of discourse being received. Westman observed that "the function of text types in linguistic communication in society is to make it possible for members of society to orient themselves as readers and to make choices as writers."[26] One way to classify discourses into types is to identify the overall speech act being performed by the speaker. One should try to determine whether the speaker is telling a story, teaching a moral, expressing an opinion, ridiculing, questioning, appeasing, teasing, lying, etc. Having made a judgment about the overall purpose of a discourse the hearer will process its successive parts in conformity with that judgment.[27]

Some discourse types have a set of formal devices that are commonly used to accomplish the speech acts being performed. Hearers use these type-specific devices to organize the information as it comes to them in the discourse into meaning consistent with the act being performed. So, if the analyst has determined that the speaker is primarily attempting to record history, for example, attention should be paid to the speaker's use of those devices that characterize historical discourse, namely, temporal and spatial devices, event indexing, agent/victim roles, and others.[28]

If the discourse type changes from historical to, say, poetic, then the esthetic, literary, and emotive effects must be assumed to have been activated in the hearer's mind. If conversation is under examination, those devices that reflect personal sentiments and attitudes should be looked at with care.

It must be kept in mind, however, that there are very few devices that can be considered exclusively historical, or poetic, or conversational. It is the

26. M. Westman, "On Strategy in Swedish Legal Texts," *Text* 4 (1984) 58.
27. On the functional classification of discourse types, see R. Jakobson, "Closing Statement: Linguistics and Poetics," in *Style in Language* (ed. T. Sebeok; Cambridge: MIT Press, 1960) 350–77; E. Gülich and W. Raible, eds., *Textsorten: Differenzierungskriterien aus linguistischer Sicht* (Wiesbaden: Athenäum, 1975); E. Werlich, *Typologie der Texte: Entwurf eines textlinguistischen Modells zur Grundlegung einer Textgrammatik* (Heidelberg: Quelle & Meyer, 1975); Longacre, *Grammar of Discourse*; D. Tannen, ed., *Spoken and Written Language: Exploring Orality and Literacy* (Norwood, NJ: Ablex, 1982); E. L. Smith Jr., "Functional Types of Scientific Prose," in *Systemic Perspectives on Discourse* (ed. J. Benson and W. Greaves; Norwood, NJ: Ablex, 1985) 2:241–57; and T. A. van Dijk, ed., *Discourse and Literature* (Amsterdam: Benjamins, 1985).
28. On the analysis of historical discourse, see W.-D. Stempel, "Erzählung, Beschreibung und der historische Diskurs," in *Geschichte—Ereignis und Erzählung* (ed. R. Koselleck and W. D. Stempel; Munich: Fink, 1973) 325–46; and N. S. Struever, "Historical Discourse," in *Handbook of Discourse Analysis.* vol. 1: *Disciplines of Discourse,* 249–72. On the elements of narrative discourse in general, see G. Prince, *Narratology: The Form and Functioning of Narrative* (Berlin: Mouton, 1982); and F. Gülich and H. M. Quasthoff, "Narrative Analysis," in *Handbook of Discourse Analysis.* vol. 2: *Dimensions of Discourse,* 169–98.

functions of linguistic forms that are characteristic of discourse types. The analyst must be slow to attribute literary values to features of a discourse of a type that does not usually activate such usage.

For example, one may find a chiastic intersentential structure in both a Hebrew historical narrative and a Hebrew poetic discourse, but the organizational function of the chiastic structure in the former may differ considerably from its function in the latter. Chiasm in Hebrew narrative may be used to delay information, to slow down the event line, to shift attention to a new topic, or to change thematic character. However, in Hebrew poetry chiasm restates, compares, and contrasts for purposes of elaboration, emphasis, or rhythm. For each type of discourse in which this device is found, one must determine what function is commonly activated in the mind of the hearers.

In addition to having specific functions for linguistic devices, each discourse type (narrating, describing, teasing, dreaming, etc.) has a set of characteristic strategies that may be used to accomplish its global speech act. These strategies have been discussed under the terminology of *macrostructures*.[29] This is familiar territory for those scholars versed in classical rhetoric. The difference is that, unlike the rhetoricians, who attempted to relate the forms of discourse to the intentions of the speaker, discourse analysts attempt to relate the patterns of discourse to the subconscious attitudes and the psychological strategies that have given rise to them.[30]

Through the centuries most Biblical Hebrew texts have served many functions: mythical, religious, ideological, historical, and literary.[31] One must determine which of the multiple speech acts that have been performed by a biblical text is to be accepted as primary. With that decided, one can then go on to analyze the function of its linguistic components.

Scripts

There is widespread uniformity of behavior among members of a society in everyday circumstances such as driving on a highway, making a bank deposit, and ordering a fast-food hamburger. In each of these circumstances there are "scripts" that we all follow. Scripts, in the sense developed by cognitive linguists,[32] form the knowledge base that needs to be shared by both a

29. On macrostructures, see van Dijk, *Macro-structures*; and L. Polanyi, *Telling the American Story*.

30. Van Dijk found that the following macrostructures are unwittingly used to disguise ethnically prejudiced speech: generalization, correction, denial, (apparent) concessions, contrast, mitigation, displacement, avoidance, and indirectness; "Cognitive and Conversational Strategies in the Expression of Ethnic Prejudice," *Text* 3 (1983) 375–404.

31. See M. Sternberg, *The Poetics of Biblical Narrative* (Bloomington: University of Indiana Press, 1985), chap. 1.

32. See especially Schank and Abelson, *Scripts, Plans, Goals and Understanding*.

speaker and a hearer of a specific communicative situation in order for the hearer to process the information of an utterance as the speaker expects. The speaker assumes that the scripts necessary to interpret the utterance are available to the hearer, and that the hearer will use them in the same way as would any other member of the same linguistic community. This freedom to assume a basic knowledge among hearers frees the speaker from the need to state all presuppositions and details about the references.[33] For example, when we hear that someone is ordering a burger to go, the picture in our minds is quite different from the one in which a customer is ordering pheasant under glass. In the former the person ordering is casually dressed, standing at a counter, reading a plastic menu on the wall behind a teenager who is standing before a cash register; in the latter the diner is dressed in formal attire, sitting at a table with a white tablecloth and shining crystal, holding a big cardboard menu, and talking to a middle-aged waiter standing next to the table.

When Rachel went to draw water from the well, we think we know what the situation entailed, but do we? In order to understand an ancient discourse as an ancient hearer would, one would have to be able to describe the scripts that were being activated by the discourse. That is, what was inferentially "obvious" to members of the originating culture because of shared knowledge may not be inferable to the modern reader, given the differences in the inventory and content of scripts in the two cultures. Biblical discourses that to us appear vague, elliptical, or even defective may be ones in which the speaker was simply assuming a high degree of overlap between his or her own scripts and those of the hearers.

Scripts help the hearer make proper inferences from one proposition to the next. Scripts that are activated early in a discourse can trigger a sequence of inferences in the mind of the hearer. This sequence of inferences will create coherency and a sense of "logicalness" for the whole discourse. If the script that the hearer is using does not allow coherent connections to be made between parts of the discourse, the hearer may be confused or have to adjust the script until it can adequately organize the incoming information. When the hearer and speaker possess different sets of interests, attitudes, beliefs, and experiences, their scripts will be different; and the hearer will probably make inferences quite different from those assumed by the speaker.

Cohesion and Coherence

In their substantial contribution to discourse grammar, Halliday and Hasan point out numerous microlinguistic devices that directly promote connectivity

---

33. On the avoidance of stating the obvious by efficient speakers, see H. P. Grice, *Studies in the Way of Words* (Cambridge: Harvard University Press, 1989), chaps. 2–3.

tures, scripts, and cohesive devices by the process of inferencing. This is the mental activity of a reader that takes place while encountering each successive sentence in the discourse.[37] Of course, large chunks of meaning are revealed once the macrostructure and script(s) of the discourse are known; but still much of the meaning peculiar to this discourse comes one piece at a time.[38]

One method that might clarify the amount of inferencing actually involved in a given discourse has been discussed by Langleben.[39] She suggests

34. Halliday and Hasan, *Cohesion in English.*
35. For discussions of the cohesive functions of many other linguistic structures, like word order, sentential adverbs, and pro-forms, see W. Gutwinski, *Cohesion in Literary Texts: A Study of Some Grammatical and Lexical Features of Discourse* (The Hague: Mouton, 1976); and various articles in Petöfi and Sözer, *Micro and Macro Connexitivity of Texts.*
36. On the concept of coherence in discourse, see N. E. Enkvist, "Coherence, Pseudo-coherence, and Non-coherence," in *Reports on Text Linguistics* (ed. J.-O. Östman; Åbo: Åbo Akademi, 1978) 109–28; E. Vasiliu, "On Some Meanings of 'Coherence,'" in *Text vs. Sentence* (ed. J. Petöfi; Hamburg: Buske, 1981) 2:450–66; M. Charolles, "Coherence as a Principle in the Interpretation of Discourse," *Text* 3 (1983) 71–97; C. Linde, *The Creation of Coherence in Life Stories* (Norwood, NJ: Ablex, 1984); and various articles in Neubauer, *Coherence in Natural-Language Texts;* and Tannen, *Coherence in Spoken and Written Discourse.*
37. For research on linear inferencing, see H. H. Clark, "Inferring What Is Meant," in *Studies in the Perception of Language* (ed. J. Levelt and G. Flores d'Arcais; New York: Wiley, 1978) 295–322; C. Linde and J. Goguen, "Structure of Planning Discourse," *Journal of Social and Biological Structures* 1 (1978) 219–51; L. Polanyi and R. J. H. Scha, "The Syntax of Discourse," *Text* 3 (1983) 261–70; G. Rickheit and H. Strohner, *Inferences in Text Processing* (Amsterdam: North-Holland, 1985); and R. G. van de Velde, *Prolegomena to Inferential Discourse Processing* (Amsterdam: Benjamins, 1984).
38. In the case of biblical interpretation, where the hearers have probably heard the discourse many times before, the linear inferencing is minimized. In fact, it is likely that the versions of these stories we have today represent tellings in which the speaker knew that the audience was familiar with the story lines even before narrating them. What effect this had on the tellings is hard to say.
39. M. Langleben, "Latent Coherence, Contextual Meanings, and the Interpretation of Text," *Text* 1 (1981) 279–313.

that, once analysts have taken the surface cohesion into consideration, they can bridge the gap between these formal factors and the scripts or underlying coherence of a discourse by what she calls "expanding." This is done by adding to each sentence comments that state explicitly any presuppositions that are needed by the hearer to understand the connection of that sentence to the rest of the discourse—especially to the prior discourse. The goal is to close any notional gaps between meaningful units (i.e., between key words, whole propositions, thematic units, and scenes). This procedure usually reveals concepts that were important for the understanding of the discourse but that are never mentioned in the discourse itself, and that come to the surface only in the mind of the inferencing hearer. Then, after the analysts understand the themes and meanings behind the discourse, they can better evaluate the meaning of the obscure parts of the discourse that initially may have appeared incoherent.

If the analysts generate massive comments, the procedure could derive meanings from the discourse that are not necessary for understanding the "point" or main speech act of the discourse. Since speakers usually have only a few speech acts to accomplish in a given discourse, and usually encode them in some way in the discourse itself, over-expansion may unnecessarily complicate the analysis. Despite this potential excess, the effort to make explicit the presuppositions of a discourse is worthwhile as a means of revealing any implicit information that is crucial to the interpretation of the discourse.

Co-text

The linguistic context of an utterance is sometimes called "co-text." Discussions of co-text usually focus on the role of the prior sections of a discourse in the interpretation of a given linguistic unit, but it can just as well include the study of all syntagmatic (i.e., linear) relations of that unit with all other parts of a discourse—both anterior and posterior. Each appearance of an element in a discourse entails the information already transmitted about it earlier in the discourse and must be interpreted in light of that prior occurrence. The co-textual effect on interpretation is that all sections of a discourse, but most strongly the previous sections, serve as the framework or field of reference for the information to be processed in later sections of the discourse.[40]

---

40. On the effect of linguistic context on understanding, see D. Swinney, "Lexical Access during Sentence Comprehension: (Re)consideration of Context Effects," *Journal of Verbal Learning and Verbal Behavior* 18 (1979) 645–59; W. L. Chafe, "The Flow of Thought and the Flow of Language," in *Discourse and Syntax* (Syntax and Semantics 12; ed. T. Givón; New York: Academic Press, 1979) 159–81; C. Marcello, "Text, Coherence and Lexicon,"

characters change, and contexts are redefined. The term *man* takes on a particular physical appearance and gets a personality in the mind of the hearer.

Topic

Although the term *topic* is universally used in discourse studies, it is rarely well defined; and even when it is, the definitions vary from study to study. What makes it so difficult to define is that topical phenomena are found on several levels of discourse: sentence, paragraph, and whole discourse.[42]

The topic of a sentence is what that sentence is about. It usually denotes something already stated in the discourse, that is, "old" information; or something that is assumed to be part of the knowledge base of the hearer, or "given" information. A topic is usually the first major constituent of a sentence; and since in most English sentences the subject is the first major constituent, the subject and topic are usually the same. The topic of a sentence is what the speaker perceives that sentence to be about and must be the starting point for all sentential interpretation.

Opposed to the topic of the sentence is the *comment* of a sentence, which identifies what it is that is said in the sentence about that topic. Whatever major sentence constituents are not part of the topic are usually designated as the comments.[43] The comment of a sentence represents the speaker's effort to

---

in *Text vs. Sentence* (ed. J. Petöfi; Hamburg: Buske, 1979) 2:618–33; and S. T. Hekkanen, *The Effects of Context on the Processing of Ambiguous Words* (Ph.D. diss., University of Southern Florida, 1981).

41. T. Ballmer, "Words, Sentences, Texts, and All That," *Text* 1 (1981) 174.

42. For more on the levels of topic in discourse, see J. E. Grimes, "Topic Levels," in *TINLAP–2* (ed. D. Waltz; New York: Association for Computing Machinery, 1978) 104–9; L. B. Jones and L. K. Jones, "Levels of Significant Information in Discourse," in *Papers of the 1978 Mid-America Linguistics Conference at Oklahoma* (ed. R. Cooley et al.; Norman: University of Oklahoma Press, 1979) 307–16; and E. Levy, "Towards an Objective Definition of 'Discourse Topic,' " in *Papers from the Eighteenth Regional Meeting, Chicago Linguistic Society* (ed. K. Tuite et al.; Chicago: Chicago Linguistic Society, 1982) 295–304.

43. For more on this bifurcation of a sentence, see M. A. K. Halliday, "The Place of Functional Sentence Perspective in the System of Linguistic Description," in *Papers on Functional Sentence Perspective* (ed. F. Daneš; the Hague: Mouton, 1974) 43–53; W. L. Chafe, "Givenness, Contrastiveness, Definiteness, Subjects, Topics, and Point of View," in *Subject*

If successive sentences have the same sentence topic, a sense of topic continuity is created.[45] In some languages, of which Biblical Hebrew is one, the syntax of a sentence is often distinctive for sentences in which old topics are repeated and sentences in which new topics are introduced.[46] This formal marking can help the interpreter of a discourse by pointing out the places in a discourse where one is most likely to find a shift in development of the discourse (e.g., shift in speech act, scene, theme, etc.).[47]

and Topic (ed. C. N. Li; New York: Academic Press, 1976) 25–56; J. Firbas, "On the Thematic and the Non-thematic Section of the Sentence," in *Style and Text* (ed. H. Ringbom; Stockholm: Språkforläget Skriptor, 1975) 317–34; F. Daneš, "Functional Sentence Perspective and the Organization of the Text," in *Papers on Functional Sentence Perspective*, 106–28; C. N. Li and S. A. Thompson, "Subject and Topic: A New Typology of Language," in *Subject and Topic*, 457–89; and P. Sgall, E. Hajičová, and J. Panevová, *The Meaning of the Sentence in Its Semantic and Pragmatic Aspects* (ed. J. L. Mey; Dordrecht: Reidel, 1986). For a comparison of the oppositions of topic vs. comment with the related oppositions of given vs. new and theme vs. rheme, see E. F. Prince, "On the Given/New Distinction," in *The Elements* (ed. P. Clyne et al.; Chicago: Chicago Linguistic Society, 1979) 267–78. She sorts out the subtle differences in the positions taken by Firbas, Daneš, Halliday, Chafe, and others.

44. Chafe, "Givenness, Contrastiveness," 50.
45. For numerous articles on topic continuity and discontinuity, see T. Givón, ed., *Topic Continuity in Discourse: A Quantitative Cross-Language Study* (Amsterdam: Benjamins, 1983).
46. In early Biblical Hebrew narratives, the difference in word order between sentences like [/way-yiqṭōl/ + subject] and [/wĕ/ + subject + /qāṭal/] (e.g., /way-yēlek Mōšeh/ vs. /wĕ-Mōšeh hālak/) is frequently controlled by considerations of continuity and discontinuity of topic and often signifies a shift in speech act; see T. Givón, "The Drift from VSO to SVO in Biblical Hebrew: The Pragmatics of Tense-Aspect," in *Mechanisms of Syntactic Change* (ed. C. N. Li; Austin: University of Texas Press, 1977) 181–254; R. E. Longacre, "A Spectrum and Profile Approach to Discourse Analysis," *Text* 1 (1981) 337–59; A. Fox, "Topic Continuity in Early Biblical Hebrew," in *Topic Continuity* (ed. T. Givón; Amsterdam: Benjamins, 1983) 217–54; and S. G. Dempster, *Linguistic Features of Hebrew Narrative: A Discourse Analysis of Narrative from the Classical Period* (Ph.D. diss., University of Toronto, 1985).
47. Such shifts can be identified by other linguistic markers as well. For shifts in forms of tense, voice, or mood see P. J. Hopper, ed., *Tense-Aspect: Between Semantics and Pragmatics*

opment than has been typical of past research.[46]

In some cases, a paragraph topic is the same as the most frequently used sentence topic in that paragraph. In other cases, it may be a complete sentence that summarizes or overlays the information or point of that paragraph, or it may be the sum of the sentence-level comments. But paragraph-level topics are often not formal units at all. They may just be concepts inferred by the reader from the semantic relatedness perceived in the vocabulary, event sequence, and character networks of that paragraph.

At the paragraph level of analysis of topic, it seems useful to turn to the more abstract notions of speech acts and macrostructures (as developed by van Dijk). To determine the topic of a discourse, van Dijk and Kintsch have developed a procedure that strips away elements from the formal and semantic structure of a discourse as a whole in order to produce abstract propositions that will represent the main concepts or main plot elements, in other words, to reduce the discourse to a single statement of just what the discourse is about.[49] These rules can be used by recursion to produce several levels of abstraction. The admitted dependence of these rules on abstract notions such as personal knowledge and awareness of various scripts means that the results of their application are likely to vary according to the person applying them.

This is not, however, a defect of the model. It is just a fact of human communication that, despite large areas of overlap in the basic knowledge of all speakers, the specific knowledge base that each hearer brings to the inter-

(Amsterdam: Benjamins, 1982). For shifts marked by special particles see R. E. Longacre, "'Mystery' Particles and Affixes," in *Papers Presented at the Twelfth Regional Meeting, Chicago Linguistic Society* (ed. S. Mufwene et al.; Chicago: Chicago Linguistic Society, 1976) 468–75; and I. Bearth, "Discourse Patterns in Toura Folk Tales," in *Papers on Discourse* (ed. J. E. Grimes; Dallas: Summer Institute of Linguistics and University of Texas at Austin, 1978) 208–25. On the use of adverbials as discourse markers see W. J. M. Bronzwaer, "A Hypothesis Concerning Deictic Time Adverbs in Narrative Structure," *Journal of Literary Semantics* 4 (1975) 53–72.

48. For some ideas along these lines, see the discussion of "rhematic progression" in Daneš, "Functional Sentence Perspective."

49. This process consists of the application of rules of selection, reduction, and generalization: see van Dijk, *Macro-structures*; T. A. van Dijk and W. Kintsch, *Strategies of Discourse Comprehension* (New York: Academic Press, 1983).

process is dynamic and impervious to any systematic description by a linguist without consultation with social psychologists, sociolinguists, cognitive scientists, historians, and literary critics.

The way real hearers arrive at the meaning of a discourse will probably always differ considerably from the way any of these analysts—even in consultation with one another—can ever describe. Real hearers have strategies that make short cuts through the theoretical processes and transformations posited by researchers. The study of these strategies is entirely outside my competence and must be left for others to characterize,[50] but their existence is here acknowledged.

I have, however, for some time taken an interest in the strategies of speakers, both conscious and subconscious, that may invest a personal touch in the structure of the discourse. This is sometimes thought of as a definition of "style," but what I am talking about is not the study of the devices and expressions that characterize a given speaker, but the study of the discourse features that relate to the beliefs and attitudes of the speaker toward what he or she is saying.

Undoubtedly, most of the forms and most of the organization of a discourse are already decided for the speaker by such factors as those just discussed in this paper: the discourse type, cohesion and coherence requirements, the specific social context, and human cognitive capabilities.[51] The characters and events that the speaker mentions in a narrative are to a large extent already determined by the world of reference; how they are arranged in the discourse is mostly determined by the conventions of plot development. However, when the arrangement of the information is not in accordance with the established patterns, that is, when it deviates from the unmarked way of structuring a sentence or a discourse, the analyst should

50. Van Dijk and Kintsch discuss this at length in *Strategies of Discourse Comprehension.*
51. Sometimes every element of an utterance is predetermined for the speaker. In uttering formulaic oaths, prayers, and toasts, the speaker must not vary at all from the prescribed wording and voice inflection lest that nullify the qualification of the utterance as a token of the intended speech act.

that norm as meaningful. These points of deviation are often identifiable by specialized structures such as negation, subordination, inverted word order, passivization, tense and mood shifts, modals, loaded adjectives, comparatives, and parallelisms.[52] Such constructions may reflect the author's personal view of the relative importance of an event being narrated to the overall speech act being performed.

Labov and Waletzky, in their study of spontaneous oral narratives, discuss a subset of these constructions, which they call "evaluative" devices.[53] Polanyi expands the notion and discusses evaluatives on all levels of language from the phonological to the discourse level.[54] In each case the evaluative is conceived of as a deviation from the established norm of expression that forces the hearer to accept the narrator's, rather than the conventional, view of the circumstances.

If an event is subject to evaluation in a discourse, the hearer would not respond to it with a usual, unmarked "uh-huh," "go on," or "I see," but instead might be a bit surprised and say "oh really?" "that's strange," "you've gotta

52. More of these special words and particles are discussed by W. Pickering, *A Framework for Discourse Analysis* (Dallas: Summer Institute of Linguistics and University of Texas at Arlington, 1978); and P. Werth, *Focus, Coherence and Emphasis* (London: Croom Helm, 1984). In Biblical Hebrew, events are frequently evaluated by such devices as negation, inverted word order, tense shifts, the use of /wa-yĕhî/, /we-hinnēh/, conjunctionless sentences, specialized conjunction, subject pronominalization, ellipsis, and syntactic subordination.

53. W. Labov and J. Waletzky, "Narrative Analysis: Oral Versions of Personal Experience," in *Essays on the Verbal and Visual Arts* (ed. J. Helm; Seattle: University of Washington Press, 1967) 12–44; see also W. Labov, "The Transformation of Experience in Narrative Syntax," in *Language in the Inner City* (ed. W. Labov; Philadelphia: University of Pennsylvania Press, 1972) 354–96. Labov and Waletzky found that in the speech of blacks in Harlem these evaluative devices clustered into special sections of the discourse—either at the beginning or at the end—and that they tended to reveal how the speaker felt about the content of the narrative. These sections may have little to do with the actual events and plot of the narrative itself. They focus on something that the speaker sees as important as a consequence of thinking about the narrative just told. The evaluative section reveals what it is that the speaker thinks the narrative is really about, what the speaker thinks the motivation of the characters was in the narrative, or what relevance the narrative has for our own day. One kind of evaluative discussed in "Transformation of Experience," intensives, is treated at greater length in W. Labov, "Intensity," in *Meaning, Form, and Use in Context* (ed. D. Schiffrin; Washington, DC: Georgetown University Press, 1984) 43–70.

54. Polanyi, *Telling the American Story*.

all about how they are presenting themselves in a discourse, others very much do. In spontaneous, face-to-face communication, speakers are more likely to reveal their attitudes and feelings by evaluative devices than they are in more controlled modes of discourse like storytelling, letter writing, or lecturing.

Yet even in the writing of discourse, speakers cannot altogether hide their attitude toward what is being discussed. For example, on the word level the speaker must choose how to refer to the characters, using a proper name for that character or simply referring to him as *a man*. During the discourse the speaker can alternate between synonyms (e.g., *the man, the king, David*, or *king David*), can simply repeat the same word each time the character is mentioned, can resort to a personal pronoun, or can even delete the reference altogether.[56] But when rules of syntax and discourse structure do not require a certain form of reference, the speaker's attitudes, ideologies, or prejudices may influence the choice of terms of reference. The choice of one noun over a less marked near synonym can reveal an attitude or a social status that would otherwise be unrecoverable.

55. Labov suggests that one might be able to determine the point of a narrative by isolating "the most reportable event" or "events," i.e., that event which makes the discourse worth telling; "Speech Actions and Reactions in Personal Narratives," in *Analyzing Discourse: Text and Talk* (ed. D. Tannen; Georgetown University Round Table on Language and Linguistics 1981; Washington, DC: Georgetown University Press, 1982) 219–47.
56. Jones and Kress assess a speaker's use of pronouns and nominalizing of people's identities as indicators of the speaker's relationship to or attitude toward these persons; G. Jones and G. Kress, "Classifications at Work: The Case of Middle Management," *Text* 1 (1981) 69–76. For example, *our* not only shows empathy and identity of the speaker with someone else, but also implies acceptance of responsibility for the beliefs and commitments of that group. For other factors that influence lexical selection, see P. Downing, "Factors Influencing Lexical Choice in Narrative," in *The Pear Stories* (ed. W. Chafe; Norwood, NJ: Ablex, 1980) 89–126; T. A. van Dijk, *Prejudice in Discourse* (Amsterdam: Benjamins, 1984); and E. Bates, W. Kintsch, C. R. Fletcher, and V. Giuliani, "On the Role of Pronominalization and Ellipsis in Texts: Some Memory Experiments," *Journal of Experimental Psychology: Human Learning and Memory* 6 (1980) 676–91.

is surprised that a possible comparison can be made. Modal verbs, auxiliaries, and verbs of mental processes such as *think, see,* and *know* can strengthen or weaken a speaker's commitment to the message. Non-present tenses distance events from the here-and-now of the speaker/hearer interaction: past tenses may evoke lack of empathy, a past/present contrast can reflect a certainty/uncertainty opposition. Using a variety of tenses and modals may imply an uncertainty of the speaker of the actual facts. Jones and Kress mention the modal particles *really, as such, pretty, a fair number of, literally, normally, usually,* and *kind of* that serve to dissociate the speaker from the literal interpretation of the utterance by lexicalizing uncertainty and vagueness.[57] This meaning is in addition to the meaning that each of these devices has on the sentence level of syntax and semantics.

On the clause level, a speaker can assign the status of sentence subject to either the actor or the victim of an action (i.e., subject position often reveals speaker empathy).[58] Or the speaker can negate the sentences (which constitutes the foregrounding of the reversal of normal expectations). On the sentence level, the speaker can put an idea or event into a main clause, or lower its importance by putting it into a subordinate clause.

The use of these devices transforms the unmarked underlying semantic structures of the discourse into a surface form that is designed to meet the special needs of speakers in their psycho-social communicative situations and to express their personal or projected-personal points of view. By the use of evaluative devices, speakers subtly exert pressure on hearers to accept the speaker's beliefs, values, and attitudes toward the characters and their actions and motives. When a speaker spends time justifying an idea or opinion through making concessions, denials, repetitions, and contrasts, we know that it is an underlying view of the subject matter that is controlling the expression and not just a matter of style or rhetorics.[59]

We must be careful not to evaluate wrongly the personality or social status of speakers in a negative way simply because their modes of discoursing

57. See Jones and Kress, "Classifications at Work," 5–64.
58. See S. Kuno and E. Kaburaki, "Empathy and Syntax," *Linguistic Inquiry* 8 (1977) 627–72.
59. See M. Kreckel, *Communicative Acts and Shared Knowledge in Natural Discourse* (London: Academic Press, 1981); I. Roeh, *The Rhetoric of News in the Israel Radio: Some Implications of Language and Style for Newstelling* (Bochum: Studienverlag Brockmeyer, 1982); and van Dijk, *Prejudice in Discourse.*

out evaluative devices, the view of the speaker remains obscure.

CONCLUSION

Biblical scholars have known for a long time that knowledge of the context of a biblical text is a prerequisite for adequate interpretation. However, they have usually discussed context in terms of the historical background, the sociocultural setting, or the literary traditions of the texts. In discourse analysis, the notion of context has been expanded to include the linguistic framework, human mental capabilities and strategies, and the modes of speaker–hearer interaction.

If the study of discourse and context continues to attract the attention of social scientists to the degree that it has in recent years, then we may some day understand the connection between discourse and its social, cultural, and cognitive contexts well enough to provide a consistent and coherent set of terms and methodologies that will help the biblical scholar understand certain aspects of the world behind a biblical text that have not been illuminated by the more traditional means of analysis; and perhaps we may even be able to catch glimpses of the attitudes and beliefs of the personalities who produced and used the biblical texts during their development.

60. D. Hymes, "On Communicative Competence," in *Sociolinguistics* (ed. H. Pride and D. Holmes; Harmondsworth: Penguin, 1972) 269–93.
61. On the difference in the modes of discoursing between Americans, Japanese, Athabaskans, and Germans, and the negative impressions they often leave on speakers of other languages, see L. Loveday, "Conflicting Framing Patterns: The Sociosemiotics of One Component in Cross-cultural Communication," *Text* 2 (1982) 359–74; and M. Clyne, "Culture and Discourse Structure," *Journal of Pragmatics* 5 (1981) 61–66.
62. R. Hunt and D. Vipond, "Evaluations in Literary Reading," *Text* 6 (1986) 56.

[November, 1986]

The purpose of this paper is to shed light on the various tense/aspect/mode forms of the verb in Biblical Hebrew, not by suggesting some new and penetrating insight into the subtle mystique of each form, but simply by placing each form in context with other forms in various types of discourse and inquiring as to the functions of each verb form within a given discourse type.[1] This is in conscious contrast to the time-honored way of attempting to describe all the uses of a given verb form in the same comprehensive write-up in one section of a grammar. Thus GKC (1910) devotes four pages to the uses of the perfect, six pages to the uses of the imperfect, four pages to the uses of the *wāw*-consecutive with the imperfect, nine pages to the uses of the imperative, etc. From the point of view of this paper, such presentation jumbles together rather distinct uses of a given verb form in different discourse types, such as narrative, predictive, procedural, hortatory, expository, and juridical—to name a few prose types without going on to consider further uses in

Author's note: The following abbreviations are used: NV, noun–verb; VSO, verb–subject–object.

1. Insofar as this is a textlinguistic approach to the structure of the verb in Biblical Hebrew, my approach is similar to that of W. Schneider, *Grammatik des biblischen Hebraisch* (Munich: Claudis, 1974), with which I am acquainted via E. Talstra's review, "Text Grammar and Hebrew Bible, Part I: Elements of a Theory," 35 (1978) 169–74; (published in 1980) and "Part II: Syntax and Semantics," *BO* 39 (1982) 26–38; and also to the current work of A. Niaccacci, *Sintassi del verbo ebraico nella prosa biblica classica* (Studium Biblicum Franciscanum Analecta 23; Jerusalem: Franciscan Printing Press, 1986). Both Schneider's and Niaccacci's works (as well as Talstra's comments) contain many germinal ideas which I am just now beginning to assimilate. My work differs from theirs mainly in regard to my sharper insistence on the relevance of discourse types to the analysis, the main point of this paper.

within such a cluster. The uses of a given tense within a given cluster may differ quite strikingly from the uses of the same tense within another cluster (discourse type).

VERB FORMS IN NARRATIVE DISCOURSE

Biblical Hebrew narrative discourse tells a story about particular people and their actions and contingencies in past time. It is agent-oriented and action-oriented—as, indeed, is narrative discourse in any language.

The backbone or storyline tense of Biblical Hebrew narrative discourse is the *wāw*-consecutive with the imperfect. Since this form is historically descended from an archaic preterite, I simply call it a preterite[2]—a form which has survived only with a waw frozen on the front of it. That this form involves a "conversion" of a present-future into a past is a quaint piece of linguistic folklore that is better forgotten. Calling it a *wāw*-consecutive with the imperfect is better than calling it a "*wāw*-conversive"—provided we simply mean that the tense form expresses sequential actions in the past (and is viewed as punctiliar). The view that the *wāw*-consecutive is necessarily consecutive on a perfect (which must obligatorily precede it) flies in the face of many counterexamples in the Hebrew Scriptures. GKC put it quite well early in this century by simply terming *wāw*-consecutive + the imperfect a special narrative tense (GKC §111a/p. 326).

The perfect in Biblical Hebrew acts like a secondary storyline. It is only weakly sequential and not necessarily punctiliar. Since preterites occur only in verb-initial clauses, the preposing of a noun (whether the subject or object) precludes the use of a preterite and makes necessary recourse to the perfect. Such use of clause-initial nouns for participant introduction or contrast determines a participant-oriented clause rather than an action-oriented one. However, a VSO clause may have a perfect when it encodes a preparatory or resultant action. Perfects may also encode a flashback. In all these respects the perfect is secondary to the preterite in Biblical Hebrew narrative. The perfect makes possible the inclusion of participant-oriented actions or back-

---

2. Alternatively, there is much to say for identifying these forms according to the Hebrew form of the paradigm verb, e.g., *wayyiqtol* for the preterite, *qatal* for the perfect, etc.

Setting is given in *hāyâ* clauses, nominal clauses (verbless), and in *yēš* (existential) clauses. Such clauses offer necessary detail as to participants, props, and circumstances without which a story cannot be adequately staged—or restaged at crucial junctions—and without which the reader might not understand what is reported as transpiring. Irrealis elements are negative. In most languages, modal elements occur as well. In Biblical Hebrew, were such elements to occur in the framework of a story (no examples at present), they would presumably emerge as modal imperfects. Irrealis elements which involve negation are events which "don't get off the ground." Significant here is the well known fact that preterites qua preterites cannot be negated. Attachment of *lō*ʾ 'not' results in a preterite being replaced by a perfect.

What then? A narrative discourse is a cluster of clause types which is characterized by several tense/aspect forms, among which the preterite predominates as primary storyline but is accompanied by perfects in secondary function; imperfects, participles, nominal, equational and existential clauses, and negative clauses further flesh out the story. These various forms do not constitute a haphazard conglomeration, but rather a structured scheme in which ever lower positions in the scheme reflect progressive degrees of departure from the storyline preterites (see diagram 1). Within narrative discourse, the tenses which are involved in it can be given somewhat precise and useful functions.

The following brief passage, Gen 40:20–23, is a fairly run-of-the-mill narrative paragraph in Biblical Hebrew.

> [20]wayhî bayyôm haššĕlîšî yôm hulledet ʾet-parᶜōh wayyaᶜaś mišteh lĕkol-ᶜăbādāyw wayyiśśāʾ ʾet-rōʾš śar hammašqîm wĕʾet-rōʾš śar hāʾōpîm bĕtôk ᶜăbādāyw. [21]wayyāšeb ʾet-śar hammašqîm ᶜal-mašqēhû wayyittēn hakkôs ᶜal-kap parᶜōh. [22]wĕʾēt śar hāʾōpîm tālâ kaʾăšer pātar lāhem yôsēp. [23]wĕlōʾ-zākar śar-hammašqîm ʾet-yôsēp wayyiškāḥēhû.

Here the initial *wayhî* 'and it came to pass' followed by the temporal expression *bayyôm haššĕlîšî* 'on the third day' (which is further identified as *yôm hulledet ʾet-parᶜōh* 'Pharaoh's birthday') provides setting for the paragraph;

Band 2: Backgrounded Activities	2.1 Noun + imperfect: implicitly durative/repetitive 2.2 *Hinnēh* + participle 2.3 Participle (explicitly durative) 2.4 Noun + participle
Band 3: Setting	3.1 Preterite of *hāyâ* 'be' 3.2 Perfect of *hāyâ* 'be' 3.3 Nominal clause (verbless) 3.4 Existential clause with *yēš*
Band 4: Irrealis	4. Negation of verb (in any band)
Band 5: (± *wayhî* + temporal phrase/clause) Cohesion (back-referential)	5.1 General reference 5.2 Script-predictable 5.3 Repetitive

the perfect form contained in the construction is in an appositional phrase and has non-storyline *flashback* meaning. The narrative storyline clauses begin with *wayyaʿaś* 'and he made', *wayyiśśāʾ* 'and he raised up', *wayyāšeb* 'and he restored', *wayyittēn* 'and he [the cupbearer] gave', and *wayyiškāḥēhû* 'and he forgot him'. The clause *weʾēt śar hāʾōpîm tālâ* 'and (but) the chief baker he hanged' focuses temporarily and contrastively on the chief baker and is participant-oriented rather than action-oriented; its perfect verb is illustrative of NV clauses found in the secondary storyline. The clause *kaʾăšer pātar lāhem yôsēp* 'just as Joseph had interpreted to them' is a flashback to an earlier event. Finally, *loʾ zākar* 'and he didn't remember' is irrealis (negative) and is off the storyline, while the positive counterpart *wayyiškāḥēhû* 'but he forgot him' is on the storyline.

Band 3: Setting		3.1 *Wāw*-consecutive perfect of *hāyâ* 'be' 3.2 Imperfect of *hāyâ* 'be' 3.3 Nominal clause (verbless) 3.4 Existential clause with *yēš*
Band 4: Irrealis		4. Negatation of verb (in any band)
Band 5: Cohesion	(± *wĕhāyâ* + temporal phrase/clause)	5.1 General reference 5.2 Script-predictable 5.3 Repetitive

VERB FORMS IN PREDICTIVE DISCOURSE

The backbone structure in predictive discourse is the *wāw*-consecutive + the perfect (an analogical creation after the *wāw*-consecutive + the imperfect). The formal analogy of the *wāw*-consecutive perfect to the *wāw*-consecutive imperfect is quite complete: (1) Both are limited to VSO clauses and may not be negated (or otherwise introduced by particles such as *kî* or *ʾîm*). (2) Both report sequential and punctiliar actions/events. (3) Just as *wāw*-consecutive imperfect (preterite) gives way to a perfect when a noun or *lōʾ* 'not' is preposed, so a *wāw*-consecutive perfect gives way to an *imperfect* when a noun or *lōʾ* is preposed to it. Semantically there is contrast: the *wāw*-consecutive perfect is projected into the future, and the *wāw*-consecutive imperfect is a past tense.

The imperfect functions as a secondary storyline in predictive discourse—where its function is quite parallel to that of the perfect in narrative.

izes predictive discourse.

In summary, predictive discourse is a cluster of clause types characterized by tense/aspect forms in which the *wāw*-consecutive perfect has preeminence with progressive degrees of departure from the *mainline of prediction* signaled by imperfects, participles, and 'be' verbs/nominal clauses. Perfects (aside from *wāw*-consecutive perfects) are rare but do occur and function much like *wāw*-consecutive perfects in a "perfect of certainty." I have emphasized above the parallel (but semantically distinct) functions of *wāw*-consecutive imperfect and *wāw*-consecutive perfect in the two discourse types, the similar parallelism (and semantic difference) of perfect to imperfect across types, and the distinct use of the imperfect in narrative as opposed to prediction (see diagram 2).

The following selection, 1 Sam 10:2–7, is a predictive discourse in which Samuel predicts what will happen to Saul after he departs from Samuel's presence.

²bĕlektĕkā hayyôm mēᶜimmādî ûmāṣāʾtā šnê ʾănāšîm ᶜim-qĕbūrat rāḥēl bigĕbûl binyāmin bĕṣelṣaḥ wĕʾāmĕrû ʾēlêkā nimṣĕʾû hāʾătōnôt ʾăšer hālaktā lĕbaqqēš wĕhinnēh nāṭaš ʾābîkā ʾet-dibrê hāʾătōnôt wĕdāʾag lākem lēʾmōr mâ ʾeᶜĕśeh libnî. ³wĕḥālaptā miššām wāhālĕʾâ ûbāʾtā ᶜad-ʾēlôn tābôr ûmĕṣāʾûkā šām šĕlōšâ ʾănāšîm ᶜōlîm ʾel-hāʾĕlōhîm bêt-ʾēl ʾeḥād nōśēʾ šĕlōšâ gĕdāyîm wĕʾeḥād nōśēʾ šĕlōšet kikkĕrôt leḥem wĕʾeḥād nōśēʾ nēbel-yāyin. ⁴wĕšāʾălû lĕkā lĕšālôm wĕnātĕnû lĕkā štê-leḥem wĕlāqaḥtā miyyādām. ⁵ʾaḥar kēn tābôʾ gibᶜat hāʾĕlōhîm ʾăšer-šām nĕṣibê pĕlištîm wîhî kĕbōʾăkā šām hāᶜîr ûpāgaᶜtā ḥebel nĕbîʾîm yōrĕdîm mēhabbāmâ wĕlipnêhem nēbel wĕtōp wĕḥālîl wĕkinnôr wĕhēmmâ mitnabbĕʾîm. ⁶wĕṣālĕḥa ᶜālêkā rûaḥ yhwh wĕhitnabbîtā ᶜimmām wĕnehpaktā lĕʾîš ʾaḥēr. ⁷wĕhāyâ kî tābōʾynā hāʾōtôt hāʾelleh lāk ᶜăśēh lĕkā ʾăšer timṣāʾ yādekā kî hāʾĕlōhîm ᶜimmak.

In this example the following *wāw*-consecutive perfect forms introduce clauses which are on the mainline of the passage: *ûmāṣāʾtā* 'and you will meet', *wĕʾāmĕrû* 'and they will say', *wĕḥālaptā* 'and you will proceed', *ûbāʾtā* 'and you will come', *ûmĕṣāʾûkā* 'and they will meet you', *wĕšāʾălû* 'and they will ask', *wĕnātĕnû* 'and they will give', *wĕlāqaḥtā* 'and you will take', *ûpāgaᶜtā* 'and you will meet', *wĕṣālĕḥâ* 'and she will come upon', *wĕhitnabbîtā* 'and you will prophesy', and *wĕnehpaktā* 'and you will be changed'. In v. 5 there is an imperfect occasioned by the preposed *ʾaḥar kēn* and functioning

VERB FORMS IN
PROCEDURAL/INSTRUCTIONAL DISCOURSE

At first blush, procedural/instructional discourse looks very similar to predictive. Both, for instance, have a mainline which consists of *wāw*-consecutive perfects. But while in predictive discourse imperfects can occur both in VSO clauses to mark a secondary storyline and in NV clauses to mark an action/event relative to a noun, in procedural discourse the imperfect occurs only in NV clauses. The rule is: Major procedures (e.g., accomplishing the major goals of a ritual) are marked by VSO *wāw*-consecutive perfect clauses, while minor procedures (e.g., having to do with necessary but less important parts of a ritual) are marked by NV clauses with the imperfect.[3]

In strictly procedural discourses, the discourse is not agent-oriented but goal-oriented; any appropriate agent may implement the procedures in order to reach the desired goal (e.g., to propitiate Yahweh, or to certify a cleansed leper for return to society). This discourse type turns mainly on the *wāw*-consecutive perfect and the noun + imperfect, as outlined above, with use of participles, 'be' clauses, and nominal clauses much as in narrative and predictive discourses.

Such a procedural discourse is contained in Lev 4:1–12, which deals with offering a sacrifice for a sin committed in ignorance.

---

3. Obviously, the departure from VSO to NV represents a kind of topicalization of a weak sort, i.e., while major procedures are VSO and are action-oriented toward major goals, minor procedures, expressed in NV clauses, focus on subordinate goals represented in clauses with initial nouns. The structure can be roughly represented as:

Do A
Do B } major procedures: *wāw*-consecutive perfect in VSO clauses
Do C

As for q, do X
As for r, do Y } minor procedures: noun + verb in the imperfect
As for s, do Z

pe amım lıpne yhwh ᵓet-pĕnê pārōket haqqōdeš. ⁷wĕnātan hakkōhēn min-had-dām ᶜal-qarnôt mizbaḥ qĕṭōret hassammîm lipnē yhwh ᵓăšer bĕᵓōhel môᶜēd wĕᵓēt kol-dam happār yišpōk ᵓel-yĕsôd mizbaḥ hāᶜōlâ ᵓăšer-petaḥ ᵓōhel môᶜēd. ⁸wĕᵓet-kol-ḥēleb par haḥaṭṭāᵓt yārîm mimmennû ᵓet-haḥēleb hamĕkasseh ᶜal-haqqereb wĕᵓēt kol-haḥēleb ᵓăšer ᶜal-haqqereb. ⁹wĕᵓēt štê hakkĕlāyōt wĕᵓet-haḥēleb ᵓašer ᶜălêhen ᵓăšer ᶜal-hakkĕsālîm wĕᵓet-hayyōteret ᶜal-hakkābēd ᶜal-hakkĕlāyôt yĕsîrennâ. ¹⁰kaᵓăšer yûram miššôr zebaḥ haššĕlāmîm wĕhiqṭîrām hakkōhēn ᶜal mizbaḥ hāᶜōlâ. ¹¹wĕᵓet-ᶜôr happār wĕᵓet-kol-bĕśārô ᶜal-rōᵓšô wĕᶜal-kĕrāᶜāyw wĕqirbô ûpiršô. ¹²wĕhôṣîᵓ ᵓet-kol-happār ᵓel-miḥûṣ lammaḥ-ăneh ᵓel-māqôm ṭāhôr ᵓel-šepek haddešen wĕśarap ᵓōtô ᶜal-ᶜēṣîm bāᵓēš ᶜal-še-pek haddešen yiśśārēp.

In v. 1 and part of v. 2 we find formulas of quotation followed by presenta-tion of the topic: 'And God said to Moses, "Speak unto the sons of Israel saying, 'As for the person who sins in ignorance . . . even if it is the anointed priest who sins. . . . ' " ' The procedure proper sets in as the apodosis of the conditional structure with which the passage opens. The onset of the proce-dural is signaled by a clause with *wāw*-consecutive perfect: *wĕhiqrîb ᶜal haṭ-ṭāᵓtô ᵓăšer ḥāṭāᵓ par* 'and he shall bring near for his sin which he has sinned a bullock. . . . ' A chain of clauses with *wāw*-consecutive perfects outlines the major procedures down through the first part of v. 7; I cite these clauses here in translation:

⁴ And he shall bring the bullock to the door of the tabernacle before YʜWʜ.
And he shall lay his hand on the head of the bullock.
And he shall kill the bullock before YʜWʜ.
⁵And he shall take, the anointed priest, some of the blood of the bullock.
And he shall bring it to the tent of meeting.
⁶And he shall dip, the priest, his finger in the blood.
And he shall sprinkle the blood seven times before YʜWʜ at the front of the veil of the sanctuary.
⁷And he shall put, the priest, some of the blood on the horns of the altar. . . .

Some minor (resultant or preparatory) procedures are given in NV im-perfect (in this case object-verb) clauses. Thus, in v. 7 such a clause specifies the procedure for disposing of the rest of the blood which was not used in the ritual proper: 'And all the blood of the bullock, he shall pour out at the base of the altar of burnt offering. . . . ' In vv. 8–9 instructions are given in con-

have not figured in the ritual. Verse 11 itself is a string of accusative phrases (skin, flesh, head, leg, intestines, and dung) for which apparently no main verb is given (the initial *wāw*-consecutive perfect of v. 12 cannot be construed with the preposed phrases). Verse 12 contains two *wāw*-consecutive perfects—'and he shall carry out . . . and he shall burn'—which tie these concluding procedures into the main parts of the ritual. The latter part of v. 12 is a chiastic sentence with 'burn' occurring first as a *wāw*-consecutive perfect and lastly as an imperfect (passive). My claim that the use of the *wāw*-consecutive perfect signals the return to a major procedure is not a piece of special pleading to bolster my theory of tense uses. On the contrary, the use of the periphrastic and chiastic sentence at the end of v. 12 is itself a witness to the importance attached to the closing procedure.

Varying somewhat in form is the instructional discourse in which instruction is given to a particular individual (e.g., Noah, Moses) to make something according to specifications, or to act as specified in a given situation. Here occasional isolated imperatives occur (but not strings of imperatives) which give (enjoin) the major goal of the procedures. For example: 'Make an ark' (Gen 6:14), 'Take for yourself provisions' (Gen 6:21), 'Make a tabernacle' (Exod 25:8), 'Make an ark [of testimony]' (Exod 25:10), 'Make one cherub on one end and the second cherub on the other end' (Exod 25:19). Aside from such isolated goal-announcing and goal-enjoining imperatives, the VSO clauses with *wāw*-consecutive perfect and NV clauses with the imperfect function as described above for procedural discourse. In one such discourse (Gen 6:13–16), we find, in fact, only one imperative followed by noun + imperfects; the imperative enjoins the main goal ('build an ark') and the NV clauses treat various details: rooms, window, door, and decks. The one *wāw*-consecutive perfect which occurs ('and you will pitch it . . . ') seems to be in construction with the previous clause. Nominal clauses specify dimensions of the ark.

Such a discourse, directed at a particular person, can be strongly second-person oriented. Gen 6:17–21 is directed at Noah and uses second-person pronouns and affixes to emphasize the second-person orientation. Neither the

types lest there be distinct uses that here have been inadvertently lumped together.

VERB FORMS IN HORTATORY
(PERSUASIVE) DISCOURSE

The hortatory discourse type is characteristic of the human situation in which one person tries to impose his or her will on another person. Imperatives, cohortatives, and jussives make up the line of exhortation/persuasion in this discourse type. Strings of "command" clauses occur; unlike the isolated clause-initial imperatives found in instructional discourse, these clauses may be verb-initial or noun-initial with the command form, as in Gen 43:11–14 and 42:18–20. The modal imperfect is characteristic of this discourse type, as are negative commands with $^{\circ}al$ + the jussive/imperfect (not always clearly distinguished), or *pen* 'lest' + the imperfect in negative purpose clauses. If the *wāw*-consecutive perfect is used, it seems quite regularly to express result. Participles, 'be' verbs, and nominal clauses continue to be used much as described above.

Gen 43:11–14 is a typical piece of hortatory discourse. Here a rather distraught Jacob has just lost the main point of his year-long argument with his sons regarding taking Benjamin to Egypt. Nevertheless, he takes charge and as clan head tells his sons what to do.

> ¹¹wayyōʾmer ʾēlēhem yiśrāʾēl ʾăbîhem ʾim-kēn ʾēpôʾ zōʾt ʿăśû qĕḥû mizzimrat hāʾāreṣ biklêkem wĕhôrîdû lāʾîš minḥâ mĕ ʿaṭ ṣŏrî ûmĕ ʿaṭ dĕbaš nĕkōʾt wālōṭ boṭnîm ûšĕqēdîm. ¹²wĕkesep mišneh qĕḥû bĕyedĕkem wĕ-ʾet-hakkesep hammûšāb bĕpî ʾamtĕḥōtêkem tāšîbû bĕyedĕkem ʾûlay mišgeh hûʾ. ¹³wĕ-ʾet-ʾăḥîkem qāḥû wĕqûmû šûbû ʾel-hāʾîš. ¹⁴wĕ-ʾēl šadday yittēn lākem raḥămîm lipnê hāʾîš wĕšillaḥ lākem ʾet-ʾăḥîkem ʾaḥēr wĕ-ʾet-binyāmîn waʾănî kaʾăšer šākōltî šākāltî.

Starting off with a generic imperative ʿăśû 'do as follows', he proceeds to issue specific commands: qĕḥû 'take (of the produce of the land)', wĕhôrîdû 'and take down (to the man a present)', wĕkesep mišneh qĕḥû 'and take double silver', wĕ-ʾet-ʾăḥîkem qāḥû 'and take your brother', wĕqûmû 'and rise up', šûbû 'return (to the man)'. Modal imperfects occur as well in v. 12 (tāšîbû 'you must return' in 'silver which was returned in the mouths of your sacks

⁹mahărû waᶜălû ᵓel-ᵓābî waᵓămartem ᵓēlāyw kōh ᵓāmar binĕkā yôsēp śāmanî
ᵓĕlōhîm lĕᵓādôn lĕkol-miṣrāyim rĕdâ ᵓēlay ᵓal-taᶜămōd. ¹⁰wĕyāšabtā bĕᵓereṣ-
gōšen wĕhāyîtā qārôb ᵓēlay ᵓattâ ûbānêkā ûbĕnê bānêkā wĕṣōᵓnĕkā ûbĕqārĕkā
wĕkol-ᵓăšer-lāk. ¹¹wĕkilkaltî ᵓōtĕkā šām kî-ᶜôd ḥāmēš šānîm rāᶜāb pen-tiwwārēš
ᵓattâ ûbêtĕkā wĕkol-ᵓăšer-lāk. ¹²wĕhinnēh ᶜênêkem rōᵓôt wĕᶜênê ᵓāḥî binyāmîn
kî-pî hamĕdabbēr ᵓălêkem. ¹³wĕhiggadtem lĕᵓābî ᵓet-kol-kĕbôdî bĕmiṣrayim
wĕᵓēt kol-ᵓăšer rĕᵓîtem ûmihartem wĕhôradtem ᵓet-ᵓābî hēnnâ.

Here Joseph, who has just revealed himself to his brothers, no longer speaks
to them in strings of imperatives (as he did in his role of grand vizier), but
now instructs them as a brother (although still ordering them around much
as before!).

Notice the initial imperative in v. 9: *mahărû* 'hurry'. This is followed by
wāw-consecutive perfects: *waᶜălû* 'and go up (to my father)', *waᵓămartem*
'and say (to him: "Thus says your son Joseph")'. The message to be relayed
to Jacob also contains an initial imperative (strengthened with -*â*), *rĕdâ* 'come
down (to me)', and is followed by a negative command: *ᵓal-taᶜămōd* 'don't
delay'. Thereafter the imperative is replaced by *wāw*-consecutive perfects:
wĕyāšabtā 'and you shall dwell (in the land of Goshen)', *wĕhāyîtā* 'and you
shall be (near me)', *wĕkilkaltî* 'and I will nourish (you there)'. With v. 13 the
exhortation to the brothers is resumed: *wĕhiggadtem* 'and you shall declare
(to my father all my glory), *ûmihartem* 'and you shall hurry', *wĕhôradtem*
'and you shall bring down (my father here)'. On both layers of the message—
to the brothers who stand before Joseph and to the father back in Canaan—
lone imperatives begin the series and *wāw*-consecutives follow. When the in-
terrupted instructions to the brothers resume, the imperative does not recur;
rather *wāw*-consecutive perfect forms do. Here the one imperative + consecutive stands in contrast to the strings of imperatives found elsewhere (e.g., in
Gen 43:11–14). Consequently, the *wāw*-consecutive perfect cannot be considered to be an automatic continuation of the imperative, but is a conscious
choice over against the imperative along with the semantic implications
which are resultant on the choice.

your eyes) are seeing . . . (that I'm the one) talking (to you)'.

To conclude the discussion of this passage, I would suggest that all the *wāw*-consecutive perfects possibly have hortative force, as in 'and you shall dwell with me', and even 'and I will nourish you' (= 'and let me nourish you . . . ').

If a more thoroughgoing mitigation was desired, a hortatory discourse could, in effect, substitute for the form of predictive discourse. A noticeable example of this is Joseph's appeal to the chief cupbearer after he interpreted the latter's dream. The thrust of the appeal to the courtier is clearly hortatory/ persuasive: 'Remember me to Pharaoh, and do something to get me out of prison.' But Joseph did not presume to use even one imperative (much less a string of them) in wording his appeal to the courtier. As a slave, and a disgraced slave at that, he was making an appeal to a high-ranking noble shortly to be returned to favor (according to Joseph's own prophecy). Joseph opted, then, for a string of *wāw*-consecutive perfects, introduced by an off-the-line future perfect and terminated with some historical perfects expressing why he found himself imprisoned. The only hortatory/persuasive trait found in the surface structure of Joseph's discourse is the use of the entreaty particle *nāʾ* with the first *wāw*-consecutive perfect. Because of space limitations I will not give this passage here nor comment further on it.

A further variety of hortatory discourse, the deferential, uses court etiquette in addressing such personages as the Pharaoh, in third-person constructions. For this reason the text approximates a string of jussives (e.g., 'Let Pharaoh find a wise man') with isolated *wāw*-consecutive perfects expressing result—as posited above for unmitigated hortatory discourse (cf. Gen 41:33–36).

VERB FORMS IN OTHER PROSE TYPES

Space limitations do not permit detailed presentation of other prose types here. Two further types can be called *expository* and *juridical* discourse.

Expository discourse takes as its line of exposition 'be' clauses and nominal clauses. In exposition, unlike the other discourse types, the most *static* elements are central. This is seen, for instance, in Joseph's interpretation of dreams, in Gen 40:12–13, beginning as it does with *zeh pitrōnô* 'This is its interpretation'. It also occurs in the speech of the brothers, in Gen 42:22, as

('he will surely die'); $l\bar{o}^{\jmath}$ + imperfect ('he will not be punished'); otherwise *wāw*-consecutive perfect (in VSO) and imperfect (in NV). Nonconditional injunctions (cf. the Decalogue) can presumably have any structure appropriate to an apodosis.

[April, 1987]

An Introduction to
Historical/Comparative Linguistics

The interest of this volume is, as specified in the title, *Linguistics and Biblical Hebrew*. But before I begin my overview of historical and comparative linguistics and what they can offer the student of the biblical text, a few words of warning are in order. The Bible may be a sacred text, but the languages in which it is written are not sacred. Biblical Hebrew is a language like any other language. Because of the nature of our primary—but not our only—text in this language, special sensitivity must be brought to its study, but not special methods. Methods used to study Biblical Hebrew, like those used to study other "dead" languages, must take into account the limited nature of the corpus; we do not have access, for example, to the complete Biblical Hebrew lexicon or to the full range of pronunciation facts about the language. Nevertheless, explanations offered for Biblical Hebrew phenomena must be commensurate with those advanced for comparable phenomena in other languages, and they must be subject to the same standards of evaluation.

The Concept of Mischsprache

A case in point is the claim, first advanced in the early years of the twentieth century, that Biblical Hebrew is a *Mischsprache*, overlaying Aramaic elements on a Canaanite foundation (BL § 2j–o / pp. 19–25). Now there is a tendency among American historical linguists, one to which Semitists are by no means immune, to assume that ordinary German words acquire, by virtue of their importation into English, technical rigor, and that they imbue scholarly discourse into which they are embedded with a corresponding degree of rigor.

191

that context (BL § 26g′ / p. 237). However, if the *Mischsprache* theory is that Biblical Hebrew is a language of truly mixed parentage, discussion of this claim must be placed in the context of a general discussion of creolization, an area of linguistics in which an extensive literature has developed. When creoles develop, they follow certain well-known patterns, and their structures differ from those of their parents in predictable ways. If Biblical Hebrew is, in fact, a creole, its structure should be similar to those of other creoles like Tok Pisin of Papua New Guinea and Jamaican Creole; and it should differ from both Phoenician and Aramaic. While detailed exploration of these patterns would be a topic for another essay, I note here the unlikelihood of a complex verbal inflectional system like that of Biblical Hebrew surviving the process of creolization; reduction or loss of inflectional systems is so common in creoles as to be near-diagnostic of past creolization.[1]

The Basis of Language Change

Theories of creolization represent an attempt to deal with a particular class of changes. While some might contend that creolization is special in that these changes differ qualitatively from the ordinary language changes treated in historical linguistics, I disagree.[2] This disagreement is based on my understanding of the nature of language change. Quite simply, language change is an inevitable consequence of the biological makeup of language users and of the social circumstances in which they use language. Given that change is inevitable, there is no need to seek nonlinguistic explanations for the fact of change in a particular instance. In the nineteenth century, some of the changes that took place in the history of Spanish were attributed to the linguistic influence of the Ibero-Celts, autochthonous residents of the Iberian peninsula about whose language, conveniently, nothing is known. In like

1. For background on creoles and creolization, see D. Bickerton, *Roots of Language* (Ann Arbor: Karoma, 1981); A. Valdman, *Le créole: Structure, statut et origine* (Paris: Klincksieck, 1978); D. DeCamp and I. F. Hancock, eds., *Pidgins and Creoles: Current Trends and Prospects* (Washington, DC: Georgetown University Press, 1974); H. E. M. Schuchardt, *The Ethnography of Variation: Selected Writings on Pidgins and Creoles* (ed. and trans. T. L. Markey; Ann Arbor: Karoma, 1979); P. Muysken and N. Smith, eds., *Substrata versus Universals in Creole Genesis* (Amsterdam: Benjamins, 1986).
2. Creoles differ, of course, from noncreoles in the extent to which they have been influenced by other languages.

(2 Kgs 18:26–37), both aware of the political and sociolinguistic consequences of their choice of parley language and of the power dynamic inherent in its selection, would have rejected *le mot juste* simply because it came from the other's language.

These two insights—that language change is inevitable and that languages are not impervious to outside influence—are at the core of historical linguistics. As a result of the inevitability of change, differentiation of a once monolithic speech community into several distinct speech communities occurs when different changes occur in different segments of the community; and changes will occur in all segments of the community. Contrary to popular opinion, there are no speakers of Elizabethan English living in the hollows of Appalachia. Appalachian English has evolved differently from other dialects of American English, but evolved it has. Thus, the inevitability of change translates into the inevitability of linguistic divergence. This divergence results in the existence of groups of related languages, all descended from a common ancestor. In the absence of direct attestation, the structure of unattested ancestor languages, generally referred to as proto-languages, must be inferred on the basis of the structures of their descendants, as well as on general linguistic principles. Likewise, the susceptibility of languages to influence from without means that languages may come to resemble each other over time, even if they are not descendants of the same linguistic stock. The permeability of languages, then, translates into the inevitability of linguistic convergence.

GRAPHIC METAPHORS FOR LANGUAGE RELATIONSHIPS

There are two graphic metaphors that are commonly used in connection with related groups of languages.[3] One metaphor, the tree, is borrowed from

3. For more extensive discussion of these metaphors, in somewhat different terms, see L. Bloomfield, *Language* (New York: Holt, Rinehart & Winston, 1933) 311–19; J. M. Anderson, *Structural Aspects of Language Change* (London: Longman, 1973) 191–94; T. Bynon,

1

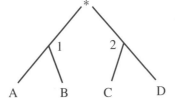

Here, * represents the earliest relevant language stage, *1* and *2* represent intermediate stages of development, and *A–D* actual languages. The vertical depth of the graph represents time, so tree 1 represents a different linguistic history from that shown in trees 2 or 3, even though the internal relationships in the trees are the same.

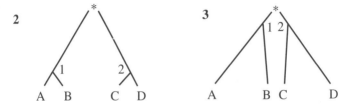

Tree 4, however, represents a different internal structure from that represented by trees 1–3:

Historical Linguistics (Cambridge Textbooks in Linguistics; Cambridge: Cambridge University Press, 1977) 171, 192.

In this diagram each of the following pairs of languages—*AD*, *AC*, and *BC*—shares a property or a set of properties. In the view of change supported by this *Wellentheorie*, changes in a linguistic territory radiate outward from their points of origin like the ripples in a pond caused by a pebble or a raindrop. The language of a given subgroup of speakers may be affected by changes rippling outward from several different points of origin.

The two metaphors that I have described differ in two crucial respects. The *Stammbaumtheorie* requires the idealization of independent development following a split, while the *Wellentheorie* does not. Likewise, the *Stammbaum* explicitly incorporates the dimension of time, while the *Wellentheorie*, again, does not. Now, it is often assumed, especially by Semitists, that the wave and tree models are competing for the same sets of facts.[4] The isolation of a set of facts that can only be incorporated within a wave model is taken as evidence against the tree model. But, given that the wave model makes no explicit mention of the time dimension, such a rejection begs the question of the original relationship among a group of languages, before the first wave, as it were. Furthermore, given the basic assumptions about language change which I discussed earlier, it is clear that the picture is more

4. See, for example, G. Garbini, *Le lingue semitiche* (Ricerche 9; Naples: Istituto Orientale di Napoli, 1972); C. Rabin, "The Origin of the Subdivisions of Semitic," in *Hebrew and Semitic Studies Presented to G. R. Driver* (ed. D. W. Thomas and W. D. McHardy; Oxford: Clarendon, 1963); and, using lexicostatistics, a method of dubious validity, C. Rabin, "Lexicostatistics and the Internal Divisions of Semitic," in *Hamito-Semitica* (Janua Linguarum Series Practica 200; ed. J. Bynon and T. Bynon; The Hague: Mouton, 1975).

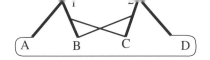

Here, the thick lines represent lines of direct descent, following split, as reflected in a pure tree model, while the thin lines represent diffused innovations, as in a pure wave model.

Possible Relationships among Languages

If a group of languages is characterized by a sufficient number of structural similarities—and I ignore for present purposes the thorny problem of determining just what constitutes a sufficiently large number of similarities—that it is possible to hypothesize a relationship among them, it is no trivial task to discover the precise nature of that relationship and the structure of the earlier, unattested language states. Yet making determinations of this sort is one of the primary tasks of historical linguists. (The other task, characterization of possible language changes, is outside the scope of this presentation.) In the remainder of this paper, I both demonstrate the importance of this task and outline some of the ways in which it can be addressed.

A linguistic feature (whether phonological, morphological, syntactic, or lexical) which recurs in two related languages but not in other languages to which both are related can come about in four distinct ways:[5]

1. The feature may be one that innovated at a point in time when the two languages were differentiated from others in their group but not yet from each other.
2. Alternatively, both of the languages might have retained the feature, unchanged, from a remote common ancestor, while the other descendants of that ancestor underwent linguistic change.
3. An additional possibility is that the feature developed in one of the languages and later spread to the other.
4. Finally, it is possible that the feature represents a coincident, convergent development. That is, the two languages might have inherited structural similarities which caused them to develop in parallel.

5. J. H. Greenberg, *Essays in Linguistics* (Chicago: University of Chicago Press, 1957) 37.

the personal pronoun *du*, beginning with a dental, immediately followed the verb.

In like vein, if two related languages differ with regard to a particular feature, either one of the languages may retain the original form while the other has innovated. It is also possible that neither language reflects the parent language with regard to this feature; that is, both languages may have changed. A final possibility is that two options existed in the parent language, each of which was preserved in one of the two languages in question.

What it Means to be a Conservative Language

Now, in neither of the above sets of circumstances is there any *a priori* means of determining which possibility is correct. This decision can only be made on the basis of study of a specific situation. In particular, the following information is needed:

1. The internal structure of the linguistic group, including the chronology of linguistic developments; in other words, the tree structure.[6]
2. The linguistic structures of the unattested stages *, *1*, and *2*.
3. The likelihood of cultural contact of the sort necessary for linguistic diffusion.
4. How the particular feature is represented in all the languages in the group, not just in the two of immediate interest.

It is particularly important to note that there is no such thing as an inherently conservative language. That is, one cannot accept claims of the following form: "Language *L* is generally a conservative language. Therefore, language *L* is conservative with regard to feature *F*." Nevertheless, investigators often work with an implicit bias that some languages in a group are better witnesses than others for the proto-language or for certain aspects of the proto-language. Thus, Indo-Europeanists used to give undue weight to Sanskrit, Greek, and Latin in their attempts to reconstruct earlier stages of the language group. This emphasis on ancient literary languages has been replaced, at least in some quarters, with a focus, equally illegitimate, on the allegedly conservative Lithuanian. Similarly, some Semitists have a tendency to rely overmuch on Akkadian, because that language is attested early, extensively, and with indications of vowel quality. The countervailing tendency is to rely heavily on Arabic, especially Bedouin Arabic, because of the allegedly conservative character of the Bedouin, uncontaminated by urbanization

---

6. As far as I know, no definitive tree has ever been developed for any major language group, with the possible exception of some American Indian language families.

cestor can only be determined on the basis of reconstruction of the ancestor, taking into account features of all its known descendants. The method by which this is done is called comparative reconstruction. This method is generally related to the *Stammbaum* model of language relatedness discussed above. That is, it assumes that language relatedness reflects descent from a common ancestor. It further assumes that the changes that occurred during the descent of each language from the proto-language were lawful changes, that is, that the changes were systematic.

THE REGULARITY OF SOUND CHANGE

The primary hypothesis regarding the systematic nature of change is generally referred to as the Neogrammarian hypothesis. This hypothesis holds that sound change is regular and exceptionless. What this means is that sound changes are statable on the basis of phonological environments. To give a slightly oversimplified example, in Hebrew, unstressed word-final vowels (preserved in Akkadian, Classical Arabic, and perhaps in Ugaritic) were lost; word-final position and lack of stress constitute the phonologically statable environment for this change. And the Neogrammarian hypothesis claims that all these unstressed, final vowels were lost at the same time. The competing hypothesis, lexical diffusion,[8] claims that change, rather than being statable in purely phonological terms, diffuses through the lexicon of a language; factors such as meaning, semantic affect, and token frequency affect the likelihood of a particular change occurring in a particular word.

Like the *Stammbaumtheorie* and the *Wellentheorie*, these two hypotheses are often conceived of as competing for the same sets of facts. And, as is the case with the *Stammbaumtheorie* and the *Wellentheorie*, such a dichotomous conception of the Neogrammarian and lexical diffusion hypotheses is simplistic and misleading. The lexical diffusion hypothesis focuses exclusively on the process of sound change, while the Neogrammarian hypothesis focuses exclusively on its outcome. Under ordinary circumstances, it is only in cases of apparent irregularity of outcome that questions of process are even

7. C. Rabin, *Ancient West-Arabian* (London: Taylor's Foreign Press, 1951) 12.
8. M. Y. Chen and W. S.-Y. Wang, "Sound Change: Actuation and Implementation," *Lg.* 51 (1975) 255–81.

reason for this requirement is simple. Given the well-known *double articulation* of language,[10] by which languages necessarily consist of a hierarchical arrangement of meaningless units (sounds) which are combined into meaningful units (morphemes, words, and sentences), it can plausibly be expected that change in one level would proceed independently of change in another. But this requirement, which serves to prevent breakdowns in communication, in no way implies that change in one level must be independent of structure in another.

The Comparative Method

With this in mind, let us now turn to the comparative method itself. Central to comparative reconstruction is the isolation of systematic, recurrent correspondences among related languages. For this to work, the units being compared must be compared in contexts. Sounds are compared in phonological environments within words; morphemes are compared in words and in syntactic contexts; words are compared in semantic fields; sentence structures are compared in discourse or paragraph contexts.[11] If a correspondence recurs in the same environment, it is systematic and can be discussed independent of the context. So, for example, on the basis of correspondences between English and French, like those listed in 7, one can say that English /f/ and French /p/ correspond.

9. H. M. Hoenigswald, "Is the 'Comparative' Method General or Language-Specific?" in *Linguistic Change and Reconstruction Methodology* (ed. P. Baldi; Berlin: de Gruyter, 1990) 375–83.

10. A. Martinet, *Économie des changements phonétiques* (Bern: Francke, 1955) 157–58.

11. R. J. Jeffers, "Syntactic Change and Syntactic Reconstruction," in *Current Progress in Historical Linguistics* (ed. W. M. Christie Jr.; North-Holland Linguistic Series 31; Amsterdam: North-Holland, 1976) 1–10, asserts that syntactic reconstruction is impossible; even if two languages share the same word order, this order cannot be attributed to the parent language. But, if two languages agree in having a distinct word order in counterfactual conditionals, surely this order in this context could safely be attributed to their parent language.

In establishing correspondences, the systematicity of a particular correspondence is more important than the phonetic transparency of the posited relationship. The classic example of an odd correspondence is Armenian initial /erk/, which corresponds to /dʷ/, /tʷ/, or /cʷ/ in other Indo-European languages, as illustrated in 8.[12]

8   English *two*
         German *zwei*
         Latin *duo*
         Armenian *erku*

Once systematic correspondences have been isolated, they can be grouped together. As 8 (in conjunction with many other examples) shows, English /t/ corresponds to German /c/ at the beginning of a word. In the middle of a word, however, English /t/ corresponds to German /s/, as in *better* and *besser*. So, even though two distinct correspondences are represented here, the fact that they do not contrast means that they can be grouped together and treated as representing one unit of the proto-language. It is typically the case that comparison within a language family will isolate more correspondence sets than proto-language phonemes; correspondence sets will often be in complementary distribution.

The Phonetic Content of Reconstructed Phonemes

The final step in comparative reconstruction is to attempt to determine the content of the reconstructed unit. In the case of English /t/ corresponding sometimes to German /c/ and sometimes to /s/, we establish a single phoneme of the proto-language and attempt to determine some of its phonetic features. In fact, given any phonological comparison, the final step is to determine the nature of the reconstructed phoneme or phonemes. In cases of lexical comparison, the final step is to attempt to determine the proto-language meaning of a word that has varied meanings in the descendant languages. Or, in case of a morpheme that has differing ranges of function in the descendant languages, the final step is to determine its function in the proto-language. In all cases, these determinations presuppose some coherent

12. H. H. Hock, *Principles of Historical Linguistics* (Berlin: de Gruyter, 1986) 583–84.

phonetic content of reconstructed phonemes, to the extent to which this is seen as possible, is outside the comparative method proper. In such a view, the phonetic symbol following the asterisk is intended merely as an abbreviation for a correspondence set or for a group of correspondence sets in complementary distribution. The difficulty with this procedure is that it is almost inevitable that asterisked symbols will be interpreted as phonetically meaningful, sometimes even by writers who specifically exclude this usage. So, for example, Moscati asserts that the three reconstructible proto-Semitic sibilants are represented, like their Hebrew descendants, *š, *ś, and *s, solely on the basis of conjecture, but then refers to the Arabic change of *š to /s/.[14] It makes no sense to say that an "abbreviation for a correspondence set" has undergone change. Yet, given that Moscati provides no defense for reconstructing *š as in Hebrew, rather than *s as in Arabic or even some third sound, no other interpretation is possible.

Now, if our interest is in determining which languages in a group are conservative and which innovative with regard to a particular feature or features, it is not enough to end with an algebraic reconstruction. Conserving the number of original phonemes in no way implies conserving the phonetic content of these phonemes. As noted above, statements about innovation and retention must be based on the relationship between the reconstructed structure of the parent language and the attested structures of the descendant languages. It is impossible to state such a relationship based on an algebraic reconstruction. But, given a reconstruction that aspires to some sort of phonetic realism, it is relatively obvious which languages have undergone change and what sort of change they have undergone. The question then becomes how to determine the phonetic content of reconstructed phonemes.

Generally, correspondence sets, on the basis of which phonemes are reconstructed for the proto-language, are of two sorts. There are sets in which all the languages have the same sound, and sets in which not all the languages have the same sound. In cases of the first sort, correspondences of identity, it is customary to reconstruct the same thing for the proto-language, so that no

13. Such as Bloomfield, *Language*, 303, 309.
14. S. Moscati, ed., *An Introduction to the Comparative Grammar of the Semitic Languages* (Wiesbaden: Harrassowitz, 1969) 34.

correspondence set of /t d θ ð/ is isolated, it will be assumed without discussion that the range of possibilities for the proto-language ancestor phoneme is restricted to one of those four sounds. Furthermore, if the correspondence set is of /t t θ d t θ/, all other things being equal, *t is treated as the reconstruction of preference, on the basis of a simplicity criterion: with the reconstruction of *t, only three changes must be stated, one each in three languages, while, with the possible alternative reconstruction of *θ, changes must be stated for four languages, and, with the reconstruction of *d, for five. If, on the other hand, only three languages are represented, with /t θ ð/, no matter which sound is reconstructed, two changes must be stated. But reconstruction of *t is preferred, because the complex of changes *t → /θ/ and *t → /d/ is simpler to state than those resulting from the possible alternative reconstructions of *d or *θ, as shown in example 9:

9 *t   *θ   *d

t → θ [+stop] → [−stop]   θ → t [−stop] → [+stop]   d → t [+vce] → [−vce]

t → d [−vce] → [+vce]   θ → d [−stop] → [+stop]   d → θ [+stop] → [−stop]

                                              [−vce]   [+vce]   [+vce]   [−vce]

A further consideration in reconstruction is the inventory of the reconstructed system. If correspondence set /t θ d/ contrasts with correspondence set /t t t/, and the latter is reconstructed *t, then *t is not available for the former; either *θ, *d, or something else must be reconstructed for that set.

As I noted above, little attention has been paid to the question of how two sounds in two different languages can be identified as the same. Yet such a determination is crucial to the analytical principles that I have outlined. In practice, identity is assumed on the basis of a phonemic transcription of the attested sounds. Two sounds transcribed ⟨t⟩ are assumed in the absence of information to the contrary to be phonetically identical. However, even the "identical" /t/'s in English and French differ. English /t/ is alveolar and aspirated, while French /t/ is dental and unaspirated. A further dimension along which /t/'s can differ is the part of the tongue effecting the oral closure, the apex or the blade.[15] If only these features are combined, as in 10, there are eight different sounds that might be represented /t/:

15. J. C. Catford, *Fundamental Problems in Phonetics* (Bloomington: Indiana University Press, 1977) 143, 145, 151–52.

lytic decision involved in deciding what kind of /t/ to reconstruct is exactly parallel to that involved in reconstructing the ancestor of corresponding /s/ and /θ/.

Kinds of Innovation

Now, on the basis of the reconstructed inventory, it is possible to outline the changes that must have occurred in the history of each of the descendant languages. It is sometimes possible to determine the relative order in which changes took place as well. For example, in Arabic, /l/ of the definite article assimilates to following dental/alveolar consonants, except for /ǰ/. /ǰ/, however, corresponds to /g/ in other Semitic languages.[16] What probably happened is that /l/ first assimilated to following dental/alveolar consonants and then *g changed to /ǰ/. /l/ does not assimilate to /ǰ/ because at the time that the assimilation was innovated, /ǰ/ was still a velar /g/ and not alveolar /ǰ/.

Once the innovations in a group of related languages have been isolated, the focus moves to those innovations that recur in the histories of more than one of the languages in the group. These innovations are of three sorts: those reflecting a shared history, those reflecting influence of one language on another, and those reflecting convergent development. Shared and convergent developments are generally differentiated on the basis of how idiosyncratic they are. For example, if a new Indo-European language were found in which the reflex of *d^w was /erk/, it would be assumed that this language shared a history with Armenian; the likelihood of any sequence of changes relating *d^w and /erk/ occurring twice, independently, is extremely slim. On the other hand, "small" natural changes like *t → /θ/ or *t → /d/ are much more likely to recur independently.

Shared innovations are further differentiated from diffused and convergent innovations on chronological grounds. All innovations in the history of a particular language that are shared with other languages must necessarily have occurred prior to any innovations that are unique to that language. If,

---

16. The discussion in the text is somewhat oversimplified. *g is preserved in some dialects of Egyptian Arabic and is realized /ž/ rather than /ǰ/ in some Levantine dialects.

they are. For example, the change of *g to /j/, already discussed on the basis of Arabic forms, recurs in Ethiopian Semitic languages. However, because the Arabic change followed the assimilation of /l/ to following dental-alveolars, a development unique to Arabic, the change of *g to /j/ cannot be treated as a joint innovation in Arabic and Ethiopian Semitic; it must represent a convergent or a diffused development. And, given the normalcy of palatalizations in a wide range of languages, the change probably was not diffused, but represents rather a convergent development.

An additional factor relevant to determining whether a particular innovation could have diffused is cultural history. In order for a feature to diffuse from one language to another, speakers of one language must have been in contact with speakers of the other. Thus, late innovations that recur in Biblical Hebrew and in Aramaic can plausibly be treated as innovations diffused from one language to the other, while innovations recurring in Phoenician and Jibbali (one of the Modern South Arabian languages) are much more likely to represent convergence.

I noted above that comparative reconstruction is commonly assumed to be based on the regular sound changes posited by the Neogrammarian hypothesis and not on the idiosyncratic products of lexical diffusion. However, if it is the case that highly idiosyncratic changes like the Armenian change of *d^w to /erk/ are better potential indicators of shared development, then idiosyncratic, "irregular" changes should be equally good indicators. In the history of English, older *o: had the regular outcome /uw/; but in a class of words that is not phonologically definable, it appears, instead, as /u/.[17] Thus *good* and *food*, which rhymed in earlier stages of English, now have different vowels. This is a textbook case of lexical diffusion. If it were to turn out that comparable changes occurred in two related languages in even partially isomorphic sets of words, this common anomaly would constitute powerful evidence indeed for shared development.

Representations like those in trees 1–4 above are constructed on the basis of shared innovations only. Diffused innovations can be charted as in tree 6, but, as they are in some sense secondary, they can be set aside and charted at a later stage. As already noted, the intermediate nodes *1* and *2* on the trees represent a period of shared development. Thus, node *1* on tree 1, dominating

17. E. Sapir, *Language* (New York: Harcourt, Brace & World, 1921) 177–78; Hock, *Principles of Historical Linguistics*, 645–46, 657–58.

Innovation vs. Retention. In the procedures that I have sketched, I have emphasized shared innovation. It is only on the basis of shared innovations that a subgroup, symbolized by a dominating node, can be posited. If /t/ in *A* and *B* corresponds to /θ/ in *C* and *D*, and the decision has been made to reconstruct *t, a change of *t to /θ/ must be posited in *C* and *D*. Now, *C* and *D* agree in having undergone this change, and, if it is determined that the change represents a shared innovation, a subgroup consisting of *C* and *D* may be posited. But, even though *A* and *B* agree in not having undergone the change, no subgrouping may be based on this agreement. Shared retention never provides the basis for positing a subgroup. Thus, on the basis of this correspondence alone, it is impossible to differentiate between tree 1 and tree 4; in both trees, a single node dominates *C* and *D*. In a more complicated tree, every single branching must be justified by its own shared innovation or innovations.

Phonological, Morphological, and Syntactic Innovation. The final area that I would like to touch on concerns structure and innovation. Earlier in this discussion I suggested that the comparative method can be based on phonological, morphological, or syntactic comparisons. But all of my examples had to do with phonological reconstruction. If our interest lies in reconstructing the proto-language sound system, such an emphasis is understandable. If, however, our interest lies in discovering the internal structure of a language family, higher-level comparison becomes necessary. Given my earlier claim that idiosyncratic, "irregular" developments provide the best diagnostic of shared history, it becomes relevant to ask which level of linguistic structure is most likely to be characterized by idiosyncratic developments. It has been claimed that arbitrary morphological features provide the best possible evidence for linguistic subgrouping and relatedness.[18] So the presence of irregular comparative and superlative forms like *better* and *best* for the adjective *good* in Indo-European languages, even if they do not have cognate words for 'good', provides solid evidence that these languages are related. Obviously, the utility of morphological comparison in a particular language group will

---

18. Greenberg, *Essays in Linguistics*, 51; R. Hetzron, "Two Principles of Linguistic Reconstruction," *Lingua* 38 (1976) 89–108.

ties. The Sino-Tibetan languages, on the other hand, typically use syntactic means to code distinctions that might be marked morphologically in other languages. It would be oversimplifying only marginally to say that these languages have virtually no morphology. As a result, morphological comparison of Sino-Tibetan languages is not likely to produce meaningful results.

CONCLUSION

Structural linguistics of any sort is based on the presumption that linguistic facts are not isolated data but rather constitute parts of systems. Given this presumption, it is illegitimate to analyze any piece of data independently of the systems of which it constitutes an element. Second-person verb suffixes cannot be understood synchronically independently of their paradigms or of the sorts of sentences in which second person verb forms are typically used. In like fashion, the diachronic development of such endings cannot be analyzed independently of developments affecting other elements in the paradigm; developments affecting the phonemes making up the ending; developments affecting the syntactic contexts in which the ending might occur; and, lastly, developments affecting cognate forms in related languages. I hope that I have provided some insight into how this analysis can be carried out.

APPENDIX: BASIC READING LIST

1. Introduction to Historical Linguistics
   Arlotto, A. *Introduction to Historical Linguistics*. Washington, DC: University Presses of America, 1981.
   Jeffers, R. J., and I. Lehiste. *Principles and Methods for Historical Linguistics*. Cambridge: MIT Press, 1979.
2. Advanced Textbooks
   Anderson, J. M. *Structural Aspects of Language Change*. London: Longman, 1973.
   Anttila, R. *Historical and Comparative Linguistics*. 2d ed. Amsterdam: Benjamins, 1989.
   Bynon, T. *Historical Linguistics*. Cambridge Textbooks in Linguistics. Cambridge: Cambridge University Press, 1977.

Hock, H. H. *Principles of Historical Linguistics*. Berlin: de Gruyter, 1986; reviewed by S. M. Embleton in *Diachronica* 3 (1986) 203–31.

3. Comparative Method and Reconstruction

Baldi, P., ed., *Linguistic Change and Reconstruction Methodology*. Berlin: de Gruyter, 1990.

Greenberg, J. H. *Essays in Linguistics*. Chicago: University of Chicago Press, 1957.

Hoenigswald, H. M. *Language Change and Linguistic Reconstruction*. Chicago: University of Chicago Press, 1960.

(See also the relevant chapters in the items under no. 2 above).

4. Development of Methodology

Anderson, S. A. *Phonology in the Twentieth Century*. Chicago: University of Chicago Press, 1985.

Lehmann, W. P., ed., *A Reader in Nineteenth Century Historical Indo-European Linguistics*. Austin: University of Texas Press, 1967.

Pedersen, H. *The Discovery of Language*. Bloomington: Indiana University Press, 1931.

Robins, R. H. *A Short History of Linguistics*. London: Longman, 1979.

[December, 1988]

John Huehnergard

Historical Phonology and the Hebrew Piel

The problem considered in this paper may be put quite simply: Why does the perfect of the Hebrew D stem have two *i*-vowels, or, why *pi^cel*? This is a venerable question, one that has figured with some prominence in literally dozens of discussions concerning the Hebrew vocalization and accent system and the Hebrew verbal system over the last century and more. Though it is, therefore, obviously a thorny problem, it is nevertheless also a fruitful one to illustrate my topic, historical and comparative linguistics, since it involves both internal, diachronic reconstruction and external, comparative data.

THE HEBREW FORMS AND THEIR RECONSTRUCTION

The forms that concern us, then, are those of the D suffix-conjugation.[1] In Tiberian Hebrew, these are, paradigmatically: 3d masc. sing. *qittel* or *qittal*,[2]

Author's note: The following abbreviations are used for the Hebrew conjugations: G, *Qal*; N, *Niphal*; D, *Piel*; Dᴾ, *Pual*; tD, *Hithpael*; C, *Hiphil*; Cᴾ, *Hophal*. Note also the following conventions for the transliteration of Tiberian vowels: *pátaḥ, a; qɔmɛṣ, ɔ; ṣere, e; sᵊḡol, ɛ; ḥirɛq, i; ḥólɛm, o; qibbuṣ* and *šurɛq, u*; simple *šwɔ* is unrepresented.

1. The semantics of the D stem are not considered in this study. The interested reader may consult, *inter alia*, the following: A. Goetze, "The So-called Intensive of the Semitic Languages," *JAOS* 62 (1942) 1–8; E. Jenni, *Das hebräische Pi^cel: Syntaktisch-semasiologische Untersuchung einer Verbalform im Alten Testament* (Zurich: EVZ, 1968); S. A. Ryder II, *The D-Stem in Western Semitic* (Janua Linguarum Series Practica 131; The Hague: Mouton, 1974); G. Steiner, "Die primären Funktionen des Intensiv- und des Zielstammes des semitischen Verbums," in *XX. deutscher Orientalistentag, Vorträge* (ed. W. Voigt; Wiesbaden: Steiner, 1980) 308–10; J. Weingreen, "The Pi^cel in Biblical Hebrew: A Suggested New Concept," *Henoch* 5 (1983) 21–29.
2. Some verbs exhibit both. There are a few forms with *sᵊḡol*: *dibbɛr, kippɛr, kibbɛs, w-kîḥɛš, (ḥ-r-p)*; see C. Rabin, "The Vocalization of the Third Singular Perfect of Pi^cél in Tiberian

in pause always *qittēl*; pl. *qittlu*, in pause again *qittēlu*;[3] before the first and second person suffixes, base *qittal-*, as in 2d masc. sing. *qittáltɔ*.[4] We have, therefore, *-i-* in the first syllable, and either *ṣere* or *páṭaḥ* in the second syllable; synchronically, the verbs that have *-a-* in the third person may be said to exhibit a uniform paradigm in the suffix-conjugation, *qittal-*, while verbs with *ṣere* may be said to exhibit stem allomorphism, *qittēl ~ qittáltɔ*.

These forms cannot, of course, be considered in isolation. We must also take into account the causative perfect, which likewise, in sound roots, exhibits both an *i* in the first syllable and stem allomorphism in the quality of the second vowel: *hiqtil*, but *hiqtáltɔ*. Some G perfects exhibit a similar variation, as in *zɔqen*, *zɔqántɔ*.

Paradigms that exhibit stem allomorphism give the historical linguist something to do. For variation within a paradigm is often the result of a change, a development away from an originally more consistent paradigm. The change may be the result of analogy to forms in another paradigm, or the result of a sound rule that, because of the conditions or environment in which it worked, affected only part of the paradigm in question. And so, given *qittēl* but *qittáltɔ*, we ask, first, Which contains the more original stem form, and second, What brought about the change that produced the other, newer base?

Perhaps the more obvious choice is to posit *qittal-* as the original base. After all, as we have already noted, there are some D verbs that exhibit only that base in the perfect.[5] Moreover, forms in the Babylonian vocalization tradition of Hebrew consistently exhibit *qittal*.[6] Thus the problem would be merely to explain why, in Tiberian, some renegade 3d person forms in con-

---

Hebrew," *Leš* 32 (1967–68) 12–26 [Hebrew]; J. Blau, "Studies in Hebrew Verb Formation," *HUCA* 42 (1971) 133–58, esp. 155. The occurrence of *sḡol* in some of these may be due in part to the phonetic environment; e.g., both *dibbɛr* and *kippɛr* are II-labial and III-*r*; cf. the effect of sonorants in second position on the development of original **qatl* and **qitl* nouns into Tiberian *qɛ́tɛl*, for which see T. O. Lambdin, "Philippi's Law Reconsidered," in *Biblical and Related Studies Presented to Samuel Iwry* (ed. A. Kort and S. Morschauser; Winona Lake, IN: Eisenbrauns, 1985) 135–45, esp. 140.

3. Similarly the fem. sing., *qittlɔ*, in pause *qittēlɔ*.

4. In pause with *-a-* or *-ɔ-*.

5. Such as *šillam*, *šillámti* (but *šillému* in pause).

6. See P. Kahle, *Masoreten des Ostens* (Leipzig: Hinrichs, 1913) 188–89; I. Yeivin, *The Hebrew Language Tradition as Reflected in the Babylonian Vocalization* (Jerusalem: Academy of the Hebrew Language, 1985) 514–15 [Hebrew]; I wish to thank I. Teshima for bringing this important work to my attention. As noted by Yeivin, the 3d masc. sing. form is also normally *qittal* in pause; the plural in pause, however, is *qittelu*, with *ṣere*. Forms in the Palestinian vocalization often exhibit *qittal* as well (also *qittēl*; see the next note); see E. J. Revell, "Studies in the Palestinian Vocalization of Hebrew," in *Essays on the Ancient Semitic World* (ed. J. W. Wevers and D. B. Redford; Toronto: University of Toronto Press, 1970) 51–100, esp. 70 n. 66.

text[7] and all 3d person forms in pause have *ṣere*. The usual explanation is to point accusingly at the imperfect, *yqattel*, and say that its *i*-vowel was simply taken over by the perfect.[8] But there is a real difficulty here, for it is not clear how the vowel could have been borrowed from the one paradigm into the other. In other words, a change of that sort requires a mechanism, an analogy that can be made in the speakers' minds that can lead to reanalysis of the underlying shape of a form. It is not enough simply to suggest that an *i* in the second stem syllable was felt to be characteristic of the D stem, because, obviously, before the change in question had occurred, that would only have been true of the imperfect and the forms related to it,[9] but not of the perfect itself.[10]

The same, or similar, difficulties attend a view of the C forms that begins with the *hiqtal-* base. And if we do not begin with the *hiqtal-* base when we begin with *qittal-*, we have divorced the development of the two stems, something that is of course possible, but less economical, since the stem allomorphisms of the D and C are so similar.

If we take the other base, *qittil-*, as our starting point, we must explain the *-a-* vowel that regularly appears in the Tiberian tradition before suffixes of the first and second persons and in a significant number of third-person masculine singular forms, and in the Babylonian tradition in all forms of the perfect. Though there is, therefore, a wider range of forms to explain, they are more easily accounted for, I believe, than is *qittel* from an earlier *qittal*.

The Babylonian forms *qittal* and *qittaltɔ* require little comment: the base *qittal-* may derive from earlier *qittil-* because short *a* (*pátaḥ*) is a regular reflex of earlier **i* in closed stressed syllables in verbal forms,[11] as well as in other environments, throughout Babylonian Hebrew.[12]

---

7. Slightly over half the roots; see Rabin, "Third Singular Perfect of *Piʿél*." Note that *qittel* also occurs in Palestinian; see A. Murtonen, *Materials for a Non-Masoretic Hebrew Grammar I: Liturgical Texts and Psalm Fragments Provided with the So-called Palestinian Punctuation* (Helsinki: Akateeminem Kirjakauppa, 1958) 44.

8. As in BL §45f/p. 325; GB pt. 2 §17/p. 97; C. Brockelmann, *Grundriss der vergleichenden Grammatik der semitischen Sprachen* (Berlin: Reuther & Reichard, 1908–13) §257Ba/1:508; F. R. Blake, "The Apparent Interchange between *a* and *i* in Hebrew," *JNES* 9 (1950) 76–83, esp. 76b.

9. Namely, the imperative, participle, and infinitive.

10. One might suggest an analogy between the plural forms, as in *yqatt(ə)lu : qitt(ə)lu :: yqattel : X = qittel*; but that presumes that the reduction to *šwɔ* in the plural forms preceded the change in the vowel of the perfect, an unlikely sequence of events. Also, such an analogy would not explain the presence of *e* in all D perfect third-person forms in pause.

11. Similarly, in Palestinian Hebrew stressed *í* often becomes *á* in closed syllables, yielding *qittal*; see Revell, "Palestinian Vocalization of Hebrew," 69–70 with n. 66.

12. The pausal plural forms *qittelu* mentioned in n. 6 are also most easily explained as Babylonian reflexes of **qittil*. The imperfect of the D is normally *yɔqattel*, with *ṣere*, while expected *yɔqattal* appears only in roots III-*r* and some III-*l* (in addition to roots III-guttural);

In Tiberian Hebrew, the forms of the first and second person may be explained as the result of a sound rule, Philippi's Law, which is usually cited,
in one version or another, to account for any instance in which short *a*
(*pátaḥ*) is the Hebrew reflex of an earlier **i* in a closed stressed syllable. The
conditions under which Philippi's Law is said to operate are notoriously
vague, since there seem to be as many counterexamples to its operation as
proper examples. In a recent review of the evidence of three traditions of
Hebrew vocalization, however—Tiberian, Babylonian, and the Greek transcriptions in the secunda of Origen's hexapla—T. O. Lambdin has suggested
that Philippi's Law operated only in one rather restricted environment. This
can be formulated as follows:

$$-\acute{\imath}C_1C_2(V)\# > -\acute{a}C_1C_2(V)\#   \quad (or, \; i > a \; / \; \underline{\;'\;} \; C_1C_2(V)\#)$$

That is, early stressed **í* became *á* before a consonant cluster, plus or minus
a following vowel, at the end of a word.[13] Further, the rule operated only in
Tiberian Hebrew; since it did not operate in the other traditions, it must be
seen as a relatively late rule in the history of Hebrew vowel development.[14]

---

see Kahle, *Masoreten des Ostens*, 189–90; Yeivin, *Hebrew Language Tradition*, 525–27.
The appearance of *yəqattal* in roots III-*r* means, if we discount the III-*l* forms, that the distribution of *yəqattel* and *yəqattal* accords with what we find in (Babylonian) Aramaic, so
that Aramaic influence on these forms is at least a possibility. T. O. Lambdin (pers. comm.)
suggests that the imperfects with *e* may also have arisen as the result of analogy with the D
participle, which, being a nominal form, properly has *e* in Babylonian (cf. the analogous
situation in III-guttural forms in Tiberian: *yśammaḥ* vs. *mśammeaḥ*).

13. Lambdin, "Philippi's Law Reconsidered." Even with Lambdin's reformulation of the rule,
the forms do not behave completely consistently: D fem. pl. (*t*)*qattélnɔ* (pause -*á*-/-*é*-); tD
titqatté/álnɔ; C *taqtélnɔ* (also pause; vs. pausal 3d masc. sing. *yaqtal*), imv. *haqtélnɔ*; but N
consistently *tiqqɔtálnɔ*. The tendency for an *i*-vowel (*é*) to appear in these forms stems in
part from paradigmatic leveling, i.e., the pressure for a uniform paradigm to be maintained
and thus for the operation of the rule to be stalled or blocked (see also the next paragraph).
Additional pressure for an -*i*- vowel comes from other forms in the relevant conjugations,
including the participle (see n. 12); note that the N participle (*niqtɔl*) does not have an *i*-
vowel between the second and third radicals, so that there is no pressure for one in
tiqqɔtálnɔ, unlike in the other conjugations.

14. Arguing from an entirely different point of view, J. Blau suggests that the operation of
Philippi's Law continued "much later than is generally assumed," though he declines to suggest its beginning; see "On Pausal Lengthening, Pausal Shift, Philippi's Law and Rule Ordering in Biblical Hebrew," *HAR* 5 (1981) 1–13. At p. 8 n. 20, Blau rejects the contention
that Philippi's Law had no validity in the hexaplaric dialect, a contention supported, as Blau
notes, by C. Sarauw, *Über Akzent und Silbenbildung in den älteren semitischen Sprachen*
(Copenhagen, 1939) 76–80; further, E. Brønno, *Studien über hebräische Morphologie und
Vokalismus auf Grundlage der Mercatischen Fragmente der zweiten Kolumne der Hexapla
des Origenis* (Leipzig: Deutsche Morgenländische Gesellschaft, 1943; repr. Nendeln: Kraus,
1966) 448, quoted by Lambdin, p. 37 n. 12; see further n. 23 below. G. Janssens, *Studies in
Hebrew Historical Linguistics based on Origen's Secunda* (Orientalia Gandensia; Louvain:

Thus, in Tiberian, *qittáltɔ* may derive from earlier **qittíltā*. Similarly, in the C stem, *hiqtáltɔ* may be the reflex of **hiqtíltā*, and in G verbs, *zɔqántɔ* of **zaqíntā*.[15]

Finally, the 3d masc. sing. forms *qittal* in Tiberian,[16] I would suggest, are simply new forms that result from analogy,[17] or, more specifically, from paradigmatic leveling; in other words, there is an observable tendency in the language toward maintaining or reinstituting consistency within paradigms.[18] Thus, given the forms *qittáltɔ*, *qittálti*, *qittálnu*, etc., that result from Philippi's Law, the third person **qittil*, unaffected by the sound rule, was nevertheless simply replaced by *qittal* in many instances,[19] though obviously not in

---

Peeters, 1982) 65–66, notes that there are no examples of the operation of Philippi's Law in the hexaplaric material, though he believes that the law must have begun to operate before the loss of case vowels; for a counterargument to the latter point, see Blau, "On Pausal Lengthening," 5 n. 11. Rather extreme is the proposal of K. Beyer, who in a brief note suggests that Philippi's Law is a purely Aramaic sound rule that operated only beginning in the 8th century c.e. and affected both Syriac and Hebrew vowel pointing; "Wann wirkte das Philippische Gesetz?" in *XX. deutscher Orientalistentag, Vorträge* (ed. W. Voigt; Wiesbaden: Steiner, 1980) 267.

15. Cf., without stress, *hiš³iltíhu* (1 Sam 1:28); cf. G *š³iltíw* (1 Sam 1:20) and *ylidtíkɔ* (Ps 2:7); note also the tD forms cited by Blake, "Apparent Interchange," 79b.

16. Blau, "Hebrew Verb Formation," 152, sees **qittala* as "due to a blend" of original **qittila* and **qattala*. Blending, however, is usually nonsystematic and nonparadigmatic and does not normally result in wholesale morphological change; see, e.g., H. H. Hock, *Principles of Historical Linguistics* (Berlin: de Gruyter, 1986) 189–92. Further, there is little evidence, *pace* Blau, for a proto-Hebrew **qattala* (see n. 28 below).

17. As an appropriate analogy, we may cite the active G perfect: *qɔtáltɔ* : *qɔtal* :: *qittáltɔ* (Philippi's Law) : *X = qittal*. In other words, given G *qɔtal ~ qɔtáltɔ*, in which one simply adds *-tɔ*, there is pressure to level *qittil ~ qittáltɔ* once the latter is created by Philippi's Law; similarly, the historically late G verbs like *qɔrab*, originally **qɔreb* (cf. pausal *qɔrébɔ*): with Philippi's Law **qaríbtā* became *qɔrábtɔ*, which by the analogy just mentioned in turn could engender *qɔrab* to replace **qɔreb*.

18. For paradigmatic leveling, i.e., pressure for a single base, for the same vowel throughout the paradigm, see also n. 13 above. In the latter case the effect of the pressure is to block the operation of a sound rule, whereas in the present situation a new form (*qittal*) is created to eliminate forms (*qittel*) that become inconsistent with the majority of forms in their paradigm because, unlike that majority, they have remained unaffected by a particular rule. Cf., e.g., Latin nominative *honos* → *honor* after a sound rule, *s > r / V_V*, caused genitive *honosis > honoris*, etc.; for this example and others, see, e.g., R. Anttila, *An Introduction to Historical and Comparative Linguistics* (New York: Macmillan, 1972) 59–60, 83; A. Arlotto, *Introduction to Historical Linguistics* (Boston: Houghton Mifflin, 1972; repr. Washington, DC: American University) 130–32.

19. Since analogy often (though not always) proceeds from a more basic form to a derived one, such as 3d masc. sing. → other, we might expect the leveling to have produced **qittíl(tɔ)* (or, to restrict/stall the operation of Philippi's Law). But in view of G *qatal ~ yiqtul / qatil ~ yiqtal* and N *niqtal ~ yiqqatil*, we may extract a tendency to maximize the distinction between perfect and imperfect; thus, given a choice of analogically leveled pairs *qittil/qittiltā*

all cases, and regularly not in pause, where we often find preservations of earlier forms. Why *qittil* was replaced by *qittal* in some roots and not others, and why some roots exhibit both, like *berek̲/berak̲*, are difficult questions. Analogy and leveling do not operate with the same consistency we find in phonological rules, as a review of the history of the shift in English of strong verbs (like *sing ~ sang ~ sung*) to the weak pattern (like *work ~ worked ~ worked*) will reveal.[20] Some of the distribution of 3d masc. sing. *qittel* and *qittal* has to do with the phonological shape of the root, and some with the contextual position of a given form, as C. Rabin showed in an article some twenty years ago:[21] *qittel* forms tend to predominate with disjunctive accents, rather like semi-pausal forms, while *qittal* is more common with conjunctive accents and with *maqqep̄*, thus where there is more closure, a contextual situation similar to the more precise phonological environment in which Philippi's Law operates. Another possible impetus for the replacement of *qittil* by *qittal* may have been the existence of synchronic phenomenon that J. L. Malone calls a flip-flop rule, by which allomorphs of words with the vowel sequence *a . . . i* alternate with allomorphs with the opposite sequence, *i . . . a*.[22] Although Malone's derivation of *qittal* more or less directly from an earlier perfect **qattil* is historically unlikely, the flip-flop rule may have had an influence on the synchronic level, given the *a . . . i* sequence in other D stem paradigms such as the imperfect, imperative, and infinitive (cf. also GB pt. 2 § 17i/ p. 97). Finally, some examples may be dialectal variants, reflecting one or more dialects of Hebrew in which the paradigmatic leveling was carried through more vigorously.

At any rate, to get back to the issue at hand, examination of the evidence indicates that all Tiberian forms exhibiting the base *qittal-* may be derived by regular historical processes from earlier **qittil-*.

Additional evidence for the original shape of the *Piel* is afforded by other forms outside the Tiberian "dialect," particularly those preserved in the hexaplaric Greek transcriptions. In D perfect forms, these generally exhibit *epsilon* in both syllables of the base, regardless of the person of the form, paradigmatically, 3d masc. sing. *qettel* and 2d masc. sing. *qettelth(a)*. Since

and *qittal/qittaltā*, the latter prevailed, perhaps because it was the more distinct from imperfect *yVqattil*, particularly in the more important vowel between the second and third radicals (see further below, with n. 22).

20. See, e.g., T. Bynon, *Historical Linguistics* (Cambridge Textbooks in Linguistics; Cambridge: Cambridge University Press, 1977) 32–39.

21. Rabin, "Third Singular Perfect." There are phonological tendencies other than those noted by Rabin, who only considered the third radical; e.g., roots II-ʾ and II-ʿ always have *e*; roots II-ḥ and II-h tend to have *e* when III-dental/alveolar, *a* otherwise.

22. J. L. Malone, "A Hebrew Flip-flop Rule and its Historical Origins," *Lingua* 30 (1972) 422–48. See also n. 19 above.

epsilon in such hexaplaric forms regularly reflects early short *i,[23] and since neither Philippi's Law nor the *qatqat* > *qitqat* dissimilation operates in the hexaplaric "dialect," these forms, as noted by Lambdin, "unambiguously require *qittil-* and not *qittal-* as a starting point."[24]

We have therefore several traditions of Hebrew vocalization; from the viewpoint of historical linguistics, these ought, a priori, to be considered equally valid dialects, parallel descendants of a proto–Biblical Hebrew that exhibit divergent developments.[25] The methodology of historical reconstruction requires that the reflexes of a form posited for the parent language be accounted for by regular processes in each of the descendant dialects. Since one of our "dialects," the hexaplaric, *requires* a base *qittil-* as its protoform, and since the attested forms in the other "dialects," Babylonian and Tiberian, may be explained as reflexes of *qittil-*, that is the form we should posit as the base of the D suffix-conjugation in proto–Biblical Hebrew.[26]

Although space does not permit a review of the evidence here, similar arguments point to similar conclusions for the causative stem, in sound roots: at one stage of proto-Hebrew, allomorphic bases *hiqtil-* before first- and second-person endings, but *hiqtīl-* (with long *ī*) otherwise; and earlier, before the intrusion of the long *ī* by analogy with the hollow verbs, a single base *hiqtil-*.[27]

To recapitulate the discussion thus far: internal reconstruction and comparative reconstruction among the dialects yield for proto-Hebrew the bases

---

23. Cf. Brønno, *Hebräische Morphologie*, 304. There are a few troublesome exceptions, in which *epsilon* apparently reflects proto-Hebrew *a; for the most part Brønno's ad hoc explanations of these exceptions are preferable to the view of Janssens, *Hebrew Historical Linguistics*, 67–75, who essentially claims that the representation of the hexaplaric reflex of proto-Hebrew *a varied freely between *alpha* and *epsilon*, so that *epsilon*, at least in some environments, may reflect either *a or *i (similarly E. A. Speiser, "The Pronunciation of Hebrew based Chiefly on the Transliterations in the Hexapla," *JQR* 24 [1933–34] 9–46, esp. 40; Blau, "On Pausal Lengthening," 8 n. 20). In any case, Janssens (p. 69) agrees with Brønno that the hexaplaric forms of the D and C perfects reflect *qittil(ta)* and *hiqtil(ta)*.

24. "Philippi's Law Reconsidered," 143.

25. See, e.g., Janssens, *Hebrew Historical Linguistics*, 11; Lambdin, "Philippi's Law," 136–37.

26. III-weak *qittɔ* (as in *gillɔ* 'he has uncovered') may derive from *qittiya* as well as *qittaya*, as noted by Blau, "Hebrew Verb Formation," 153. For Samaritan *qattel*, see Lambdin, "Philippi's Law Reconsidered," 143 n. 31. Since only Hebrew *qittal* forms exhibit *i . . . a* for the D suffix-conjugation in Semitic, and since these can be shown to be variants of earlier *qittil*, it goes without saying that it is unlikely that *qittal* is proto-Semitic, as suggested by A. Ungnad, "Zum hebräischen Verbalsystem," *Beiträge zur Assyriologie und semitischen Sprachwissenschaft* 6/3 (1907) 55–62, esp. 57–60.

27. In all but I-*w hošib* < *hawθiba*, probably also I-*y heniq* < *hayniqa*, relic forms that continue to exhibit the proto-Northwest Semitic shape *haqtila* (see below); even geminate *hesab* is probably < *hisibba* (*pace* Blau, "Hebrew Verb Formation," 153), for which see further below.

*qittil- for the D stem perfect and *hiqtil- for the C stem. As will be seen below, it is likely that this was the situation already in the proto-Canaanite period.

A PROTO-CANAANITE SOUND CHANGE

To this point only the vowel patterns *i . . . i* (as in *qittil-) and *i . . . a* (as in qittal-) have been considered. To account for the historical development of the allomorphs under discussion within Hebrew, it simply has not been nec-essary to refer to other patterns, such as *a . . . i* and *a . . . a*.[28] But even within Hebrew, and especially when we move beyond Hebrew to consider the other Semitic languages, we do find other patterns in the paradigms of the D and C suffix-conjugations: Aramaic *qattil and *h/ʾaqtil; Arabic and Ethiopic qattala and ʾaqtala; and in the formally equivalent verbal adjective (stative) in Akkadian, quttul and šuqtul (in Babylonian and Old Akkadian; qattul and šaqtul in Assyrian). Even leaving aside the Akkadian for the moment as ob-viously distinct, the correct reconstruction of the original pattern of these forms is not readily apparent. Many scholars simply posit *qattala on the ba-sis of Arabic and Ethiopic.[29] The original *qattala is presumed to have be-

28. Blau, "Hebrew Verb Formation," 152–58/ §§ 2.1–4, posits both *qittila and *qattala for proto-Hebrew, suggesting "plurilinear" development. Blau's evidence for proto-Hebrew *qattala, however, fails to convince. The use of Arabic and Ethiopic qattala (§ 2.1) as evi-dence of the early Hebrew situation is not helpful, since it entails a tacit assumption that the former languages must preserve proto-Semitic forms, an assumption that is unproved and to be greeted, a priori, with the same skepticism that meets the Hebrew or Aramaic forms (see further below). The C forms of verbs I-*w* (§ 2.2), like holiḏ, probably do indicate earlier *haqtil, but not *haqtal; so also perhaps the *Poel* and *Polel* forms (again, with *i* in the sec-ond syllable, since *Poal/Polal* is passive), although, despite Blau's arguments (pp. 147–51), the origin of these forms remains obscure, so that it is difficult to use them as evidence for earlier vocalization with any confidence. Blau maintains (§ 2.3) that attested qittal forms reflect original qittala rather than innovations due to analogy or leveling; yet G forms like qɔraḇ, which certainly derives from earlier *qariba, must reflect the same type of paradig-matic leveling that Blau here considers unlikely in the case of the D forms (see above, at nn. 13, 18, 19). The C of geminate verbs (§ 2.4), hesaḇ, shows the effect of Philippi's Law, while forms such as 2d masc. sing. hᵃsibbóṯɔ preserve the original second vowel; forms like heseḇ are then based on the latter, through paradigmatic leveling, so that Philippi's Law is blocked (or reversed). Finally, one must question the validity of "plurilinear development" as a tool in reconstruction (see also Blau's "Some Difficulties in the Reconstruction of 'Proto-Hebrew' and 'Proto-Canaanite,'" in *In Memoriam Paul Kahle* [ed. M. Black and G. Fohrer; Berlin: Töpelmann, 1968] 29–43, esp. 42–43), since an essential condition for its use is the reconstruction of byforms in the proto-language (here *qittila and *qattala), a practice that should, if possible, generally be avoided, as noted recently, e.g., by R. Steiner, "*Lulav* versus *lu/law: A Note on the Conditioning of *aw > ū in Hebrew and Aramaic," *JAOS* 107 (1987) 121–22.

29. E.g.: GB pt. 2 § 17i/p. 97; BL § 14v/p. 193; Brockelmann, *Grundriss*, § 52g/1:146–47, § 257Ge/1:524–25; Blake, "Apparent Interchange," 77; note also Blau, "Hebrew Verb For-mation," 152–58, whose arguments for proto-Hebrew *qattala are taken up in the preceding note.

come **qittala* in Hebrew by the attenuation of *a* to *i*. That change, however, does not operate across a doubled consonant (cf. *dayyɔn* < **dayyan-*; *mattɔn* < **mantan-*); further, and more important, the change *qatqat* > *qitqat* is a strictly Tiberian rule,[30] and therefore does not explain the existence of *qittal* in Babylonian and *qettel* in the hexaplaric transcriptions.[31] Besides the phonological difficulties caused by positing protoforms with *a . . . a*,[32] there is a significant methodological problem: proceeding directly from an assumed proto-Semitic **qattala* to proto-Hebrew bypasses several necessary intermediate stages of reconstruction, the most significant of which in the present context is proto–Northwest Semitic,[33] where, as we will see presently, **qattala* cannot be posited. We should therefore aim first for that intermediate stage, proto–Northwest Semitic, the more immediate ancestor of Hebrew and Aramaic. The goal here, of course, is to reconcile proto-Hebrew **qittil-* and **hiqtil-* with proto-Aramaic **qattil-* and **haqtil-*.[34]

30. As noted by Lambdin, "Philippi's Law Reconsidered," 138–39.

31. It must be admitted that a similar sound change may also have occurred in an earlier period, since the N suffix-conjugation, which is *niqtal* in all dialects, must apparently be derived from **naqtala*, in view of weak forms such as *nɔkon*, *nɔsab̠*, *nolad̠*, and probably of *naqtala* in Ugaritic; for the latter, see my *Ugaritic Vocabulary in Syllabic Transcription* (Harvard Semitic Studies 32; Atlanta: Scholars Press, 1987) 321. Cf. Lambdin, "Philippi's Law Reconsidered," 143–44, who also notes that the rule would have to be formulated so as not to affect *maqtal* nouns.

32. See also n. 28 above. Other forms that would be difficult to explain if we begin with *qattala/haqtala* are the C perfects of hollow verbs, *heqim*: were the C perfect originally **haqtala*, we might expect a development **haqyama* > **haqāma* (cf. Arabic *ʔaqāma*, Ethiopic *ʔaqo/ama*). Thus it is more economical to assume **haqtila*, i.e., **haqyima* > **haqīma*. It should be noted that the *i*-vowel in the second syllable of **haqīma*, later **hiqīma*, cannot be the result of analogy with sound roots; on the contrary, the analogical lengthening of **i* to **ī* in the second syllable of sound roots (**hiqtil-* → **hiqtīl-*) is contingent upon the earlier presence of that *ī* in **hiqīma*.

33. For the genetic subgrouping of the Semitic languages I now follow, to a certain point, the classification scheme proposed in a number of very insightful essays by R. Hetzron, including *Ethiopian Semitic: Studies in Classification* (JSS Monograph 2; Manchester: Manchester University Press, 1972) 15–16; "La division des langues sémitiques," in *Actes du premier congrès international de linguistique sémitique et chamito-sémitique* (ed. A. Caquot and D. Cohen; Janua Linguarum Series Practica 159; The Hague: Mouton, 1974) 181–94; "Two Principles of Genetic Reconstruction," *Lingua* 38 (1976) 89–108; "Semitic Languages," in *The World's Major Languages* (ed. B. Comrie; New York: Oxford, 1987) 654–57. Where I must disagree with Hetzron is in the internal subdivision of Central Semitic: where Hetzron posits an Arabo-Canaanite group over against an Aramaic group, I would maintain a more traditional partition into Arabic on the one hand and the so-called Northwest Semitic languages on the other, the latter group consisting of at least three coordinate members, viz., Aramaic, Canaanite, and Ugaritic. Space does not permit a review of the evidence here, for which the reader is referred instead to my forthcoming study, "Central Semitic and Northwest Semitic."

34. In doing so, obviously, it is unlikely that we will come up with the base *qattal-* that we find in Arabic and in Ethiopic. For proto–Central Semitic and proto–West Semitic, see further below.

The less likely choice for the ancestors of these forms are the Hebrew forms with two *i*-vowels. Quite simply, there is no convincing way to derive proto-Aramaic **qattil-* from an earlier **qittil-*; a rather vague and unlikely comparison involving the prefix-conjugation **yVqattil-* and imperative **qattil-* is not satisfactory, since there would have been no available analogy or other mechanism to bring about the necessary change.[35]

The evidence for proto–Northwest Semitic suffix-conjugation forms **qattila* and **haqtila*, on the other hand, is fairly impressive. First of all, if we begin with those bases, we obviously have the proto-Aramaic forms immediately. There is also new evidence that in Ugaritic, another Northwest Semitic language,[36] the D suffix-conjugation was likewise *qattila*: a form in an Akkadian text written at Ugarit, *šal-li-ma* (also *ša-li-ma*), is most easily translated 'has paid'; since the form cannot be parsed as Akkadian, it must be taken as a Ugaritic D suffix-conjugation, *šallima*.[37] Finally, there is evidence within Hebrew itself of the *a . . . i* sequence, not in any D forms, but in C perfects of roots originally I-*w*, like *hošib*; with J. Blau,[38] I would suggest that **hawθib-*, the ancestor of *hošib*, reflects an earlier Northwest Semitic vocalization and is not an innovation derived analogically from the imperfect *yošib*.[39]

In any case, the evidence suggests strongly that the bases of the suffix-conjugations of the D and C stems in proto–Northwest Semitic[40] had the vowel sequence *a . . . i*, as in **qattila* and **haqtila* (Ugaritic presumably **šaqtila*).[41] In this reconstruction it is necessary only to account for the

---

35. *Pace* H. Torczyner (N. H. Tur-Sinai), "Zur Bedeutung von Akzent und Vokal im Semitischen," *Zeitschrift der Deutschen Morgenländischen Gesellschaft* 64 (1910) 269–311, who posited *qittila* for proto-Semitic.

36. In my opinion Ugaritic represents a separate strain of Northwest Semitic, not directly ancestral to either Canaanite or Aramaic, and should accordingly be considered a coordinate branch in parallel with proto-Canaanite and proto-Aramaic in the reconstruction of proto–Northwest Semitic.

37. The form occurs in *Ugaritica* 5 (ed. J. Nougayrol et al.; Paris: Imprimerie Nationale, 1968) 187–89, text 96:passim; see my *Ugaritic Vocabulary in Syllabic Transcription*, 182.

38. Blau, "Hebrew Verb Formation," 153.

39. So, e.g., S. Izre'el, "The Gezer Letters of the el-Amarna Archive—Linguistic Analysis," *IOS* 8 (1978) 13–90, esp. 77 n. 244; the difficulty here is that if the perfect originally exhibits *hiqtil*, there is no set of forms on which to base an analogy by which *yošib* might generate *hošib*. Blau (among others) also notes converted perfects of I-guttural roots, such as *w-ha²aḇaḏti*, as relics of an original *a* in the first stem syllable, but the phonetic interpretation of such forms is difficult, and they should probably be used with caution.

40. The linguistic position vis-à-vis Central Semitic and Northwest Semitic of the early West Semitic dialects reflected in "Amorite" personal names remains unclear. In any case, such names offer no clear evidence for the vocalization of the D suffix-conjugation.

41. It might be objected that we should not begin, as suggested here, with identical bases for the suffix- and prefix-conjugations in proto–Northwest Semitic (see also n. 72 below). Compare,

changes **qattila* > **qittila* and **haqtila* > **hiqtila* as we move down toward proto-Hebrew; we need only move, in fact, into proto-Canaanite, the immediately preceding phase, since evidence for one or both of the forms **qittila*, **hiqtila* is attested both in Phoenician[42] and in a form in one of the el-Amarna Akkadian texts from Syria-Palestine that exhibit a Canaanite substratum.[43]

It may be suggested that the change of the sequence *a . . . i* to the sequence *i . . . i* began with the D forms and that it simply reflects the operation of a proto-Canaanite sound rule, a rule of regressive vowel assimilation:

proto–Northwest Semitic **qattil-* > proto–Canaanite **qittil-*

Note that the second vowel is short **i*; conversely, the pattern **qattīl*, with long *ī*, remained unchanged, at least in proto-Hebrew.[44]

When a phonological rule is proposed, several procedures must be undertaken: First, one must discover whether its operation can be detected anywhere else in the language; second, one must look for counterexamples; third, if counterexamples are found, one must determine whether they vitiate

---

however, the Hebrew Dᵖ forms: the identical bases in the Dᵖ forms *quttal ~ yquttal* must either be original or have arisen by analogy. If they are original in proto-Hebrew, they constitute a precedent for positing D **qattila ~ *yVqattil-* with the same base; if they result from analogy, they must be analogous to D **qattila ~ *yVqattil-*, in which case again we must take the latter as a starting point. (On the Kāmid el-Lōz D passive form *tuwaššar*, see n. 53 below, end.)

42. For the Phoenician D suffix-conjugation *qittil* note Greek *sillēch* and Latin *sillec* = /šillik/ as the second element of personal names, and late Punic writings like *ḥydš* for /ḥiddiš/ 'he renewed'; see S. Segert, *A Grammar of Phoenician and Punic* (Munich: Beck, 1976) 137–38. The Phoenician C suffix-conjugation began with *y* rather than *h* and was apparently pronounced *yiqtil*; see ibid., 142–43. (It is unclear whether the palatalization of the original initial *h* to *y* in the latter form resulted from the following *i*-vowel (i.e., **hiqtil > yiqtil*) or occurred first in forms following the negative **ʾi* (i.e., **ʾi-h . . . > ʾi-y . . .*); for the former view, see most recently W. R. Garr, *Dialect Geography of Syria-Palestine, 1000–586 B.C.E.* [Philadelphia: University of Pennsylvania Press, 1985] 58–59; for the latter, see T. O. Lambdin, "The Junctural Origin of the West Semitic Definite Article," in *Near Eastern Studies in Honor of William Foxwell Albright* [ed. H. Goedicke; Baltimore: Johns Hopkins University Press, 1971] 315–33, esp. 330 n. 25.)

43. The form occurs in a letter of Mut-Baᶜli of Piḥilu (Pella), EA 256:7: *ḫi-iḫ-bi-e* 'he concealed', corresponding to Hebrew *heḥbiʾ*. (For EA 256 see W. F. Albright, "Two Little Understood Amarna Letters from the Middle Jordan Valley," *BASOR* 89 [1943] 7–17.) The writing *ḫi-iḫ-bi-e* is usually taken to represent [hiḫbē]. It is more likely, however, that it denotes [hiḫbiʾe] < /hiḫbiʾa/, with the expected final *-a* of the suffix-conjugation 3d masc. sing. form (*qatal-a*) assimilated to the preceding high vowel; cf. vowel assimilation around gutturals in Ugaritic (albeit regressive rather than progressive, as here), for which see my *Ugaritic Vocabulary in Syllabic Transcription*, 271–75.

44. Perhaps also in Phoenician; see Segert, *Grammar of Phoenician and Punic*, § 43.25 / p. 84. **qattīl* also remained unchanged in proto-Aramaic but became *qittīl* in both Ugaritic and Arabic; see my *Ugaritic Vocabulary in Syllabic Transcription*, 269–70.

the rule entirely, or instead lead one to define with more precision the phonological environment in which the rule operated.

First, then: Are there other forms in Canaanite that may reflect the operation of the rule? I believe there are, namely, the Hebrew adjectives of the pattern *qittel*;[45] many of these, such as ⁽iwwer 'blind' and ʾiṭṭer 'lame', denote bodily defects, though not all do: geʾε 'proud', *piqqeaḥ* 'open (of eyes, ears)'.[46] These forms must, of course, derive from an immediately earlier *qittil.[47] But since a noun or adjective pattern *qittil* is otherwise unattested among the Semitic languages, one naturally wonders whether it represents a development from some other, earlier pattern. Two possibilities present themselves.

One possibility is to derive *qittil*, both in these adjectives and in the D suffix-conjugation, from earlier *quttul* as we find in Akkadian. Already seventy-five years ago, N. H. Tur-Sinai (Torczyner) noted that the *qittel* adjectives seem to correspond to Akkadian *quttul* adjectives.[48] More recently, both E. Y. Kutscher and J. Blau have suggested that *qittel* is actually the phonological reflex in Hebrew of earlier *quttul*, via an intermediate stage *quttil.[49] Blau goes further, and suggests that the *Piel* and *Hiphil* perfects with *i*-vowels in both syllables also derive from *quttul- and *huqtul-, that is, from the patterns that correspond to the Akkadian D and Š verbal adjectives. As attractive as these derivations may be in some ways, they are difficult to accept: While it is true that *quttul* forms do occur in Akkadian to denote bodily defects and diseases,[50] these are in fact merely a subset of the common *quttul* pattern, which is essentially the D stem verbal adjective; such forms are, in origin at least, passive, a semantic feature not shared by either the *qittel* adjectives or the *Piel* perfect in Hebrew.[51] While there may be

---

45. This has also been suggested by Lambdin, "Philippi's Law Reconsidered," 144 with n. 36.

46. There are some fifteen of these in Biblical Hebrew; still others, like *higger* 'lame' and *ṭippeš* 'stupid', occur in Mishnaic Hebrew. As BL § 61cγ / p. 477 pointed out, not all of these were necessarily *qittil* originally; some may have shifted to this pattern as it became semantically marked. Note also some Mishnaic Hebrew *qittel* nouns, whose relevance to the present discussion is uncertain: *dibber* (pl. *dibbrot*) 'speech'; *ribbit* 'usury' (perhaps also ⁽iddit 'choice land'); for *kisseʾ* see further below with n. 54. Other Canaanite dialects offer no evidence for the patterns *qattil*, *qittil*.

47. Note also Hexaplaric *ekkēs* = ⁽iqqeš (Ps 18:27); for *qittel* in Babylonian Hebrew see Yeivin, *Hebrew Language Tradition*, 963–64.

48. Torczyner (Tur-Sinai), "Zur Bedeutung von Akzent und Vokal," 286–87.

49. E. Y. Kutscher, in a long section on the sound change *u > i* in *The Language and Linguistic Background of the Isaiah Scroll (I Q Isaᵃ)* (Leiden: Brill, 1974) 463–64; Blau, "Hebrew Verb Formation," 157.

50. W. von Woden, *Grundriss der akkadischen Grammatik* (Analecta Orientalia 32/47; Rome: Pontifical Biblical Institute, 1969) § 55n #22b/ p. 62.

51. *Pace* Torczyner (Tur-Sinai), "Zur Bedeutung von Akzent und Vokal" (especially at the end of the article). On the semantics of Akkadian *quttul* as other than a form for defects, see also C. Wilcke, "Zur Deutung der sɪ.ʙɪ-Klausel in den spätbabylonischen Kaufverträgen aus Nordbabylonien," *Die Welt des Orients* 9 (1977–78) 207 n. 3.

some connection between Akkadian *quttul* and the Hebrew forms under discussion, it is a connection in the remote past, in an early phase of proto-Semitic, not something that may be subjected to phonological analysis at the much later proto-Canaanite or proto-Hebrew phase. More significant, perhaps, is the phonological difficulty encountered in attempting to derive the proto-Hebrew pattern **qittil* from earlier **quttul*.[52] Despite Kutscher's and Blau's arguments for it, an intermediate change of **quttul* to **quttil* is very hard to explain, as even Kutscher noted.[53] The reflex of proto-Semitic **quttul*

---

52. Note also the possibility that proto-Akkadian had **qattul* as in Assyrian; *quttul* in Old Akkadian and in Babylonian may be the result of assimilation, as perhaps also in proto-Hebrew; see below.

53. Kutscher, *Language and Linguistic Background of the Isaiah Scroll*, 463–64; so too Izre'el, "Gezer Letters of the el-Amarna Archive," 77 n. 246, who nevertheless also accepts it. As evidence for such an intermediate stage, Blau and Izre'el (pp. 74–78) cite the suffix-conjugation forms that appear in Canaanizing Amarna letters with the apparent vocalization *quttil*. These are said to reflect the actual form of the Canaanite D suffix-conjugation in this period. But despite the fact that the D infinitive in Ugaritic had a *u*-vowel, *quttalu* (probably semantically equivalent to Akkadian *pa/urrus*, and the Hebrew D^p infinitive *gunnob* and perfect *quttal*, i.e., the "passive" form, originally, like all verbal nouns, voiceless), I find it very difficult to accept the Amarna *quttil* forms as real, spoken Canaanite forms; as mentioned in n. 43, the actual Canaanite pronunciation of the C suffix-conjugation appears in an Amarna text as *ḫi-iḫ-bi-e* (Blau's attempt to account for the distinction between this form and *quttil*, "Hebrew Verb Formation," 157 n. 109, is not convincing). In all probability the *quttil* forms are, like so many other forms in the Canaanizing Amarna texts, Akkadian bases altered by the overlaying of the minimal amount of information required to make them comprehensible in terms of Canaanite morphology. Thus, all that the *quttil* forms tell us is the quality of the vowel in the second stem syllable in the dialect of these scribes or of their school, since that is the only feature in which the forms differ from the underlying Akkadian *quttul*. A similar explanation was suggested already a century ago by H. Zimmern, "Palästina um das Jahr 1400 vor Chr. nach neun Quellen," *Zeitschrift des Deutschen Palästina-Vereins* 13 (1890) 141 n. 5; followed by F. M. Th. Böhl, *Die Sprache der Amarnabriefen* (Leipzig: Hinrichs, 1909) § 27i/ p. 45; and Brockelmann, *Grundriss*, § 264fα Anm./1:583. Blau's rejection of this explanation, "Hebrew Verb Formation," 156, is unwarranted, in my view. As other instances in which only part of an Amarna form represents the underlying Canaanite morphology, we may cite, e.g., forms such as *tišpurūna* for 'they will send' (EA 138:137), where the *-i-* vowel of the prefix is not Canaanite but is rather part of a paradigmatic base {išpur} to which Canaanite prefix consonants and endings are added (see A. F. Rainey, "Observations on Ugaritic Grammar," *UF* 3 [1971] 164; idem, "The Barth-Ginsberg Law in the Amarna Tablets," *ErIsr* 14 [1978] 9*–13*); note also the C suffix-conjugation *šumrir* EA 185:74, in which Izre'el, "Gezer Letters of the el-Amarna Letters," 76 n. 239, takes only the vowels, but not the preformative *š* to reflect the Canaanite form; further, note the Amarna *iparras* forms that are intended as preterites rather than duratives, since they bear the Canaanite *-ø* ending that indicates *yaqtul* preterite (see A. F. Rainey, "Morphology and the Prefix-Tenses of West Semitized el-ʿAmarna Tablets," *UF* 7 [1975] 395–432). (Similarly, perhaps *tuwaššaru* in a text from Kāmid el-Lōz is not necessarily evidence of **yuqattal* for the D passive, with Arabic and against Hebrew, as suggested by Rainey in "KL 72:600 and the D-Passive in West Semitic," *UF* 8 [1976] 337–41. This form may simply be the Akkadian active *tuwaššir* modified by one specifically passive feature of

in proto-Hebrew, rather, is **qittul*, the result of a phonological process traditionally labeled the dissimilation of two *u*-vowels, though W. R. Garr in a recent study would prefer to call it reduction of the first *u*.[54] In any case, proto-Hebrew **qittul* undergoes no further changes apart from the later lowering of the stressed second vowel to *o*, as in words like *gibbor*[55] 'warrior', *ṣippor* 'bird', *šikkor* 'drunk', and *šibbólɛt* 'ear of grain'. Finally, deriving the D suffix-conjugation *qittil* from passive **quttul* as in Akkadian means that we would have to posit two very different bases, **quttul-* and **qattil-*, for proto–

---

the Canaanite D passive, viz., *-a-* between R_2 and R_3; the vowel between R_1 and R_2, therefore, cannot be established with this form.)

54. W. R. Garr, "On Vowel Dissimilation in Hebrew," *Bib* 66 (1985) 572–79. I am not entirely convinced by Garr's analysis of the forms he considers.

(1) The word *kisseʾ*, mentioned by many, is unique in Biblical Hebrew, and since it is a loanword of uncertain date (and even of uncertain immediate provenance), its form is ad hoc and not really relevant to a discussion of sound changes.

(2) If we omit *kisseʾ* from consideration, we have **u > i/ə/__C(C)u/ū/o*, except across certain morpheme boundaries (see under [3] below); we may therefore suggest the following chronologically ordered rules:

(*a*) **u > i/(#C?)__C(C)ŭ/o* (not across some morpheme boundaries), a change that is best described as dissimilation: **quttŭl > *qittŭl*; **qutŭl > *qitŭl* (cf. perhaps Amarna *ki-lu-bi* = Hebrew *k(ə)lub* 'cage', EA 74:46, 79:36, 81:35, all from Byblos); **qutāl > *qitōl*; so also **tōkōn > tikon* and any original **qutlān > qitlon* (see below under [3]);

(*b*) *i > ∅/(#C?) __ CV̄[+hi]*, also a process of dissimilation: **qitūl > q(ə)tul*; **qitūl*, **qitōl > q(ə)tol*; **piry > *piri > p(ə)ri*; ?**niṣīb > n(ə)ṣib* (probably Aramaic); note also, however, the Jerusalem form *zu-ru-uḥ* 'arm' < **ðirāᶜ-* (cf. Hebrew *z(ə)roaᶜ*; EA 286:12, 287:27, 288:14, 288:34), apparently reflecting a dialect in which assimilation took place, viz., = /ðorōᶜ/, although one may also conclude that the first *u* simply reflects a reduced vowel, as suggested by R. Steiner, "Yuqaṭṭil, Yaqaṭṭil, or Yiqaṭṭil: D-Stem Prefix-Vowels and a Constraint on Reduction in Hebrew and Aramaic," *JAOS* 100 (1980) 513–18.

(3) Given the existence of *qatlon* and *qitlon*, we might a priori expect to find *qutlon*; the fact that no examples of the latter are attested may be the result of dissimilation after all (*pace* Garr); the morpheme boundary in these forms may not have presented an obstacle:

(*a*) not all boundaries affect phonological changes in the same way (cf. the effects on Babylonian Akkadian assimilation of *a* to *e* in *erb=et*, *erb=ēta*, *erb=ā*, etc.);

(*b*) (**-ān >) -on* was not a very productive morpheme, unlike *-ot* (in *qolot̠*, *ḥūṣot̠*, cited as counterexamples by Garr).

55. In view of Syriac *gabbār*, Hebrew *gibbor* is, not surprisingly, usually labeled a *qattāl* form (see, e.g., BL § 61hγ–jγ/pp. 478–79; note that Arabic *jabbār* is a loan from Aramaic, while Biblical and later Jewish Aramaic *gibbār* owes its initial vowel to the Hebrew form). There are several difficulties with such a derivation, however: (1) in other forms, **qattāl > qattol*, as expected, e.g., *qannoʾ*; (2) the putative dissimilation in *qattol > qittol* is unexpected; and (3) the normal pattern corresponding to the Aramaic *qattāl* in Hebrew is *qattɔl* < proto-Hebrew **qattal* (see n. 59 below). Despite the Syriac, therefore, it is more likely that *gibbor* derives from **gubbur*. (It might be expected that the original short **u* of the second syllable should become *šwɔ* in certain environments, such as the construct plural *gibbore* [cf. *yiqtol* ~ *yiqt(ə)lu*]; *o* < **u* in nominal forms, however, eventually merged morphophonemically with *o* < **ā*, becoming in the process an irreducible vowel in such forms, as in **gadul-ay > gdole*, vs. **ðaqin-ay > *zəqəne > ziqne* and **yašar-ay > *yəšəre > yišre*.)

Northwest Semitic, since Ugaritic and Aramaic *qattil-* obviously cannot be derived from **quttul-*; and the existence of two distinct proto–Northwest Semitic forms, of course, is unlikely.[56]

The second possibility is that the Hebrew adjectives **qittil* derive instead from **qattil*,[57] and this is by far the more likely. The form *qattil* admittedly is not very common as a nominal pattern elsewhere in Semitic,[58] having been replaced generally by the form *qattīl*.[59] It is attested in Akkadian, however, in what von Soden calls "Gewöhnlichkeitsadjektive," for example, *gammilu* 'friendly', *šaggišu* 'murderous'.[60]

When we look for counterexamples to a rule of assimilation, we seem at first to be inundated by them:

1. The D forms other than the perfect—imperfect *yqattel*, imperative and infinitive *qattel*, participle *mqattel*—remain unchanged; similarly the corresponding forms of the causative, assuming this rule to have operated before the intrusion of the long *ī*.
2. Forms of the tD stem, including the perfect *hitqattel*, seem to violate the rule.
3. Nouns of the pattern **maqtil* appear in Hebrew as *maqtel* (as in *mapteah* 'key') and not as *miqtel*, as we might expect.[61]

---

56. So, too, is the existence of two proto-Hebrew forms, **qattala* and **qittila*, as suggested by Blau, "Hebrew Verb Formation," 152–58 (see n. 28 above, end). Note further that there is no happy way to derive a form like *hošīb* from either **hawθab* or **hiwθib/huwθub* at any stage of the developments that have to be assumed by Blau, so that *qattil* in **hawθib* must be called a "blend" form in his reconstruction.

57. So also, more or less, BL § 61cγ / p. 477. Note that apart from D infinitives, for which see below, no forms **qattil* are attested in Hebrew (having, if I am correct, become **qittil*); an apparent exception is *ʾaher* < **ʾaḥḥir*, whose plural *ʾaherim*, however, suggests that the word may have been *qatil* originally, with unexplained ad hoc doubling of *h* in the singular, as in the numeral 'one': **ʾahad* → **ʾaḥḥad* > *ʾɛḥɔd*, vs. pl. *ʾahɔdim* < **ʾahadīm*.

58. Arabic *ṭayyib* 'good', *hayyin* 'easy' are II-weak reflexes of *qatil*.

59. Likewise *qattūl* is rare (see n. 71 below), generally → *qattūl*. Similarly *qattāl* elsewhere in Semitic corresponds to proto-Hebrew **qattal* (cf. fem. forms like *qaššέbɛt* 'attentive' < **qaššab-t*, Mishnaic *gaddέlɛt* 'hairdresser' < **gaddal-t*; note also Akkadian *qattal* as in *šarraqu* 'thief': Assyrian *šarruqu*, with vowel harmony, shows that the second vowel is short, at least in this form).

60. Von Soden, *Grundriss*, § 55m/pp. 61–62. Note also substantivized *zammiru* 'singer', *zabbilu* 'porter'.

61. Although there are, naturally, two very odd exceptions, in Tiberian only: *mizbeah* 'altar' and *misped* 'wailing' (Babylonian *mazbeh*; construct *maspad*). In both of these it is likely that the *i* of the first syllable arose first in construct forms: **mazbah* > *mizbah* on the pattern of construct *midbar*. *Maqtil* forms also appear unchanged in Canaanite Amarna texts: e.g., *maqqibu* 'hammer' in EA 120:11 (from Byblos); *matniʾu* 'supplies', EA 337:9, 21; see W. L. Moran, "A Note on igi-kár, 'Provisions, Supplies,'" *Acta Sumerologica* 5 (1983) 175–77; D. Sivan, *Grammatical Analysis and Glossary of the Northwest Semitic Vocables in Akkadian Texts of the 15th–13th c.b.c. from Canaan and Syria* (Alter Orient und Altes Testament 214; Kevelaer/Neukirchen-Vluyn: Butzon & Berker/Neukirchener Verlag, 1984) 95.

4. Also, though they are not traditionally so taken, I would assume that at least some of the abstract nouns associated with the *qittel* adjectives, such as *ᶜawwérɛṯ* 'blindness', *gabbáḥaṯ* 'baldness', *qɔráḥaṯ* 'bald spot', were originally simply the feminine singular forms of the adjective, namely, **qattil-t*;[62] yet in these too no assimilation took place.

Most of these counterexamples can be accounted for if we define the conditions under which our rule operated more precisely.

1–2: It is likely that the D imperfect and participle remained unaffected simply because of the presence of a preceding syllable; in other words, the *a*-vowel affected by the rule had to be the *first* vowel in the form. The same restriction may account for the tD forms, although it is unlikely that they had the requisite *i*-vowel in the final stem syllable in this early period; more likely the tD was **hitqattal*, **yitqattal*, etc., as elsewhere in Semitic. The remaining D forms, the imperative and infinitive construct, do not have a preceding syllable, yet they also fail to exhibit assimilation. In these the operation of the phonological rule was undoubtedly *blocked* (or reversed) because of their close relationship, both historically and synchronically, to the imperfect, a relationship that can be observed in all conjugations, including the G.[63]

3: Since the rule failed to operate on *maqtil* nouns, we must probably assume a further restriction in the environment of the rule, namely, that the consonants between the two vowels had to be identical, thus, a geminate consonant rather than a consonant cluster.[64] If that is the case, then the rule would obviously not have affected the causative suffix-conjugation **haqtila*.[65] It may therefore be suggested that the rule affected only the suffix-conjugation of the D directly; the change of **haqtila* to **hiqtila* then probably came about as the result of analogy with the D stem, probably proceeding from the prefix-

---

62. Brockelmann's suggestion, *Grundriss*, § 150/1:361, that *qattélɛṯ*, the regular abstract of *qittel*, derives from **qattalat*, has little to recommend it. Note also the many *qattélɛṯ* nouns for diseases, etc.: *ṣɔráᶜaṯ*, *šaḥép̄ɛṯ*, *yabbélɛṯ*, *yallép̄ɛṯ*, *bahérɛṯ* (pl. *bɛhɔroṯ*, adj. *bɔhir*), *dalléqɛṯ*, *ᶜaṣṣébɛṯ* (construct *ᶜaṣṣbaṯ*, pl. *ᶜaṣṣɔḇoṯ*), *qaddáḥaṯ*; cf. also *ᵓaddérɛṯ* 'glory, cloak' (suffixed *ᵓaddarto*, adj. *ᵓaddir*). Some of these were undoubtedly **qattal-t* originally, as their allomorphs indicate (unless the latter have been re-formed later), but perhaps others derive from **qattil-t*.
63. For example, **yVqtul-* ~ **q(u)tul* ~ **qutul*, i.e., there is a pronounced tendency to have the same base in the imperfect, imperative, and infinitive in all conjugations.
64. It must be admitted, however, that *maqtil*s of I-*n* roots would continue to be exceptional, apparently because of pressure for a uniform *maqtil* pattern: instead of attested *mappeṣ*, etc., we expect *miCC-*.
65. Except perhaps in roots I-*n*. The Mishnaic Hebrew abstracts of the pattern *hɛqtel* must derive from the earlier C infinitive absolute *haqtel* (the construct apparently remained *haqtel*); the date of this change and its relationship to the other forms under consideration here are unclear to me.

conjugation (C still has *yVhaqtil-* in this early period) to the suffix-conjugation, as follows:

$$\text{*}yVqattil\text{- : *}qittil\text{- :: *}yVhaqtil\text{- : } X = \text{*}hiqtil\text{-}[66]$$

4: The nonoperation of my rule on the substantivized feminine singular forms *qattil-t* is rather more difficult to explain, but it may be suggested that the *bête noire* of Semitic historical phonology, stress, had something to do with it. If we assume that stress in this early period of Northwest Semitic was like what we find in Akkadian and Arabic, an assumption I find quite plausible, then the masculine forms *qáttil-* would have been stressed on the first stem syllable, while the feminine singular forms would have been stressed on the second stem syllable, *qattíl-t-*. Perhaps, therefore, the rule operated only on a stressed first vowel. Thus, the masculine form *qáttil-* became *qíttil-*, while the feminine singular at first would have remained unaffected, *qattíl-t-*.[67] At some point, probably not long afterward, morphological pressure would begin to generate other feminine singular forms whose bases mirrored their masculine counterparts,[68] that is, *qittíl-t-*. The competing feminine singular forms *qattíl-t-* and *qittíl-t-* then probably underwent a common development, a functional semantic split, whereby the new form came to be used as the regular feminine adjective while the older form assumed the more restricted role of an abstract noun.[69] If stress did affect the operation of the rule as I have suggested, then also in the D stem perfect the first- and second-person forms, like *qattíl-tă*, would likewise have been unaffected by the rule; in other words, only third-person forms would have acquired the *i* of the first stem syllable at first. But again analogy, or paradigmatic leveling, will have eliminated the new allomorphism in the paradigm, replacing *qattíl-tă* with *qittíl-tă*, etc.

Thus, what produced the distinctive vocalization of the Hebrew *Piel* and *Hiphil* perfects was a proto-Canaanite phonological rule, which we may now formulate more precisely as follows:[70]

$$a > i \; / \; \#C\text{\_}C_1C_1i$$

66. It would probably only be later that the long *i* invaded the causative forms of the sound verb.

67. Note that likewise no assimilation to the stressed vowel took place in the forms *qattíl* and *qattúl* in the dialects ancestral to Hebrew; see also n. 71 below, on *qattólet* < *qattúl-t*.

68. So also in the plural forms.

69. Cf. J. Kuryłowicz, "La nature des procès dits 'analogiques,'" *Acta Linguistica* 5 (1945–49) 15–37, esp. 30–31. The noun *ʾiwwélet* (suffixed *ʾiwwalti*) is probably a later substantivization of a feminine adjective (cf. *ʾᵉwil*).

70. This is, obviously, a rule of rather restricted application, one that affected directly only the third-person forms of the D perfect and the masculine singular of *qattil* nominal forms. Nevertheless, the validity of a proposed sound rule does not, ultimately, depend on the extent

The phonological process under discussion here may actually have been more general. It was noted earlier that the Hebrew noun pattern *qittol* in some instances derives from early Hebrew **qittul*, which in turn derives from proto-Canaanite **quttul*. It may further be suggested that some (though certainly not all) examples of the latter, proto-Canaanite **quttul*, are reflexes of a still earlier, that is, proto–Northwest Semitic, pattern **qattul*, just as proto-Canaanite **qittil* is the reflex of proto–Northwest Semitic **qattil*. Note that there are no clear reflexes in Hebrew of a pattern **qattul*.[71] If, as just suggested, proto–Northwest Semitic **qattul* became proto-Canaanite **quttul*, then a more general proto-Canaanite rule may be proposed:

$$a > V_1 \; / \; \#C \, \underset{\_}{'} \, C_1 C_1 V_1$$

THE EARLIER SEMITIC SITUATION

In the discussion thus far, reconstruction of the D and C suffix-conjugations has been taken back to proto–Northwest Semitic, where, in all likelihood, we find **qattila* and **haqtila* (/ **šaqtila*). These forms, it must be admitted, are

---

of its application; Philippi's Law as reformulated by Lambdin, for example, (see n. 2 above), also operated, much later, in a very restricted environment.

Objections concerning the actual environment of the rule as written here can also be answered by reference to similar conditions under which other rules operate. As an example of rules in which the initial morpheme boundary is an integral feature, we may cite Ugaritic *a* > *i/u* / #C __ *w/y*; see my *Ugaritic Vocabulary in Syllabic Transcription*, 275–77. As examples of the assimilation of a stressed vowel to an unstressed one, we may note, *inter alia*, the following: the development of the *i*-class perfect from Classical to Syro-Lebanese Arabic, *šáriba* 'he drank' > *šírib*, for which see H. Grotzfeld, *Syrisch-arabische Grammatik (Dialekt von Damaskus)* (Wiesbaden: Harrassowitz, 1965) 11; similarly roots II-guttural in Classical Ethiopic (Geᶜez), **káhida* 'he denied' > **kíhida* > **kíhda* > *kéhda*; cf. Babylonian Akkadian **tášmaᶜ* 'you heard' > **tášmeᶜ* > *tášme* > *téšme* and **baᶜlátum* 'ladies' > **beᶜlátum* > **bēlátum* > *bēlétum*.

A sound rule similar to the one posited above is probably responsible for the fact that, at least in Hebrew (no evidence from Phoenician or from Amarna Canaanite texts), *qatl* nouns of roots III-*y* behave like *qitl* forms. For example, a form like *gdi* 'kid' reflects an intermediate form **gidi* (not **gadi*; cf. also pausal forms such as *gédi*), which in turn must derive from **gidy-*, whereas comparative evidence suggests a proto–Northwest Semitic form **gady-*. Thus, it would seem that proto–Northwest Semitic *a* > proto-Canaanite (or proto-Hebrew) *i* / #C __ *Cy*; i.e., proto–Northwest Semitic *qaty* > proto-Canaanite *qity*. (Forms like *békɛ*, whether they derive ultimately from *qatl* or *qitl*, are innovations patterned after forms from sound roots.)

71. The form *qanno³* probably derives from **qannā³*. Feminine nouns such as *bassórɛt* 'dearth' and *kappórɛt* 'cover' do undoubtedly reflect **qattúl-t*. The nonassimilation of the unstressed **a* in these forms parallels the nonassimilation in fem. **qattíl-t* forms, discussed above. For *qattul* elsewhere in Semitic, cf. the Assyrian D verbal adjective and infinitive *parrus* (older or later than Old Akkadian/Old Babylonian *purrus*?), Ugaritic *bahhuru³* 'youth' (see my *Ugaritic Vocabulary in Syllabic Transcription*, 270).

not easily reconciled with those in Arabic and Ethiopic, *qattala* and *ʾaqtala*. For the sake of completeness, however, a proposal may be offered. If we posit **qattala* for proto–West Semitic and proto–Central Semitic, it is difficult, if not impossible, to account for proto–Northwest Semitic **qattila*. The *i*-vowel of the second syllable cannot be derived by appealing to the *i*-vowel of the prefix-conjugation: as was noted near the beginning of the discussion in connection with the suggestion that the second vowel of the Hebrew perfect *qittel* was somehow "borrowed" from the imperfect *yqattel*, there is no mechanism to trigger such a borrowing. And it is difficult to envisage any other means by which a proto–West/Central Semitic **qattila* would have become **qattila* in proto–Northwest Semitic. It may be proposed, therefore, that the proto–Northwest Semitic suffix-conjugation forms **qattila* and **haqtila* (/ **šaqtila*) were inherited from proto–West/Central Semitic, and that, accordingly, the Arabic and Ethiopic forms with *a* in both stem syllables are parallel innovations. The change of **qattila* to **qattala* in those areas may have come about through analogy to G forms. In G verbs, the suffix- and prefix-conjugation bases for most roots exhibit different vowels, as in *qatala ~ yaqtul-* or *~ yaqtil-* and *qatila ~ yiqtal-* (the main exceptions are a small class of *u ~ u* verbs and roots II- and III-guttural). It is possible that this tendency in the G stem for the theme vowel of the suffix-conjugation to differ from that of the prefix-conjugation was felt to be pronounced enough to become generalized in other stems, and thus bring about, for example in the D stem, a shift from *yuqattil- ~ qattila* to *yuqattil- ~ qattala*, with *a . . . a* in the suffix-conjugation as in the majority of transitive G verbs.[72]

72. J. Barth, "Zur vergleichenden semitischen Grammatik, I: Die Vocale der vermehrten Perfecta," *Zeitschrift der Deutschen Morgenländischen Gesellschaft* 48 (1894) 1–4 (see also idem, *Die Nominalbildung in den semitischen Sprachen* [2d ed.; Leipzig: Hinrichs, 1894] xxii–xxiii with n. 1), suggested that the Northwest Semitic suffix-conjugation forms were unlikely to be original, arguing that since the different vocalizations of the prefix- and suffix-conjugations in the G stem (i.e., *yVqtV₁l* vs. *qatV₂la*) must reflect the proto-Semitic situation, we should likewise posit, as the proto-Semitic D and C suffix-conjugation forms, those in which the vocalization differs from that of the prefix-conjugation, i.e., *qattala* and *yuqattil*, as in Arabic and South Semitic; in other words, the difference in vocalism between the prefix- and suffix-conjugation forms should be taken as characteristic of their opposition. We do not, however, know a priori that the various derived conjugations came into existence at the same time or out of the same morphological categories as the G verb. An analogical development in the opposite direction, as suggested here, is thus no less likely.

On p. 4 of his article, Barth also mustered D and L (form III) suffix-conjugation forms from some modern Egyptian and related dialects of Arabic, such as *ʿallim* 'he taught', *qātil* 'he fought', as further documentation of a development *qattal(a) > qattil* under the influence of the prefix-conjugation. In this case, however, and unlike the situation in proto–Northwest Semitic, a productive analogy was available: in the prefix-conjugation of a large group of verbs, viz., those whose second or third radical was either a guttural or an emphatic, the original *i* of the last syllable became *a*, i.e., **yuʿallim > yiʿallim* 'he teaches', but **yunazzif >*

At least, that is one possible line of development. But we are now almost far enough back in time to be quite uncertain about the shape of the entire verbal system, for example, about the very existence yet of an active suffix-conjugation, the origin and vocalization of which is not entirely clear in any conjugation; even the existence of discrete conjugations as morphological categories becomes fuzzy at some point.[73] All these factors, as well as passive forms and relevant *t*-forms, must be considered together, since they are all part of an interrelated, developing system in the proto-Semitic period.

SUMMARY OF THE PROPOSED DEVELOPMENT

In concluding this paper I offer a summary of the development of the D and C suffix-conjugation forms as outlined above, but now moving forward in time.

The earliest bases reconstructed here are **qáttil-* and **háqtil-* (/ **šáqtil-*), which may be present already in proto–West/Central Semitic, and are certainly present in proto–Northwest Semitic. At some point, in at least part of the Canaanite dialect area, a sound change caused **qáttil-* to become **qíttil-* in third-person forms. Paradigmatic pressure then leveled these bases through all persons, such as **qittíltă*. Other forms subject to the sound rule, the imperatives and verbal nouns, remained unchanged because of the close formal relationship of those forms, throughout the language, to the imperfect, which was not affected by the rule. By analogy with the corresponding D forms, the C suffix-conjugation also acquired an *i*-vowel in its first syllable, so that **háqtil-* was replaced by **híqtil-*. This replacement affected nearly all C verbs, even those of weak roots whose phonological shape was significantly different from that of sound roots; thus, for example, middle-weak **haqíma* became **hiqíma*, and geminate **hasíbba* became **hisíbba*;[74]

---

yinaddaf 'he cleans' (see M. Woidich, "Das Ägyptisch-Arabische," in *Handbuch der arabischen Dialekte* [ed. W. Fischer and O. Jastrow; Wiesbaden: Harrassowitz, 1980], esp. 224–25); the many available examples of the contrast *yinaddaf* : *naddaf* then generated contrasts of the type *yi^callim* : X = *^callim*. For uncertain reasons, the sound change did not occur in L forms II/III-guttural/emphatic, but the analogy of the new D forms also eradicated the contrasting vocalism in those forms as well: *yi^callim* : *^callim* :: *yiqātil* : X = *qātil*. (Similar D suffix-conjugation forms *qattil* or *qattəl* in the Anatolian Arabic dialects of Diyarbakır and Siirt [noted by Fischer and Jastrow, 72], in which the phonetic environment is not significant, probably reflect early borrowings from Syriac.)

73. This is especially true of the D stem, which in view of its absence from other members of the Afro-Asiatic phylum must be considered a proto-Semitic innovation. It may even be suggested that the "D" base was originally lexical (*qatta/i/ul*), like that of the G (it seems likely that C was originally {*3d masc. sing. pronoun + G base}).

74. Blau, "Hebrew Verb Formation," 156, notes that the initial *-i-* of these forms cannot be due to attenuation.

only I-*w* forms like *háwθiba retained the original *a*-vowel. Still later, the
second stem vowel in open syllables in all causative forms was replaced
with long *ī*, on the analogy of the forms of hollow verbs (**hiqī́ma* ~
**hiqímtă̆*), so that *híqtila became **hiqtī́la*, *háwθiba became **hawθī́ba*,
while forms like **hiqtī́ltă̆* and *hisíbba remained unchanged.

With the loss of final short vowels and the shift of stress to the final
syllable, we arrive at what can probably be labeled proto-Hebrew forms: D
**qittī́l* ~ **qittī́lt(ā̆)*; C **hiqtī́l* ~ **hiqtī́lt(ā̆)*. The subsequent development of
these forms in the various traditions of Biblical Hebrew was as follows: In
the hexaplaric transcriptions, they are essentially unchanged; short *i is
written as *epsilon*: *qettel* ~ *qettelth*(*a*); (*h*)*eqtil* ~ (*h*)*eqtelth*(*a*). In the Babylonian tradition, stressed short *i in verbal forms essentially merged with
*a: *qittal* ~ *qittaltɔ*; *hiqtīl* ~ *hiqtaltɔ*. The Tiberian tradition, as usual, is
more complicated: A sound rule, Philippi's Law as reformulated by Lambdin, changed stressed short *i before a consonant cluster at word end to *á*:
qittáltɔ; *hiqtáltɔ*; otherwise, stressed short *i became *ṣere*: *qittel*. But some
examples of *qittel* either alternate with or are replaced by *qittal*, particularly
in contextual situations that parallel the environment in which Philippi's
Law operates, namely, close juncture, as before *maqqep̄* and with conjunctive accents; the same phenomenon is probably the source of geminate
causative forms like *hesaḇ* rather than *heseḇ*, both from *hisíbb (cf. especially *hᵃsibbótɔ*). Still other instances of 3d masc. sing. *qittal* must be ascribed to paradigmatic leveling.

There are, to be sure, a few forms not accounted for by the developments proposed here; one thinks particularly of the causative participles of
hollow and geminate roots, *meqim* and *mese/aḇ*, the first vowel of which we
expect to be *ɔ*, not *e*.[75] Nevertheless, I believe the developments outlined
here to be the most economical and consistent explanation of how the *Piel*
got its vowels.

---

75. Despite the fact that some "Amorite" names exhibit a form *mekīn*; the latter simply follows
the general paradigm of some (but not all) dialects represented by such names in which
meqtil was apparently the C participle for all roots. BL § 56x′ / p. 397 suggested that the
shape of Hebrew *meqim* is due to analogy with verbs I-*y* (*heniq* : *meniq* :: *heqim* : *X*), but
this seems unlikely, given the rarity of roots I-*y* (in Mishnaic Hebrew, in fact, participles of
roots I-*y* behave as if from hollow roots and exhibit reduction in the first syllable, e.g.,
mniqɔ 'nursing').

[May, 1989]

M. O'Connor

Writing Systems and
Native-Speaker Analyses

PROLEGOMENA

The general framework of this paper follows from a concern with semiotic-as-communication rather than semiotic-as-signification. In American linguistics such a framework is associated with E. Sapir and B. L. Whorf, and with the general rubric of anthropological linguistics.[1] I have scanted strictly formalist approaches,[2] not for lack of interest but in order to keep such approaches in their place. I am trying to shift emphasis away from regarding

Author's note: I undertook this brief introduction to writing systems for "biblical scholars with an interest in, but little familiarity with, linguistics" at the suggestion of Walter R. Bodine and Edward L. Greenstein. Some of the material was presented, under the title "Understanding Writing and Understanding Culture," at the conference on "The Alphabet as a Technology in the West" sponsored by the Institute of Semitic Studies, Princeton, October 1988, organized by Ephraim Isaac. I have proceeded with assistance from Yoël L. Arbeitman, Mark Aronoff, Alexander Borg, Paul E. Dion, Suzette Haden Elgin, Shlomo Izre'el, Edmund S. Meltzer, Tova Meltzer, Loraine K. Obler, Keith H. Palka, Pierre Swiggers, and, as always, the late Li Chi; all of them commented on drafts and versions. To all of them my thanks, and special thanks to Peter T. Daniels, who commented, it seems, on all drafts and versions. A brief version of this paper appeared under the present title in *Society of Biblical Literature Seminar Papers, 1986*, 536–43.

1. A major contemporary contribution is M. Silverstein, "Language Structure and Linguistic Ideology," in *The Elements: A Parasession on Linguistic Units and Levels* (ed. P. R. Clyne et al.; Chicago: Chicago Linguistic Society, 1979) 193–247. For a survey and samples of recent work in the area, largely lexical, see C. H. Brown, "Where Do Cardinal Directions Come From?" *Anthropological Linguistics* 25 (1983) 121–61; and idem, *Language and Living Things: Uniformities in Folk Classification and Naming* (New Brunswick: Rutgers University Press, 1984).

2. See, e.g., R. A. Hall Jr., "Graphemics and Linguistics," in *Symposium on Language and Culture* (ed. V. E. Garfield and W. Chafe; Seattle: University of Washington Press, 1963) 53–59.

language (and related phenomena) primarily as a code and toward thinking of it as a factor in human action and interaction.[3] An anthropologically oriented view of writing systems as a whole may allow us to sidestep the false dichotomy between philology as the study of what-happens-in-text and historical linguistics as the study of why-it-happens.[4]

Two facets of standard expositions of writing systems absent from this essay deserve special mention. First, I have eschewed the functionalist view of writing as distinct from and an intrinsic complement to speech, best known from the neo-Praguian work of J. Vachek.[5] I find insupportable his view that no language attains its full existence in the absence of writing ("Those language communities which still lack the written norm have not yet fully developed all the latent possibilities of language" [p. 45]. It is the case that writing is now part of the environment of many languages and has a role to play in their development, but to extend the connection to all languages at all times is profoundly ahistorical, a manifestation of the modernistic tendency of much of social science.

Second, I have left aside the phoneme as a primary concept, in part because there are other questions I take to be more important and in part because the phoneme is itself a by-product of the alphabetic system it is so often made to explain. A major juncture in the history of phonological theory was compassed in the 1934 paper of Y. R. Chao, "The Non-uniqueness of Phonemic Solutions of Phonetic Systems,"[6] and Chao's work was in part the result of native familiarity with a nonalphabetic writing system. The crucial point was made more recently by a historical linguist of Chinese, E. G. Pulleyblank: "The phoneme is really only a more sophisticated form of the 'letter' as a phonological unit. We still tend to assume, for example, that consonants and vowels are units (segments) of essentially the same kind. The way in which our Graeco-Roman alphabets represent them—as units of the

---

3. In this sense, the goal of this essay is not far removed from that of my *Hebrew Verse Structure* (Winona Lake, IN: Eisenbrauns, 1980).

4. See, e.g., K. Koerner, "On the Historical Roots of the Philology/Linguistics Controversy," and W. M. Christie Jr., "On the Relationship between Philology and Linguistics," both in *Papers from the Fifth International Conference on Historical Linguistics* (ed. A. Ahlqvist; Amsterdam Studies in the Theory and History of Linguistics 4, Current Issues in Linguistic Theory 21; Amsterdam: Benjamins, 1982) 404–13, 414–24; W. R. Bodine, "Linguistics and Philology in the Study of Ancient Near Eastern Languages," in *"Working with No Data": Semitic and Egyptian Studies Presented to Thomas O. Lambdin* (ed. D. M. Golomb and S. T. Hollis; Winona Lake, IN: Eisenbrauns, 1987) 39–54.

5. See, e.g., J. Vachek, "English Orthography: A Functionalist Approach," in *Standard Languages: Spoken and Written* (ed. W. Haas; Manchester: Manchester University Press, 1982) 37–56; see also Bodine, "Linguistics and Philology," 42–44.

6. Reprinted in *Readings in Linguistics One* (ed. M. Joos; Washington, DC: American Council of Learned Societies, 1957; repr. Chicago: University of Chicago Press, 1966) 38–54.

same kind strung in a line—predisposes us to this assumption."[7] Appreciation of this point has recently spread among general linguists.[8] The dominant role of phonemics in "explaining" the alphabet is a prime example of
the way writing enters into the texture of language and language study.

I have also scanted many political aspects of the study of writing systems, bound up as it is in the history of commerce, travel, empire, and col-
ony. The coincidence of popular interest in archaic Mesoamerican culture
and postcolonialist ravaging of their successors seems not to be having as
positive an effect as one might hope.

The scholarly literature on writing systems is enormous, but pride of
place still belongs to I. J. Gelb's *Study of Writing*, though it is outdated in
many particulars.[9] Three other scholars of the Near East, Février, Friedrich,
and Gordon, have also written useful manuals on writing and decipherment;[10] G. Sampson offers a "linguistic introduction" to writing systems,[11]
and P. T. Daniels deals specifically with Semitic scripts.[12] More lavishly illustrated and more up-to-date historically than the manuals is the catalog of
the University of Wisconsin exhibit "Sign, Symbol, Script."[13] Since "ten
hearings are not equal to one seeing" (to give a well-known proverb its

7. "Linguistic Reconstruction: An Historical Problem," paper presented at the Second Annual
   Conference on Sino-Tibetan Reconstruction, Columbia University, 1969.
8. See, e.g., D. G. Frantz, "Abstractness of Phonology and Blackfoot Orthography Design," in
   Approaches to Language: Anthropological Issues (ed. W. C. McCormack and S. A. Wurm;
   The Hague: Mouton, 1978) 307–25; K. H. Campagna, "Recognizing Alphabetics," *General
   Linguistics* 25 (1985) 75–91; as well as the crucial paper of J. L. Malone, "Systematic vs.
   Autonomous Phonemics and the Hebrew Grapheme *Dagesh*," *AAL* 2 (1975) 113–29.
9. I. J. Gelb, *A Study of Writing: The Foundations of Grammatology* (2d ed.; Chicago: Univer-
   sity of Chicago Press, 1963); see also his general papers: "Written Records and
   Decipherment," in *Current Trends in Linguistics*, vol. 11: *Diachronic, Areal, and Typological Linguistics* (ed. T. A. Sebeok; The Hague: Mouton, 1973) 253–84; "Records, Writing,
   and Decipherment," *Visible Language* 8 (1974) 293–318, revised in *Language and Texts:
   The Nature of Linguistic Evidence* (ed. H. H. Paper; Ann Arbor: Center for Coördination of
   Ancient and Modern Studies, The University of Michigan, 1975) 61–86 (citations below are
   from the revised version).
10. J. G. Février, *Histoire de l'écriture* (2d ed.; Paris: Payot, 1959); J. Friedrich, *Entzifferung
    verschollener Schriften und Sprachen* (2d ed.; Berlin: Springer, 1966); and C. H. Gordon,
    Forgotten Scripts: Their Ongoing Discovery and Decipherment (2d ed.; New York: Basic
    Books, 1982).
11. G. Sampson, *Writing Systems* (Stanford: Stanford University Press, 1986).
12. P. T. Daniels, "Semitic Scripts," in G. Bergsträsser, *Introduction to the Semitic Languages*
    (trans. P. T. Daniels; Winona Lake, IN: Eisenbrauns, 1983) 236–60; and idem, "Semitic
    Writing," in *The Semitic Languages* (ed. R. Hetzron; London: Routledge, forthcoming).
13. M. L. Carter and K. N. Schoville, eds., *Sign, Symbol, Script* (Madison: Department of
    Hebrew and Semitic Studies, University of Wisconsin, 1984); a series of lectures presented
    in conjunction with the exhibit is gathered in W. Senner, ed., *The Origins of Writing* (Lin-
    coln: University of Nebraska Press, 1989).

proper form), note also the fine set of illustrations in J. B. Pritchard's *Ancient Near East in Pictures* (2d ed., 71–89, 348–49). There are some important collections of scholarly papers.[14] On the methodology of decipherment, see the papers of Gelb (n. 9 above); the handbooks (n. 10 above) provide accounts of the "great decipherments." Specialized studies abound.[15] The popular literature is also abundant and, alas, riddled with errors as well as insights and illustrations.

This paper is in some ways a prequel to an earlier study, on early alphabetic orthography, and some of the technical literature cited there is also relevant here.[16]

ETHNOSCIENCE

Human knowledge tends to be schematized: fact and observation, memory and fancy articulate in a complex structure which yet moves, if often the joints crack, the tendons tighten. There are various ways of classifying and clarifying the schematizations of knowledge: true and false, preliminary and precise, functional and nonfunctional. One of the most useful clarifications distinguishes "science" from "folk science" or, as anthropologists prefer to term it, *ethnoscience*. Ethnoscience is preliminary and functional but not necessarily therefore false; science, as the term is usually understood, is taken as true, aims to be precise, and is often alarmingly dysfunctional. Science and ethnoscience sometimes yield comparable results. Pharmacology is a scientific discipline based in folk observation, and indeed pharmacology has made a child out of its parent by adopting it and calling it pharmacognosy. But the women and men who, studying flowers, recognized the cardio-

14. W. Haas, ed., *Writing without Letters* (Manchester: Manchester University Press, 1976); idem, *Standard Languages: Spoken and Written* (Manchester: Manchester University Press, 1982); J. A. Fishman, ed., *Advances in the Creation and Revision of Writing Systems* (The Hague: Mouton, 1977). Psychologically oriented: W. Frawley, ed., *Linguistics and Literacy* (New York: Plenum, 1982); M. Martlew, ed., *The Psychology of Written Language: Developmental and Educational Perspectives* (Chichester: Wiley, 1983). C. Read's paper "Orthography" in the latter (143–62) is particularly useful. J. Oates has edited a special issue of *World Archaeology*, 17/3 (Feb. 1986), on "Early Writing Systems."

15. Such as P. T. Daniels, " 'Shewing of Hard Sentences and Dissolving of Doubts': The First Decipherment," *JAOS* 108 (1988) 419–36, on J.-J. Barthélemy; P. Swiggers, "La base leibnizienne des déchiffrements de G. F. Grotefend," *Orientalia Lovaniensia Periodica* 10 (1979) 125–32; and J. Chadwick, "Linear B," in *Current Trends in Linguistics*, 11:537–68, on Michael Ventris, with extensive quotations from his notes.

16. M. O'Connor, "Writing Systems, Native Speaker Analyses, and the Earliest Stages of Northwest Semitic Orthography," in *The Word of the Lord Shall Go Forth: Essays in Honor of David Noel Freedman in Celebration of His Sixtieth Birthday* (ed. C. Meyers and M. O'Connor; Winona Lake, IN: Eisenbrauns, 1983) 439–65.

tonic properties of the leaves of certain species of foxglove were not strictly pharmacognosists; they were rather ethnoscientists. They knew that digitalis herbs relieved pain, specifically the pain of sluggish heartbeat, and although pharmacologists are able to control the purity and dosage of the drugs, and to explain the action of the glycosides, the humanly important insight remains the ethnoscientific one. Science in this case merely schematizes.

Science and ethnoscience are not always so closely allied. Our ethnoscience distinguishes living things which move from those that do not, but science has many more qualifications about separating animals and plants; most of us do not see methanogens, so whether they are plant or animal does not trouble us. Science sees no basic difference between a cat and a tiger, but the split between the class of wild animals and the class of domesticated (including domestic) animals is intuitively clear and part of many cultures' way of accounting for the world. When children say dolphins are not "really" fish, they mean that dolphins share the major property of fish, an aqueous environment, but are not gill-breathing and cold blooded. Zoologists worry, with some justice, about lots of quite small animals, but ethnoscience recognizes that chickens are more important than anything much smaller.

LANGUAGE ETHNOSCIENCE

The scheme of science/ethnoscience can be applied to the chief instrument of human knowledge, language. The science of language is roughly what is known as linguistics, while the ethnoscience involves various native-speaker analyses of language. The domain of language folklore usually recognized as such is quite small and involves, for example, notions about accent ("Southerners speak slowly"),[17] grammar ("People who use double negatives are ignorant"), and lexicon ("People who use 'big words' are smart"). As the examples suggest, no scientific linguist would find these folkloric beliefs worthy of serious scrutiny except as a source of dangerous and foolish prejudices. The ethnoscience of language is, however, vastly more complex than the small nexus of these beliefs might suggest: these beliefs tend to concern how other speakers use language,[18] but the more interesting side of

---

17. The incident in Judg 12:6 is a biblical example; see, e.g., P. Swiggers, "The Word *šibbōlet* in Jud. XII.6," *JSS* 26 (1981) 205–7.

18. There is also interlingual folklore, some of it Jewish. The Modern Hebrew poet C. N. Bialik, for example, is reported to have said, "Hebrew one talks, but Yiddish talks itself" (quoted, in English, by C. Rabin, "The Ancient in the Modern: Ancient Source Materials in Present-Day Hebrew Writing," in *Language and Texts*, 149–76, at 157); reported for Yiddish as *"Hebraish redt man, Yiddish redt sikh"* (A. Norich).

language ethnoscience focuses on how speakers use their own variety of language.

Native-speaker analyses may involve the speech stream itself,[19] and almost all effective use of language reflects such analyses.[20] The creativity evident in slang formation, wordplay,[21] and poetry is grounded in often quite complex notions about how language works. To recognize the half-rhyme in the Vietnam marching song, "If I die in a combat zone, / Box me up and ship me home,"[22] the phonological class of nasals must be taken as providing the basis of the *on/om* half-rhyme. The slang use of *wheels* is based on metonymy, of *walking point* on metaphor. Indeed, the whole of traditional rhetoric is a form of language ethnoscience, for it is an inventory not of what can be done with language but of what has been done and found to work, namely, found to make people believe arguments and act on those beliefs. The ethnoscience of language can involve remarkably precise judgments as well as the broader notions of rhetoric. The half-rhyme example is only a small sample of the careful phonological evaluations native speakers routinely make. No speaker of English would hesitate over judging that *ndo* and *ngo* are not possible words of English, nor would any speaker not be able to produce a strategy to make them English words, introducing a vowel to accommodate the unacceptable segment(s). English is a language with a sufficiently complex sound inventory and phonology to accept a great many loanwords with little modification, as well as the semantic flexibility to be "willing" to do so. Almost all loans in Modern English reflect some degree of phonological reshaping by native speakers, and these countless reformations are a good index to English phonology.[23] Thus native-speaker analyses

19. I refer here and below to the speech stream but do not wish to exclude languages not based in the speech stream, notably American Sign Language; cf. N. S. Baron, *Speech, Writing, and Sign: A Functional View of Linguistic Representation* (Bloomington: Indiana University Press, 1981).

20. This topic is treated in several of the essays in the collection of L. Menn and L. K. Obler, *Exceptional Language and Linguistics* (Perspectives in Neurolinguistics, Neuropsychology, and Psycholinguistics; New York: Academic Press, 1982), including my own, " 'Unanswerable the Knack of Tongues': The Linguistic Study of Verse" (143–68). The ongoing psycholinguistic validation of the Chinese view of the syllable as *onset + rhyme* (or *nucleus*) is a striking example of the vindication of native-speaker analyses.

21. Wordplay is associated with writing systems by, e.g., A. Parpola, "The Indus Script: A Challenging Puzzle," *World Archaeology* 17 (1986) 399–419, at 409.

22. The title of a memoir by Tim O'Brien (New York: Bantam, 1973).

23. On loanwords, see M. O'Connor, "Arabic Loanwords in Nabatean Aramaic," *JNES* 45 (1986) 213–29 and references. S. J. Lieberman, *The Sumerian Loanwords in Old-Babylonian Akkadian*, vol. 1: *Prolegomena and Evidence* (Missoula: Scholars Press, 1977), is confined to nouns (14–18), the largest class of loans, but note his general remarks on loans (21–24); note also some of the unusual examples in W. Bright, *American Indian Languages and*

can range from phonology through the lexicon, involving persuasive, poetic, and playful language use.

The native-speaker analyses mentioned so far involve the speech stream and may be called nonmaterial in the limited sense of not using material foreign to speech itself. One case of private twin speech (cryptophasia or idiophasia) is an instructive nonmaterial example. A set of twins was observed to be speaking what was thought to be a private language, presumably of their own invention; on investigation, however, it emerged that the twins were speaking their native language (English) at an incredibly high rate.[24] The girls had performed an analysis of the language that allowed them to eliminate much of the redundancy required for ordinary conversation and create a form of speech that only they could understand; the acuity of the twins in tackling English is remarkable.[25] The stripping away they performed in speech served only private goals, but such stripping away is crucial to any embodiment of a native-speaker analysis in a medium other than speech. No medium can approach the flexibility of the voice (or the signing body), but other media have certain features the voice lacks; these may be adapted for language but only after rigorous analysis and simplification.

The two disadvantages of the voice that may be ameliorated by the use of other media involve time and space. The speech stream can only be heard within a limited area, and so to pass speech over a greater distance, drum

---

Literatures (Berlin: Mouton, 1984). To the references on loans in the eastern Mediterranean in my "Arabic Loanwords in Nabatean Aramaic," add H. Rosén, "The Stele of Lemnos, Its Text and Alphabetic System," originally 1954; repr. in his *East and West: Selected Writings in Linguistics*, pt. 1: *General and Indo-European Linguistics* (Munich: Fink, 1982) 212–302; and J. Barr, *Comparative Philology and the Text of the Old Testament* (Oxford: Clarendon, 1968; repr., Winona Lake, IN: Eisenbrauns, 1987) 101–11, 121–24. On the use of loans in historical linguistics, see E. G. Pulleyblank, "The Reconstruction of Han Dynasty Chinese," *JAOS* 105 (1985) 303–11.

24. The twins cited here, of Anglo-Jamaican birth, are the subject of M. Wallace, *The Silent Twins* (London: Chatto & Windus, 1985). Most twins show slow language development, and many show cryptophasia or private languages. For the popular literature, see P. Watson, *Twins* (London: Hutchinson, 1981) 90; E. M. Bryan, *The Nature and Nurture of Twins* (London: Baillière Tindall, 1983) 126–30. For reports of cryptophasia in 40 percent of all twins, see S. Savić, *How Twins Learn to Talk* (New York: Academic Press, 1980); in 48 percent of monozygotic ("identical") twins and 27 percent of dizygotic ("fraternal") twins, see R. Zazzo, "The Twin Condition and the Couple Effect on Personality Development," *Acta geneticae medicae et gemellologiae* (Rome) 25 (1976) 343–52, and cf. his *Les jumeaux: Le couple et la personne* (Paris: Presses Universitaires de France, 1960) 340–77, and "Genesis and Peculiarities of the Personality of Twins," in *Twin Research* (ed. W. E. Nance et al.; New York: Liss, 1978) 1–11.

25. The Anglo-Jamaican twins have had rather desperate lives; one killed herself, and the other is hospitalized in an institution for the criminally insane.

and whistle "languages" have developed.[26] The telephone and broadcasting signals are modern analogs. Similarly, the speech stream can only be heard for a limited time, and so to pass speech over time, writing systems have developed.[27]

Language ethnoscience has two domains, stock folkloric beliefs, for the most part concerned with the funny ways other people talk, and a larger realm of notions of how a speech community itself uses language. Native-speaker analyses may involve the speech stream, or they may emerge in an alien medium. The alien media may extend speech across space, as with drums or whistling, or across time, as with writing. The results of analyses using alien media are considered by some scholars to be themselves linguistic systems, but many, realizing the distance between the language material and the results of the analysis, prefer to regard them as delinguistic, derived from language but not strictly part of it.[28]

WRITING AS LANGUAGE ETHNOSCIENCE

Writing may be described as the expression of the results of native-speaker analysis of a language in such a way that the results can be preserved and understood (by others) over time.[29] A linguistically informed inquiry into writing will consider three questions: (a) What sort of analysis is involved?

26. The major literature on drum and whistle languages is collected in T. A. Sebeok and D. J. Umiker-Sebeok, eds., *Speech Surrogates: Drum and Whistle Systems* (The Hague: Mouton, 1976). Not all drum communication systems reflect a single language; indeed such systems may serve to bridge language gaps as well as gaps in space. Dell Hymes, in a brief but important review of *Speech Surrogates*, asks, "Is it coincidental that drum and whistle systems have so largely a complementary distribution with writing systems (despite non-identity of function)?"; see *Language in Society* 6 (1977) 436–37, at 437.

27. Baron deals with the relationship of writing to other forms of "durable visible representation" (*Speech, Writing, and Sign*, 149–75) in approaching the question of the role of writing (cf. 175–88).

28. See, e.g., Gelb, "Records, Writing, and Decipherment," 64–66.

29. Thus no writing system "writes down everything." Students of early cuneiform tend to refer to the limited material of the records they study as an indication that the system in question is minimal, reduced, or the like (e.g., H. Nissen, "The Archaic Texts from Uruk," *World Archaeology* 17 [1986] 317–34, at 329–30); this needs to be understood as a relative, not an absolute claim. Unfortunately this question tends to get muddled with another, which is completely distinct, that of the way a text is used. Any piece of writing can be used as a mnemonic or *aide-mémoire* for recitation or review; technically, it could be claimed that a piece of writing is thereby made into a piece of a precursor system (see below for this term), but it seems to me unwise to make the definition of writing depend on notions of the psychology of reading. For nineteenth-century Native American mnemonics, used in reciting sacred and treaty texts, see W. Walker, "Literacy, Wampums, the gúdəbuk, and How Indians in the Far Northeast Read," *Anthropological Linguistics* 26 (1984) 42–52.

(b) How are the results expressed? (c) How are they preserved? Or again: The scribe for intelligence, the script for form, and the scroll for matter.[30] Before considering the three objects cited, some consequences of the description of writing here proposed should be mentioned. The most important is the role of language; there is no end to the confusion created by approaches to writing systems grounded in elementary typologies of sign and symbol systems rather than in language. Writing is a sign system that has only one reading in only one language; such is a good rule of thumb. There are exceptions, most of them puzzles and riddles; cases in which only a small amount of text is available tend to be indeterminate. These marginal phenomena do not provide sufficient justification to discard the notion of writing as based in language. Historically obscure cases likewise offer us no such warrant.

Some native-speaker analyses are homogeneous, that is, they use and extend the speech stream itself: others, like writing, use alien media. All languages reflect homogeneous analyses, for wordplay is known in all languages, the inevitable result of the redundancy of the linguistic code. Further, poetry, the numerical regulation of language material that grows out of wordplay and schematizes it, is also universal.[31] All languages also have their own rhetoric and their own way of regulating and advancing the changes going on within them. In contrast, heterogeneous analyses are not at all universal: relatively few language communities have ever created a drum "language," a whistle "language," or even a writing system. But the few speech communities in human history that have had writing have been powerful, and, although universal literacy is not to be looked for, the ability to use writing is now quite common throughout the world.[32]

Two concepts essentially foreign to this account have just been introduced: The notion of speech community, which becomes problematic in looking at such very large "speech communities" as the Roman Empire, the Chinese Empire under the T'ang Dynasty, or the British Empire under

---

30. As I noted after drafting the paper, this scheme is vaguely Aristotelian; a corresponding medieval Jewish scheme, found in the *Sepher Yeṣirah* and Ibn Gabirol, involves scribe/script/scroll.

31. See O'Connor, *Hebrew Verse Structure*; and "Unanswerable the Knack of Tongues."

32. On the ethnography of writing, see, e.g., the brief essay of K. Basso, "The Ethnography of Writing," in *Explorations in the Ethnography of Speaking* (ed. R. Bauman and J. Sherzer; Cambridge: Cambridge University Press, 1974) 425–32, who treats the folk taxonomy of writing in modern American culture. The ethnography of writing in the children of that culture is treated by C. de Góes and M. Martlew, "Young Children's Approach to Literacy," in *The Psychology of Written Language* (ed. M. Martlew; Chichester: Wiley, 1983) 217–36. There is a "linguistic folklore" of writing, too; some native speakers(-and-writers) of both French and Spanish believe that those languages are spelled as they are pronounced; native speakers of English believe this of Spanish, but not of French.

Victoria; and, more importantly, the notion of history. History is not merely
involved with writing: on many accounts, history is defined in terms of
written documentary evidence. The trapdoor down the rabbit hole of history
is disguised in the description of writing by reference to "time," but time as
a perceptual category of modern Western ethnoscience exists only because
of writing. There are ways to circumvent or undermine the circularity of inquiry here, but they tend to end in very dark warrens favored by philosophers and, lately, literary critics.[33]

The human use of language predates the advent of writing time out of
mind, but almost all familiar understandings of language involve writing to
some extent. This reflects the fact that, although a heterogeneous native-
speaker analysis is not necessary for a language, where such is present it becomes an element in the speech community's self-understanding. Indeed,
writing can be seen as so powerful a force in such self-understanding as to
justify drafting the history of consciousness in terms of literacy and related
technologies. This approach segments the history of southwestern Asia, Europe, and the dependencies into phases corresponding to early stages of literacy, the era of widespread chirographic use, the era of printing by movable
type, and the current era of electronic manipulation of information. These
phases are readily associated with other decisively important historical
events, most conspicuously the European use of printing with the Renaissance and Reformation, that congeries of events which created the civiliza-
tional base of all that is called modern.[34] The association of literacy and the
Euroamerican colonial mission is so strong that the naïve commentator is
sometimes misled into making false, not to say meaningless, claims about

33. The problematic alluded to here is deconstruction, chiefly associated with J. Derrida and the
    late P. de Man.
34. This project, the tracing of the history of consciousness as it has been influenced by media,
    is centrally associated with the work of W. J. Ong; see, e.g., *The Barbarian Within and
    Other Fugitive Essays and Studies* (New York: Macmillan, 1962); *Rhetoric, Romance, and
    Technology: Studies in the Interaction of Expression and Culture* (Ithaca: Cornell Univer-
    sity Press, 1971); *Orality and Literacy: The Technologizing of the Word* (London: Methuen,
    1982). Also relevant is the work of M. McLuhan, e.g., *Understanding Media: Extensions of
    Man* (New York: McGraw-Hill, 1964). The related work of E. A. Havelock is marred by
    serious misunderstandings of the ancient world and of language; see *Preface to Plato* (Cam-
    bridge: Harvard University Press, 1963) and *The Literate Revolution in Greece and Its
    Cultural Consequences* (Princeton: Princeton University Press, 1982). A qualified reconsid-
    eration of the earliest era of printing is afforded by E. Eisenstein, *The Printing Press as an
    Agent of Change: Communications and Cultural Transformations in Early Modern Europe*
    (New York: Cambridge University Press, 1979), valuable for its detailed record of what
    came into print. For related reflections from an anthropologist linguist, see W. Bright, "The
    Virtues of Illiteracy," in *American Indian Languages and Literatures*, 149–59. On the
    alphabet and democracy, see the remarks of G. E. Mendenhall, *The Syllabic Inscriptions
    from Byblos* (Beirut: American University of Beirut, 1985) 149–57.

some favored or disfavored segments of the past; the twin dangers of nationalistic puffery and racist denigration lie in wait for all whose historical interests range far. The project of research into the history of consciousness is a bold one, correlating as it does the material aspects of writing with intellectual and spiritual consequences; it can serve as a corrective to many forms of devouring dullness, not least the dullness of meliorism.

The role of writing in the self-understanding of a speech community is necessarily historical, and, as has been remarked, this quality is an explication of the reference to time in the definition of writing. This link to consciousness does not, however, exhaust the role of history in considering a writing system. If a piece of writing represents the form of speech used at a particular time, it will do the job of representation less adequately at some later time, since language is constantly changing. Since language change occurs in unpredictable ways and probably at unpredictable rates, a given convention or system of writing will fail to preserve language through time in unpredictable ways. There are two varieties of change here. The first of them, language change, is absolute: the two forms of a language used by, say, two generations are different, the later an outgrowth of the earlier, one of a plethora of possible outgrowths. The later form of the language can be characterized in terms of the earlier (by historical linguistics), and some of the changes that have taken place can be accounted for (by comparative linguistics). The two forms of the language probably do similar but slightly different social duties, probably with similar but slightly different felicities and gaps. It makes no sense to say one of them is better than the other, however; thus the change or complex of changes involved can be called absolute.

The kind of change involved in writing systems is deforming, for a writing system is a *dependent* phenomenon with an *independent* dynamic. A piece of writing which perfectly represents a sample of an earlier form of a language cannot lose that hypothetical perfection, but the perfection of the system behind that piece of writing for that form of the language will not obtain for a later form; the language change does not trigger exactly matching changes in the writing system, for changes in the writing system follow from the dynamic of that system, not the language it represents. A writing system starts out with a *fit* to the language; as the language changes, the fit grows looser and looser, almost always entropically, that is, in the direction of chaos.[35] To be sure, not all change in writing systems is deformational; there are directed changes—instances, that is, of reformational change—but script

---

35. Gelb, "Records, Writing, and Decipherment," 65. Thus "the writing system takes on a life of its own, separate and apart from the 'life' of the language and with no reference to it" (K. H. Palka, pers. comm.). The changes in language and the changes in script are both somewhat systematic—Why do the systems virtually never mesh? Why does fit almost always degenerate? Because the systems are of essentially different phenomena.

and spelling reform are usually erratic and intermittent.[36] Any student of the history of English knows, however, that spelling reform is usually a lost cause.[37]

The two crucial facts of historical involvement in writing are its role in the evolution of consciousness and its role in degenerating fit. There is a temptation to see them as broadly complementary, for the first seems to involve an increase (in the amount of information processed) and the second a decrease (in the basic harmonic of how the information is recorded). Such a vision would require a careful scrutiny of the notion of speech community. The combination is clearly counterintuitive for the individual, since each person is proprioceptively complete, but may provide a sense of the broader human entity, an entity now speaking and being spoken by, reading and being read by an interpenetrating web of global languages.[38]

COMPONENTS OF WRITING

The three components of a linguistically oriented consideration of a writing system are, it was suggested earlier, the analysis of the language, the expression of the results of the analysis, and the preservation of the expression. The native-speaker analysis of a language shares with all linguistic science a weary, eager, and anxious resignation to the elephantine character of the object of study. Phonologists hang off the tusks, syntacticians poke the hide trying to count the ribs, lexicographers fiddle with the tail, and all intermittently crosscheck their findings and adjust their descriptions accordingly. Linguists prefer to regard language as stratified in more or less separate components or levels, but that is as much a metaphor as the more organic elephant. Writing systems, too, operate with various components, in that certain features of the system schematize certain aspects of the language.[39] There is no writing system that fully integrates all aspects of the analyses in-

36. Early changes, when they can be traced, often have a more complex relation to fit; on the early stages of Cherokee spelling, see W. L. Chafe and J. F. Kilpatrick, "Inconsistencies in Cherokee Spelling," in *Symposium on Language and Culture* (ed. V. E. Garfield and W. Chafe; Seattle: University of Washington Press, 1963) 60–63.
37. Script reform has been successful in Japan (see the work in Chris Seeley, ed., *Aspects of the Japanese Writing System*, published as *Visible Language* 18/3 [1984]) and China, the chief efforts involving the simplification of characters. Recent Dutch spelling reforms are reputed to have been effective; Noah Webster reformed English spelling in the United States.
38. I have in mind Teilhard de Chardin's eschatology.
39. As already noted, all writing systems omit material present in the speech stream. All aspects of a writing system derive ultimately from linguistic analysis, and the signs refer ultimately to linguistic units and features.

volved, that is, a writing system always involves subsystems. The major subsystem, the one popularly identified with the speech stream (or sign stream, for sign languages) is often taken as crucial or definitional, but other coordinate subsystems cannot therefore be ignored. Readers of English think they are reading the words, but they are also reading the spaces between them, the marks of punctuation, the patterns of capitalization, italics, and hyphenation, etc.

The first facet of a writing system is the analysis involved. The major subsystem may be based primarily on lexical analysis and secondarily on phonological analysis, or vice versa. No writing system uses only one sort of analysis to the absolute exclusion of the other, though there are cases that come close to this exclusion. If a writing system was invented for a language, it involves an analysis that reflects the character of the language recorded.[40] A language in which root morphemes are kept intact and grammatically modified by agglutination or juxtaposition tends to favor a lexical analysis. A language like Hebrew or Tigre in which root morphemes undergo extensive modification tends to favor a phonological analysis. An analysis that is apt for the original language recorded is often not apt for another, and, since writing systems are almost never borrowed for linguistic reasons, they have often been modified extensively in the borrowing process.[41]

Alongside the major subsystem, there are one or more lesser subsystems, based on suprasegmental features of speech. Such subsystems, because they are less extensive, tend to be more simply structured and may be based, for example, exclusively on such phenomena as utterance-level stress. A language like English or Hebrew that uses word stress would tend to favor a writing system that distinguishes words; a language like Chinese that does not use word stress would tend not to represent words as units graphically. Other subsystems may be based almost exclusively on syntax, as modern punctuation tends to be. A language which uses relatively few different syntactic structures tends to require fewer marks of punctuation than a language which uses relatively many.

40. The process of innovating a writing system is roughly analogous to the advent of human language in the remote past, the process called glottogenesis, probably to be dated after the Neanderthals, who, if they had speech, used few of the contrasts requisite for human speech; Cro-Magnon anatomy corresponds to our own in terms of speech facilities. See, e.g., P. Lieberman and E. S. Crelin, "On the Speech of Neanderthal Man," *Linguistic Inquiry* 11 (1971) 203–22; Lieberman served as the linguistic consultant on the movie *Ice Man*, which depicts the resuscitation of a Neanderthal.

41. The more common case of innovation is the adaptation of a writing system to a language. This process is roughly analogous to the creation of new languages (in the presence of and drawing on existing languages), the process called language genesis or creolization; see the papers in K. C. Hill, ed., *The Genesis of Language* (Ann Arbor: Karoma, 1979).

The second facet of a writing system is the expression of the results of the analysis. The fused and juxtaposed results of the analyses are expressed in groups of signs arranged along one major axis, with coordinate axes sometimes used for subsystems. The signs of the major subsystem may be lexical or (morpho)phonological, and the major sign type follows from the linguistic analysis involved. Lexical signs, called logograms, dominate in an innovating writing system if the analysis is strongly lexical, while phonological signs or phonograms dominate if the analysis is strongly phonological. There are at base two varieties of logogram: primary logograms, designating the word for the type of thing "pictured," and redundant logograms, designating a homonym of the thing pictured; because the second class is larger than the first, such a system has an intrinsic degree of economy, though a limited one. Phonograms may be primarily syllabic or alphabetic; syllabic-dominated systems tend to be more economical than systems that use logograms, and alphabetic systems tend to be more economical than syllabic systems.

One type of sign tends to dominate in the major subsystem of a given system; this has led to the creation of an evolutionary typology which collapses the historical order in which various types of signs are first attested (logograms, syllabograms, alphabetic signs) with an evaluation nominally based on an efficiency metric (the more efficient the better).[42] The typology has several unfortunate corollaries. First, it has tended to absolutize the various categories of writing system, disguising several important facts: (a) there are no purely logographic systems and arguably few pure types at all;[43] (b) the dominant subsystem is always articulated with some lesser subsystem, even if of the most rudimentary type; and (c) the efficiency metric undervalues features of a system which do not reflect the speech stream in a simple way, such as determinatives. Second, the typology collapses diachronic and synchronic measures. It is historically true that logogram-and-syllabogram-dominated writing systems preceded syllabogram-dominated systems, and that alphabets come last. This priority does not mean that the later types of system are superior or are features of superior cultures. To believe in such superiority is at base naïve ethnocentrism. A special form of the typology adds on a rigid distinction between unvocalized alphabetic systems (taken as systems of syllabic signs with variable vowels)[44] and vocalized alphabetic

42. The typology goes back to the father of modern anthropology, Edward Burnett Tylor (1832–1917), who included as a first stage pictographic writing. On the dangers of the typology, see, e.g., M. Bernal's review of *Sign, Symbol, Script* in *JAOS* 105 (1985) 736–37.
43. On historical relations among writing systems, see the next section of this essay. The nearly pure alphabetic systems usually cited are Finnish, Hungarian, and Spanish; Russian and French spelling systems are morphophonemic.
44. There are substantive issues involved in so describing unvocalized alphabetic scripts but no space here to treat them.

systems. The specious historical corollary of this distinction leads to sharp separations among the cultures of the eastern Mediterranean basin, and the forms of ethnocentrism at hand can be named with an unfortunate precision: colonialism, Eurocentrism, anti-Semitism.

The signs used to express features of writing other than the dominant subsystem tend to be either bigger or smaller than the bulk of the signs, either a cartouche or a comma, a block or a bullet. The larger signs group together signs of the dominant subsystem, whether in small rectangles or long lines. The smaller signs function by standing within, above, or below the sequence of dominant signs.[45]

The third and most straightforward facet of a writing system is the preservation of the analysis. The written signs expressing the result of native-speaker analysis can be preserved in various ways. The marking process may be subtractive (e.g., carving out signs), additive (e.g., laying signs on with graphite or ink), or manipulative (e.g., pushing clay or plaster around to shape signs). The material marked may be hard, or soft and perishable. Perishable materials may be vegetable or animal. Animal materials may be prepared with inorganic agents (tawing with alum and salt produces parchment

---

45. On cases and columns in archaic cuneiform, see M. W. Green, "The Construction and Implementation of the Cuneiform Writing System," *Visible Language* 15 (1981) 345–72, at 349–56. In Hittite, one line occasionally expresses one clause; often tablet rulings separate off sentences; see C. F. Justus, "Visible Sentences in Cuneiform Hittite," *Visible Language* 15 (1981) 373–408. The compartments in Maya writings have played an important role in decipherment; see D. H. Kelley, *Deciphering the Maya Script* (Austin: University of Texas Press, 1976) 7; and L. Schele, *Maya Glyphs: The Verbs* (Austin: University of Texas Press, 1982) 5. The phonetic complements in Maya texts are smaller than the logograms, as are the glossing signs in Japanese (*furigane*)—see M. Paradis, H. Hagiwara, and N. Hildebrandt, *Neurolinguistic Aspects of the Japanese Writing System* (New York: Academic Press, 1985) and Chinese (*bopumofu*)—see O'Connor, "Writing Systems, Native Speaker Analyses," 452–55. Among early alphabetic texts, Hebrew and Moabite inscriptions tend to use word dividers, while Aramaic epigraphs tend to favor word spacing and Phoenician tends to be written solid. On the basic structural features of Greek inscriptions (a corpus of ca. 20,000 monuments, dated 625 B.C.E.–300 C.E.), see L. Threatte, *The Grammar of Attic Inscriptions*, vol. 1: *Phonology* (Berlin: de Gruyter, 1980): on direction of writing (pp. 52–57), layout (pp. 58–64), and punctuation, with a single mark, the interpunct (pp. 73–98). Most smaller signs, including marks of punctuation, are involved with the general problem of diacritics.

Some markings of larger units can be of the same order as the dominant subsystem: Cherokee uses a character for sentence beginning, of the same shape as the syllabograms (see Chafe and Kilpatrick, "Cherokee Spelling," 61). Most descendants of the Roman alphabet use majuscule letters for sentence beginning and in other ways; German *Grossschreibung* 'capitalization' marks all nouns and also gives a clue to noun-phrase structure (i.e., in the string *die meisten Dialekte = art adj Noun*, only the head, i.e., the noun, is capitalized), though an imperfect clue (cf. the string *ein weiteres, der jüngeren Forschung diskutiertes Problem = art adj art adj Noun adj Noun*). (Examples chosen almost at random from R. Degen, *Altaramäische Grammatik*, 1–2.)

or vellum; the distinction between these two depends on the age of the animal from which the skin is taken) or organic agents (tanning with the common vegetable acid tannin produces leather). The joining together of pieces of perishable writing materials in the scroll and the codex, ultimately the book, involves complexities outside the scope of this paper; but the role of such developments in stimulating refinements in writing systems cannot be ignored.[46]

FEATURES OF THE HISTORY OF WRITING

A review of some features of a proper history of writing and its precursors will help balance the abstract historical correctives noted above and situate some related materials. The geographical horizons are these:

Old World   A. Egypt
                 B. The Levant (*sensu largo*)
                 C. Mesopotamia and Iran
                 D. South Asia (the Indian subcontinent)
                 E. East Asia
New World[47]   A. North America (north of the Rio Grande)
                 B. Mexico
                 C. The Maya lands/Mesoamerica
                 D. South America

In the Old World the relevant series is laid out west-to-east. In the New World, the relevant schema involves a series of regions defined north-to-south. Writing systems were invented in all the cited sections of the Old World and in the Maya lands in the New World.

The first complex of materials to be treated involves precursors of writing, systems reflected in the winter-count hides of North America, potters'

---

46. Writing instruments are less discussed than writing materials, although P. T. Daniels, "A Calligraphic Approach to Aramaic Paleography," *JNES* 43 (1984) 55–68, has shown the enormous contribution the study of applied paleography can make. General surveys of ancient writing materials are provided by R. J. Williams, "Writing and Writing Materials," in *Interpreter's Dictionary of the Bible* (ed. G. A. Buttrick; Nashville: Abingdon, 1962) 4:909–21, esp. 916–20, and K. Galling, "Tafel, Buch und Blatt," in *Near Eastern Studies in Honor of William Foxwell Albright* (ed. H. Goedicke; Baltimore: Johns Hopkins Press, 1971) 207–23.

47. The recent and on-going decipherment of Maya writing makes it necessary to consider New World data: "Since Maya is the *only* writing system we know for absolutely *certain* is totally independent of all the others, it is our only chance of seeing alternative ways of recording language (until the little green persons get here) and thus can *never* be left out of treatments of writing anymore" (P. T. Daniels, pers. comm.).

marks in the Old World, and the like. These sign and symbol systems are generally related to writing systems but lack the basic representational features of them.[48] The term *precursor system* is unsatisfactory, but the alternatives are worse: precursors are not consistently "semasiographic," and to call them "writing" as opposed to "true writing" is to court utter confusion. Such systems are typologically precursors.[49] The presence of a precursor system does not necessarily lead to the development of writing. The chronographic systems of the New World outside the Maya sphere do not differ extensively from Maya chronography, but in the New World only the Mayas appear to have developed true writing. Similarly, the absence of a precursor system may reflect historical accident, but even so such absence does not seem revealing. The difference between precursor systems and writing systems is both formal and functional, since it appears that precursor systems serve one purpose (economic [Old World] or chronographic [New World]),[50] while writing systems serve many purposes. The traditional insistence on a gap between the two sets of systems remains valid.

The history of writing systems proper is an elaborate skein of crosscultural borrowings and influence. Two types of borrowings are attested: the outright borrowing of a writing system (the Germanic and Celtic peoples of northern Europe taking over the Latin alphabet) and the borrowing of one or other element of the idea of writing.[51] Total borrowing is commoner. Other

---

48. On some precursor systems, see Gelb, *Study of Writing.*

49. Some of the alternatives to the term *precursor system* are grounded in the spurious view that simple representation of objects is based on a visual code comprehensible across the entire range of the human species. If such a code exists, it is quite limited. Philologists like to say, You can't read a text unless you know what it says. The parallel rule of thumb—You can't recognize a picture unless you know what it shows—is less true, but not entirely misleading. For "semasiographic," see, e.g., Gelb, "Records, Writing, and Decipherment," 68; I doubt that his further classification into descriptive-representational and identifying-mnemonic systems is workable. "Picture writing," as the term is usually meant, seems not to exist.

50. There are New World economic records, but they are "rare and late" (J. S. Justeson, "The Origin of Writing Systems: Preclassic Mesoamerica," *World Archaeology* 17 [1986] 437–58, at 445), except in Peru.

51. The relationship between script borrowing and language learning could profitably be explored: How much exposure to writing is needed for the two types of borrowing? Does limited exposure lead to fuller innovation (as in Sequoyah's case, apparently)?

The rather rare cases of *script crossing* should be distinguished from script borrowing: in these a language is written in a system for which it has not been adapted—the crossing is brief and sociologically anomalous. I have in mind cases like the Aramaic text written in Demotic, P. Amh. Eg. 63, and the Akkadian texts written in Greek. On P. Amh., see C. F. Nims and R. C. Steiner, "A Paganized Version of Psalm 20:2–6 from the Aramaic Text in Demotic Script," *JAOS* 103 (1983) 261–74; Steiner and Nims, "Ashurbanipal and Shamash-Shum-Ukin: A Tale of Two Brothers from the Aramaic Text in Demotic Script," *Revue biblique* 92 (1985) 60–81; S. P. Vleeming and J. W. Wesselius, "An Aramaic Hymn from the Fourth Century B.C.," *BO* 39 (1982) 501–9; K. A. D. Smelik, "The Origin of Psalm 20,"

forms of borrowing testify to the power of the idea of a permanent record of a native-speaker analysis, as well as to the fact that the analysis involved in writing must be to some extent of a piece with other knowledge speakers have of their language. The best-known cases of modern script innovation, the Hangŭl syllabary of Korean (1443) and the Cherokee syllabary of Sequoyah (1825),[52] also reveal that script innovation has the character of an invention, a major device instituted in a short time by a single person.[53]

The innovation of writing in the late fourth and third millennia presents a major puzzle, a specific form of the anthropologists' polarity of independent innovation and cultural diffusion. Writing appears in Mesopotamia and Egypt around the same time and in China and the Indus Valley thereafter: Is the innovation dependent in all four areas? Or the first two only? Or only in Mesopotamia?[54] Given that New World writing must be an independent

---

Journal for the Study of the Old Testament 31 (1985) 75–81. On the Akkadian texts, see E. Sollberger, "Greco-Babyloniaca," *Iraq* 24 (1962) 63–72; M. J. Geller, "More Greco-Babyloniaca," *Zeitschrift für Assyriologie* 73 (1983) 114–20; J. A. Black and S. M. Sherwin-White, "A Clay Tablet with Greek Letters in the Ashmolean Museum, and the 'Graeco-Babyloniaca' Texts," *Iraq* 46 (1984) 131–40. G. J. P. McEwan's suggestion that Akkadian was regularly written in Greek script has been rejected by M. W. Stolper, reviewing *Texts from Hellenistic Babylonian in the Ashmolean Museum* (Oxford Editions of Cuneiform Texts 9; Oxford: Clarendon, 1982), in *JAOS* 105 (1985) 141–42. The Greco-Babyloniaca texts and P. Amh. Eg. 63 are more or less contemporary.

52. On Sequoyah, see W. Walker, "The Design of Native Literacy Programs and How Literary Came to the Cherokees," *Anthropological Linguistics* 26 (1984) 161–69.

53. The notion that a given writing system was invented is remarkably popular, given that there is no relevant evidence (and what would constitute relevant evidence?). W. G. Boltz, "Early Chinese Writing," *World Archaeology* 17 (1986) 42–35, at 432, allows that Chinese writing was invented in "relatively [?] quick" order. M. A. Powell, "Three Problems in the History of Cuneiform Writing: Origins, Direction of Script, Literacy," *Visible Language* 15 (1981) 419–40, opines that cuneiform was invented by one person, albeit one familiar with the token system of accounting. J. D. Ray, "The Emergence of Writing in Egypt," *World Archaeology* 17 (1986) 307–16, opts for a single inventor for hieroglyphs. The alphabet is a favorite candidate for invention; see, e.g., A. R. Millard, "The Infancy of the Alphabet," *World Archaeology* 17 (1986) 390–98, at 394.

On the pre-modern cultural history of writing, see O'Connor, "Writing Systems, Native Speaker Analyses," 452–55, adding for Egypt a reference to Thoth as inventor in pre-Hellenistic times (Ray, "Emergence of Writing in Egypt," 311) and to Isis and Hermes as joint inventors in the Hellenistic age (G. H. R. Horsley, *New Documents Illustrating Early Christianity* [North Ryde: The Ancient History Documentary Research Centre, Macquarie University, 1981] 1:10–21).

54. The general sense of scholars is that Egyptian and Mesopotamian writing systems have some common origin. Most would say that Mesopotamia influenced Egypt (perhaps via the Red Sea and Wadi Hammamat), be they Assyriologist (e.g., Powell, "Three Problems") or Egyptologist (e.g., Ray, "Emergence of Writing in Egypt"), though C. T. Hodge (reviewing B. Watterson, *Introducing Egyptian Hieroglyphics*, in *Anthropological Linguistics* 26

innovation, what factors are involved in historical judgments of the Old World cases? The next stage in the history of Old World writing is well known: the Egyptian writing system in the process of fine-tuning its fit to the complex morphology of the Egyptian language developed and sporadically implemented various strategies for simplified writing which provided a base for innovation in the Levant. Virtually all associated notions must be scrapped, however. The Proto-Sinaitic inscriptions are not crucial in the transition to the alphabet, and Egypt was probably not the only major influence. The recent archaeological investigations into the history of the Levant make it increasingly difficult to distinguish it clearly from Mesopotamia, and so the influence of Akkadian syllabographic adaptations of the Sumerian writing system cannot be ruled out in the Levant. The notion of the Sinai as a crucial transfer point, an interlocking piece culturally as well as geologically, can no longer be sustained, though the documentation of Egyptian-Levantine trade contact long predating the Serabit el-Khadem mines should have made that notion unlikely. In fact, Egyptian group spellings and syllable-based signs (both CVC and CV) were important in the transition, but probably only indirectly.

Two well-developed writing systems are used for West Semitic in the Late Bronze Age: the wedge alphabet and the linear alphabet.[55] Of the two forms of the wedge alphabet, the better known, the Ugaritian, is partially syllabographic. The Levant is usually recognized as a source for writing systems in the Aegean sphere: Linear A and B are innovations based on Levantine (and perhaps also Egyptian) notions of writing, as is the later

---

[1984] 240–43, at 241) has preferred to speak of both as being under the influence of a third, as yet unidentified *Kulturkreis*. The indigenous origins of hieroglyphs has recently been defended by W. S. Arnett, *The Predynastic Origin of Egyptian Hieroglyphs* (Washington, DC: University Press of America, 1983).

Few scholars dispute that the Indus Valley script reflects Mesopotamian influence, probably mediated by maritime (rather than overland) trade contact.

The Chinese connection can scarcely even be called disputed: It is my sense that no Sinologist would allow for outside influence (for which there is no evidence, cf. Boltz, "Early Chinese Writing," 429; again I am forced to ask, what form would the evidence take?), and no scholar of Western Asia would fail to assume that outside influence was involved (e.g., Powell, "Three Problems"). That is, we have a contest of prejudices.

55. There is some confusion over these forms of the alphabet and the issue of alphabetic order that needs cleaning up. The Ugaritian abecedaries show an alphabetic order for the wedge alphabet in which *i̯*, *u̯*, and *s̀* are placed last; indeed in one text (RS 24.492) there is a word divider after *t* and before the last three units (see P. Bordreuil, "Quatre documents en cunéiformes alphabétiques mal connus ou inédits," *Semitica* 32 [1982] 5–14, at 9–10). This shows that these final units are secondary to the alphabetic order, but not necessarily secondary to the alphabetic system. The common view that the alphabet was "enlarged" at Ugarit (e.g., Millard, "Infancy of the Alphabet") seems dubious.

Cypriot syllabary, while the Greek alphabet represents a borrowing, whether of the Late Bronze or Iron Age, whether direct or via Anatolian routes.

By the time of the Axial Age, around the middle of the first millennium B.C.E., the history of writing systems had entered into well-understood patterns, though the evaluation of those patterns remains complex.[56] Between the fall of Rome and the Renaissance the great innovations proceed in remarkably interlaced patterns. Two paradigmatically complex points stand out. The innovation of papermaking in China was followed by its transfer to the House of Islam and thence to Europe; this chain of events binds up the whole of the Old World, both at war (the Battle of Samarqand, 856, between Chinese and Muslim forces) and in peace.[57] The Old World is apparently fissured by the invention of printing from movable type, first in Korea and later in Germany (in 1453).[58] The fifty years after Gutenberg's innovation are, in the history of books, the incunable years, the years of swaddling clothes, and it is claimed that printing these days has a whole nursery of young electronic siblings, all loud in their swaddling clothes.

56. One outcome of the patterns is clear: The present status of the Latin alphabet as the writing system of the future is suggested by its status in the People's Republic of China as the resource, both before and after the Cultural Revolution, for orthographies of previously unwritten languages, be they Turkic (which might historically use the Arabic alphabet) or Sinic (Sino-Burmese) (which might use Chinese characters). See Fu Maoji, "Language Policies Toward National Minorities in China," *Anthropological Linguistics* 27 (1985) 214–21, for a report. Christian missionaries are likewise committed to the Latin alphabet; for useful notes on script innovation, particularly on the effect of other orthographies in the environment, see E. A. Nida, "Practical Limitations to a Phonemic Alphabet," *Bible Translator* 32 (1981) 204–9; and D. Kenrick, "The Development of a Standard Alphabet for Romani," *Bible Translator* 32 (1981) 215–19.

57. M. F. Jamil, *Islamic* wirāqah *"Stationery" during the Early Middle Ages* (Ph.D. diss., University of Michigan, 1985); J. Pedersen, *The Arabic Book* (trans. G. French, from Danish original of 1946; Princeton: Princeton University Press, 1984).

58. The earliest printing, of Taoist charms from wood blocks, took place in China in the seventh century (late Sui Dynasty); the earliest surviving examples date to the ninth century (T'ang Dynasty: a *Diamond Sutra* of 868 found at Tunhuang by A. Stein). Printing reached Japan by 770 C.E. Movable type of wood and later ceramic was invented in China, by the Sung engineer Pi Sheng (990–1051); printing with movable metal type was in use in Korea by 1234. See S. S. Chweh, "In Search of the Origin of Metal Type Printing," *Gutenberg-Jahrbuch* 60 (1985) 15–18; M. Pye, "Chinese Script and the Invention of Printing," *Rocznik Orientalistyczny* 44 (1985) 5–19; Tsien Tsuen-Hsien, *Science and Civilization in China*, vol. 5: *Chemistry and Chemical Technology*, pt. 1: *Paper and Printing* (ed. Joseph Needham; Cambridge: Cambridge University Press, 1985). The possibility of Oriental influence on Gutenberg cannot be ruled out: note the careful formulation of G. W. Williams: "The invention of printing in Western Civilization should be attributed to Johann Gensfleisch zum Gutenberg, a patrician of Mainz (1394–1468)" (*The Craft of Printing and the Publication of Shakespeare's Works* [Washington, DC: The Folger Shakespeare Library, 1985] 29). Hebrew was first printed in 1475 (p. 40). Williams provides a brief introduction to European printing.

APPENDIX: THE HEBREW WRITING SYSTEM

There are three subsystems used in the writing of Biblical Hebrew: the dominant (or skeletal) subsystem, the consonantal text; and two diacritic systems, the vowel signs and the accents. Direct study of the system necessarily involves reconstruction, since the language is, in some sense, a written language, and the writing system is no longer used. The sources for the reconstruction grow less diverse and more reliable as the subsystems grow closer to us in terms of time and tradition.

The first task, assessing the consonantal units, is aided in part by a large fund of epigraphic materials, essential in distinguishing the various uses certain units are put to. The six plain stops (*p t k b d g*) and the six plain fricatives (*s z l r n m*) present no basic problems on the consonantal level. The remaining ten units are more difficult; it is possible to follow Jewish tradition in handling them, but there is reason to look at a broader range of materials in considering the four remaining groups of segments. (1) The emphatics are, according to most scholars, a single class of secondarily articulated sounds, whether pharyngealized, as cognates are in Arabic, or glottalized (glottalic ejectives), as in some Ethiopic languages.[59] R. C. Steiner has demonstrated that ancient *ṣ* was probably not a fricative (as in Arabic), but an affricate (*ts* or *c*, as in Jewish tradition).[60] (2) The next-to-last unit of the Hebrew alphabet is known to be of unclear denotation both from the later diacritical marking and from evidence of scribal confusion and later glossing. A system of two voiceless sibilants should involve *s* (Hebrew *sāmek*) and *š*, the role assigned the more common form of *šîn/śîn*; what role should be assigned the less common? A three-way system of plain voiceless sibilants is possible,[61] but evidence suggests that *ś* was a fricative lateral—the simplest example is *kaśdîm* 'Chaldeans.'[62] According to Steiner's review, in earlier Semitic *ś* was the voiceless counterpart of *l*, with *ḏ* an emphatic lateral. (3) The extrabuccal sounds designated by *ʾ* and *h* (glottalics) and *ḥ* and *ʿ* (uvulars) are of interest for two reasons. The latter two are usually reconstructed on the basis of comparative data; they are unusual segments, both typologically and phonologically. The glottalic signs, along with (4) the semivowel signs, are part of the system of vowel letters.

59. See R. D. Hoberman, "The Phonology of Pharyngeals and Pharyngealization in Pre-Modern Aramaic," *JAOS* 105 (1985) 221–31, for discussion of the problem in comparative Semitic perspective.

60. R. C. Steiner, *Affricated Ṣade in the Semitic Languages* (American Academy for Jewish Research Monograph 3; New York: AAJR, 1982).

61. Examples in W. Bright, "Sibilants and Naturalness in Aboriginal California," in *American Indian Languages and Literatures*, 31–54.

62. R. C. Steiner, *The Case for Fricative-Laterals in Proto-Semitic* (AOS 59; New Haven: American Oriental Society, 1977).

The problem of ghost sounds, that is, sounds distinguished in the language but not notated distinctively, arises occasionally; the strongest evidence is for the preservation of *ġ* (cognate to Arabic *ġayin*) down to the time of portions of the Septuagint. (Similar preservations are clearer in Old Aramaic: *ḏ* written *z* but later *d*; *ḏ* written *q* but later *ʿ*; *ẓ* written *ṣ* but later *ṭ*; and *ṯ* written *š* but later *t*.)[63]

Epigraphic data have enabled the reconstruction of the development of the vowel letter system. I have outlined the linguistic bases.[64] The epigraphic findings continue to accumulate, but new information is unlikely to change the basic picture of the dynamic.[65] The literary implications of the system's history remain controversial.[66]

There are a number of Hebrew spelling patterns that require special comment. Root morphemic spellings are found, notably in the retention of the *y* in nouns derived from middle-weak roots: *ʿyn* and *byt* are almost invariant. Affix morphemic spellings are also used, the best known being the third masculine singular suffix on masculine plural nouns, spelled *-yw* at the cost of a number of *Kethiv/Qere* "corrections." The existence of etymological spellings is not certain; the examples brought into discussion generally involve the glottal stop *ʾalep*, but certainty regarding the lenition of that segment is impossible. Its phonology is complex,[67] and direct evidence is slight.[68] Comparative evidence, even from closely related languages, is problematic.

The diacritics involved with consonantal discriminations are the *śîn/šîn* dot and the *dāgēš*. The usual treatment of the latter as two signs, *qal* (*lene*) vs. *ḥāzāq* (*fortis*), is an expression of post-Masoretic despair at the workings of the unitary sign. As Malone has shown, the phonology of *dāgēš* illustrates in acute form the difference between the systematic phoneme (as in generative phonological theory) and the autonomous phoneme (as in neo-Bloomfieldian linguistics).[69] Malone argues that the linguistic analysis reflected in the use

63. See, e.g., P. Swiggers, "The Notation System of the Old Aramaic Inscriptions," *Archív Orientálñi* 51 (1983) 378–81; J. Blau, *On Polyphony in Biblical Hebrew* (Jerusalem: Israel Academy of Science and Humanities, 1982).
64. O'Connor, "Writing Systems, Native Speaker Analyses."
65. See, e.g., D. M. Gropp and T. J. Lewis, "Notes on Some Problems in the Aramaic Text of Hadd-Yithʿi Bilingual," *BASOR* 259 (1985) 45–61.
66. See, e.g., James Barr, "Hebrew Orthography and the Book of Job," *JSS* 30 (1985) 1–33, on D. N. Freedman, "Orthographic Peculiarities in the Book of Job," *ErIsr* 9 (1969) 35*–44*.
67. See, e.g., J. L. Malone, "Textually Deviant Forms as Evidence for Phonological Analysis: A Service of Philology to Linguistics," *JANESCU* 11 (1979) 71–79, at 73–74; idem, "Classical Mandaic Radical Metathesis, Radical Assimilation and the Devil's Advocate," *General Linguistics* 25 (1985) 92–122, at 101–4; E. J. Revell, "Stress and the Waw 'Consecutive' in Biblical Hebrew," *JAOS* 104 (1984) 437–44, at 442–43.
68. E.g., *makkolet* in 1 Kgs 5:25.
69. Malone, "Systematic vs. Autonomous Phonemics."

of *dāgēš* is an autonomous phonemic understanding of gemination and spirantization.

The two systems of diacritics are usually lumped together, but the vowel-sign system is earlier. It is known in various forms, the simplex and complex Babylonian forms representing one tradition and the Palestinian and various Tiberian forms (the victorious Ben Asher, the defeated Ben Naphtali) another. The older view that the Palestinian system was more primitive than the Tiberian and less sophisticated linguistically must be rejected.[70]

The structure of the Tiberian vowel system is widely agreed to involve seven, not five, full vowels and to distinguish primarily vowel color. (The Babylonian is a six-vowel system.) The grammarians of the Qimḥi dynasty several centuries later treated the language as having five full vowels and using a systematic long/short distinction. The prestige of the Qimḥis combined with typographical convenience has led to widespread adoption of a misleading transliteration (by, e.g., the Society of Biblical Literature). The full vowels are *u* (*šûreq* and *qibbûṣ*), *o* or *ọ* (*ḥôlem*), *ɔ* or *å* (*qāmeṣ*), *a* (*pataḥ*), *ɛ* or *ẹ* (*sĕgôl*), *e* or *ẹ* (*ṣērê*), and *i* (*ḥîreq*); all except *pataḥ* can occur long or short.

i			u
	e (ẹ)		o (ọ)
	ɛ (ẹ)		ɔ (å)
	a		

There are also four *ḥātûp* or reduced vowels, *ɔ̆*, *ă*, *ɛ̆* or *ĕ*, and *ə* (*šĕwā⁾ mobile*; graphically the same as *šĕwā⁾ quiescens* and *šĕwā⁾ medium*); the reduced vowels are all low-mid (*ɛ̆*, *ə*, *ɔ̆*) or low (*ă*). The five-vowel system does have several recent defenders, but their arguments have not stood up to close scrutiny.[71]

In strict terms, current practice in the field of biblical studies fits the definition of transliteration, the "unambiguous replacement of one set of signs by another,"[72] but the use of *ē* for *ṣērê* certainly suggests that the segment is always long, even if defenders of the practice could plausibly call this a misunderstanding. One alternative would be to use four signs for the

---

70. E. J. Revell, "The Hebrew Accents and the Greek Ekphonetic Neumes," *Studies in Eastern Chant* 4 (1974) 140–70.

71. J. L. Malone, "Issues in the Morphophonology of Tiberian Hebrew" (ms., 1980), and "Messrs. [John] McCarthy and [Alan S.] Prince, and the Problem of Hebrew Vowel Color" (ms., 1980). See further his *Tiberian Hebrew Phonology* (Winona Lake, Ind.: Eisenbrauns, 1993).

72. Daniels, "Semitic Scripts," 250.

four mid-vowel signs (and a circumflex for most matres lectionis), which would yield a reasonably conservative transliteration, with length unindicated. The other would be to mark length regularly and use a transcription, an "interpretation of the original writing . . . according to a particular understanding of the grammar."[73] Both approaches could be used profitably; the current creeping conformism in the matter is disturbing, though the current practice does have advantages and need not be abandoned entirely.[74]

The accentual system probably grew out of musical notation and so better reflects cantillation than speech contour.[75] The view that the imposition of the accent system led to the creation of pausal forms is as unacceptable as other earlier views of the Masoretes as innovators.[76] The pause system, a direct reflection of the syntax in phonology, antedates the accents as much as other features of the syntax. The Masoretes were grammarians who formalized a syntactic native-speaker analysis; Aronoff's recent study of the Tiberian accents is a preliminary survey.[77] A broader view is afforded by Revell's ongoing work.[78] The diacritical system of accents cannot be separated too rigidly from other internal Masoretic markings, such as paragraphing[79] and the various *puncta extraordinaria* and the like, nor from the marginal notes and apparatus. These markings grew out of older scribal practices.[80]

---

73. Ibid. Actually this is done in the SBL system by authors who mark defectively written, etymologically long *i* and *o* with a macron.

74. On some related points, see J. C. L. Gibson, "The Massoretes as Linguists," *Oudtestamentische Studiën* 19 (1974) 86–96.

75. See Revell, "Hebrew Accents"; and idem, "Syntactic/Semantic Structure and the Reflexes of Original Short *a* in Tiberian Pointing," *HAR* 5 (1981) 75–100, esp. 97.

76. E. J. Revell, "Pausal Forms and the Structure of Biblical Poetry," *VT* 31 (1981) 186–99.

77. M. Aronoff, "Orthography and Linguistic Theory: The Syntactic Basis of Masoretic Hebrew Punctuation," *Language* 61 (1985) 28–72.

78. In addition to papers cited in notes 67, 70, 75, and 76, see "Pausal Forms in Biblical Hebrew," *JSS* 25 (1980) 165–79.

79. F. Langlamet, "Les divisions massorétiques du livre de Samuel," *Revue biblique* 91 (1984) 481–519.

80. See, e.g., A. R. Millard, "In Praise of Ancient Scribes," *Biblical Archaeologist* 45 (1982) 143–53.

[November, 1989]

Stephen J. Lieberman†

Toward a Graphemics of the Tiberian Bible

אמר ר(בי) שפטי(ה) אמר ר(בי) יוחנן
הקורא בלא נעימה ו(ה)שונה בלא
זמ(י)רה עליו הכתוב אומר וגם אני
נתתי להם חוקים לא טובים ומשפטים
לא יחיו בהם

R. Shiftiyah quoted R. Yochanan:
"One who reads (Scripture) without a
melody or studies (the Oral Law)
without song—of him Scripture says,
'I too gave them laws which were not
pleasant and decrees by which they
do not live.'" (Ezek 20:25)

—Babylonian Talmud, *Megilla* 32a

I approach the question of the writing system used for the Hebrew Bible somewhat diffidently.[1] To attempt a complete description would require a multivolumed book, not an article. Many preliminary matters must be reviewed before such a treatment could be presented, and if one thing is clear, it is that a great deal of groundwork remains to be done. If, nonetheless, I address the topic from my perspective as a Semitic linguist, I do so in the spirit attributed to R. Tarfon in ʾAbot 2:16: "You are not required to finish (the) task, but are not at liberty to furlough."

A complete study would have to review many issues which are not usually considered by linguists and which are likewise commonly left out of the

---

1. The bibliographical references provided here are intended only as an initial guide to the reader. I have usually tried to light the way with a single recent or excellent study (which will point to earlier work), rather than blind with an excess of small blazes. Given the bounds of the present effort, there can be but little hope of expanding the bibliography to the extent that would be needed to try to illumine the whole. Providing much beyond a single source leaves one focusing on the many single flowers and mistaking their individuality for a garden. S. Z. Leiman has reprinted some of the important articles in *The Canon and Masorah of the Hebrew Bible: An Introductory Reader* (New York: Ktav, 1974).

curricula of schools which teach the Hebrew Bible. Of particular importance are questions related to the Masorah. I must perforce treat of some relevant issues, but a mention will have to suffice where a thorough investigation is really what is required.

For purposes of the present discussion, I accept the terms set by the present volume, and treat "Biblical Hebrew" as a category, even if we all know that the language of the books of the Bible is not uniform; I prefer a periodization not based on literary criteria.[2]

My objective is to point toward some of the basic features of the system, rather than to describe it fully. A synchronic rather than a diachronic approach seems appropriate at this stage, particularly given the fact that one must describe before one explains. Nonetheless, I make some historical observations to bolster one or two of my contentions. After introducing the topic, I turn to what graphemics is, and how some of the principles of this branch of semiotics or linguistics can be seen in features of the system used to record the Bible. Then I review the varieties of graphemes used by the Tiberian Masoretes to write the Bible and the structure of those graphemes, and conclude with an overall characterization of the system.

WHY TIBERIAN?

One might well ask why I chose to study the writing system used in the Hebrew Bible in the Tiberian tradition, rather than one of the other possibilities. I could well have focused on a different variety of Hebrew: the ancient inscriptions contemporary with the time the Bible is thought to have been written,[3] the spelling found in the biblical and other texts found at Qumran,[4] or one of the supralinear systems of voweling: the Palestinian[5] or the

2. See S. J. Lieberman, "Response [On the Historical Periods of the Hebrew Language]," in *Jewish Languages: Theme and Variations* (ed. H. H. Paper; Cambridge, Massachusetts: Association for Jewish Studies, 1978) 21–28.

3. See Z. Zevit, *Matres Lectionis in Ancient Hebrew Epigraphs* (American Schools of Oriental Research Monograph 2; Cambridge: ASOR, 1980), with references to earlier literature; see also n. 48 below.

4. See E. Qimron, *The Hebrew of the Dead Sea Scrolls* (Harvard Semitic Studies 29; Atlanta: Scholars Press, 1986), and E. Tov, "The Orthography and Language of the Hebrew Scrolls Found at Qumran and the Origin of the Scrolls," *Textus* 13 (1986) 31–57.

5. See E. J. Revell, *Biblical Texts with Palestinian Pointing and Their Accents* (Society of Biblical Literature Masoretic Series 4; Missoula: Scholars Press, 1977); and B. Chiesa, *L'Antico Testamento Ebraico secondo la tradizione palestinese* (Turin: Bottega d'Erasmo, 1978). Y. Yahalom has reviewed the study of Palestinian pointing in "The Palestinian Vocalization—Its Investigation and Achievements," *Leš* 52 (1988) 112–43 [Hebrew]; the article is to appear in English as an introduction to his *Palestinian Vocalized Piyyuṭ Manuscripts in the Cambridge Genizah Collections*.

Babylonian.[6] The secunda, that is, the column of Origen's Hexapla in which he records the Hebrew text in Greek characters,[7] and the various transliterations into other writing systems (including cuneiform, Egyptian, and Latin) are also of relevance, if one is trying to reconstruct the history of the phonology of the Hebrew Bible. Surely one of the ultimate goals of the graphemic description of a language no longer spoken is to refine our understanding of its sounds, so all of these are of some relevance.

I have chosen the Tiberian tradition for a simple reason: all the grammars of Biblical Hebrew are based on it, and it is the only voweled system which is currently in use. The Palestinian tradition gave way to the Tiberian before the turn of the second millennium C.E., and the Yemenite Jews who kept the supralinear Babylonian pointing in use following the triumph of the Tiberian finally adopted it under the influence of Maimonides. There is no complete biblical text, including points, other than the Tiberian. Nonetheless, the failure of modern dictionaries even to record the Babylonian or Palestinian voweling for their entries is a lack which must surely be remedied by the current generation of scholars.

One simply cannot reconstruct a grammar of Hebrew without vowels, and all who carry out examinations of unvocalized texts do so based on their prior knowledge of Hebrew. While none of the Ashkenazic, Sephardic, or Yemenite varieties of pronunciation of Hebrew is identical with the sound system which underlies Tiberian vocalization, it is taken as a norm. For each of these types of pronunciation, the deviations from Tiberian can be predicted with a small number of linguistic rules which are, largely, quite simple (though some of them are best described in morphophonemic, not mere phonological terms).

Since treatments of Hebrew must be based on Tiberian,[8] it should be the object of a thorough description if we are to approach more closely that

---

On the Palestinian vocalic system expressed in Tiberian graphemes, see most recently Y. Bentolila, *A French-Italian Tradition of Post-Biblical Hebrew* (Publications of the Hebrew University Language Traditions Project 14; Jerusalem: The Hebrew University Language Traditions Project/Beer Sheva: Ben-Gurion University of the Negev Press, 1989) 2–5 [Hebrew], with references to the earlier literature.

6. See the excellent study of I. Yeivin, *The Hebrew Language Tradition as Reflected in the Babylonian Vocalization* (Texts and Studies 12; Jerusalem: Academy of the Hebrew Language, 1985) [Hebrew].

7. See G. Janssens, *Studies in Hebrew Historical Linguistics Based on Origen's Secunda* (Orientalia Gandensia 9; Louvain: Peeters, 1982).

8. M. H. Goshen-Gottstein, "The Rise of the Tiberian Bible Text," in *Biblical and Other Studies* (ed. A. Altmann; Lown Institute Studies and Texts 1; Cambridge: Harvard University Press, 1963) 79–122 (repr. in Leiman, *Canon and Masorah*) has given ample reason to ignore the aspersions cast by P. Kahle on the value of the Tiberian Masoretes as recorders of a living linguistic tradition.

el Dorado of a precise Hebrew phonology; so I have chosen to center my remarks on it. It may be noted that, as a result of their rarity and great interest, thorough listings of the biblical manuscripts which use the Palestinian and Babylonian systems have been compiled,[9] but I know of no comparable recent listing of the manuscripts that follow the Tiberian traditions, though the earliest preserved witnesses are well known. Perhaps this is because of the large number of such manuscripts.

Masorah is the body of traditions which was inherited, collected, formulated, and developed by a variety of individuals whom we dub Masoretes in accord with their activities.[10] It encompasses a variety of topics not immediately germane to a linguistic description of Biblical Hebrew, since the Masoretes commonly focused on questions which were of seemingly little import in their attempt to safeguard the text of the Bible and pass it on in the form they received it. They frequently noted when a spelling or form occurred only a single time in the text (*měsôrâ qěṭannâ* = *masorah parva*), or collected unusual orthographies in their longer notes at each occurrence of such rare forms (*měsôrâ gědolâ* = *masorah magna*), and provided lists of various peculiarities of the text. Thus they largely focused on the particular rather than the general, but they also prepared works describing their system or parts of it.[11] They worked to preserve all the oddities of the text they inherited, rather than imposing some grammatical theory on it.

While this results in the fact that much of their work has held but little interest for the modern linguist, an understanding of this basic thrust of their task is essential to an assessment of it. Many modern scholars think that the anomalies which the Masoretes recorded are simple errors, and as a result they commonly dismiss the details, while they build their grammars on those forms which are common. Nonetheless, since, as Sapir put it, "all grammars leak,"[12] such exceptions to the "rules" of grammar they record may be taken as some indication of the Masoretes' fidelity in attempting to record what

9. Cf. nn. 5 and 6 above.

10. The comprehensive book of I. Yeivin, *Introduction to the Tiberian Masorah* (trans. E. J. Revell; Society of Biblical Literature Masoretic Series 5; Missoula: Scholars Press, 1980), can be recommended as an introduction to the field of Masoretic studies. It has an extensive bibliography. A. Dotan's summary "Masorah," in *EncJud* 16:1401–82, can also be used with profit.

11. See A. Dotan, *The Diqduqé Haṭṭě ʿamim of Ahǎron ben Moše ben Ašér* (Jerusalem: Academy of the Hebrew Language, 1967) [Hebrew]; N. Allony, "Rabbi Yehuda Ibn Balaam's Book 'Horayat Hakore'," in *Jubilee Volume in Honor of Moreinu Hagaon Rabbi Joseph B. Soloveitchik* (ed. S. Israeli, N. Lamm, and Y. Raphael; Jerusalem: Kook/New York: Yeshiva University, 1984) 2:644–80 [Hebrew]; and the literature referred to by I. Eldar, "Biblical Orthöepy," *Tarbiẓ* 54 (1985) 225–43 [Hebrew]. N. Allony's Masoretic studies have been collected in the second volume of his *Mḥqry lšwn wsprwt*, ed. J. Tubi and S. Morag (Jerusalem: Ben Zvi Institute, 1988).

12. E. Sapir, *Language: An Introduction to the Study of Speech* (New York: Harcourt, Brace & World, 1921) 38.

they heard, even if one must be skeptical concerning the historical provenance of all such peculiarities.[13]

Just as Masoretic notes recounting whether a form is found only once or
a few times in the biblical text are, by and large, ignored by linguists,[14] so
are other parts of the Masorah. I refer particularly to neumes or signs which
record the cantillation of the text. Since contemporary exegetes are most frequently interested in the "original" meaning of a biblical passage, they commonly ignore the neumes. Thus in grammars used to teach Biblical Hebrew,
the neumes are often not even listed—except for those which radically
change the vocalization since they indicate pause. I will presently show why
I think this is a linguistic error.

The Masoretes' attempt to prevent change was aimed foremost at the
consonantal text, and the fact that other parts of the biblical text, such as the
vowels, were not preserved in a wholly uniform way is admitted even by
scholars (such as M. Breuer) who think that this attempt was highly successful through the ages, and who hold that the received text as verified by such
latter-day scholars as R. Menahem ben Judah de Lonzano (1556–ca. 1623)
and R. Jedediah Solomon Raphael ben Abraham Norzi (1560–1616) differed
but little from the Bible as it issued from the hands of Aaron ben Asher.[15]
Breuer admits that H. Orlinsky's insistence that we not speak of *the* Masoretic text, but of many such texts,[16] is therefore justified.

WHICH TIBERIAN TEXT?

There is, alas, no complete collation of the Tiberian manuscripts of the Hebrew Bible, let alone a proper critical reconstruction. The collation of C. D.
Ginsburg did not include those texts which are now considered the most authentic representatives of the tradition.[17] Ginsburg's edition added variants

---

13. *Pace* S. Morag, "On the Historical Validity of the Vocalization of the Hebrew Bible," *JAOS* 94 (1974) 307–15; idem, "The Tiberian Tradition of Biblical Hebrew—Homogeneous and Heterogeneous Features," *P'raqim* 2 (1969–1974) 105–44.

14. Modern scholars prefer to rely on concordances rather than the Masoretes' listings of passages in their work.

15. M. Breuer, *The Aleppo Codex and the Accepted Text of the Bible* (Jerusalem: Kook, 1976) xxix–xxx.

16. H. M. Orlinsky, "The Origin of the Kethib-Qere System: A New Approach," in *Congress Volume: Oxford 1959* (Vetus Testamentum Supplement 7; Leiden: Brill, 1960) 184–92; and idem, apud C. D. Ginsburg, *Introduction to the Massoretico-Critical Edition of the Hebrew Bible* (repr. with a prolegomenon by H. M. Orlinsky; New York: Ktav, 1966); both essays are reprinted in Leiman, *Canon and Masorah.*

17. C. D. Ginsburg, *The Pentateuch; The Earlier Prophets; The Later Prophets; The Writings, Diligently Revised according to the Massorah* (London: British & Foreign Bible Society, 1926), a work which has been reprinted more than once.

from some manuscripts and early printings to the biblical text which was, largely, simply a printing of the Rabbinic Bible which had been supervised by Jacob ben Hayim ibn Adonijah and issued in Venice in the sixteenth century.[18] The edition does not include the Masoretic notes, and Ginsburg's alphabetic rearrangement of those notes largely left out indication of the printed and manuscript sources on which the individual traditions were based.[19] We have no complete biblical text based on collations of the relevant manuscripts which can serve as a basis for linguistic study. Even the Hebrew University Bible Project, which when completed will be a giant step forward, employs a diplomatic method of text criticism and prints as its text the Aleppo Codex (including both its *masorah magna* and *parva*) as well as recording variants from the versions, scrolls from the Judean desert, rabbinic literature, and medieval Bible manuscripts.[20]

Instead of studying such a critical text, I have (reluctantly) followed the scholarly consensus and selected a single manuscript. There were a few possible manuscripts which could have been chosen. The Aleppo Codex used for the Hebrew University project lays claim to having been endorsed by Maimonides.[21] It has been the subject of meticulous studies by I. Yeivin and M. Breuer[22] and was largely adopted by the latter in the printing of the Bible

18. A facsimile of this printing was issued, with an introduction by M. H. Goshen-Gottstein, as *Biblia Rabbinica: A Reprint of the 1525 Venice Edition* (Jerusalem: Makor, 1972).

19. C. D. Ginsburg, *The Massorah* (London/Vienna: Brög/Fromme, 1880–1905; repr. Jerusalem: Makor, 1980; repr. with a prolegomenon by A. Dotan: New York: Ktav, 1975). See also S. Frensdorff, *Die Massora Magna* (Hanover and Leipzig: Cohen & Reisch, 1876; repr. with a prolegomenon by G. E. Weil as *The Massorah Magna*: New York: Ktav, 1968); and idem, *Das Buch Ochlah W'ochlah* (Hanover: Hahn, 1864; repr. New York: Ktav, 1972).

20. Thus far, M. H. Goshen-Gottstein, *The Book of Isaiah: Sample Edition with Introduction* (Jerusalem: Magnes, 1965), vol. 1 (Jerusalem: Magnes, 1975), and vol. 2 (Jerusalem: Magnes, 1981), have issued from the project. The scope of the critical apparatus is described in the first of these, but it should be noted that the format in the later publications has changed somewhat.

21. There is a large literature on the pedigree of the Aleppo manuscript, from which I single out the following as advocates of the manuscript: I. Ben-Zvi, "The Codex of Ben Asher," *Textus* 1 (1960) 1–16 (repr. in Leiman, *Canon and Masorah*); M. H. Goshen-Gottstein, "The Authenticity of the Aleppo Codex," *Textus* 1 (1960) 17–58 (repr. in Leiman, *Canon and Masorah*); idem, *Text and Language in Bible and Qumran* (Jerusalem and Tel Aviv: Orient, 1960); D. S. Loewinger, "The Aleppo Codex and the Ben Asher Tradition," *Textus* 1 (1960) 59–111 (repr. in Leiman, *Canon and Masorah*); and J. S. Penkower, "Maimonides and the Aleppo Codex," *Textus* 9 (1981) 39–128. Scholars who think the pointing did not come from the hand of ben Asher include J. Teicher, "The Ben Asher Bible Manuscripts," *Journal of Jewish Studies* 2 (1950) 17–25 (repr. in Leiman, *Canon and Masorah*); and A. Dotan, "Was the Aleppo Codex Actually Vocalized by Aharon ben Asher?" *Tarbiẓ* 34 (1965) 136–55.

22. I. Yeivin, *The Aleppo Codex of the Bible: A Study of its Vocalization and Accentuation* (Hebrew University Bible Project Monograph Series 3; Jerusalem: Magnes, 1968); M. Breuer, *Aleppo Codex*. M. Breuer's טעמי המקרא בכ"א ספרים ובספרי אמ"ת (Jerusalem: Ḥorev, 1989) appeared as a second edition of his earlier פיסוק טעמים שבמקרא, revised on the basis of the Aleppo Codex and expanded to cover all the books of the Hebrew Bible.

issued under his editorship,[23] while the *masorah magna* was published by
D. S. Loewinger.[24] Sadly, it was damaged in 1948 and is not whole, as anyone who looks at the published facsimile will discover.[25]

The earliest completely preserved manuscript is Leningrad B 19ᵃ. This
text was completed in 1009 c.e. and served as the basis for the second edition
of the *Biblia Hebraica*,[26] as well as for the *Biblia Hebraica Stuttgartensia*[27]
and an edition by A. Dotan.[28] The Stuttgart edition is that which is now used
by the majority of critical scholars in the United States and Europe. Even
those who are highly critical of the accuracy of the manuscript's consonantal

23. M. Breuer, תורה נביאים כתובים :נביאים (Jerusalem: Kook, 1979); and idem, תורה נביאים
כתובים :כתובים (Jerusalem: Kook, 1982). Breuer's תורה :כתובים נביאים (Jerusalem:
Kook, 1977) is not based (in any fashion) on Aleppo, which is not preserved for most of the
Pentateuch, but on Breuer's eclectic methods of selecting a small number of witnesses
and reconstructing the text found in a majority of them and on "the Masorah." For the non-
pentateuchal parts of the Bible, his text (determined by the same method) was identical with
Aleppo (with respect to questions of plene spelling), except for five words (Breuer, כתובים,
395). His pentateuchal text, he writes, is identical, letter for letter, with the model text used
for writing Torah scrolls by Yemenite scribes. At any rate, the difference between such texts
is statistically quite small. The Leningrad manuscript which Breuer considers inferior (but
which he uses, nonetheless, when Aleppo fails) has, according to his count, 370 words which
differ from the text he reconstructs with respect to plene spelling. This is out of a total of
more than one million letters in the Hebrew Bible, so that there is—seemingly—an error rate
of less than 0.037 percent, and the inaccuracies involved are all purely matters of orthography on which the texts which issued from the hands of Masoretes were not consistent.
24. D. S. Loewinger, *Massorah Magna of the Aleppo Codex* (Jerusalem: Orient and Occident
and the Shrine of the Book, 1977).
25. M. H. Goshen-Gottstein, *The Aleppo Codex Originally with Masoretic Notes and Pointed by
Aaron ben Asher* (part 1: plates; Jerusalem: Magnes, 1976), published the extant part of the
manuscript; and M. Beit-Arié, "A Lost Leaf from the Aleppo Codex Recovered," *Tarbiz* 51
(1982) 171–74 [Hebrew] recognized and published an additional page. W. Wickes, *A Treatise on the Accentuation of the Twenty-One So-called Prose Books of the Old Testament*
(Oxford: Clarendon, 1887), published a photograph of a page which is no longer extant as a
frontispiece, and that page has been reproduced elsewhere (but is omitted from the reprint,
see n. 60 below); M. Benayahu noted that J. Segall, *Travels through Northern Syria* (London: London Society for Promoting Christianity, 1910) 99, published a photograph of two
more pages which are now lost; cf. M. H. Goshen-Gottstein, "A Recovered Part of the
Aleppo Codex," *Textus* 5 (1966) 53–59. R. Zer, "R. Yaᶜaqov Sappir's Meoroth Nathan,"
Leš 50 (1986) 151–213 [Hebrew], has now published an edition of a copy of a letter which
gives collations of some passages in the Aleppo Codex, including parts now lost. A. Sha-
mosh, *Ha-Keter: The Story of the Aleppo Codex* (Jerusalem: Ben Zvi Institute, 1987) [He-
brew] has told the story of this manuscript.
26. R. Kittel et al., eds., *Biblia Hebraica* (11th ed.; Stuttgart: Würtembergische Bibelanstalt
Stuttgart, 1971). Editions later than the second were based on the manuscript.
27. K. Elliger and W. Rudolph et al., eds., *Biblia Hebraica Stuttgartensia* (Stuttgart: Deutsche
Bibelstiftung, 1967–1977).
28. A. Dotan, תורה נביאים וכתובים מדוקים היטב על פי הניקוד הטעמים והמסורה של אהרן
בן משה בן אשר בכתב יד לנינגרד (Tel Aviv: Ady, 1973). The biblical text has been reprinted, sometimes with a brief Hebrew commentary.

text admit to the excellence of its vocalization.[29] It is, fortunately, available in facsimile edition,[30] and parts of its *masorâs* have been printed.[31]

It is essential that one investigating the spelling used by the Tiberian Masoretes base the study on the manuscripts themselves. One of the reasons I have picked Leningrad B 19[a] is that the casual reader would expect it to be precisely represented by the printed editions based on it, but this is not the case. For instance, the manuscript marks certain letters with *rāpeh*, a superscript horizontal line. This can be seen in the first line of the biblical text (Gen 1:1), where *ʾālep*, which does not normally take *dāgeš*, is so marked in the third letter of the first word, as is *tāw* at the end of the word (בראשׁית). Other *ʾālep*s on the line are not so marked, however, despite the fact that in the second word (ברא) *ʾālep* is, surely, not consonantal (see the frontispiece). I return to this graphemic issue presently, but this difference may be taken as an emblem for the need to check the originals when one is working toward a graphemics, since *Biblia Hebraica Stuttgartensia*, the second edition of the *Biblia Hebraica*, and Dotan's edition all omit the *rāpeh* in these cases. All these consider *rāpeh* otiose, but if we are interested in the system which the Tiberian Masoretes used to represent the text, we cannot ignore it.[32] It is

---

29. Breuer, *Aleppo Codex*, xxx. A. Dotan considers this manuscript a fitting base for Masoretic investigations (cf. his edition, referred to in n. 28), despite his conclusion that the codex preserves some uncorrected traces of a stage of Tiberian pointing earlier than the completely fixed form which was normative and (virtually) universal. See his "Deviation in Gemination in the Tiberian Vocalization," in *Estudios masoreticos* (*V Congreso de la IOMS*) *dedicados a Harry M. Orlinsky* (ed. E. Fernández Tejero; Textos y Estudios "Cardinal Cisneros" 33; Madrid: Instituto "Arias Montano" C.S.I.C., 1983) 63–77, with references to his earlier articles expounding the same view.

30. D. S. Loewinger, *Pentateuch, Prophets and Hagiographa: Codex Leningrad B19 A* (facsimile with introduction; Jerusalem: Makor, 1971).

31. G. Weil, בית צפורה: *Massorah Gedolah iuxta codicem Leningradensem B 19 a* (Rome: Pontificium Institutum Biblicum, 1971–); A. Dotan, *Thesaurus of the Tiberian Masora, Sample Volume: The Masora to the Book of Genesis in the Leningrad Codex* (Tel Aviv: Tel Aviv University Press, 1977) arranges the Masorah to Genesis in alphabetical order. A. Dotan, "Studies in the Massorah of the Leningrad Manuscript," in *Studies in the Hebrew Language and the Talmudic Literature, Dedicated to the Memory of Dr. Menaḥem Moreshet* (ed. M. Z. Kad-dari and S. Sharvit; Bar-Ilan Departmental Researches: Department of Hebrew and Semitic Languages 3; Ramat-Gan: Bar-Ilan University Press, 1989) 75–82, reports on his continuing work on the manuscript and particularly the practices of the scribes who copied its *masorah parva*.

32. There is a variety of systems of pointing derived from the Tiberian, which need not detain us here. In addition to the most common—those which are used for nonbiblical texts and employ the Tiberian vowels (with the addition of some other signs)—there have been various attempts to remove certain of the "ambiguities" of Tiberian script in the printing of certain prayer books. I mention only the American *Shilo Prayer Book* (New York: Shilo, 1960; I consulted the sixth edition, 1972), which puts a horizontal line above letters pointed with a *šĕwâ* if it was *mobile* (vocalic) rather than "quiescent" (= /∅/), since this eliminates the

worth noting that, in addition to the biblical text with surrounding *masorôt*, Leningrad B 19[a] contains a variety of Masoretic lists[33] and a number of illuminations in the form of "carpet pages."[34]

Linguists' descriptions of the grammar of Hebrew have thus far been based either on the sixteenth-century Venice printing or some devolution of it on the one hand, or—since the second edition of *Biblia Hebraica*—on a form of the Leningrad manuscript. Clearly, the Aleppo Codex and other early manuscripts (such as Moshe ben-Asher's 895 c.e. copy of the Prophets)[35] are viable alternatives, but the fact that these do not preserve the whole of the Hebrew Bible means that a choice of one of them would force one to base a grammar at least partly on another manuscript. Clearly, Leningrad B 19[a] remains a prime candidate for the principal manuscript on which to ground grammatical studies.

All three of these texts represent the ben-Asher tradition. There were apparently two leading Tiberian Masoretes: Abū Saᶜīd, Aaron ben Moshe ben Asher; and Abū Imrān Moshe ben David ben Naphtali. The differences between their texts are celebrated, and are listed by a number of medieval Jewish scholars.[36] A complete study of Hebrew graphemics (and of Tiberian phonology) would have to include the views of both of these scholars, as well as other Tiberians, including additional members of the prestigious ben-Asher family.

---

major ambiguity for those who pronounce in the Ashkenazic tradition (a convention which is fairly common, though some use an asterisk instead of *rāpeh*); and S. Tal, סדור רינת ישראל (Jerusalem: Moreshet, 1963), which uses *qāmeṣ* with a long vertical to mark *qāmeṣ qāṭān* to simplify reading (see p. 6) for those using Sephardic pronunciation (certain other aids for the reader were also added by Tal, who has also edited a series of holiday prayer books). Accent is also commonly marked in such variations on the Tiberian system.

I must also leave aside the work of Karaite scribes who copied the Bible using Arabic letters instead of Hebrew—but with Tiberian pointing; this has now been edited by G. Khan, *Karaite Bible Manuscripts from the Cairo Genizah* (Cambridge University Library Genizah Series 9; Cambridge: Cambridge University Press, 1990).

33. For publication of these, see Weil, בית צפורה.

34. I am unaware of any thorough art-historical study of Leningrad B 19[a], but it is treated among the comparative materials in L. Avrin, *The Illuminations in the Moshe Ben-Asher Codex of 895 c.e.* (Ph.D. diss., University of Michigan, 1974). She comments on the micrography of the colophons in C. Sirat and L. Avrin, *La lettre hébraïque et sa signification [and] Micrography as Art: Etudes de paléographie hébraïque* (Paris: C.N.R.S. / Jerusalem: Israel Museum, Department of Judaica, 1981) 101/47.

35. D. S. Loewinger, *Codex Cairo of the Bible from the Karaite Synagog[u]e at Abbasiya* (Jerusalem: Makor, 1971).

36. See L. Lipschütz, "Kitāb al-Khilaf, the Book of the Ḥillufim," *Textus* 4 (1964) 1–27; repr. as *Kitāb al-Khilaf: Mishael ben Uzziel's Treatise on the Differences between Ben Asher and Ben Naphtali* (Hebrew University Bible Project 2; Jerusalem: Magnes, 1965).

SOME PRINCIPLES OF GRAPHEMICS

Turning to the study of graphemics, I note three principles on which such investigations must be based. These are the autonomy of graphemic systems, the primacy of speech, and the force of tradition.[37]

By "autonomy of graphemic systems" I mean that writing systems must be studied as sign systems in their own right. It is true that they derive from an attempt to represent speech in permanent media, but once they have been created, they have a structure of their own. It is this independent system that constitutes the writing. Graphemics should be viewed, eventually, in the light of phonology, but first it must be described. If we want to forge beyond the current oral traditions to the language recorded by the Tiberian Masoretes, we must first look at their writing system alone.

"Primacy of speech" refers to the fact that written or printed symbols are "symbols of symbols." Writing imitates speech, at least originally, rather than vice versa. Speech is a result of human convention, and writing is a conventional, that is, learned, accidental, way to represent it.

By "force of tradition" I mean the culture lag between things as they are at a given time and as they are represented. Writers commonly reproduce the forms taught, rather than considering anew the spelling of each word while writing.

H. J. Polotsky succinctly stated the basic approach to understanding writing systems as autonomous entities when he wrote of Coptic: "Was wir vor uns haben, ist eine Orthographie, in der ein anonymer Sprachgelehrter . . . seine phonologische Analyse . . . niedergelegt hat. Wir können nicht mehr tun als seine Analyse zu verstehen suchen. Sollte er seine Sache nicht gut gemacht haben, so können wir nicht weit über ihn hinaus."[38] One must not, however, take the term *Analyse* in his formulation too seriously.[39] There is,

---

37. For the following, see my treatment of cuneiform script in *The Sumerian Loanwords in Old-Babylonian Akkadian* (Harvard Semitic Studies 22; Missoula: Scholars Press, 1977) 40–42.

38. H. J. Polotsky, Review of Till, *Koptische Grammatik*, *Orientalische Literaturzeitung* 52 (1957) 219–34, at 221; repr. in idem, *Collected Papers* (Jerusalem: Magnes, 1971) 227.

39. S. Morag, *The Vocalization Systems of Arabic, Hebrew, and Aramaic* (Janua Linguarum Series Minor 13; The Hague: Mouton, 1962) 61 paraphrases Polotsky's statement as "An analysis of a vocalization system—like that of an orthographical system—is, in fact, simply an attempt at a reconstruction of the phonemic analysis which was carried out by the inventors of the system," and assures us that this principle "has general validity" (n. 1). There is, however, neither any argumentation or evidence to show that the system was "phonemic" (see below). M. Aronoff, "Orthography and Linguistic Theory: The Syntactic Basis of Masoretic Hebrew Punctuation," *Lg.* 61 (1985) 28–72, anachronistically (or vacuously) takes the "accents" as "a purely theoretical notation . . . based on a theory of syntactic analysis" (p. 70). A reading of the Masoretes' own treatises would have kept him from such a conclusion.

no doubt, a taxonomy inherent in any group of symbols viewed as a set; but that is not the same as the examination which is implied by the term *analysis*.

In the case of the Tiberian system of representing Hebrew, as in a number of other writing systems, there is a peculiar relationship between speech and writing.[40] These systems were not created by "native speakers," but rather by scholars who were trying to record and preserve the proper pronunciation of sacred texts which had been handed down to them. In the case of Tiberian Hebrew, the inventors of those parts of the writing system other than the "letters" were not native speakers of Hebrew, but rather of Arabic, and perhaps of Aramaic, for "Biblical" Hebrew had not been spoken for a millennium, and "Mishnaic" Hebrew for at least half a millennium. More importantly, all the Masoretes felt at liberty to do was to add certain marks to one form of the text which they received and—what was, no doubt, more important to them—to devise methods of seeing to it that the received text itself was not altered in any fashion.

One of the ways that they did this was with the well-known means of *Qere* and *Kethiv*. The Masoretes kept the written text as they inherited it but indicated that another form was to be substituted when reading. The device was commonly used to correct seeming (or actual) imprecisions in the spelling recorded by the letters, but it was also used to change or add whole words. When used with words, the word written in the text was replaced, commonly, with a semantically related term—a device which may be loosely compared with the use of semantically determined graphemes in cuneiform (particularly so-called Diri words)[41] or with our reading of *e.g.* as "for example" or "for instance." This peculiarity of Tiberian spelling was used for linguistic forms which were not used, whether the received word had become taboo (such as some terms no longer considered polite and the tetragrammaton) or represented an archaic form which had gone out of use (as in the case of the second-person feminine singular, whether independent pronoun or suffixed verb, where the *Kethiv* sometimes reflects the original יִ, but the *Qere* is always ן).

GRAPHEMES AND PHONEMES

The basic unit used in writing Tiberian Hebrew, the grapheme, was, of course, smaller than the word. I have defined *grapheme* as "a contrastive

---

40. O'Connor (above, pp. 231–524) considers writing systems to be equivalent to "native-speaker analyses." I must demur. One cannot ignore the question of where such a definition puts Tiberian Hebrew, or Sanskrit *devanāgarī*, etc. I do not see how one can consider these to be either an analysis or the product of a "native" speaker.
41. Cf. Lieberman, *Sumerian Loanwords*, 49–56, on word graphemes.

(significant) unit used in any writing system. Like phonemes, graphemes are defined by contrast and constitute a class of marks."[42] The comparison with phonemes is imprecise for a variety of reasons. Segmental phonemes have an internal structure based on their substance—the sounds with which they are realized—but graphemes need not have any such structure. Segmental phonemes can be analyzed into "distinctive features," but this is not necessarily true of graphemes. Both types of units are symbols, that is, both are defined by human convention. Both speech and writing are primarily symbolic, but they are not purely symbolic. That is, aspects of them have a "real," not an imputed relationship to the universe. For instance, in the case of speech, the plurals of nouns are, by and large, longer in duration than their singular forms; and, commonly, a word which is longer in speech is represented by a larger form or more forms in writing. At the least, these two aspects of the two semiotic systems are thus indexical rather than symbolic, in the terms of C. S. Peirce.[43]

Despite their differences, however, many of the terms in which the phoneme has been described can be used to elucidate features of graphemes. I illustrate a few of these concepts with features of the writing system used by the Tiberian Masoretes.

Phonemes are defined by contrast. If two phone types are in complementary distribution, one sort always occurring at the beginning and middle of words and another at the end, as in the case of aspirated [p^h] versus unaspirated [p] in English, they can be grouped together into a single phoneme, and each of the two called an *allophone*. The final and nonfinal letters in Tiberian square script are thus correctly described as *allographs*, since their usage is completely predictable from the context: the use of a final letter at the end of a word gives the reader no information that was not available from the following blank space (or *maqqēp* or *sōp pāsûq*). (The spellings in Isa 9:6 and Neh 2:13 result from *Qere* vs. *Kethiv*).

It is usually said that *rāpeh* is used in Tiberian script to indicate the absence of *dāgēš* (for those letters which can bear *dāgēš*). First, it must be noted that in Leningrad B 19ª, as in the Aleppo Codex, it would be more precise to say that it indicates the absence of a dot in the middle of a letter, since it is used over *hē^ɔ* in word-final position to show that there is no *mappîq*. If it were true that one always found either a dot or *rāpeh* in the appropriate places, then the two marks could be considered to be a single grapheme with two forms and it would be legitimate to omit occurrence of *rāpeh* when we reproduce the Tiberian text. A belief that this was the case led, no doubt, to

42. Ibid., 42 n. 112.
43. A. W. Burks, ed., *The Collected Papers of Charles Sanders Peirce* (Cambridge: Harvard University Press, 1957) 8:228–29.

the complete omission of *rāpeh* by those who have printed a form of Leningrad B 19ᵃ,[44] who thus conform to the almost universal practice of printers since the sixteenth century. Masoretic scholars are in apparent agreement that *rāpeh* is used "inconsistently." Such a nonsystematic usage of a graph means that the occurrences must be recorded, so that one can investigate further. If the two were really allographs, the omission might be defensible.

It must be admitted that the usage of *rāpeh* is puzzling. If one looks at contexts which seem to be linguistically identical, its motivation is unclear. For instance, in the first chapter of Genesis, the divine creating for each day (after the first) starts out with the same phrase: ויאמר אלהים 'God said/commanded'. The first word is always identically pointed and always has the same cantillation mark, *mûnāḥ*, but *ʾālep* bears *rāpeh* only for days three and six. *Dāgēš* and *rāpeh* are, then, not allographs, and the omission of *rāpeh* from a printing which attempts to represent the Leningrad manuscript is imprecise (see the frontispiece).

The features that distinguish phonemes one from another, such as the voicing which separates /b/ from /p/, can be irrelevant in certain contexts; but if there are *minimal pairs* of words which have only this contrast, then the loss of contrast in certain positions is called *neutralization*. In word-final position in a number of languages, such as German, Russian, Turkish, voicing does not distinguish words. There is a comparable neutralization in the usage of some graphemes in Hebrew. For instance, in post-vocalic position, *hēʾ* may not be distinguished from *ʾālep*, as in the words קרא 'read' versus קרה 'happen'. By and large the script—if not the language during all periods—kept these two separate, but in at least some instances, a form with *ʾālep* is used for the other verb.

The Masoretes' use of *ḥôlem*, either over *wāw* found in the received text or over the left of a letter if there was no *wāw*, shows their need to render neutral a distinction between the two spellings, since there was no phonemic difference between them. Here, they were able to retain the ideal of representing a single phoneme with a single grapheme for the vowel. With /u/, however, this could not be done, since the distinction between a dot to the left of the midpoint of letter (*šûreq*) and to the left of the top of a letter (*ḥôlem*) was too small. We find, then, two graphemes (*šûreq* when *wāw* was present, *qibbûṣ* otherwise) representing a single phoneme—as a result of the "force of tradition" which did not allow the addition of *wāw*.

On the other hand, there are a number of instances in which a single mark was used with many meanings. Some of these depended on the height of the mark with respect to the letters, as in the case of the single dot, which

---

44. See Kittel, *Biblia Hebraica*, xxvii; Elliger and Rudolph, *BHS*, xii ("almost consistently omitted as before"); likewise omitted in Dotan's printing of the text.

represented *ḥôlem* when it was over the left of a letter, and *dāgēš* when it was in its middle, but *ḥîreq* when it was below a letter. Even in the same relative physical position, in the middle of a letter, a single dot could stand for *mappîq* when it was within final *hē*ᵓ. Since this letter could not be doubled, and the dot would not confuse anyone, it merely indicated the consonantal nature of *hē*ᵓ.

The interpretation of even a dot in the middle of a letter is, in Tiberian Hebrew, dependent on context, that is, on position within a word. If it is in *wāw*, it can stand for either *dāgēš forte*, doubling of the consonant, or it can represent the vowel *qibbûṣ*. At the beginning or end of a word there can be no doubling, so it must always represent the vowel. To represent a double consonant in the middle of a word, it must be accompanied by a vowel sign or immediately followed by a *mater lectionis* that bears the vowel for it.

There are also characteristics of Tiberian graphemes which contrast with phonemes as usually conceived. For instance, some, such as *ḥāṭēp* vowels, are composed of two graphemes.

In the case of phonemes, we distinguish between segmental phonemes, those which are most frequently treated, and so-called suprasegmental phonemes, such as stress, pitch, and tone. Likewise, in graphemics, we must distinguish between different types of graphemes. In Tiberian Hebrew, there are four types: letters, neumes, diacritics, and vowels. I presently take a brief look at each of these. (My listing of the accentual marks—neumes—before the other parts of the pointing is quite intentional; I show that they are both linguistically and historically anterior to the consonantal diacritics and the vowels.)

Just as suprasegmental phonemes occur simultaneously with segmental phonemes, more than one of the types of Tiberian graphemes may occupy a single slot or writing segment. In fact, it is not at all unusual for a segment to have all four in a single horizontal slot, showing that they record the form of a single syllable.

Each (linguistic) syllable begins with a consonant and a vowel. Except in final position, the consonant written is to be pronounced before the vowel, but in final position, when *hē*ᵓ, *ḥêt*, or *ᶜayin* is pointed with *pataḥ*, the vowel precedes. (This is another instance of the context-dependent nature of the pointing.) The neumes record the suprasegmental features of the word (and the syllable) where they are written, and the diacritic marks distinguish consonants. Words are marked by beginning with a horizontal space; each word unit is accompanied by a single neume, which marks the accented syllable. It must be noted, however, that the neume which goes with a word may consist of two separated marks, and that two linguistic units can be joined by *maqqēp*, in which case they count as but a single word (and are accompanied by only one neume). *Maqqēp* thus marks enclisis. The opposite phenomenon, separation of two words, is marked with a vertical line, known as *pāsēq* ('). This shows a pause between two words which was shorter than that which would be required by a disjunctive accent.

A word at the end of a verse bears the neume *sillûq* (ֽ); it is identical in form to *pāsēq*, but below the letters. Such a word is usually—but not always—followed by two dots which look like a raised shewa, and are commonly called *sôp pāsûq*. (The printings of Leningrad B 19ᵃ have the two dots in places where the manuscript omits them.) Within a verse, a major phrase division is marked with *ʾatnāḥ*. A blank space three letters wide (or an empty line if space does not suffice) regularly marks off the groupings of verses into larger units of discourse ("paragraphs"). This feature is known as a *pĕtûḥâ* when the new line begins at the right, and commonly marked פ in printed texts; when the space is in the middle of a line or to the right of the first word in the next line, it is known as *sĕtûmâ* and abbreviated ס in printings. (Dotan's edition uses the system of the manuscript for both of these.) Since the ends of lines do not always come out even, various marks are added to fill in such spaces.

THE FOUR TYPES OF GRAPHEMES

We call the first type of grapheme *letters*. These constitute all the consonants and semivowels, including the *matres lectionis*. As the principle object of preservation by the Masoretes, they are the central core of the transmitted text and they form the skeleton of the word—except when that skeleton is replaced by a *Qere*. The Tiberian system of pointing was meant to make it clear how that skeleton was to be fleshed out with a trope and vowels.

It may be of interest to note that for many biblical manuscripts the duties of writing the various parts of the text were undertaken by more than one scribe: one wrote the text (כתב), a second person pointed it (נקד) and added the Masorah, but according to the colophons[45] of the Leningrad manuscript,[46]

---

45. The first page was printed by E. M. Pinner, "Nachtrag," in his *Prospectus der Odessaer Gesellschaft für Geschichte und Alterthumer gehörenden ältesten hebräischen und rabbinischen Manuscripte: Ein Beitrag zur biblischen Exegese* (Odessa: Odessaer Gesellschaft, 1845) 81–92 (while the manuscript was in Odessa), and the colophons added by A. Harkavy and H. L. Strack, *Catalog der hebräischen Bibelhandschriften der Kaiserlichen Öffentlichen Bibliothek in St. Petersburg*, parts 1, 2 (Catalog der Hebräischen und Samaritanischen Handschriften der Kaiserlichen Öffentlichen Bibliothek in St. Petersburg 1; St. Petersburg: Ricker / Leipzig: Hinrichs, 1875) 263–74; they also translated the first page.

46. Harkavy and Strack, *Catalog der hebräischen Bibelhandschriften* 269, colophons 2 and 3, which are reproduced in the facsimile by Loewinger, *Codex Leningrad*, 3:294 (in Sirat and Avrin, *La lettre hébraïque* pl. 10) and 326. The latter colophon (formulated in the third person) refers to the text relying on Aaron ben Asher.

all three of these were completed by Samuel ben Jacob.[47]

The letters of the text included forms which were quite inconsistently spelled, particularly with respect to the inclusion and omission of the subcategory of letters known as vowel letters or *matres lectionis* (א, ה, ו, י). These, from a Tiberian perspective, before pointing, could represent either a consonant or a vowel without a consonant. The development of the use of *matres* in Hebrew is a topic with a large literature which cannot be explored here.[48] Viewing the Tiberian Bible as a synchronic whole (as the Masoretes did), one can only say that, in a number of words, spellings with and without *matres* were in free variation. The contention that the inconsistencies resulted from historical development is irrelevant to Tiberian graphemics, though the usual explanation of them seems correct. Thus, the presence or absence of *ʾālep* in some forms (such as שלתך in 1 Sam 1:17 vs. שאלתך elsewhere, 'your [fem.] request'), viewed synchronically, must be described simply as free variation.

The letters which were in the text inherited by the Masoretes had more than purely phonemic information: in some instances, morphemic information was conveyed in the letter chosen, so that the system cannot be judged to be "purely" phonological. For instance, though word-final *ʾālep* and word-final *hēʾ* (without *mappîq*) were alike unpronounced, only the latter was regularly used when the preceding syllable was the feminine stem afformative or the 3d person fem. sing. of the suffixed verb.

The second type of grapheme in the Tiberian system was the (musical) *neumes*, which were written to indicate the cantillation of the text. This part of the system is more central, linguistically, than the voweling, as we shall see. M. L. Margolis put the matter succinctly: "Without some sort of knowledge of the Hebrew system of accentuation, an understanding of Hebrew

---

47. According to the colophon of the Aleppo manuscript (now lost), the letters were written by Solomon ben Buyāᶜa and the pointing added by Aaron ben Asher himself. It is agreed, however, even by advocates of this manuscript, that the colophon was added some time after it was written, by a different scribe. On such questions, see B. Narkiss, "The Relationship between the Author, Scribe, Massorator and Illuminator in Medieval Manuscripts," in *La paléographie hébraïque médiévale* (ed. J. Glénisson; Colloques Internationaux du C.N.R.S. 347; Paris: C.N.R.S., 1974) 79–84, with plates following.

48. See W. Weinberg, *The History of Hebrew Plene Spelling* (Cincinnati: Hebrew Union College, 1985; repr. from *HUCA* 46–50 [1975–1980]), which covers the whole history of Hebrew. F. I. Andersen and A. D. Forbes, *Spelling in the Hebrew Bible* (Biblica et Orientalia 41; Rome: Pontifical Biblical Institute, 1986), describe the use of *matres lectionis* in the Bible and assess the value of the orthography for questions of dating and transmission on a "statistical" basis; J. Barr, *The Variable Spellings of the Hebrew Bible* (Schweich Lectures 1986; Oxford: Oxford University Press, 1989), has introduced a number of new concepts into the study of *matres*. Unfortunately, the perspectives of these last two volumes have not been informed by any comparison with spelling variation in the writing of other languages.

phonology and morphology becomes nugatory."[49]

Let us recall first that the consequences of the fact that the voweling of Biblical Hebrew reflects the pronunciation of a sung or cantillated text have not received proper attention. Anyone familiar with the singing of English[50] or French[51] knows full well that there are quite important differences between the pronunciation of such languages when they are sung as compared with their spoken forms.[52] It is true that for other languages, such as Italian, the differences between speech and singing are smaller; but unfortunately for our ability to use the Tiberian pointing as an accurate guide for the pronunciation of spoken Biblical Hebrew, Hebrew seems to have been closer to the English or French model than the Italian one. This increases the importance of the cantillation system for our understanding of the vocalic system and its pointing,[53] but it puts limitations on the value of the pointing as a guide to the pronunciation of spoken Hebrew.

A moment's reflection by those who are familiar with Biblical Hebrew as usually taught will make evident the centrality of the sentence-intonation patterns of Hebrew as recorded in the neumes. If we are confronted with a word, say one spelled פני, there is a variety of ways to vocalize it. We can take it as a verb, a form of פנה 'turn', and read *pĕnî* 'face [fem. sing. imv.]' or *pannî* 'spread open [fem. sing. imv.]'. We could also understand it as being a form of the noun *pānîm* 'front [pl. tantum]'. If we take it thus, there are two different possible relations it could have to the surrounding context: it could either be joined to what follows as a construct, in which case it would have to be vocalized as *pĕnê*, and translated as 'front of', or it could be separated from what follows and independent, in which case it would be vocalized as *pānay* and it would mean 'my front'. If it is not dependent on what follows, its use could coincide with the end of a phrase or sentence, in which case it would be in pausal form, *pānāy*, but the translation would be the same.

With an unpointed spelling, the choice between these four possibilities can be made only after one deciphers the surrounding context. When we know what the sentence-intonation pattern was, however, we can easily

---

49. M. Margolis, "The Place of the Word Accent in Hebrew," *JBL* 30 (1911) 29–43, at 30; on the importance of accent in the historical development of Hebrew, see A. Goetze, "Accent and Vocalism in Hebrew," *JAOS* 59 (1939) 431–59.

50. See M. Marshall, *The Singer's Manual of English Diction* (New York: G. Schirmer, 1946); and D. Uris, *To Sing in English: A Guide to Improved Diction* (London: Boosey & Hawkes, 1971).

51. See P. Bernac, *The Interpretation of French Song* (New York: Praeger, 1970), particularly p. 18 on diphthongs.

52. W. Vennard has discussed the differences in *Singing: The Mechanism and the Technic* (5th ed.; New York: Fischer, 1967) 135–36 § 481, 160–61 § 576, 184–85 § 682, etc.

53. The distinction between spoken and sung Hebrew is critical for a proper evaluation of the spellings of Hebrew not in its usual script as witnesses to the history of its vocalization.

determine which of the vocalizations is correct. Without prior consideration, if we do not even know where sentences ended, there is little chance of getting a word right. In short, one must understand a passage before it can be vocalized. Such an understanding is recorded in the neumes. The Tiberian system of pointing was aimed at making it possible for a reader to pronounce a text correctly without any prior understanding, and the sentence-intonation rules came first.

Just as the rules of syntactic interpretation precede the choice of vocalization in a synchronic interpretation of an unpointed Hebrew text, the setting of tropes for the text preceded the historical fixing of its vocalization.[54] The text was cantillated long before the Tiberian system of recording the vowels was perfected.[55] We all know that setting a text to music will facilitate its memorization, and clearly the cantillation of the biblical text helped in the retention of its vocalization before the Masoretic inventions of written vocalic systems. It is well known that the Tiberian Masoretes distinguished two different systems of tropes: one for Psalms, Proverbs, and Job with twenty neumes; and another with twenty-six neumes for the rest of the biblical text.

54. E. J. Revell, "The Oldest Evidence for the Hebrew Accent System," *Bulletin of the John Rylands Library* 54 (1971–1972) 214–22, at 214–15, refers to the marking of divisions of phrase in Qumran manuscripts. E. Tov, *The Greek Minor Prophets Scroll from Naḥal Ḥever* (Discoveries in the Judaean Desert 8; Oxford: Clarendon, 1990) 9–12, has elaborated the comparisons between the indications of divisions in the manuscript he edits and those in the Leningrad manuscript, whether they were larger or smaller than a verse. A. Dotan, "The Relative Chronology of Hebrew Vocalization and Accentuation," *Proceedings of the American Academy of Jewish Research* 48 (1981) 87–99, and "The Relative Chronology of the Accentuation System," *Language Studies* 2–3 (1987) 355–65 [Hebrew], has argued that the setting of tropes before the vowels was true for the Tiberian system, where one can not be certain; and he has compared the histories of the Babylonian and Palestinian systems, where it is clear that this was the case. Dotan assumes that the Talmudic and Midrashic citations refer to written neumes, but there is no proof, and *b. Ber.* 62a contradicts this conclusion.

55. See *b. Meg.* 32a, cited above as an epigraph. Some philological comments are in order. The printed editions add כל before הקורא; the Munich manuscript replaces זמ(י)רה with אמירה, and Vatican Hebr. 134 writes the form with a *mater lectionis*, as indicated. See H. L. Strack, *Talmud Babylonicum Codicis Hebraici Monacensis 95* (Leiden: Sijthoff, 1912; repr. as *Babylonian Talmud: Codex Munich (95)* [Jerusalem: Sefer, 1971]) 243 (cited from the reprint); A. F. Sherry, *Manuscripts of the Babylonian Talmud from the Collection of the Vatican Library* (Jerusalem: Makor, 1972) 2:231. The scriptural citation is briefer in printed editions. The Munich manuscript (and printed editions) add וגו(מר); the Parma manuscript is as cited; see R. Rabbinovicz, *Variae Lectiones in Mischnam et in Talmud Babylonicum* (Munich: Huber, 1877), 8:159 *ad loc.*; Vatican Hebr. 134 writes out the whole of the biblical verse, but imprecisely. E. L. Segal has presented his reasons for thinking the Columbia manuscript of Megillah superior to others in "The Textual Tradition of Ms. Columbia University to TB Megillah," *Tarbiẓ* 63 (1983) 41–69. I have not had access to the manuscript itself, but J. J. Price, *The Yemenite Manuscript of Megilla* (Toronto: Rosenberg, 1916; repr. Jerusalem: Makor, 1970), records only that it omits the כל, like all the other manuscripts to which I have had access.

In doing this, they surely recorded the transmitted musical patterns rather than inventing them, but how had those musical patterns been preserved up until the time of the Masoretes?

Let us consider the problem of reading the Pentateuch as it confronted Jews before the invention of systems of pointing. An individual was called to read from the Pentateuch before a congregation. (The general European practice of having a special reader is clearly late.) He was unprepared and had he wanted to ready himself, he would not have been able to look up the correct vocalization in a convenient printed text: printing had not yet been invented and even the scarce manuscripts gave minimal help with the vowels. The only way he could know how to pronounce was by having already listened to a master and learned the text from him. His memory was imperfect, and he had to "read" accurately: the correct grouping of words into phrases and sentences was clearly critical to a proper interpretation of the text, and as he went along he did not want to stumble or mislead his hearers. Interposed in his reading of the original was the verse-by-verse Aramaic (or, earlier, Greek) interpretation which clarified the text for those whose Hebrew was imperfect.

Clearly, the man reading had to be given some sort of help by an aide who oversaw the reading of the Torah, but the guide was not permitted to lead the reader by whispering to him. He helped the reader by showing him with a series of hand signals what the correct grouping of the words in the text was, that is, what the tropes for each word were. The technical term for such signals is *cheironomy* (also spelled chironomy).[56] Jewish cheironomy and its history are not well known (at least among biblical scholars), but a recognition of it is crucial for evaluation of the antiquity of the system of neumes, so I must briefly review it.

There are two types of evidence for the signaling of tropes with the hand. First, there are reports of its use by various Jewish communities, starting at the latest in the eleventh century.[57] To these general reports of cheironomy

---

56. See E. Gerson-Kiwi, "Cheironomy," in *The New Grove Dictionary of Music and Musicians* (ed. S. Sadie; London: Macmillan, 1980) 4:191–96.

57. Saadiyah Gaon (882–942) apparently refers to the practice in his Prayer Book; see I. Davidson, S. Assaf, and B. I. Joel, eds., *Siddur R. Saadja Gaon* (2d ed.; Jerusalem: Mass, 1963) 360, lines 12–13, a reference I owe to S. Cohen. The earliest absolutely unequivocal description is found in the commentary of Rashi (1040–1105) on *b. Ber.* 62a (in the Bomberg 1520 edition, repr. Makor, the passage is on 64a), who reports on his observation of Palestinian practice (whether this is the intent of the Talmudic text being commented upon cannot be determined with total certainty). R. Pethahyah saw hand signals as a part of instruction during his time (1180) in Iraq, see *Die Rundreise des R. Petachjah aus Regensburg* (ed. L. Grünhut; Frankfurt and Jerusalem: Kauffman, 1904–5; repr. Jerusalem, 1967) 24. In the description of his travels, Jacob Saphir (1822–1885) adds a report on his observations in Yemen, refers to Rashi, and records the use of the hands in teaching the tropes, in his אבן

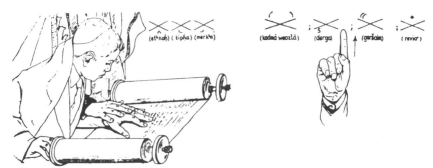

Figure 1. Roman Hand Signals for Cantillation (reprinted from Jacques Porte [ed.], *Encyclopédie des Musiques Sacrées* [Paris: Labergerie, 1968] 1:472–73).

may be added the medieval books of instruction in cantillation and grammars which include some specifics of the technique,[58] a technique which still has some currency. In the case of contemporary usage one can easily determine the specifics of the hand signals, but I know of descriptions of the particulars and illustrations for only a few Jewish communities (see fig. 1).[59] The second

ספיר (Lyck: M'kize Nirdamim, 1866–1874; repr. Jerusalem, 1967) 1:56b. Simeon Duran (1361–1444) cites Rashi in his מגן אבות in a passage which has been included in *Hebrew Writings Concerning Music in Manuscripts and Printed Books from Geonic Times up to 1800* (ed. I. Adler; Répertoire international des sources musicales B 9²; Munich: Henle, 1975) 137 250 B [60]. B. Chiesa, *The Emergence of Hebrew Biblical Pointing: The Indirect Sources* (Judentum und Umwelt, 1; Frankfurt: Lang, 1979) 37, has translated relevant texts, depending on the listing of them in Dotan, "Masorah."

58. Note particularly that ben Asher's work on the tropes refers to some hand signals (Dotan, *Diqduqé Haṭṭě ᶜamim*, 106–7; note the comments in vol. 2). The eleventh-century manual published by J. Dérenbourg, "Manuel du lecteur d'un auteur inconnu," *Journal Asiatique* ser. 6, vol. 16 (1870) 390–550, at 416; repr. as a separate volume (Paris: Imprimerie Nationale, 1871), where the passage is on p. 108, refers to the practice and gives the signals; see A. Neubauer, *Petite grammaire hébraïque provenant de Yemen* (Leipzig: Harrassowitz, 1891), esp. 35–37. On this literature, see Eldar, "Biblical Orthöepy," with references, as well as his various articles in *Lešonénu*, particularly his new edition of "The Reader's Guide," the introduction to which has now appeared as "Mukhtaṣar Hidāyat al-Qāri," in *Leš* 50 (1986) 214–31; 51 (1987) 3–41.

59. Cf. I. Adler, "Histoire de la musique réligieuse juive," in *Encyclopédie des musiques sacrées* (ed. J. Porte; Paris: Labergerie, 1968) 1:469–92, esp. 472–73; S. Levin, "The Traditional Chironomy of the Hebrew Scriptures," *JBL* 87 (1968) 59–70; and particularly A. Laufer, "Hand- and Head-Movements during the Reading of the Pentateuch," in *Proceedings of the Fifth World Congress of Jewish Studies, 1969* (ed. A. Shinan; Jerusalem: World Union of Jewish Studies, 1973) 93–101, with 6 plates; and Gerson-Kiwi, "Cheironomy." A. Herzog, "The Emergence of an Old Tradition—Reading the Torah with the Aid of Hand Movements," in *Proceedings of the Ninth World Congress of Jewish Studies* (Jerusalem:

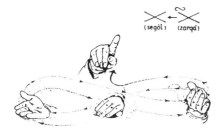

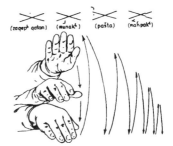

type of evidence is the names of the tropes themselves. As Wickes and others have seen,[60] the names used for at least some of the neumes point towards the hand signals; and this makes their historical origin clear.[61] The hand signals for tropes, then, preceded the written neumes, and their use continued past the introduction of the Tiberian system, down to the present day.

The most important distinction between accentual units which the reader had to make was between those words that were joined to what follows and those that were separated from subsequent words. This is the distinction

---

World Union of Jewish Studies, 1986) D/2:97–104 [Hebrew], writes of recently innovated prompting of the Torah reader and refers to the available films of the traditional usages (p. 104 n. 7). There has obviously been development in the hand signals used, so that the reconstruction of their original forms would be a complex undertaking which would have to take account of the written sources and the changes in the forms of the various neumes and tropes, as well as current practice.

60. See W. Wickes, *Two Treatises on the Accentuation of the Old Testament* (prolegomenon by A. Dotan; New York: Ktav, 1970) 2:18 § 5–6; A. Z. Idelsohn, *Jewish Music in Its Historical Development* (New York: Holt, Rinehart & Winston, 1929; New York: Schocken, 1967) 67–68.

61. It seems to me that a number of the names of neumes taken by Wickes as referring to a trope can just as well be taken as referring to the music or its hand signal, but, given the congruence between the (musical, cheironomic, and written) shapes of a trope, there need be no differences between them, and no *etymological* way of proving which came first. For instance, רביעי 'staying' (also called מיושב 'settled' and תקף 'firm') meant that the note was sustained, which was doubtless indicated with an unmoving hand, and is written in the manuscripts as a simple dot. This point had the same form as the period (known in England as the "full stop") which comes at the end of our sentences. Under the influence of homophony with the Aramaic word for 'four', it developed into a four-sided mark and a four-toned trope.

between "conjunctive" and "disjunctive" tropes known to students of the Masorah.[62]

Before I turn from the neumes used in the Tiberian system, I should mention that the musical forms which they have gained in European communities are much more elaborate than those which one finds in Sephardic and Yemenite groups,[63] and that the simpler forms are closer to their original realizations and to the suprasegmental patterns of speech.[64]

Various rabbinic texts are also found in manuscript forms which include neumes,[65] and these texts are traditionally recited with melodies, but their printed versions do not include neumes, so that the tropes used have been preserved by oral tradition alone. The (contemporary) study of such texts is also accompanied by gesticulation (even in Jewish communities which do not use hand signals when reading the Pentateuch), but I know of no attempt to record such accompaniments to recitation.

The third type of grapheme used by the Tiberian Masoretes is the consonantal diacritics. Except for *rāpeh*, which as I have mentioned is supposedly (but not actually) in complementary distribution with *dāgēš*, all the consonantal diacritics consist of a single dot. Placed in the middle of a letter the dot is *dāgēš* or *mappîq* with *hē*ʾ, and above ש it distinguishes *śîn* and *šîn*.

The fourth variety of graphemes consists of the vowels. The symbols used for vowels had to be designed to conform to the letters from the inherited text. This meant, as we have noted, that two different means of writing /u/ had to be employed: one, *šûreq*, when there was *wāw* in the text; and an-

---

62. For the Yemenite terminology see S. Morag, *The Hebrew Language Tradition of the Yemenite Jews* (Academy of the Hebrew Language Studies 4; Jerusalem: Academy of the Hebrew Language, 1963) 214.

63. Cf. A. Z. Idelsohn, *Hebräisch-Orientalischer Melodienschatz* (Leipzig: Breitkopf & Härtel, 1914; Berlin: Harz, 1922–1929; Leipzig: Hofmeister, 1932; repr. as *Thesaurus of Hebrew-Oriental Melodies* [New York: Ktav, 1973]) passim; and idem, *Jewish Music*, 35–71.

64. G. Weil, P. Rivière, and M. Serfaty, *Concordance de la cantilation du Pentateuque et des cinq Megillot* (Documentation de la Bible 1; Paris: C.N.R.S., 1978); and idem, *Concordance de la cantilation des prèmieres prophètes, Josue Juges, Samuel et Rois* (Documentation de la Bible 2; Paris: C.N.R.S., 1982), present surveys of the distributions of the neumes.

There is in progress a major musicological study of the neumes by D. Weil and his collaborators. Some of the preliminary results of the study have been published: D. Cohen and D. Weil, "The Original Realization of the Tiberian Masoretic Accents—A Deductive Approach," *Leš* 53 (1988–1989) 7–31 [Hebrew]; D. Weil, "Tentative Reconstruction of Masoretic Cantillation," in *Proceedings of the Tenth World Congress of Jewish Studies,* division D, vol. 2, *Art, Folklore and Music* (ed. D. Assaf; Jerusalem: World Union of Jewish Studies, 1990) 157–64; D. Cohen, A. Herzog, U. Sharvit, and D. Weil, "Characterization of the System of Teʿamim in Practice in Light of Theoretical Findings about the Original Performance," *ibid.*, 149–56, with further references.

65. See I. Yeivin, "The Cantillation of the Oral Law," *Leš* 24 (1960) 47–69, 167–78, 207–31; D. Zlotnick, "Memory and the Integrity of the Oral Tradition," *JANESCU* 16–17 (1984–1985) 229–41, esp. 231–33.

other, *qibbûṣ*, when there was none. In instances where the vowel required was at odds with a vowel letter (*mater lectionis*) in the inherited text, the vowel overrides the letter.[66]

In addition to these four well-known types of graphemes and the circles above words referring to the marginal Masoretic comments, various marks in the text seem to be of a text-critical nature. These symbols include the dots on letters, upside-down *nûn*, and the large and small letters, as well as suspended letters.[67] They seem not to refer to the underlying language but to the text itself, or to make some nonlinguistic comment on the text, and need not detain us here.

The Tiberian system of writing consists, then, of four hierarchically arranged types of graphemes: the letters, which came from the tradition; the neumes, which reflected sentence intonation patterns and the syntactic interpretation of the text; consonantal diacritics, which depend in part on how the words were grouped (for spirantization and *dāgeš lene*); and vowels, some of which were dependent on the way the sentence was construed.

VOCALIC OVERDETERMINATION

The vowels were dependent on the tropes; and the system is *not* phonemic, but differentiates between phone types which depended on the phonetic context. The Tiberian system may be described as providing considerably more information than was necessary to read the text correctly. This overdetermination of vowels is evident, for instance, in the distinction between *ḥāṭēp* vowels. The Masoretes tried to record what they heard, and they could hear distinctions which were not linguistically significant. If one takes the opposite view and assumes a perfect congruence between the phonological system and the graphemic system, one will quickly find contradictions.

This overdetermination can be contrasted with the system usually employed to write Russian. With Russian, one cannot know how to pronounce a written word without knowing where the accent lies, but accent is not normally marked in writing. For instance, without knowing the pronunciation beforehand, one will not know whether the last vowel of the name Jakobson, which is spelled with ⟨o⟩, is pronounced as /o/, /yəkabsón/, or as schwa, /yákəbsən/. Russian marks neither the accent nor the potentially reduced nature of the vowel.

---

66. G. M. Schramm, *The Graphemes of Tiberian Hebrew* (University of California Publications Near Eastern Studies 2; Berkeley and Los Angeles: University of California, 1964) provides a useful survey of the distributions of letters and vowels which occur in the biblical text, but he leaves the neumes aside.

67. See Dotan, "Masorah," 1407–10; and Yeivin, *Introduction to the Tiberian Masorah*, 44–48.

On the other hand, the Tiberian system of writing Hebrew, with its over-determination, records both the accent, with a neume, and whether or not the vowel has been reduced or lengthened. This means that one can ignore the tropes when one reads and still pronounce the individual words correctly. This feature of the Tiberian graphemic system allowed later devolutions from it to ignore the neumes, just as most modern biblical scholars do.

The written vowels of Hebrew thus represent the surface forms of words, while those of Russian represent underlying forms.[68]

The central enigma of the Tiberian system is the question of which usages of the graphemes are merely features of the writing and which represent significant characteristics of the language, that is, phonemics. The analysis of a "vocalization" system is not identical to a phonological reconstruction;[69] a graphemic analysis cannot be assumed to be identical with a phonemic analysis. This may be illustrated by referring to the problem of the interpretation of *šĕwâ*, which is a thorny issue, as every student of Hebrew knows. The Masoretes surely intended it to represent but a single vowel, or rather, no vowel at all,[70] but modern scholars differentiate it not only into *šĕwâ quiscens*, that is zero, and *šĕwâ mobile*, that is a phonetic schwa, /ə/, but have also invented *šĕwâ medium*, for those instances where a phonetically and phonemically zero *šĕwâ* is held to have spirantized a following consonant. Clearly, such an analysis mistakenly shifts questions of the forms of words from morphology and morphophonemics (where analogy plays an important role) to the writing system, where it does not belong.[71] Tiberian spelling, like all systems of writing, omitted information which the reader must add. Trisecting the two-dotted *šĕwâ* thus cannot serve as an adequate basis on which to base Hebrew phonology, even if three points determine a plane.

The Tiberian system for writing Hebrew may be summed up with a paradox: Before context-based interpretation of its symbols, many marks are ambiguous; after the individual meanings of the signs have been discerned, it is overly determined.

---

68. Cf. J. L. Malone, "Systematic vs. Autonomous Phonemics and the Hebrew Grapheme *dagesh*," *AAL* 2 (1975) 113–29, whose conclusion about the status of Tiberian *dāgēš* is dependent on this feature of the graphemics.

69. *Pace* Morag, *Vocalization Systems*, 61.

70. See I. Garbell, "The Phonemic Status of *šĕwâ*, the *ḥăṭēpîm*, and the Fricative *begadkepat* in Masoretic Hebrew," *Leš* 23 (1959) 152–55, at 153 [Hebrew].

71. The paradox adumbrated by E. H. Sturtevant, *An Introduction to Linguistic Science* (New Haven: Yale, 1947) 109, is important for understanding the *šĕwâs*: "Phonetic laws are regular but produce irregularities. Analogic creation is irregular but produces regularity."

[December, 1986]

Bibliography

REFERENCE

"Bibliographische Dokumentation." *Zeitschrift für Althebräistik* 1 (1988–).

"Elenchus bibliographicus." *Biblica* 1 (1920–).

Hospers, J. H., compiler. "Biblical and Epigraphical Hebrew." Pp. 176–211 in *A Basic Bibliography for the Study of the Semitic Languages*, vol. 1. Leiden: E. J. Brill, 1973.

Old Testament Abstracts 1 (1978–).

Rabin, Chaim. "Hebrew." Pp. 304–46 in *Current Trends in Linguistics*, vol. 6: *Linguistics in South West Asia and North Africa*. Edited by Thomas A. Sebeok et al. The Hague: Mouton, 1970.

"Sprache." *Internationale Zeitschriftenschau für Bibelwissenschaft*, 1951–.

Téné, David, and James Barr. "Linguistic Literature, Hebrew." Cols. 1352–1401 in *Encyclopedia Judaica*, vol. 16. Jerusalem: Keter, 1971.

Waldman, Nahum M. "The Hebrew Tradition." Pp. 1285–1330 in *Current Trends in Linguistics*, vol. 13: *Historiography of Linguistics*. Edited by Thomas A. Sebeok. The Hague: Mouton, 1975.

_____. *The Recent Study of Hebrew: A Survey of the Literature with Selected Bibliography*. Bibliographica Judaica 10. Winona Lake, IN: Eisenbrauns/Cincinnati: Hebrew Union College, 1989.

GENERAL

Barr, James. "The Ancient Semitic Languages—The Conflict Between Philology and Linguistics." *Transactions of the Philological Society* (1968) 37–55.

Battle, John. "Deep Structure Concepts As Seen in the Hebrew Text of the Psalms." Pp. 20–36 in *Papers from the Fourth Annual Kansas Linguistics Conference.* Edited by H. Harris. Lawrence: University of Kansas Linguistics Students Association/Department of Linguistics, 1970.

_____. "Transformational Concepts in the Hebrew Text of the Psalms." Pp. 8–17 in *Papers From the Fifth Annual Kansas Linguistics Conference.* Edited by Frances Ingemann. Lawrence: University of Kansas Linguistics Students Association/Department of Linguistics, 1971.

Bauer, Hans, and Pontus Leander. *Historische Grammatik der hebräischen Sprache des Alten Testaments.* Halle: Niemeyer, 1922. Rpt., Hildesheim: Olms, 1962.

Bergsträsser, Gotthelf. *Hebräische Grammatik.* 2 vols. Leipzig: Hinrichs, 1918–29. Rpt., Hildesheim: Olms, 1962.

_____. "Hebrew." Pp. 50–71 in *Introduction to the Semitic Languages: Text Specimens and Grammatical Sketches.* Translated and Supplemented by Peter T. Daniels. Winona Lake, IN: Eisenbrauns, 1983. Originally Munich: Hueber, 1928.

Blau, Joshua. *A Grammar of Biblical Hebrew.* Porta Linguarum Orientalium N.S. 12. Wiesbaden: Harrassowitz, 1976.

Bodine, Walter R. "Linguistics and Philology in the Study of Ancient Near Eastern Languages." Pp. 39–54 in *Working with No Data: Semitic and Egyptian Studies Presented to Thomas O. Lambdin.* Edited by David M. Golomb. Winona Lake, IN: Eisenbrauns, 1987.

_____. "Linguistics and Biblical Studies." Pp. 327–33 in *Anchor Bible Dictionary,* vol. 4. Edited by David Noel Freedman. New York: Doubleday, 1992.

Conrad, Edgar W., and Edward G. Newing. *Perspectives on Language and Text: Essays and Poems in Honor of Francis I. Andersen's Sixtieth Birthday, July 28, 1985.* Winona Lake, IN: Eisenbrauns, 1987.

Cotterell, Peter, and Max Turner. *Linguistics and Biblical Interpretation.* Downers Grove: InterVarsity, 1989.

Erickson, Richard J. "Linguistics and Biblical Language: A Wide-Open Field." *Journal of the Evangelical Theological Society* 26 (1983) 257–63.

Gleason, H. A., Jr. "Linguistics and Philology." Pp. 199–212 in *On Language, Culture, and Religion: In Honor of Eugene A. Nida.* Edited by Matthew Black and William A. Smalley. The Hague: Mouton, 1974.

_____. "Linguistics in the Service of the Church." *Hartford Quarterly* 1 (1960) 7–27.

_____. "Some Contributions of Linguistics to Biblical Exegesis." *Hartford Quarterly* 4 (1963) 47–56.

Harris, Zellig S. "Linguistic Structure of Hebrew." *Journal of the American Oriental Society* 61 (1941) 143–67.

Hetzron, Robert. "Hebrew." Pp. 686–704 in *The World's Major Languages.* Edited by Bernard Comrie. London: Croom Helm, 1987.

Jenni, Ernst. *Lehrbuch der hebräischen Sprache des Alten Testaments.* Basel: Helbing und Lichtenhahn, 1981.

Joüon, Paul. *Grammaire de l'hébreu biblique.* Rome: Pontifical Biblical Institute, 1923.

Kautzsch, Emil. *Gesenius' Hebrew Grammar.* Translated and revised by A. E. Cowley. Oxford: Clarendon, 1910.

Kieffer, Rene. "Die Bedeutung der modernen Linguistik für die Auslegung biblischer Text." *Theologische Zeitschrift* 30 (1974) 223–33.

König, Edward. *Historisch-kritisches Lehrgebäude der hebräischen Sprache.* 2 vols. in 3. Leipzig: Hinrichs, 1881–97.

Lambdin, Thomas O. *Introduction to Biblical Hebrew.* New York: Scribner, 1971.

Levin, Saul. *Hebrew Grammar: An Objective Introduction to the Biblical Language.* Binghamton: State University of New York at Binghamton, 1966.

_____. "The Hebrew of the Pentateuch." Pp. 291–323 in *Fucus: A Semitic/ Afrasian Gathering in Remembrance of Albert Ehrman.* Edited by Yoël Arbeitman. Amsterdam: Benjamins, 1988.

Meyer, Rudolf. *Hebräische Grammatik.* 4 vols. Berlin: de Gruyter, 1966–72.

Nida, Eugene A. "Implications of Contemporary Linguistics for Biblical Scholarship." *Journal of Biblical Literature* 91 (1972) 73–89.

Rabin, Chaim. "The Emergence of Classical Hebrew." Pp. 71–78 in *The World History of the Jewish People*, vol. 5. Jerusalem: Massada, 1979.

Richter, Wolfgang. *Grundlagen einer althebräischen Grammatik.* 3 vols. Arbeiten zu Text und Sprache im Alten Testament 8, 10, 13. St. Ottilien: EOS, 1978–80.

Rosén, H. B. *East and West: Selected Writings in Linguistics*, vol. 2: *Hebrew and Semitic Linguistics.* Munich: W. Fink, 1984.

Sawyer, John F. A. *A Modern Introduction to Biblical Hebrew.* Stocksfield: Oriel, 1976.

Schneider, Wolfgang. *Grammatik des biblischen Hebräisch.* Munich: Claudius, 1974.

Silva, Moisés. *God, Language, and Scripture: Reading the Bible in the Light of General Linguistics.* Foundations of Contemporary Interpretation 4. Grand Rapids: Zondervan, 1990.

Talstra, Eep. "Exegesis and the Computer: Questions for the Text and Questions for the Computer." *Bibliotheca Orientalis* 37 (1980) 121–28.

Ullendorff, Edward. *Is Biblical Hebrew a Language? Studies in Semitic Languages and Civilizations.* Wiesbaden: Harrassowitz, 1977.

van der Merwe, C. H. J. "An Adequate Linguistic Framework for an Old Hebrew Linguistic Database: An Attempt to Formulate Some Criteria." *Journal of Semitics* 2 (1990) 72–89.

PHONOLOGY

Barr, James. "St. Jerome's Appreciation of Hebrew." *Bulletin of the John Rylands Library* 49 (1966–67) 281–302.

_____. "St. Jerome and the Sounds of Hebrew." *Journal of Semitic Studies* 12 (1967) 1–36.

_____. "Vocalization and the Analysis of Hebrew Among the Ancient Translators." Pp. 1–11 in *Hebräische Wortforschung: Festschrift . . . Walter Baumgartner.* Vetus Testamentum Supplement 16. Leiden: E. J. Brill, 1967.

Birkeland, Harris. *Akzent und Vokalismus im Althebräischen.* Oslo: Dybwad, 1940.

Blake, Frank R. "The Apparent Interchange Between *a* and *i* in Hebrew." *Journal of Near Eastern Studies* 9 (1950) 76–83.

_____. "The Hebrew Hatephs." Pp. 329–43 in *Oriental Studies Published in Commemoration of the Fortieth Anniversary of Paul Haupt, 1883–1923.* Baltimore: Johns Hopkins University, 1926.

_____. "Pretonic Vowels in Hebrew." *Journal of Near Eastern Studies* 10 (1951) 243–55.

Blau, Joshua. "Hebrew Stress Shifts, Pretonic Lengthening and Segolization: Possible Cases of Aramaic Interference in Hebrew Syllable Structure." *Israel Oriental Studies* 8 (1978) 91–106.

_____. "Non-Phonetic Conditioning of Sound Change and Biblical Hebrew." *Hebrew Annual Review* 3 (1979) 7–15.

_____. "On Pausal Lengthening, Pausal Stress Shift, Philippi's Law and Rule Ordering in Biblical Hebrew." *Hebrew Annual Review* 5 (1981) 1–13.

_____. *On Polyphony in Biblical Hebrew.* Proceedings of the Israel Academy of Sciences and Humanities 6/2. Jerusalem: Israel Academy of Sciences and Humanities, 1982.

_____. "Some Remarks on the Prehistory of Stress in Biblical Hebrew." *Israel Oriental Studies* 9 (1979) 49–54.

_____. "'Weak' Phonetic Change and the Hebrew *śîn*." *Hebrew Annual Review* 1 (1977) 67–119.

Brockelmann, Carl. "Neuere Theorien zur Geschichte des Akzents und des Vokalismus im Hebräischen und Aramäischen." *Zeitschrift der deutschen morgenländischen Gesellschaft* 94 (1940) 332–71.

Cantineau, J. "Élimination des syllabes brèves en hébreu et en araméen biblique." *Bulletin d'études orientales de l'Institut Francais de Damas* 2 (1932) 125–44.

_____. "Essai d'une phonologie de l'hébreu biblique." *Bulletin de la Société de Linguistique de Paris* 46 (1950) 82–122.

_____. "De la place de l'accent de mot en hébreu et en araméen biblique." *Bulletin d'études orientales de l'Institut Francais de Damas* 1 (1931) 81–98.

Deist, Ferdinand E. "Did Gemination Have Phonemic Status in Classical Hebrew?" *Journal of Northwest Semitic Languages* 7 (1979) 13–15.

Faber, Alice. "On the Origin and Development of Hebrew Spirantization." *Mediterranean Language Review* 2 (1986) 117–38.

Fellman, Jack. "A Note on the Phonemic Status of the Ultrashort Vowels in Tiberian Hebrew." *Journal of Northwest Semitic Languages* 4 (1975) 9–10.

_____. "On the Phonemic Status of Gemination in Classical Hebrew." *Journal of Northwest Semitic Languages* 5 (1977) 19.

Garbell, I. "Quelques observations sur les phonèmes de l'hebreu biblique et traditionnel." *Bulletin de la Société de Linguistique de Paris* 50 (1954) 231–43.

Garr, W. Randall. "Pretonic Vowels in Hebrew." *Vetus Testamentum* 37 (1987) 129–53.

_____. "The *Seghol* and Segholation in Hebrew." *Journal of Near Eastern Studies* 48 (1989) 109–16.

_____. "On Vowel Dissimilation in Hebrew." *Biblica* 66 (1985) 572–79.

Gibson, J. C. L. "Stress and Vocalic Change in Hebrew: A Diachronic Study." *Journal of Linguistics* 2 (1966) 35–56.

Hoberman, Robert D. "Initial Consonant Clusters in Hebrew and Aramaic." *Journal of Near Eastern Studies* 48 (1989) 25–29.

Kuryłowicz, Jerzy. "The Accentuation of the Verb in Indo-European and in Hebrew." *Word* 15 (1959) 123–29.

Lambdin, Thomas O. "Philippi's Law Reconsidered." Pp. 135–45 in *Biblical and Related Studies Presented to Samuel Iwry*. Edited by Ann Kort and Scott Morschauser. Winona Lake, IN: Eisenbrauns, 1985.

Levin, Saul. "The Accentual System of Hebrew in Comparison with the Ancient Indo-European Languages." Pp. 71–77 in *Proceedings of the Fifth World Congress of Jewish Studies, 1969*, vol. 4. Jerusalem: World Union of Jewish Studies, 1973.

Malone, Joseph L. "Geminates, the Obligatory Contour Principle, and Tier Conflation: The Case of Tiberian Hebrew." *General Linguistics* 29 (1989) 112–30.

_____. " 'Heavy Segments' vs. the Paradoxes of Segment Length: The Evidence of Tiberian Hebrew." *Linguistics* Special Issue (1978) 119–58.

_____. "A Hebrew Flip-Flop Rule and Its Historical Origins." *Lingua* 30 (1972) 422–48.

_____. "The Isolation of 'Schematisierung': A Service of Linguistics to Philology." *Journal of the American Oriental Society* 94 (1974) 395–400.

_____. "Messrs. Sampson, Chomsky and Halle, and Hebrew Phonology." *Foundations of Language* 14 (1976) 251–56.

_____. "Phonological Evidence for Syntactic Bracketing: A Surprise from Tiberian Hebrew." Pp. 486–94 in *Papers from the Twelfth Regional Meeting of the Chicago Linguistic Society*. Edited by Salikoko S. Mufwene et al. Chicago: Chicago Linguistic Society, 1976.

_____. "Pretonic Lengthening: An Early Hebrew Sound Change." *Journal of the American Oriental Society* 110 (1990) 460–71.

_____. "Rules of Synchronic Analogy: A Proposal Based on Evidence from Three Semitic Languages." *Foundations of Language* 5 (1969) 534–59.

_____. *Tiberian Hebrew Phonology*. Winona Lake, IN: Eisenbrauns, 1993.

Margolis, Max L. "The Place of the Word-Accent in Hebrew." *Journal of Biblical Literature* 30 (1991) 29–43.

McCarthy, John J. *Formal Problem in Semitic Phonology and Morphology*. Bloomington: Indiana University Linguistics Club, 1982. Rpt., New York: Garland, 1985.

Morag, Shelomo. "On the Historical Validity of the Vocalization of the Hebrew Bible." *Journal of the American Oriental Society* 94 (1974) 307–15.

_____. "Some Aspects of the Methodology and Terminology of the Early Massoretes." *Leshonenu* 38 (1973–74) 49–77 [Hebrew].

_____. "The Tiberian Tradition of Biblical Hebrew: Homogenous and Heterogenous Features." *P'raqim* 2 (1969–74) 105–44 [Hebrew].

_____. "The Vocalization of Codex Reuchliniaus: Is the 'Pre-Masoretic' Bible Pre-Masoretic?" *Journal of Semitic Studies* 4 (1959) 216–37.

_____. *The Vocalization Systems of Arabic, Hebrew, and Aramaic: Their Phonetic and Phonemic Principles*. Janua Linguarum 13. The Hague: Mouton, 1962.

Murtonen, A. "Biblical Hebrew Phonology." Pp. 309–13 in *Proceedings of the Sixth World Congress of Jewish Studies*, vol. 1. Edited by Avigdor Shinan. Jerusalem: World Union of Jewish Studies, 1977.

Ornan, Uzzi. "The Tiberian Vocalization System and the Principles of Linguistics." *Journal of Jewish Studies* 15 (1964) 109–23.

Rabin, Chaim. "Archaic Vocalization in Some Biblical Hebrew Names." *Journal of Jewish Studies* 1 (1948–49) 22–26.

Revell, E. J. "The Nature of *Resh* in Tiberian Hebrew." *Association for Jewish Studies Review* 6 (1981) 125–36.

_____. "The Oldest Evidence for the Hebrew Accent System." *Bulletin of the John Rylands Library* 54 (1971) 214–22.

_____. "Pausal Forms in Biblical Hebrew: Their Function, Origin and Significance." *Journal of Semitic Studies* 25 (1980) 165–79.

_____. "Syntactic/Semantic Structure and the Reflexes of Original Short *a* in Tiberian Pointing." *Hebrew Annual Review* 5 (1981) 75–100.

_____. "The Tiberian Reflexes of Short **i* in Closed Syllables." *Journal of the American Oriental Society* 109 (1989) 183–203.

Sampson, Geoffrey. "Duration in Hebrew Consonants." *Linguistic Inquiry* 4 (1973) 101–4.

Schramm, Gene M. "The Chronology of a Phonemic Change." Pp. 276–82 in *Symbolae Linguisticae in Honorem Georgii Kuryłowicz*. Edited by Stanislaw Drewniak. Warsaw: Polskiej Akademii Nauk, 1965.

Speiser, Ephraim A. "The Pronunciation of Hebrew According to the Transliterations in the Hexapla." *Jewish Quarterly Review* 16 (1925–26) 343–82; 23 (1932–33) 233–65; 24 (1933–34) 9–46.

Weinstock, Leo I. "Sound and Meaning in Biblical Hebrew." *Journal of Semitic Studies* 28 (1983) 49–62.

Wernberg-Møller, P. "Aspects of Masoretic Vocalization." Pp. 121–30 in *1972 and 1973 Proceedings of the International Organization for Massoretic Studies*. Edited by Harry M. Orlinsky. Masoretic Studies 1. New York: Ktav, 1974.

Wevers, J. W. "*Ḥeth* in Classical Hebrew." Pp. 101–12 in *Essays on the Ancient Semitic World*. Edited by J. W. Wevers and D. B. Redford. Toronto: University of Toronto, 1970.

MORPHOLOGY

Andersen, Francis I. "Biconsonantal Byforms of Weak Hebrew Roots." *Zeitschrift für die alttestamentliche Wissenschaft* 82 (1970) 270–74.

_____. "Passive and Ergative in Hebrew." Pp. 1–15 in *Near Eastern Studies in Honor of William Foxwell Albright*. Edited by Hans Goedicke. Baltimore: Johns Hopkins University, 1971.

_____. "A Short Note on Construct *k* in Hebrew." *Biblica* 50 (1969) 68–69.

Andersen, Francis I., and A. Dean Forbes. "Prose Particle Counts of the Hebrew Bible." Pp. 165–83 in *The Word of the Lord Shall Go Forth: Essays in Honor of David Noel Freedman*. Edited by Carol L. Meyers and M. O'Connor. Winona Lake, IN: Eisenbrauns, 1983.

Barr, James. "Determination and the Definite Article in Biblica Hebrew." *Journal of Semitic Studies* 34 (1989) 307–35.

Ben-Asher, Mordechai. "Causative *Hip^c îl* Verbs with Double Objects in Biblical Hebrew." *Hebrew Annual Review* 2 (1978) 11–19.

Birkeland, Harris. "Ist das hebräischen Imperfectum consecutivum ein Präteritum? Eine Untersuchung dergegen den präteritalen Character der Form angeführten Stellen." *Acta Orientalia* 13 (1935) 1–34.

Blake, Frank F. "Hebrew חֲמִשִּׁים, חֲמִשָּׁה." *Journal of the American Oriental Society* 26 (1905) 117–19.

_____. "The Hebrew *Waw* Conversive." *Journal of Biblical Literature* 63 (1944) 271–95.

_____. *A Resurvey of Hebrew Tenses*. Rome: Pontifical Biblical Institute, 1951.

_____. "The So-called Intransitive Verbal Forms in Hebrew." *Journal of the American Oriental Society* 24 (1903) 145–204.

Blau, Joshua. "Pronominal Third Person Singular Suffixes with and without *N* in Biblical Hebrew." Pp. 125–31 in *Eretz-Israel: H. L. Ginsberg Volume*, vol. 14. Jerusalem: Israel Exploration Society, 1978 [Hebrew].

_____. "Redundant Pronominal Suffixes Denoting Intrinsic Possession." *Journal of the Ancient Near Eastern Society* 11 (1979) 31–37.

_____. "Remarks on the Development of Some Pronominal Suffixes in Hebrew." *Hebrew Annual Review* 6 (1982) 61–67.

_____. "Studies in Hebrew Verb Formation." *Hebrew Union College Annual* 42 (1971) 133–58.

_____. "Über die *t*-Form des Hip^c il im Bibelhebräisch." *Vetus Testamentum* 7 (1957) 385–88.

Bloch, Ariel. "Zur Nachweisbarkeit einer hebräischen Entsprechung der akkadischen Verbalform iparras." *Zeitschrift der deutschen morgenländischen Gesellschaft* 113 (1963) 41–50.

Cantineau, J. "L'enclise au verbe en hébreu biblique." *Annuaire de l'Institut de Philologie et d'Histoire Orientalis et Slave* 13 (1953) 35–41.

Finley, Thomas J. "The WAW-Consecutive with 'Imperfect' in Biblical Hebrew: Theoretical Studies and Its Use in Amos." Pp. 241–62 in *Tradi-

tion and Testament: Essays in Honor of Charles Lee Feinberg. Edited by John S. Feinberg and Paul D. Feinberg. Chicago: Moody, 1981.

Gai, Amikam. "The Reduction of the Tense (and Other Categories) of the Consequent Verb in Northwest Semitic." *Orientalia* 51 (1982) 254–56.

Gevirtz, Stanley. "Formative ע in Biblical Hebrew." Pp. *57–*66 in *Eretz-Israel: Harry M. Orlinsky Volume*, vol. 16. Jerusalem: Israel Exploration Society, 1982.

Glinert, Lewis H. "The Preposition in Biblical and Modern Hebrew: Towards a Redefinition." *Hebrew Studies* 23 (1982) 115–25.

Gordon, Amnon. "The Development of the Participle in Biblical, Mishnaic, and Modern Hebrew." *Afroasiatic Linguistics* 8 (1982) 121–79.

Goshen-Gottstein, Moshe. "Der Qumrân-Typus yᵉqotlehu und das hebräische Verbalsystem." *Revue de Qumran* 2 (1959–60) 43–46.

_____. "Semitic Morphological Structures: The Basic Morphological Structure of Biblical Hebrew." Pp. 104–16 in *Studies in Egyptology and Linguistics in Honour of H. J. Polotsky*. Edited by H. Blanc. Jerusalem: Israel Exploration Society, 1964.

Greenstein, Edward. "On the Prefixed Preterite in Biblical Hebrew." *Hebrew Studies* 29 (1988) 7–17.

Gross, Walter. "Das nicht substantivierte Partizip als Prädikat im Relativsatz hebräisches Prosa." *Journal of Northwest Semitic Languages* 4 (1975) 23–47.

_____. "Otto Rössler und die Diskussion um das altehebräische Verbalsystem." *Biblische Notizen* 18 (1982) 28–78.

_____. *Verbform und Funktion: Wayyiqtol für die Gegenwart? Ein Beitrag zur Syntax poetischer althebräische Texte.* Arbeiten zu Text und Sprache im Alten Testament 1. St. Ottilien: EOS, 1976.

Harris, Zellig S. "Componential Analysis of a Hebrew Paradigm." *Language* 24 (1948) 87–91.

Huehnergard, John. "The Early Hebrew Prefix-Conjugations." *Hebrew Studies* 29 (1988) 19–23.

Jenni, Ernst. "Faktiv und Kausativ von אבד 'Zugrunde gehen.'" Pp. 143–57 in *Hebräische Wortforschung: Festschrift . . . Walter Baumgartner.* Vetus Testamentum Supplement 16. Leiden: E. J. Brill, 1967.

_____. "Zur Funktion der reflexiv-passiven Stammformen im Biblisch-Hebräischen." Pp. 61–70 in *Proceedings of the Fifth World Congress of Jewish Studies*, vol. 4. Jerusalem: World Congress of Jewish Studies, 1973.

_____. *Das hebräische Piᶜel: Syntaktisch-semasiologische Untersuchung einer Verbform im Alten Testament.* Zurich: EVZ, 1968.

Kaddari, Menahem Z. "The Double Adverb in Biblical Hebrew." *Semitics* 8 (1982) 106–23.

_____. "Dvandra-Type 'Composite' Substantives in Biblical Hebrew." *Leshonenu* 30 (1966) 113–35 [Hebrew].

Koskinen, K. "Kompatibilität in den dreikonsonantigen hebräischen Wurzeln." *Zeitschrift der deutschen morgenländischen Gesellschaft* 114 (1964) 16–58.

Lambdin, Thomas O. "The Junctural Origin of the West Semitic Definite Article." Pp. 315–33 in *Near Eastern Studies in Honor of William Foxwell Albright*. Edited by Hans Goedicke. Baltimore: Johns Hopkins University, 1971.

Levin, Saul. "The Correspondence Between Hebrew and Arabic Pausal Verb-Forms." *Zeitschrift der deutschen morgenländischen Gesellschaft* 131 (1981) 231–33.

_____. "The Plural of 'Segholate' Nouns." *The Journal of Hebraic Studies* 1 (1970) 41–46.

Loprieno, Antonio. "The Sequential Forms in Late Egyptian and Biblical Hebrew: A Parallel Development of Verbal Systems." *Afroasiatic Linguistics* 7 (1980) 143–62.

Malone, Joseph L. "Wave Theory, Rule Ordering, and Hebrew-Aramaic Segolation." *Journal of the American Oriental Society* 91 (1971) 44–66.

McFall, Leslie. *The Enigma of the Hebrew Verbal System: Solutions from Ewald to the Present Day*. Historical Texts and Interpreters in Biblical Scholarship 2. Sheffield: Almond, 1982.

Mettinger, Tryggve N. D. "The Hebrew Verb System: A Survey of Recent Research." *Annual of the Swedish Theological Institute* 9 (1973) 64–84.

_____. "The Nominal Pattern qᵉtulla in Biblical Hebrew." *Journal of Semitic Studies* 16 (1971) 2–14.

Meyer, Rudolf. "Aspekt und Tempus im althebräischen Verbalsystem." *Orientalische Literaturzeitung* 59 (1964) 117–26.

_____. Das hebräische Verbalsystem im Lichte der gegenwärtigen Forschung." Pp. 309–17 in *Congress Volume: Oxford 1959*. Vetus Testamentum Supplement 7. Leiden: E. J. Brill, 1960.

Müller, Hans-Peter. "Das Bedeutungspotential der Afformativkonjugation: Zum sprachgeschichtlichen Hintergrund des Althebräischen." *Zeitschrift für Althebräistik* 1 (1988) 74–98.

_____. "Zur Geschichte des hebräischen Verbs: Diachronie der Konjugationsthemen." *Biblische Zeitschrift* 27 (1983) 34–57.

_____. "Die Konjugation von Nomina im Althebräischen." *Zeitschrift für die alttestamentliche Wissenschaft* 96 (1984) 245–63.

Muraoka, Takamitsu. "The *Nun Energicum* and the Prefix Conjugation in Biblical Hebrew." *Annual of the Japanese Biblical Institute* 1 (1975) 63–71.

_____. "On the So-Called *Dativus Ethicus* in Hebrew." *Journal of Theological Studies* 29 (1978) 495–98.

_____. "The Status Constructus of Adjectives in Biblical Hebrew." *Vetus Testamentum* 27 (1977) 375–80.

Rabin, Chaim. "*L-* with Imperative (Gen xxiii)." *Journal of Semitic Studies* 13 (1968) 113–24.

Rainey, Anson F. "The Ancient Hebrew Prefix Conjugation in the Light of Amarnah Canaanite." *Hebrew Studies* 27 (1986) 4–19.

_____. "Further Remarks on the Hebrew Verbal System." *Hebrew Studies* 29 (1988) 35–42.

Rendsburg, Gary. "Dual Personal Pronoun and Dual Verbs in Hebrew." *Jewish Quarterly Review* 73 (1982) 38–58.

_____. *Linguistic Evidence for the Northern Origin of Selected Psalms.* Society of Biblical Literature Monograph Series 43. Atlanta: Scholars, 1990.

Revell, E. J. "The Battle with Benjamin (Judges xx 29–48) and Hebrew Narrative Techniques." *Vetus Testamentum* 35 (1985) 417–33.

_____. "The Conditioning or Stress Position in *Waw* Consecutive Perfect Forms in Biblical Hebrew." *Hebrew Annual Review* 9 (1985) 277–300.

_____. "First Person Imperfect Forms with *Waw* Consecutive." *Vetus Testamentum* 38 (1988) 419–26.

_____. "First Person Imperfect Forms with *waw* Consecutive-Addenda." *Vetus Testamentum* 41 (1991) 127–28.

_____. "Stress Position in Verb Forms with Vocative Affix." *Journal of Semitic Studies* 32 (1987) 249–71.

_____. "Stress and the *Waw* 'Consecutive' in Biblical Hebrew." *Journal of the American Oriental Society* 104 (1984) 437–44.

_____. "The System of the Verb in Standard Biblical Prose." *Hebrew Union College Annual* 60 (1989) 1–37.

_____. "The Vowelling of '*i* type' Segolates in Tiberian Hebrew." *Journal of Near Eastern Studies* 44 (1985) 319–28.

Rössler, Otto. "Zum althebräischen Tempussystem: Eine morpho-syntaktische Untersuchung." Pp. 33–57 in *Hebraica.* Edited by Otto Rössler. Marburger Studien zur Afrika und Asienkunde, Serie B: Asien, Band 4. Berlin: Reimer, 1977.

Rubinstein, Eliezar. "Adjectival Verbs in Biblical Hebrew." *Israel Oriental Studies* 9 (1979) 55–76.

Rundgren, Frithiof. *Das althebräische Verbum: Abriss der Aspektlehre.* Uppsala: Almqvist & Wiksell, 1961.

Schneider, Wolfgang. "Geisterformen." *Biblische Notizen* 53 (1990) 26–29.

Schramm, Gene. "A Reconstruction of Biblical Hebrew Waw Consecutive." *General Linguistics* 3 (1957) 1–8.

Segert, Stanislav. "Aspekte des althebräischen Aspekt-Systems." *Archiv Orientálni* 33 (1965) 93–104.

Sheehan, J. F. X. "Conversive Waw and Accentual Shift." *Biblica* 51 (1970) 545–48.

_____. "Egypto-Semitic Elucidation of Waw Conversive." *Biblica* 52 (1971) 39–43.

Steiner, Richard C. "From Proto-Hebrew to Mishnaic Hebrew: The History of הָ‎ and הָ‎." *Hebrew Annual Review* 3 (1979) 157–74.

_____. "On the Origin of the *ḥéḏer~ḥăḏár* Alternation in Hebrew." *Afroasiatic Linguistics* 3 (1976) 85–102.

_____. "Yuqaṭṭil, yaqaṭṭil, or yiqaṭṭil: D-Stem Prefix-Vowels and a Constraint on Reduction in Hebrew and Aramaic." *Journal of the American Oriental Society* 100 (1980) 513–18.

Talstra, Eep. "The Use of כֵּן‎ in Biblical Hebrew." *Oudtestamentsche Studiën* 21 (1981) 228–39.

Wernberg-Møller, P. "Observations on the Hebrew Participle." *Zeitschrift für die alttestamentliche Wissenschaft* 71 (1959) 54–67.

_____. "Pronouns and Suffixes in the Scrolls and the Masoretic Text." *Journal of Biblical Literature* 76 (1957) 44–49.

Williams, Ronald J. "Energic Verbal Forms in Hebrew." Pp. 75–85 in *Studies on the Ancient Palestinian World Presented to Professor F. V. Winnett.* Edited by J. W. Wevers and D. B. Redford. Toronto: University of Toronto, 1972.

_____. "The Passive *Qal* Theme in Hebrew." Pp. 43–50 in *Essays on the Ancient Semitic World.* Edited by J. W. Wevers and D. B. Redford. Toronto: University of Toronto, 1970.

Yannay, Igal. "Augmented Verbs in Biblical Hebrew." *Hebrew Union College Annual* 45 (1974) 71–95.

Zevit, Ziony. "Talking Funny in Biblical Henglish and Solving a Problem of the YAQTÚL Past Tense." *Hebrew Studies* 29 (1988) 25–33.

SYNTAX

Andersen, Francis I. *The Hebrew Verbless Clause in the Pentateuch.* Journal of Biblical Literature Monograph Series 14. Nashville: Abingdon, 1970.

_____. *The Sentence in Biblical Hebrew.* Janua Linguarum, Series Practica 231. The Hague: Mouton, 1974.

Avinun, Sarah. "Syntactic, Logical, and Semantic Aspects of the Division of Verses According to the Biblical Accents." *Leshonenu* 53 (1988–89) 159–92 [Hebrew].

Blau, Joshua. *An Adverbial Construction in Hebrew and Arabic: Sentence Adverbials in Frontal Position Separated from the Rest of the Sentence.* Proceedings of the Israel Academy of Sciences and Humanities 6/1. Jerusalem: Israel Academy of Sciences and Humanities, 1977.

_____. "Asyndetic Prepositional Clauses Opening with a Substantive in Biblical Hebrew." Pp. 277–86 in *Bible Studies: Y. M. Grintz in Memoriam.* Edited by Benjamin Uffenheimer. Tel Aviv: Tel Aviv University, 1982 [Hebrew, English summary pp. xxiv–xxv].

_____. "Notes on Relative Clauses in Biblical Hebrew." *Shnaton* 2 (1977) 50–53 [Hebrew, English summary p. xi].

_____. "On the Repetition of the Predicate in the Bible." Pp. 234–40 in *Bible and Jewish History.* Edited by Benjamin Uffenheimer. Tel Aviv: Tel Aviv University, 1971.

Bodine, Walter R. Review of Bruce K. Waltke and M. O'Connor, *An Introduction to Biblical Hebrew Syntax. Hebrew Studies* 31 (1990) 253–59.

Brockelmann, Carl. *Hebräische Syntax.* Neukirchen: Neukirchener, 1956.

Dorn, Louis. "Chronological Sequences in Two Hebrew Narratives." *The Bible Translator* 29 (1978) 316–22.

Finley, Thomas J. "The Proposal in Biblical Hebrew: Preliminary Studies Using a Deep Structure Model." *Zeitschrift für Althebräistik* 2 (1989) 1–13.

Forbes, A. Dean. "Syntactic Sequences in the Hebrew Bible." Pp. 59–70 in *Perspectives on Language and Text: Essays and Poems in Honor of Francis I. Andersen.* Edited by E. W. Conrad and E. G. Newing. Winona Lake, IN: Eisenbrauns, 1987.

Givón, Talmy. "Complex NP's Word-Order and Resumptive Pronouns in Hebrew." Pp. 135–46 in *You Take the High Node and I'll Take the Low Node.* Edited by Caudia Corum et al. Chicago: Chicago Linguistic Society, 1973.

_____. "The Drift from VSO to SVO in Biblical Hebrew: The Pragmatics of Tense-Aspect." Pp. 181–254 in *Symposium in the Mechanisms of Syntactic Change.* Edited by Charles N. Li. Austin: University of Texas, 1977.

_____. "Topic, Pronoun and Grammatical Agreement." Pp. 149–88 in *Subject and Topic.* Edited by Charles N. Li. New York: Academic, 1976.

Goshen-Gottstein, M. H. "Afterthought and the Syntax of Relative Clauses in Biblical Hebrew." *Journal of Biblical Literature* 68 (1949) 35–47.

_____. "Hebrew Syntax and the History of the Bible Text: A Pesher in the MT of Isaiah." *Textus* 8 (1973) 100–106.

Greenstein, Edward L. "The Syntax of Saying 'Yes' in Biblical Hebrew." *Journal of the Ancient Near Eastern Society of Columbia University* 19 (1989) 51–59.

Gross, Walter, "Die Herausführungsformel: Zum Verhältniss von Formel und Syntax." *Zeitschrift für die alttestamentliche Wissenschaft* 86 (1974) 425–53.

_____. *Die Pendenskonstrucktion im biblischen Hebräisch.* Arbeiten zu Text und Sprache im Alten Testament 27. St. Ottilien: EOS, 1987.

Hoftijzer, Jacob. *The Function and Use of the Imperfect Forms with Nun Paragogicum in Classical Hebrew.* Studia Semitica Neerlandica 21. Assen: Van Gorcum, 1985.

_____. "The Nominal Clause Reconsidered." *Vetus Testamentum* 23 (1973) 446–510.

Joseph, Brian. "Recovery of Information in Relative Clauses: Evidence from Greek and Hebrew." *Journal of Linguistics* 16 (1980) 237–44.

Kaddari, Menahem Z. "Concessive Relation in Biblical Hebrew." Pp. 325–48 in *Bible Studies: Y. M. Grintz in Memoriam.* Edited by Benjamin Uffenheimer, Tel Aviv: Tel Aviv University, 1982 [Hebrew, English Summary p. xiii].

_____. "Construct Infinitive as Time Adverbial in Biblical Hebrew." Pp. 132–36 in *Eretz-Israel: H. L. Ginsberg Volume,* vol. 14. Jerusalem: Israel Exploration Society, 1978 [Hebrew, English summary p. 128*].

_____. "Problems in Biblical Hebrew Syntax (On the So-Called 'Double Object')." *Leshonenu* 34 (1969–70) 245–56 [Hebrew].

_____. "Syntactic Presentation of a Biblical Hebrew Verb (MṢ᾿)." Pp. 18–25 in *Studies in Hebrew and Semitic Languages Dedicated to the Memory of Prof. Eduard Yechezkel Kutscher.* Edited by G. Sarfatti et al. Ramat Gan: Bar-Ilan University, 1980.

_____. *Studies in Biblical Hebrew Syntax.* Ramat Gan: Bar-Ilan University, 1976 [Hebrew].

_____. "Wann erfolgt die Determination des Nomen Regens im Hebräischen?" *Beth Mikra* 11 (1965–66) 42–57.

Lòde, Lars. "Postverbal Word Order in Biblical Hebrew: Structure and Function." *Semitics* 9 (1984) 113–64.

Michel, Diethelm. *Grundlegung einer hebräischen Syntax.* Teil 1: *Sprachwissenschaftliche Methodik: Genus und Numerus des Nomens.* Neukirchen-Vluyn: Neukirchener, 1977.

Müller, Hans-Peter. "Die Konstruktionen mit *hinne* 'siehe' und ihr sprachgeschichtlicher Hintergrund." *Zeitschrift für Althebräistik* 2 (1989) 45–76.

Muraoka, Takamitsu. *Emphatic Words and Structures in Biblical Hebrew.* Jerusalem: Magnes/Leiden: E. J. Brill, 1985.

_____. "On Verb Complementation in Biblical Hebrew." *Vetus Testamentum* 29 (1979) 425–35.

Revell, E. J. "The Conditioning of Word Order in Verbless Clauses in Biblical Hebrew." *Journal of Semitic Studies* 34 (1989) 1–24.

Richter, Wolfgang. "Verbalvalenz und Verbalsatz: Ein Beitrag zur syntaktischen Grundlegung einer alttestamentliche Literaturwissenschaft." *Journal of Northwest Semitic Languages* 4 (1975) 61–69.

Rubinstein, Eliezar. "Adjectival Verbs in Biblical Hebrew." *Israel Oriental Studies* 9 (1979) 55–76.

_____. "Double Causation in a Sentence: A Syntactic-Semantic Study in Biblical Hebrew." *Israel Oriental Studies* 5 (1975) 32–44.

Sappan, Raphael. *The Typical Features of the Syntax of Biblical Poetry in the Classical Period.* Jerusalem: Kiryat-Sefer, 1981 [Hebrew, with English summary].

Schwarzschild, Roger. "The Syntax of אשר in Biblical Hebrew with Special Reference to Qoheleth." *Hebrew Studies* 31 (1990) 7–39.

_____. "Sentence Modifiers and Verb Modifiers and Their Position in the Sentence." *Leshonenu* 35 (1970–71) 60–74 [Hebrew].

Silverman, Michael H. "Syntactic Notes on the *waw Consecutive*." Pp. 167–75 in *Orient and Occident: Essays Presented to Cyrus H. Gordon on the Occasion of His Sixty-fifth Birthday.* Edited by H. A. Hoffner. Alter Orient und Altes Testament 22. Kevelaer: Butzon und Bercker, 1973.

Steiner, Richard C. Review of Joshua Blau, *An Adverbial Construction in Hebrew and Arabic: Sentence Adverbials in Frontal Position Separated from the Rest of the Sentence. Afroasiatic Linguistics* 6 (1979) 5–10.

Talstra, Eep. "Towards a Distributional Definition of Clauses in Classical Hebrew." *Ephemerides Theologicae Lovanienses* 63 (1987) 75–105.

Thorion, Y. *Studien zur klassichen hebräischen Syntax.* Berlin: Dietrich Reimer, 1984.

Vetter, Dieter. "Satzformen prophetischer Rede." Pp. 174–93 in *Werden und Wirken des Alten Testaments: Festschrift für Claus Westerman zum 70. Geburtstag.* Edited by Rainer Albertz et al. Göttingen: Vandenhoeck und Ruprecht, 1980.

Waltke, Bruce K., and M. O'Connor. *An Introduction to Biblical Hebrew Syntax.* Winona Lake, IN: Eisenbrauns, 1990.

Weiss, R. "On the Use of the Negative in the Bible." Pp. 148–54 in *Eretz-Israel: H. L. Ginsberg Volume*, vol. 14. Jerusalem: Israel Exploration Society, 1978 [Hebrew, English summary, p. 128*].

Wevers, John W. "Semitic Bound Structures." *Canadian Journal of Linguistics* 7 (1961) 9–14.

Williams, Ronald J. *Hebrew Syntax: An Outline.* 2d edition. Toronto: University of Toronto, 1976.

SEMANTICS AND LEXICOGRAPHY

Barr, James. *Biblical Words for Time.* 2d edition. London: SCM, 1969.

_____. "Etymology and the Old Testament." *Oudtestamentische Studiën* 19 (1974) 1–28.

_____. "Hebrew Lexicography." Pp. 103–26 in *Studies on Semitic Lexicography.* Edited by Pelio Fronzaroli. Florence: Istituto di Linguistica e di Lingue Orientali, 1973.

_____. "Limitations of Etymology as a Lexicographical Instrument in Biblical Hebrew." *Transactions of the Philological Society* (1985) 41–65.

_____. *The Semantics of Biblical Language.* New York: Oxford University, 1961.

_____. "Semantics and Biblical Theology—a Contribution to the Discussion." Pp. 11–19 in *Congress Volume.* Vetus Testamentum Supplement 22. Leiden: E. J. Brill, 1972.

Berlin, Adele. "Lexical Cohesion and Biblical Interpretation." *Hebrew Studies* 30 (1989) 29–40.

_____. "On the Meaning of *pll* in the Bible." *Revue Biblique* 96 (1989) 345–51.

Botha, P. J. "The Measurement of Meaning—An Exercise in Field Semantics." *Journal of Semitics* 1 (1989) 3–22.

Brett, Mark G. "Motives and Intentions in Genesis I." *The Journal of Theological Studies* 42 (1991) 11–16.

Gibson, Arthur. *Biblical Semantic Logic.* New York: St. Martin's, 1981.

Holman, J. "A Semiotic Analysis of Psalm CXXXVIII (LXX)." *Oudtestamentische Studiën* 26 (1990) 84–100.

Jenni, Ernst. "Zur Semantik der hebräischen Pensonen-, Tier- und Dingvergleiche." *Zeitschrift für Althebräistik* 3 (1990) 133–66.

_____. "Zur Semantik der hebräischen Vergleichssatze." *Zeitschrift für Althebräistik* 2 (1989) 14–44.

Kedar-Kopfstein, Benjamin. *Biblische Semantik: Eine Einführung.* Stuttgart: Kohlhammer, 1981.

_____. "Semantic Aspects of the Pattern qôṭēl." *Hebrew Annual Review* 1 (1977) 155–76.

Leslau, Wolf. *Ethiopic and South Arabic Contributions to the Hebrew Lexicon.* Berkeley: University of California, 1958.

Lübbe, J. C. "Hebrew Lexicography: A New Approach." *Journal of Semitics* 2 (1990) 1–15.

_____. "Old Testament Sample Studies." Pp. 118–37 in *Lexicography and Translations with Special Reference to Bible Translation.* Edited by J. P. Louw. Cape Town: Bible Society of South Africa, 1985.

Morag, Shelomo. "On Some Semantic Relationships." Pp. 137–47 in *Eretz-Israel: H. L. Ginsberg Volume*, vol. 14. Jerusalem: Israel Exploration Society, 1978 [Hebrew, English summary p. 128*].

Mitchell, Christopher. "The Use of Lexicons and Word Studies in Exegesis." *Concordia Journal* 11 (1985) 128–34.

Rabin, Chaim. "Is Biblical Semantics Possible?" *Beth Miqra* 14 (1962) 17–27 [Hebrew].

_____. "Lexical Emendation in Biblical Research." Pp. 379–418 in *Fucus: A Semitic/Afrasian Gathering in Remembrance of Albert Ehrman*. Edited by Yoël L. Arbeitman. Amsterdam: Benjamins, 1988.

_____. "Towards a Descriptive Semantics of Biblical Hebrew." Pp. 51–52 in *Proceedings of the Twenty-sixth International Congress of Orientalists, 1964*, vol. 2. New Delhi: International Congress of Orientalists, 1968.

Rubinstein, Eliezar. "'Causation' and 'Volition' as Semantic Components of Verbs: A Study of the Biblical Verb בקשׁ." *Israel Oriental Studies* 6 (1976) 122–30.

_____. "On the Mechanism of Semantic Shift: Causation of Symmetric Locativity." *Afroasiatic Linguistics* 3 (1976) 133–42.

_____. "Semantic Transparence and Semantic Opacity: A Study of Locative Verbs in Biblical Hebrew." Pp. 349–60 in *Bible Studies: Y. M. Grintz in Memoriam*. Edited by Benjamin Uffenheimer. Tel Aviv: Tel Aviv University, 1982 [Hebrew, English summary p. xliii].

Sawyer, John F. A. "Root-Meanings in Hebrew." *Journal of Semitic Studies* 12 (1967) 37–50.

_____. *Semantics in Biblical Research: New Methods of Defining Hebrew Words for Salvation*. Studies in Biblical Theology, Second Series 24. Naperville: Alec R. Allenson, 1972.

Silva, Moisés. *Biblical Words and Their Meaning: An Introduction to Lexical Semantics*. Grand Rapids: Zondervan, 1983.

Tångberg, K. Arvid. "Linguistics and Theology: An Attempt to Analyze and Evaluate James Barr's Argumentation in *The Semantics of Biblical Language* and *Biblical Words for Time*." *The Bible Translator* 24 (1973) 301–10.

Thiselton, Anthony C. "The Semantics of Biblical Language as an Aspect of Hermeneutics." *Faith and Thought* 103 (1976) 108–20.

van Wolde, E. J. *A Semiotic Analysis of Genesis 2–3*. Studia Semitica Neerlandica 25, Assen/Maastricht: Van Gorcum, 1989.

Wyk, W. C. van. "The Present State of OT Lexicography." Pp. 82–96 in *Lexicography and Translation with Special Reference to Bible Translation*. Edited by J. P. Louw. Cape Town: Bible Society of South Africa, 1985.

DISCOURSE ANALYSIS

Altpeter, G. *Textlinguistische Exegese alttestamentlicher Literatur: Eine Dekodierung.* Bern: Lang, 1978.

Baker, David W. "Diversity and Unity in the Literary Structure of Genesis." Pp. 189–205 in *Essays on the Patriarchal Narratives.* Edited by A. R. Millard and D. J. Wiseman. Leicester: InterVarsity, 1980/Winona Lake, IN: Eisenbrauns, 1983.

_____. "Division Markers and the Structure of Leviticus 1–7." Pp. 9–15 in *Studia Biblica 1978, 1: Papers on Old Testament and Related Themes.* Edited by Elizabeth E. Livingston. Journal for the Study of the Old Testament Supplement Series 11. Sheffield: JSOT, 1979.

Bergen, Robert D. "The Role of Genesis 22:1–19 in the Abraham Cycle: A Computer-Assisted Textual Interpretation." *Criswell Theological Review* 4 (1990) 313–36.

_____. "Text as a Guide to Authorial Intention: An Introduction to Discourse Criticism." *Journal of The Evangelical Theological Society* 30 (1987) 327–36.

Berlin, Adele. *Poetics and Interpretation of Biblical Narrative.* Sheffield: Almond, 1983.

Claassen, W. T. "Speaker-Oriented Functions of /kî/ in Biblical Hebrew." *Journal of Near Eastern Studies* 11 (1983) 29–46.

Clark, David J. "Discourse Structure in Zechariah 7:1–8:23." *The Bible Translator* 36 (1985) 328–35.

Clendenen, E. Ray. "Discourse Strategies in Jeremiah 10:1–16." *Journal of Biblical Literature* 106 (1987) 401–8.

_____. "The Structure of Malachi: A Textlinguistic Study." *Criswell Theological Review* 2 (1987) 3–17.

Conroy, Charles. *Absalom, Absalom: Narrative and Language in 2 Sam. 13–20.* Analecta Biblica 81. Rome: Pontifical Biblical Institute, 1978.

Ehrlich, K. "Deixis und Anapher." Pp. 79–97 in *Essays on Deixis.* Edited by Gisa Rauh. Tübinger Beiträge zum Linguistik 188. Tübingen: Narr, 1983.

_____. *Verwendungen der Deixis beim sprachlichen Handeln: Linguistisch-philologische Untersuchungen zum hebräischen deiktischen System.* 2 vols. Forum Linguisticum 24. Frankfurt am Main: Lang, 1979.

Floss, Johannes P. "Die Wortstellung des Konjugationsystems in Jes 24: Ein Beitrag zur Formkritik poetischer Texte im AT." Pp. 227–44 in *Festgabe für G. Johannes Botterweck zum 60. Geburtstag dargebracht von seinen Schülern.* Edited by Heinz-Josef Fabry. Bonner Biblische Beiträge 50. Cologne: Hanstein, 1979.

Fox, Andrew. "Topic Continuity in Biblical Hebrew Narrative." Pp. 215–54 in *Topic Continuity in Discourse: A Quantitative Cross-Language Study*. Edited by T. Givón. Amsterdam: Benjamins, 1983.

Givón, Talmy. "From Discourse to Syntax: Grammar as a Processing Strategy." Pp. 81–112 in *Discourse and Syntax*. Edited by Talmy Givón. Syntax and Semantics 12. New York: Academic, 1979.

_____. "Topic Continuity in Discourse: An Introduction." Pp. 1–41 in *Topic Continuity in Discourse: A Quantitative Cross-Language Study*. Edited by T. Givón. Amsterdam: Benjamins, 1983.

Gross, Walter. "Syntaktische Erscheinungen am Anfang althebräisches Erzählungen: Hintergrund und Vordergrund." Pp. 131–45 in *Congress Volume*. Edited by J. A. Emerton. Vetus Testamentum Supplement 32. Leiden: E. J. Brill, 1981.

Hardmeier, Christof. *Texttheorie und biblische Exegese: Zur rhetorischen Funktion der Trauermetaphorik in der Prophetie*. Beiträge zur evangelischen Theologie 79. Munich: Kaiser, 1978.

Jensen, Hans Jorgen Lundager. "Reden, Zeit und Raum in Genesis 28:10–15: Textlinguistische und textsemiotische Exegese eines Fragments." *Linguistica Biblica* 49 (1981) 54–70.

Junger, J. "Aspect and Cohesion in Biblical Hebrew Narratives." *Semitics* 10 (1989) 71–130.

Longacre, Robert E. "The Discourse Structure of the Flood Narrative." *Journal of the American Academy of Religion* 47 Supplement B (1979) 89–133.

_____. "Interpreting Biblical Stories." Pp. 169–85 in *Discourse and Literature: New Approach to the Analysis of Literary Genres*. Edited by Teun A. van Dijk. Critical Theory 3. Amsterdam: Benjamins, 1985.

_____. *Joseph, a Story of Divine Providence: A Text-Theoretical and Text-linguistic Analysis of Genesis 37 and 39–48*. Winona Lake, IN: Eisenbrauns, 1989.

_____. "A Spectrum and Profile Approach to Discourse Analysis." *Text* 1 (1981) 337–59.

_____. "Two Hypotheses Regarding Text Generation and Analysis." *Discourse Processes* 12 (1989) 413–60.

Payne, G. "Functional Sentence Perspective: Theme in Biblical Hebrew." *Scandinavian Journal of the Old Testament* 1 (1991) 62–82.

Parunak, H. Van Dyke. "Oral Typesetting: Some Uses of Biblical Structure." *Biblica* 62 (1981) 153–68.

_____. "Transitional Techniques in the Bible." *Journal of Biblical Literature* 102 (1983) 525–48.

Rabin, Chaim. "Discourse Analysis and the Dating of Deuteronomy." Pp. 171–77 in *Interpreting the Hebrew Bible: Essays in Honour of E. I. J.*

Rosenthal. Edited by J. A. Emerton and Stefan Reif. Cambridge: Cambridge University, 1982.

Rebera, Basil A. "Identifying Participants in Old Testament Dialogue." *The Bible Translator* 33 (1982) 201–7.

_____. "Yahweh or Boaz? Ruth 2:20 Reconsidered." *The Bible Translator* 36 (1985) 317–27.

Schicklberger, Franz. "Biblische Literarkritik und linguistische Texttheorie: Bemerkungen zu einer Textsyntax von hebräischen Erzähltexten." *Theologische Zeitschrift* 34 (1978) 65–81.

_____. "Jonatans Heldentat: Textlinguistische Beobachtungen zu 1 Sam. xiv 1–23a." *Vetus Testamentum* 24 (1974) 324–33.

Schweizer, Harold. "Determination, Textdeixis—Erläutert an Genesis xviii 23–33." *Vetus Testamentum* 33 (1983) 113–18.

_____. *Metaphorische Grammatik: Wege zur Integration von Grammatik und Textinterpretation in der Exegese.* Arbeiten zu Text und Sprache im Alten Testament 15. St. Ottilien: EOS, 1981.

_____. "Prädikationen und Leerstellen im 1. Gottesknechtslied (Jes 42,1–4). *Biblische Zeitschrift* 26 (1981) 251–58.

_____. "Texttheorie und Beelzebub: Die Impulse Christof Hardmeiers für die Methodik der Exegese." *Biblische Notizen* 9 (1979) 26–44.

Segert, Stanislav. "Syntax and Style in the Book of Jonah: Six Simple Approaches." Pp. 121–30 in *Prophecy: Essays Presented to Georg Fohrer.* Edited by J. A. Emerton. Beihefte zur Zeitschrift für die alttestamentliche Wissenschaft 150. Berlin: de Gruyter, 1980.

Sternberg, Meir. "Deictic Sequence: World, Language and Convention." Pp. 277–316 in *Essays on Deixis.* Edited by Gisa Rauh. Tübingen: Narr, 1983.

_____. *The Poetics of Biblical Narrative: Ideological Literature and the Drama of Reading.* Bloomington: Indiana University, 1985.

Talstra, Eep. "Text Grammar and Hebrew Bible, I: Elements of a Theory." *Bibliotheca Orientalis* 35 (1978) 169–74; II: "Syntax and Semantics," 39 (1982) 26–38.

Wirklander, Bertil. *Prophecy as Literature: A Text-linguistic and Rhetorical Approach to Isaiah 2–4.* Coniectanea Biblica, Old Testament Series 22. Uppsala: CWK Gleerup, 1984.

Zatelli, Ida. "La chiamata dell'uomo da parte di Dio nella Bibbia al vaglio della 'discourse analysis.'" *Rivista Biblica* 38 (1990) 13–26.

HISTORICAL/COMPARATIVE LINGUISTICS

Aristar, A. M. R. "The II*wy* Verbs and the Vowel System of Proto-West Semitic." *Afroasiatic Linguistics* 6 (1979) 209–25.

Barr, James. *Comparative Philology and the Text of the Old Testament.* Oxford: Oxford University, 1968; rpt., Winona Lake, IN: Eisenbrauns, 1987.

Blau, Joshua. "Hebrew and North West Semitic: Reflections on the Classification of the Semitic Languages." *Hebrew Annual Review* 2 (1978) 21–44.

———. "The Historical Periods of the Hebrew Language." With responses by Yehiel Hayon and Stephen J. Lieberman. Pp. 1–28 in *Jewish Languages: Theme and Variations.* Edited by Herbert H. Paper. Cambridge, MA: Association for Jewish Studies, 1978.

———. "Some Difficulties in the Reconstruction of 'Proto-Hebrew' and 'Proto-Canaanitic.'" Pp. 29–43 in *In Memoriam Paul Kahle.* Edited by Matthew Black and Georg Fohrer. Beihefte zur Zeitschrift für die alttestamentliche Wissenschaft 103. Berlin: Töpelmann, 1968.

Boyd, Jesse L., III. "The Development of the West Semitic Qal Perfect and the Double-ʿAyin Verb with Particular Reference to its Transmission into Syriac." *Journal of Northwest Semitic Languages* 10 (1982) 11–23.

Fellman, Jack. "Sociolinguistic Notes on the History of the Hebrew Language." *Journal of Northwest Semitic Languages* 6 (1978) 5–7.

Garr, W. Randall. *Dialect Geography of Syria-Palestine, 1000–586 B.C.E.* Philadelphia: University of Pennsylvania, 1985.

Ginsberg, H. L. "The Northwest Semitic Languages." Pp. 102–24 in *The World History of the Jewish People*, vol. 2. Edited by Benjamin Mazar et al. New Brunswick: Rutgers University, 1970.

Givón, Talmy. "Verb Complements and Relative Clauses: A Diachronic Case Study in Biblical Hebrew." *Afroasiatic Linguistics* 1 (1974) 1–22.

Goshen-Gottstein, M. H. "The Rise of the Tiberian Bible Text." Pp. 79–122 in *Biblical and Other Studies.* Edited by Alexander Altman. Cambridge: Harvard University, 1963.

Greenstein, Edward L. "Another Attestation of Initial *h* > *ʾ* in West Semitic." *Journal of the Ancient Near Eastern Society of Columbia University* 5 (1973) 157–64.

Harris, Zellig S. *Development of the Canaanite Dialects.* American Oriental Series 16. New Haven: American Oriental Society, 1939.

Hetzron, Robert. "Third Person Singular Pronoun Suffixes in Proto-Semitic (with a Theory on the Connective Vowels in Tiberian Hebrew)." *Orientalia Suecana* 18 (1969) 101–27.

Hurvitz, Avi. "The Chronological Significance of 'Aramaisms' in Biblical Hebrew." *Israel Exploration Journal* 18 (1968) 234–41.

_____. "The Data of the Prose Tale of Job Linguistically Reconsidered." *Harvard Theological Review* 67 (1974) 17–34.

_____. "The Evidence of Language in Dating the Priestly Code: A Linguistic Study in Technical Idioms and Terminology." *Revue Biblique* 81 (1974) 24–56.

_____. *A Linguistic Study of the Relationship Between the Priestly Source and the Book of Ezekiel.* Cahiers de la Revue Biblique 20. Paris: Gabalda, 1982.

_____. "The Usage of *šēš* and *bûṣ* in the Bible and Its Implications for the Date of P." *Harvard Theological Review* 60 (1967) 117–21.

_____. "Wisdom Vocabulary in the Hebrew Psalter: A Contribution to the Study of 'Wisdom Psalms.'" *Vetus Testamentum* 38 (1988) 41–51.

Janssens, G. *Studies in Hebrew Historical Linguistics Based on Origen's Secunda.* Orientalia Gandensia 9. Leuven: Peeters, 1982.

Kopf, L. "The Arabic Dictionary as a Tool for Hebrew Philology." *Leshonenu* 19 (1953–54) 72–82 [Hebrew].

_____. "Arabische Etymologien und Parallelen zum Bibelwörterbuch." *Vetus Testamentum* 8 (1958) 161–215; 9 (1959) 247–87.

Kutscher, E. Y. "Contemporary Studies in North-Western Semitic." *Journal of Semitic Studies* 10 (1965) 21–50.

_____. *A History of the Hebrew Language.* Edited by Raphael Kutscher. Jerusalem: Magnes/Leiden: E. J. Brill, 1982.

Meyer, Rudolf. "Zur Geschichte des hebräischen Verbums." *Vetus Testamentum* 3 (1953) 225–35.

_____. "Zur Geschichte des hebräischen Verbums." *Forschungen und Fortschritte* 40 (1966) 241–43.

Moran, William L. "The Hebrew Language and Its Northwest Semitic Background." Pp. 54–72 in *The Bible and the Ancient Near East: Essays in Honor of William Foxwell Albright.* Edited by G. Ernest Wright. Garden City: Doubleday, 1961; rpt., Winona Lake, IN: Eisenbrauns, 1980.

Rabin, Chaim. *A Short History of the Hebrew Language.* Jerusalem: Orot, 1973.

Rendsburg, Gary A. *Diglossia in Ancient Hebrew.* American Oriental Series 72. New Haven: American Oriental Society, 1990.

_____. "Diglossia in Ancient Hebrew as Revealed Through Compound Verbs." Pp. 665–77 in *Bono Homini Donum: Essays in Historical Lin-*

guistics in Memory of J. Alexander Kerns. Edited by Yoël Arbeitman and Allen R. Bomhard. Amsterdam: Benjamins, 1981.

Rooker, Mark F. "The Diachronic Study of Biblical Hebrew." *Journal of Northwest Semitic Languages* 14 (1988) 199–214.

_____. "Ezekiel and the Typology of Biblical Hebrew." *Hebrew Annual Review* 12 (1990) 133–55.

Sapir, Edward. "Hebrew 'Helmet,' a Loanword, and Its Bearing on Indo-European Phonology." Pp. 285–88 in *Selected Writings of Edward Sapir in Language, Culture, and Personality.* Edited by David G. Mandelbaum. Berkeley: University of California, 1949.

Segert, Stanislav. "Hebrew Bible and Semitic Comparative Lexicography." Pp. 204–11 in *Congress Volume, Rome 1968.* Vetus Testamentum Supplement 17. Leiden: E. J. Brill, 1969.

Téné, David. "The Earliest Comparisons of Hebrew with Aramaic and Arabic." Pp. 355–77 in *Progress in Linguistic Historiography.* Edited by K. Koerner. Amsterdam: Benjamins, 1980.

GRAMMATOLOGY

Andersen, Francis I., and A. Dean Forbes. *Spelling in the Hebrew Bible.* Biblica et Orientalia 41. Rome: Pontifical Biblical Institute, 1986.

Aronoff, Mark. "Orthography and Linguistic Theory: The Syntactic Basis of Masoretic Hebrew Punctuation." *Language* 61 (1985) 28–72.

Barr, James. "The Nature of Linguistic Evidence in the Text of the Bible." Pp. 35–57 in *Language and Texts: The Nature of Linguistic Evidence.* Edited by Herbert H. Paper. Ann Arbor: Center for Coordination of Ancient and Modern Studies, University of Michigan, 1975.

_____. "Reading a Script Without Vowels." Pp. 71–100 in *Writing Without Letters.* Edited by W. Haas. Manchester: Manchester University, 1976.

_____. *The Variable Spellings of the Hebrew Bible.* Sehweich Lectures 1986. London: Oxford University, for the British Academy, 1989.

Costacurta, Bruna. "Implicazioni semantiche in alcuni casi di *Qere-Ketib*." *Biblica* 71 (1990) 226–39.

Cross, Frank M., and David N. Freedman. *Early Hebrew Orthography: A Study of the Epigraphic Evidence.* American Oriental Series 36. New Haven: American Oriental Society, 1952.

Daniels, Peter T. "Fundamentals of Grammatology." *Journal of the American Oriental Society* 110 (1990) 727–31.

_____. "'Proto-Euphratic' and the Syllabic Origin of Writing." *Proceedings Eastern Great Lakes and Midwest Biblical Societies* 9 (1989) 23–33.

Gibson, John C. L. "Hebrew Writing as a Subject of Linguistic Investigation." *Glasgow University Oriental Society Transactions* 20 (1963–64) 49–62.

_____. "On the Linguistic Analysis of Hebrew Writing." *Archivum Linguisticum* 17 (1969) 131–60.

_____. "The Massoretes as Linguists." *Oudtestamentische Studiën* 19 (1974) 86–96.

Levin, Saul. "The מתג According to the Practice of the Early Vocalizers." *Hebrew Annual Review* 3 (1979) 129–39.

_____. Review of *Spelling in the Hebrew Bible* by Francis I. Andersen and A. Dean Forbes. *Hebrew Studies* 30 (1989) 96–100.

_____. "An Unattested 'Scribal Correction' in Numbers 26,59?" *Biblica* 71 (1990) 25–33.

Malone, Joseph L. "Systematic vs. Autonomous Phonemics and the Hebrew Grapheme *dagesh*." *Afroasiatic Linguistics* 2 (1975) 113–29.

_____. "Textually Deviant Forms as Evidence for Phonological Analysis: A Service of Philology to Linguistics." *Journal of the Ancient Near Eastern Society of Columbia University* 11 (1979) 71–79.

O'Connor, M. "Writing Systems, Native Speaker Analyses, and the Earliest Stages of Northwest Semitic Orthography." Pp. 439–65 in *The Word of the Lord Shall Go Forth: Essays in Honor of David Noel Freedman in Celebration of His Sixtieth Birthday.* Edited by Carol L. Meyers and M. O'Connor. Winona Lake, IN: Eisenbrauns, 1983.

Revell, E. J. "Biblical Punctuation and Chant in the Second Temple Period." *Journal for the Study of Judaism* 7 (1976) 181–98.

_____. "Nesiga and the History of the Masoreh." Pp. 37–48 in *Estudios Masoreticos . . . dedicados a Harry M. Orlinsky.* Edited by E. Fernández Tejero. Textos y Estudios "Cardenal Cisneros" 33. Madrid: Instituto "Arias Montano," 1983.

Richter, Wolfgang. *Transliteration und Transkription: Objekt- und metasprachliche Metazeichensysteme zur Wiedergabe hebräischer Texte.* St. Ottilien: EOS, 1983.

Schramm, Gene. *The Graphemes of Tiberian Hebrew.* University of California Publications, Near Eastern Studies 2. Berkeley: University of California, 1964.

Zevit, Ziony. *Matres Lectiones in Ancient Hebrew Epigraphs.* American Schools of Oriental Research Monograph Series 2. Cambridge: American Schools of Oriental Research, 1980.

POETRY

Berlin, Adele. *The Dynamics of Biblical Parallelism*. Bloomington: Indiana University, 1985.

_____. "Grammatical Aspects of Biblical Parallelism." *Hebrew Union College Annual* 50 (1979) 17–43.

_____. "Motif and Creativity in Biblical Poetry." *Prooftexts* 3 (1983) 231–41.

Cooper, Alan. "Two Recent Works on the Structure of Biblical Hebrew Poetry." *Journal of the American Oriental Society* 110 (1990) 687–90.

Garr, W. Randall. "The Qinah: A Study of Poetic Meter, Syntax and Style." *Zeitschrift für die alttestamentliche Wissenschaft* 95 (1983) 54–75.

Greenstein, Edward L. "Aspects of Biblical Poetry." *Jewish Book Annual* 44 (1986–87) 33–42.

_____. "How Does Parallelism Mean?" Pp. 41–70 in *A Sense of Text: The Art of Language in the Study of Biblical Literature*. Jewish Quarterly Review Supplement 1982. Winona Lake, IN: Eisenbrauns, 1983.

_____. "Two Variations of Grammatical Parallelism in Canaanite Poetry and Their Psycholinguistic Background." *Journal of the Ancient Near Eastern Society of Columbia University* 6 (1974) 87–105.

Kaddari, Menahem Z. "A Semantic Approach to Biblical Parallelism." *Journal of Jewish Studies* 24 (1973) 165–75.

O'Connor, M. *Hebrew Verse Structure*. Winona Lake, IN: Eisenbrauns, 1980.

_____. "'I only am escaped alone to tell thee': Native American and Biblical Hebrew Verse." *Religion and Intellectual Life* 3 (1986) 121–32.

_____. "The Pseudosorites in Hebrew Verse." Pp. 239–53 in *Perspectives on Language and Text: Essays and Poems in Honor of Francis I. Andersen*. Edited by E. W. Conrad and E. G. Newing. Winona Lake, IN: Eisenbrauns, 1987.

_____. "The Pseudosorites: A Type of Paradox in Biblical Hebrew Poetry." Pp. 161–72 in *Directions in Biblical Hebrew Poetry*. Edited by Elaine B. Follis. Journal for the Study of the Old Testament Supplement Series 40. Sheffield: JSOT, 1987.

_____. "'Unanswerable the Knack of Tongues': The Linguistic Study of Verse." Pp. 143–68 in *Exceptional Language and Linguistics*. Edited by L. K. Obler and L. Menn. New York: Academic, 1982.

Pardee, Dennis. *Ugaritic and Hebrew Poetic Parallelism: A Trial Cut [ᶜnt and Proverbs 2]*. Vetus Testamentum Supplement 39. Leiden: E. J. Brill, 1988.

Revell, E. J. "Pausal Forms and the Structure of Biblical Poetry." *Vetus Testamentum* 31 (1981) 186–99.

Robertson, David A. *Linguistic Evidence in Dating Early Hebrew Poetry.* Society of Biblical Literature Dissertation Series 3. Missoula: Scholars Press, 1972.

Schramm, Gene. "Poetic Patterning in Biblical Hebrew." Pp. 167–91 in *Michigan Oriental Studies in Honor of George E. Cameron.* Edited by Louis L. Orlin et al. Ann Arbor: Dept. of Near Eastern Studies, University of Michigan, 1976.

Segert, Stanislav. "Problems of Hebrew Prosody." Pp. 283–91 in *Congress Volume, Oxford 1959.* Vetus Testamentum Supplement 7. Leiden: E. J. Brill, 1960.

_____. "Versbau und Sprachbau in der Altehebräischen Poesie." *Mitteilungen des Instituts für Orientforschung* 15 (1969) 312–21.

Zevit, Ziony. "Roman Jakobson, Psycholinguistics, and Biblical Poetry." *Journal of Biblical Literature* 109 (1990) 385–401.

TRANSLATION

Beckman, John, and John Callow. *Translating the Word of God.* Grand Rapids: Zondervan, 1974.

Callow, Kathleen. *Discourse Considerations in Translating the Word of God.* Grand Rapids: Zondervan, 1974.

Carson, D. A. "The Limits of Dynamic Equivalence in Bible Translation." *ERT* 9 (1985) 200–214.

Catford, J. C. *A Linguistic Theory of Translation: An Essay in Applied Linguistics.* London: Oxford University, 1965.

Crim, Keith R. "Hebrew Direct Discourse as a Translation Problem." *The Bible Translator* 24 (1973) 311–16.

Franklin, Karl J., and Kenneth A. McElhanon. "Bible Translation and Linguistics." *Journal of the American Scientific Affiliation* 31 (1979) 13–19.

Greenstein, Edward L. *Essays on Biblical Method and Translation.* Brown Judaic Studies 32. Atlanta: Scholars, 1989.

_____. "Theories of Modern Bible Translation." *Prooftexts* 3 (1983) 9–39.

Kedar-Kopfstein, Benjamin. "Synasthesien im biblischen Althebräisch in Übersetzung und Auslegung." *Zeitschrift für Althebräistik* 1 (1988) 47–60, 147–58.

Longacre, Robert E. "Items in Context: Their Bearing on Translation Theory." *Language* 34 (1958) 482–91.

Larson, Mildred. *A Manual for Problem Solving in Bible Translation.* Grand Rapids: Zondervan, 1975.

_____. "The Relevance of Sentence Structure Analysis to Bible Translation." *Notes on Translation* 40 (1971) 16–23.

Louw, J. P. "A Semiotic Approach to Discourse Analysis with Reference to Translation Theory." *The Bible Translator* 36 (1981) 101–7.

Malone, Joseph L. *The Science of Linguistics in the Art of Translation: Some Tools from Linguistics for the Analysis and Practice of Translation.* Albany: State University of New York, 1988.

Mounin, Georges. "Hebraic Rhetoric and Faithful Translation." *The Bible Translator* 30 (1979) 336–40.

Nida, Eugene A. "Problems of Cultural Differences in Translating the Old Testament." Pp. 297–307 in *Melanges Dominique Barthélemy.* Edited by Pierre Casetti et al. Orbis Biblicus et Orientalis 38. Göttingen: Vandenhoeck und Ruprecht, 1981.

_____. *Toward a Science of Translating, With Special Reference to Principles and Procedures Involved in Bible Translating.* Leiden: E. J. Brill, 1964.

Nida, Eugene A., and William D. Rayburn. *Meaning Across Cultures.* Maryknoll: Orbis, 1981.

Nida, Eugene A., and Charles R. Taber. *The Theory and Practice of Translation.* Helps for Translators 8. Leiden: E. J. Brill, 1982.

Nida, Eugene, and Jan de Waard. *From One Language to Another: Functional Equivalence in Bible Translating.* Nashville: Thomas Nelson, 1986.

Rabin, C. "The Linguistics of Translation." Pp. 123–45 in *Aspects of Communication.* Studies in Communication 2. London: Secker and Warburg, 1958.

Smalley, William A. "Discourse Analysis and Bible Translation." *The Bible Translator* 31 (1980) 119–25.

_____. "The Place of Linguistics in Bible Translation." *The Bible Translator* 16 (1965) 105–12.

_____. "Restructuring Translations of the Psalms as Poetry." Pp. 337–71 in *On Language, Culture, and Religion: In Honor of Eugene A. Nida.* Edited by Matthew Black and William A. Smalley. The Hague: Mouton, 1974.

Waard, Jan de. "Do You Use 'Clean Language'? Old Testament Euphemisms and Their Translation." *The Bible Translator* 22 (1971) 107–16.

Wonderly, William L. "Poetry in the Bible: Challenge to Translators." *The Bible Translator* 38 (1987) 206–13.

Indexes

Index of Authorities

Index of Scripture References

320